Early Childhood Mathematics Education Research

Research on the mathematical thinking and learning of young children is one of the most productive and exciting areas in education and psychology. Today, researchers from mathematics, mathematics education, developmental psychology, cognitive psychology, and neuroscience, among others, are exploring similar questions, creating a critical mass of theory and empirical evidence that has the potential to re-energize each of these fields.

This important new book synthesizes relevant research on the learning of mathematics from birth into the primary grades from the full range of these complementary perspectives. At the core of early math experts Julie Sarama and Douglas Clements' theoretical and empirical frameworks are learning trajectories—detailed descriptions of children's thinking as they learn to achieve specific goals in a mathematical domain, alongside a related set of instructional tasks designed to engender those mental processes and move children through a developmental progression of levels of thinking. Rooted in basic issues of thinking, learning, and teaching, this groundbreaking body of research illuminates foundational topics on the learning of mathematics with practical and theoretical implications for all ages. Those implications are especially important in addressing equity concerns, as understanding the level of thinking of the class and the individuals within it is key in serving the needs of all children.

Julie Sarama is an Associate Professor of Mathematics Education at the University at Buffalo, State University of New York.

Douglas H. Clements is SUNY Distinguished Professor of Early Childhood, Mathematics, and Computer Education at the University at Buffalo, State University of New York.

Studies in Mathematical Thinking and Learning

Alan H. Schoenfeld, Series Editor

Early Childhood Mathematics Education Research

Learning Trajectories for Young Children

Julie Sarama and Douglas H. Clements
University at Buffalo, State University of New York

Routledge
Taylor & Francis Group
NEW YORK AND LONDON

KH

First published 2009
by Routledge
270 Madison Ave, New York, NY 10016

Simultaneously published in the UK
by Routledge
2 Park Square, Milton Park, Abingdon, Oxon OX14 4RN

Routledge is an imprint of the Taylor & Francis Group, an informa business

© 2009 Taylor & Francis

Typeset in Minion by
RefineCatch Limited, Bungay, Suffolk
Printed and bound in the United States of America on acid-free paper by
Edwards Brothers, Inc

Library of Congress Cataloging-in-Publication Data
Sarama, Julie.
Early childhood mathematics education research : learning trajectories for young children / Julie Sarama, Douglas H. Clements.—1st ed.
    p. cm.—(Studies in mathematical thinking and learning)
    1. Mathematics—Study and teaching (Early childhood)   2. Early childhood education—Research.
3. Educational psychology.   4. Child development.   I. Clements, Douglas H.   II. Title.
    QA135.6.S27 2009
    372.701′9—dc22

                                                                                    2008033303

ISBN10: 0–8058–6308–7 (hbk)
ISBN10: 0–8058–6309–5 (pbk)
ISBN10: 0–203–88378–0 (ebk)

ISBN13: 978–0–8058–6308–6 (hbk)
ISBN13: 978–0–8058–6309–3 (pbk)
ISBN13: 978–0–203–88378–5 (ebk)

7/5/11

Contents

Preface

Research on the mathematical thinking and learning of young children is one of the most productive and exciting areas in educational psychology. Although mathematics researchers have studied young children's learning for some time, much of the research originated in fields such as developmental psychology. Today, researchers from mathematics, mathematics education, developmental psychology, cognitive psychology, and neuroscience, among others, are exploring similar questions, creating a critical mass of theory and empirical evidence that has the potential to energize each of these fields.

Our goal is to synthesize relevant research on the learning of mathematics from birth into the primary grades from all these complementary perspectives. At the core of our theoretical and empirical frameworks are *learning trajectories*—descriptions of children's thinking as they learn to achieve specific goals in a mathematical domain, and a related, conjectured route through a set of instructional tasks designed to engender those mental processes or actions hypothesized to move children through a developmental progression of levels of thinking. Rooted in basic issues of thinking, learning, and teaching, this body of research illuminates foundational themes on the learning of mathematics, with practical and theoretical implications for all ages. Those implications are especially important in addressing equity concerns. Understanding the level of thinking of the class *and* individuals in that class is key in serving the needs of all children.

Background

In 1998, we began a four-year project funded by the National Science Foundation. The purpose of *Building Blocks—Foundations for Mathematical Thinking, Pre-Kindergarten to Grade 2: Research-based Materials Development* was to create and evaluate mathematics curricula for young children based on a theoretically sound research and development framework. More than a decade later, we are still finding new opportunities for exciting research and development in early mathematics.

Funding from the U.S. Department of Education's Institute of Education Sciences (IES) has allowed us to work closely with hundreds of teachers and thousands of children over the past 10 years. All these agencies and individuals have contributed ideas to these books. In addition, these projects have increased our confidence that our approach, based on learning trajectories and rigorous empirical testing at every step, can in turn make a contribution to all educators in the field of early mathematics. The model for working with educators in all positions, from teachers to administrators to trainers to researchers, has been developed with IES funding to our TRIAD project, an acronym for Technology-enhanced, Research-based, Instruction, Assessment, and professional Development.[1]

The "Companion" Books

We believe that our successes are due to the people who have contributed to our projects and to our commitment to grounding everything we have done in research. Because the work has been so heavily researched, we decided to publish two books. The first book—this one—reviews the research underlying our *learning trajectories*. The second book, the companion to this one, *Learning and Teaching Early Math: The Learning Trajectories Approach* (Clements & Sarama, 2009), describes and illustrates how these learning trajectories can be implemented in the classroom.

Because it is in the classroom that mathematics comes alive, we urge those most interested in this, the research review book, to read the companion book as well. The illustrations of children's wonder, excitement, and especially thinking and problem-solving, help prevent the research reviews from giving the mis-impression that the main story of learning trajectories is children marching through a series of learning levels. Such a dreary picture is the opposite of that we are trying to paint, which is of children filled with curiosity and creative ideas, and teachers excited about helping them see the world through mathematical lenses.

Reading *this* Book

The first chapter of this research book introduces the area of early mathematics, our theoretical framework, and the construct of learning trajectories. Most of the chapters are content-specific and follow similar formats. Each chapter focuses on one or more related domains of early mathematics. For each domain, we describe theories and empirical evidence on children's learning of these ideas, and then on the role of education and experience. Each of these chapters concludes with a description of the research basis for the learning trajectory for that specific topic. The focus in this book is on the developmental progressions of levels of thinking children develop as they learn each topic. Although the important role of *processes* such as problem-solving, reasoning, representing, and communicating mathematics ideas is a consistent theme throughout the book, Chapter 13 summarizes research focused on these processes. The last chapter, 14, discusses the research-based approaches to scaling up, particularly the critical component of professional development, we used in the TRIAD projects.

The implications for education are detailed in the companion book. This book also elaborates the learning trajectories for each topic, emphasizing multiple instructional tasks matched to each developmental level. It also includes chapters on "Cognition, Affect, and Equity"; "Early Childhood Mathematics Education: Contexts and Curricula"; and "Instructional Practices and Pedagogical Issues". Another reason the companion book is an essential complement to this book is that only the companion book reviews research on these essential topics.

Appreciation to the Funding Agencies

We wish to express our appreciation for the funding agencies that have not only provided financial support, but intellectual support in the form of guidance from program officers (most notably and recently, Caroline Ebanks), opportunities to collaborate with other projects, and attend conferences to exchange ideas with colleagues. The ideas and research reported here has been supported by all of the following grants. Any opinions, findings, and conclusions or recommendations expressed in this material are those of the authors and do not necessarily reflect the views of the funding agencies.

1. Clements, D. H., & Sarama, J. *Scaling Up TRIAD: Teaching Early Mathematics for Understanding with Trajectories and Technologies—Supplement.* Awarded by the U.S. Department of Education, IES (Institute of Education Sciences; as part of the Interagency Educational Research Initiative, or IERI program, a combination of IES, NSF, and NIH).
2. Clements, D. H., Sarama, J., & Lee, J. *Scaling Up TRIAD: Teaching Early Mathematics for Understanding with Trajectories and Technologies.* Awarded by the U.S. Department of Education, IES (Institute of Education Sciences; as part of the Interagency Educational Research Initiative, or IERI program, a combination of IES, NSF, and NIH).
3. Clements, D. H., Sarama, J., Klein, A., & Starkey, Prentice. *Scaling Up the Implementation of a Pre-Kindergarten Mathematics Curricula: Teaching for Understanding with Trajectories and Technologies.* Awarded by the National Science Foundation (NSF, as part of the Interagency Educational Research Initiative, or IERI program, a combination of NSF, U.S. Dept. of Education IES, and NIH).
4. Starkey, Prentice, Sarama, J., Clements, D. H., & Klein, A. *A Longitudinal Study of the Effects of a Pre-Kindergarten Mathematics Curriculum on Low-Income Children's Mathematical Knowledge.* Awarded by OERI, Department of Education as Preschool Curriculum Evaluation Research (PCER) project.
5. Clements, D. H. *Conference on Standards for Preschool and Kindergarten Mathematics Education.* Awarded by the ExxonMobil Foundation.
6. Clements, D. H. *Conference on Standards for Preschool and Kindergarten Mathematics Education.* Awarded by the National

Science Foundation, Elementary, Secondary, and Informal Science Education.

7. Clements, D. H., & Sarama, J. *Building Blocks—Foundations for Mathematical Thinking, Pre-Kindergarten to Grade 2: Research-Based Materials Development.* Awarded by the National Science Foundation, Instructional Materials Development.

8. Sarama, J., & Clements, D. H. *Planning for Professional Development in Pre-School Mathematics: Meeting the Challenge of Standards 2000.* Awarded by the National Science Foundation, Teacher Enhancement Program.

Part I
Introduction

1
Early Childhood
Mathematics Learning

"It seems probable that little is gained by using any of the child's time for arithmetic before grade 2, though there are many arithmetic facts that he [*sic*] can learn in grade 1."

(Thorndike, 1922, p. 198)

"Children have their own preschool arithmetic, which only myopic psychologists could ignore."

(Vygotsky, 1935/1978, p. 84)

For over a century, views of young children's mathematics have differed widely. The recent turn of the century has seen a dramatic increase in attention to the mathematics education of young children. Our goal is to synthesize relevant research on the learning of mathematics from birth into the primary grades from multiple perspectives. This reveals a field that is fascinating in its new findings, that promises practical guidelines and suggestions for teaching and advances in theory. As just one example, Jean Piaget's genetic epistemology, as the study of the origins of knowledge itself, has never been more deeply developed or empirically tested than in recent research on early mathematics learning.

In this chapter, we begin with a brief overview of mathematics in early childhood and young children's learning of mathematics. In the several chapters that follow, we discuss children's learning of mathematical ideas and skills that are important for young children's learning (Clements & Conference Working Group, 2004; NCTM, 2006; NMP, 2008), because it is most fruitful for teachers and children to focus on the big ideas of mathematics (Bowman, Donovan, & Burns, 2001; Clements, 2004; Fuson, 2004; Griffin, Case, & Capodilupo, 1995; Tibbals, 2000; Weiss, 2002).

This organization based on content should not be taken as a de-emphasis on other critical components of high-quality mathematics education. For example, *processes* are discussed within every chapter, because processes are just as important as "facts" and concepts in understanding mathematics. Further, Chapter 13 focuses on specific processes. "As important as mathematical content are general mathematical processes such as problem solving, reasoning and proof, communication, connections, and representation; specific mathematical processes such as organizing information, *patterning*, and composing, and habits of mind such as curiosity, imagination, inventiveness, persistence, willingness to experiment, and sensitivity to patterns. All should be involved in a high-quality early childhood mathematics program" (Clements & Conference Working Group, 2004, p. 57). This structure of goals is consistent both with recommendations of the National Council of Teachers of Mathematics (NCTM, 2000) and with research on young children's development of a network of logical and mathematical relations (Kamii, Miyakawa, & Kato, 2004). Finally, it is consistent with the conclusions of another review, that: "The overriding premise of our work is that throughout the grades from pre-K through 8 all students can and should be mathematically proficient" (Kilpatrick, Swafford, & Findell, 2001, p. 10), including conceptual understanding, procedural fluency, strategic competence, adaptive reasoning (capacity for logical thought, reflection, explanation, and justification), and a productive disposition.

That last thread—productive disposition—must also be highlighted. The "habits of mind" named previously, including curiosity, imagination, inventiveness, risk-taking, creativity, and persistence—are components of the essential *productive disposition*. Children need to view mathematics as sensible, useful, and worthwhile and view themselves as capable of thinking mathematically. All these should be involved in a high-quality early childhood mathematics program. (The companion book includes chapters on learning and teaching contexts, including early childhood school settings and education, equity issues, affect, and so forth that speak to developing children's productive disposition.)

Mathematics in Early Childhood

There are at least eight reasons for the recent surge of attention to mathematics in early childhood. First, increasing numbers of children attend early care and education programs. In 1999, 70 percent of four-year-olds and 93 percent of five-year-olds were enrolled in preprimary education, up from 62 and 90 percent, respectively, in 1991 (U.S. Department of Education, 2000, p. 7). Several states are instituting universal pre-K,[1] with about 1 million children enrolled in 1999, and that number is increasing (Hinkle, 2000). In 2001, about two-thirds of all four-year-olds were enrolled in universal pre-K, with that ratio increasing (Loeb, Bridges, Bassok, Fuller, & Rumberger, in press; Magnuson, Meyers, Rathbun, & West, 2004). Various government agencies, federal and state, provide financial support for pre-K programs designed to facilitate academic achievement, particularly programs for low-income children.

Second, there is an increased recognition of the importance of mathematics (Doig, McCrae, & Rowe, 2003; Kilpatrick et al., 2001). In a global economy with the vast majority of jobs requiring more sophisticated skills than in the past,

American educators and business leaders have expressed strong concern about students' mathematics achievement.

Third, the mathematics achievement of American students compares unfavorably with the achievement of students from several other nations, even as early as first grade and kindergarten (Stigler, Lee, & Stevenson, 1990). Some cross-national differences in informal mathematics knowledge appear as early as three to five years of age (Starkey et al., 1999; Yuzawa, Bart, Kinne, Sukemune, & Kataoka, 1999). Children in East Asia and Europe learn more advanced math than most children in the U.S. are taught (Geary, 2006). (Similar contrasts appear between East Asian and other Western countries as well: Aunio, Ee, Lim, Hautamäki, & Van Luit, 2004.)

Fourth, the knowledge gap is most pronounced in the performance of U.S. children living in economically deprived urban communities (Geary, Bow-Thomas, Fan, & Siegler, 1993; Griffin, Case, & Siegler, 1994; V. E. Lee & Burkam, 2002; Saxe, Guberman, & Gearhart, 1987; Siegler, 1993). That is, differences are not just between nations, but also between socioeconomic groups within countries. A stark example occurred in our own research project when a child stepped up to research assistant grinning and showing her "Happy Birthday" crown. The assistant asked how old she was. The girl stared without responding. "Can you show me on your fingers?" The girl slowly shook her head "no." Cross-cultural differences raise concerns of equity regarding children's pre-K experiences and elementary schools' readiness to adapt instruction to children at different levels of mathematical development. Many government-funded programs serve low-income children, who often experience difficulties in mathematics and are at increased risk of school failure (Bowman et al., 2001; Natriello, McDill, & Pallas, 1990). These children need to build the informal knowledge that provides the basis for later learning of mathematics. Thus, equity demands that we establish guidelines for quality early mathematics education for *all* children.

Fifth, researchers have changed from a position that very young children have little knowledge of, or capacity to learn mathematics (e.g., Piaget, Inhelder, & Szeminska, 1960; Piaget & Szeminska, 1952; Thorndike, 1922) to theories that posit competencies that are either innate or develop in the first years of life (Baroody, Lai, & Mix, 2006; Clements, Sarama, & DiBiase, 2004; Doig et al., 2003; Gelman & Gallistel, 1978; Perry & Dockett, 2002). We will discuss these issues in more depth; here, it suffices to say that it is clear that young children can engage with substantive mathematical ideas.

Sixth, early knowledge strongly affects later success in mathematics (Denton & West, 2002). Specific quantitative and numerical knowledge in the years before first grade has been found to be a stronger predictor of later mathematics achievement than tests of intelligence or memory abilities (Krajewski, 2005). What children know early affects them for many years thereafter (Horne, 2005; NMP, 2008). Mathematics knowledge on school entry is a stronger predictor than any of a host of social-emotional skills. The most powerful preschool avenue for boosting fifth grade achievement appears to be improving the basic academic skills of low-achieving children prior to kindergarten entry (Claessens, Duncan, & Engel, 2007).

Seventh, research indicates that knowledge gaps appeared in large part due to the lack of connection between children's informal and intuitive knowledge (Ginsburg & Russell, 1981; Hiebert, 1986) and school mathematics. This is especially detrimental when this informal knowledge is poorly developed (Baroody, 1987; Griffin et al., 1994). High-quality experiences in early mathematics can ameliorate such problems (Doig et al., 2003; Thomson, Rowe, Underwood, & Peck, 2005).

Eighth, traditional approaches to early childhood, such as "developmentally appropriate practice" (DAP) have not been shown to increase children's learning (Van Horn, Karlin, Ramey, Aldridge, & Snyder, 2005). We need ways to keep the probable benefits of DAP, such as socioemotional growth (Van Horn et al., 2005), and yet infuse the young child's day with interesting, equally appropriate, opportunities to engage in mathematical thinking (cf. Peisner-Feinberg et al., 2001).

For these reasons, there has been much recent interest in, and attention to, the learning and teaching of mathematics to the young.

Young Children and Mathematics Learning

Given the opportunity, young children possess an informal knowledge of mathematics that is surprisingly broad, complex, and sophisticated (Baroody, 2004; B. A. Clarke, Clarke, & Cheeseman, 2006; Clements, Swaminathan, Hannibal, & Sarama, 1999; Fuson, 2004; Geary, 1994; Ginsburg, 1977; Kilpatrick et al., 2001; NCES, 2000; Piaget & Inhelder, 1967; Piaget et al., 1960; Steffe, 2004; Thomson et al., 2005). For example, preschoolers engage in substantial amounts of foundational free play.[2] They explore patterns, shapes, and spatial relations, compare magnitudes, and count objects. Importantly, this is true for children regardless of income level and gender (Seo & Ginsburg, 2004). They engage in mathematical thinking and reasoning in many contexts, especially if they have sufficient knowledge about the materials they are using (e.g., toys), if the task is understandable and motivating, and if the context is familiar and comfortable (Alexander, White, & Daugherty, 1997).

What do children know about math *before* they come to school? More than a century ago, G. Stanley Hall (1891) included specific mathematics skills in his survey of the "content of children's minds upon entering school." About 40 years later, Buckingham and MacLatchy (1930) similarly surveyed the number abilities of entering first graders. Since then, several reports have described what children know as they enter school, providing valuable data for writers of standards, goals, and curricula, as well as for teachers. A brief review of previous surveys of mathematics knowledge at school entry indicates that children generally are acquiring mathematical knowledge at earlier ages, but that children have never entered schools as *tabulae rasae*. The following is a brief discussion; some results are summarized in Table 1.1 to provide another view of the pattern of these findings.

Number

Of children entering first grade in Berlin, Hall (1891) reported that the percentages of children that "had the idea of" two, three, and four were 74, 74, and 73, respectively. Except for a handful of questions on shapes, these were the only questions asked concerning mathematics. Buckingham and MacLatchy (1930) reported that entering first graders possessed "remarkable" ability with counting, reproducing and naming numbers, and number combinations. At least 90 percent could verbally count to 10, 60 percent to 20. The majority of the 1,356 children enumerated objects to 20. Success in reproducing numbers declined with increasing number size, yet over 75 percent were successful with each of the numbers five, six, seven, eight, and 10 at least once; 70 percent identified a set of 10 at least once. Similarly, Brownell (1941) concluded that about 90 percent of first grade entrants could count verbally and count objects to 10 (his review of previous research revealed that about 10 percent could verbally count to 100 and between half and two-thirds could count to 20); about 60 percent could identify groups up to 10 represented concretely without pattern; over 50 percent could reproduce sets up to 10 given verbal directions; about 80 percent could identify the number which was "more"; about 75 percent could reproduce a set of four or five given a model set, whereas about 50 percent were successful with a set of seven; and about 75 percent dealt successfully with number combinations with small numbers of visible objects and from 38 to 50 percent with verbal presentations. More recently, Callahan and Clements (1984), in a survey of 4,722 first graders entering urban schools in the years 1976 to 1980, found that a relatively high percentage of children stopped verbal counting in the 10–19, 20–29 and 30–39 intervals, but beyond 50 most counted until the interviewer stopped them at 100.

A recent study found that by the end of the school year, a large percentage (88 percent) of kindergarten children understood the concept of relative size (e.g., can count beyond 10 and understand and can use nonstandard units of length to compare objects). By the spring of first grade, most children (96 percent) mastered ordinality and sequence (the understanding of the relative position of objects); and about three-quarters (76 percent) demonstrated proficiency in adding and subtracting basic whole units. Moreover, by the spring of first grade, about one-quarter (27 percent) demonstrated proficiency in multiplying and dividing simple whole units (Denton & West, 2002).

In a Netherlands study, entering first graders scored an average of 75 percent on the researchers' assessment (Heuvel-Panhuizen, 1996). Most children had mastered relational concepts and were quite familiar with numerals (written symbols, "1," "2," "3" ...) to 10 (97 percent; 81 percent for "14"). On a pictured board game, the great majority could identify numbers that come after or before another number. An even higher percentage could color two (99 percent) to nine (84 percent) pictured marbles. Performance on addition and subtraction problems was variable, from 80 percent on a countable board game problem, to 39 percent on a noncountable, open-ended subtraction problem, with performance on countable problems solved by about 79 percent, and others solved by about 50 percent. An interesting addition to this study was that several categories of experts in education were asked to predict these scores. They expected mastery of the relational concepts, but their predictions of number abilities were substantially lower. For example, they thought about half the children would know numbers to 10, compared to the actual average of 97 percent. They predicted 25 percent for numbers before and after, compared to the actual 59 percent to 86 percent. Their estimates for addition and subtraction were proportionately less accurate, often a mere tenth of the actual averages. The children's scores—and substantially lower estimates of them by experts—were substantiated by replications in Germany and Switzerland (although the estimations tended to be somewhat higher, proportionately).

Many studies have been conducted of kindergartners (for a review, see Kraner, 1977). In 1925, children 4.6 to 6 years showed 100 percent performance for naming the number of items in collections of one and two, from 85 percent to 95 percent on three, 15 percent to 65 percent for four, and 0 percent to 12 percent for five (Douglass, 1925). When not correct, most children's estimates were within one to two for numbers up to 10. These skills improved with age. Bjonerud (1960) reported the average performance of children (from a public and university demonstration school) for both rote and rational counting was 19, although there was little facility with number sequences other than the sequence of numbers by one (about 25 percent could count by tens). All were able to recognize sets of less than four immediately; some were able to recognize sets up to nine, mostly by counting. Almost 90 percent solved simple addition word problems and approximately 75 percent solved subtraction problems. Rea and Reys (Rea & Reys, 1971; Reys & Rea, 1970) assessed the mathematical competencies of 727 entering metropolitan kindergartens. Skills in counting, recognizing, and comparing small groups were generally well developed, more so than ordinal concepts. Over 50 percent counted beyond 14 and over 75 percent beyond 10 (rote and rational). Between 70 and 95 percent successfully identified the number of objects in groups containing from one to eight objects. The task of forming groups of three, seven, and 13 was performed successfully by 82, 55, and 34 percent respectively. When three numbers in sequence were provided, approximately 90 percent of the children could supply the next number; however, providing only one number cue and asking for the number before or after greatly decreased the percentage of correct responses. Kraner (1977) concluded that the average kindergartner possessed mathematics knowledge on a par with that of the average first grader of earlier years.

A few studies have surveyed the prekindergarten child's mathematical knowledge. McLaughlin (1935) investigated the number abilities of children from three to five years of age. The average verbal and object counting (without checking the cardinal principle) was to 4.5 and 4.4 for three-year-olds and 17.6 and 14.5 for four-year-olds (which included children up to 60 months). There was no substantial ability to count backwards. Only some three-year-olds could match groups of two or three whereas most four-year-olds were beginning to count as a means of matching, forming, naming, or combining number groups (percentages were not provided). In his investigation of the acquisition age (defined as an 80 percent success rate) of number concepts of three- to six-year-olds from five middle-class locations, Kraner (1977) reported the following ages of concept attainment: verbal counting to three, 3-6; to four, 4-0; to nine, 4-6; and to 18, 5-0; object counting to two, 3-6; to eight, 4-6; and to 20, 5-6; recognizing and comprehending cardinal numbers to five, 5-0; to 10, from 5-6 to 6-0; and identifying more than, 5-6, less than, 6-6, and one more or less, above 6-6. Clements (1984b) identified the following abilities of middle-class entering four-year-olds, in average accuracy: object counting to 10, 59 percent; choosing more, 51 percent; after, before, between, 30 percent; counting on and back, 19 percent; equalizing, 20 percent one-to-one correspondence, 58 percent; identity conservation, 72 percent; equivalence conservation, 62 percent; verbal arithmetic problems, 49 percent; concrete arithmetic problems, 46 percent.

An Australian study showed that most entering preschoolers could count eight objects and between 25 and 41 percent could tell what one more or one less would be (Thomson et al., 2005). Less competence was reported for Scandinavian prekindergarteners, who did not master any of the assessed counting skills (Van de Rijt & Van Luit, 1999). Preschoolers show a wide range of competencies (Aubrey, 1997). Verbal counting ranged from four to more than 100, with 80 percent counting to at least 10, and 15 percent counting to within the range of 21 to 30. Reading numerals showed variable performance, with 50 percent recognizing five to more than eight numerals, a further 31 percent recognizing two to four numbers, and 19 percent recognizing none or one number. For giving the number after another number, 25 percent could manage four to seven numbers, 27 percent one to three numbers, and 36 percent eight to 10 numbers. For addition with concrete objects, 51 percent accurately answered four or five out of five problems. For a simple division by social sharing task, 73 percent scored four or five out of five on tasks calling for simple distribution of sweets among two and three bears. For multiplication by simple addition, 66 percent were able to carry out two simple tasks checking children's understanding of a small set being repeated.

Table 1.1 Historical Patterns of Average Percent Correct of Children at School Entry

Topic	Grade 1				K					Pre-K					
Number	Hall (1891)	Buckingham and MacLatchy (1930)	Brownell (1941)	Douglass (1925)	Bjonerud (1960)	Rea and Reys (1971; 1970)	Kraner (1977)	NCES (2000)	Clarke & Clarke (2006)	McLaughlin (1935)	Kraner (1977)	Clements (1984b)	Aubrey (1997)	Clements et al. (1999)	Sarama and Clements, Study 1 (2005)[g]
Recognize 2	74			100	100				95						2–14
3	74			85–95	100				84						0–5
4	73			15–65					71						0–1
5				0–12			80		43						0–1
6–10	70[a]	60				70–95	80[b]		9						
Verbally count															
to 10	90	90						94[c]		50–70[c]	80[d]		80		44
to 20	60	47 (rural) 57 (city)			50		80	58[c,e]	57				15		
Object counting															
to 10		90				75	80[b]		41[f]	40–60[c]	80[d]	59			14–45
to 20	51					50			39						
Produce															
to 5	75[a]	75				82			85						
to 10	75[a]	50				55			67						

										Range
Identify which is more		80					84	51	51	40–48
Add w/ objects		75	90					46		2–16
verbally		38–50						49		2–12
Geometry										
Name shapes	49	75	91	50+	80[b]	94[c]	80		92	
circle										
square	54	75	76	50+	80	94[c]			82	39–84
triangle	51			38		94[c]			60	26–86
rectangle				11	80				51	32–82
Identification of sides and corners				80	80[b]					

---

[a] credit was given if the child was correct "at least once"; [b] age = 5–6; [c] estimated; [d] count to 8 or 9, age 4–6; [e] average; 79% for higher SES vs. 32% for lower SES; [f] counting 9 dots but also had to match to numeral "9."; [g] low SES children only (ranges were from different populations, for geometry, they also were for prototypical shapes—the higher percentages—and shapes that were not typical).

There is a vast related literature on children's understanding of number (e.g., Baroody, 1992; Fuson, 1992; Fuson & Hall, 1982; Gelman & Gallistel, 1978; Ginsburg & Russell, 1981). For example, Fuson (1988) presented an extensive report focusing on children's counting. The reports, especially of children's errors, are too complex to summarize here. Fuson summarized, "By age 3 counting is already very organized and exhibits the general structure of mature, effective, counting" (p. 186). Relevant findings include counting up from a number well established by age 4-6, errors when counting disorganized arrays decreasing at about the same age, and most correspondence errors decreasing sharply while children are four years of age. Because these were not general surveys, often did not disaggregate by age, and did not assess children explicitly upon school entrance, they will be discussed in other sections of the book.

Geometry

Although there is less information on geometry than number, we know something about children's competencies in that domain. Hall (1891) reported that the percentage of children entering first grade that "had the idea of" circle, square, and triangle were 49, 54, and 41, respectively. Brownell (1941) reviewed research indicating that about 75 percent of first graders understood the terms square and circle, but few understood triangle.

Bjonerud (1960) reported that 91 percent of entering kindergarteners named a circle and 76 percent named a square. Although kindergarteners could easily match shapes (97 percent), Rea and Reys (Rea & Reys, 1971; Reys & Rea, 1970) reported that only slightly more than 50 percent correctly named a circle and square. The triangle, rectangle, and diamond were named by 38, 11, and 23 percent of the children. Correct identification of line, sides, and corners was made by over 80 percent. At least 50 percent could tell how many sides these figures had (children's difficulties were not in counting, but in leaving out the side closest to them).

Regarding knowledge of preschoolers, Kraner (1977) reported the average acquisition age for circle to be 4-6, square and rectangle, 5-0, and number of sides, 5-6. Fuson and Murray (1978) reported that by three years of age over 60 percent of children could name a circle, square, and triangle. Recently, using a complex array of shapes of different sizes and shapes, middle-class four-year-olds' accuracy of identification was 92 percent for circles, 82 percent for squares, 60 percent for triangles, and 51 percent for rectangles (Clements et al., 1999). Apparently, differences in tasks or populations characteristics affect results.

Young children develop beginning ideas not just about shapes, but also about congruence and transformations. Although many young children judge congruence based on whether they are, on the whole, more similar than different (Vurpillot, 1976), four-year-olds can generate strategies for verifying congruence for some tasks. Preschoolers often try to judge congruence using an edge matching strategy, although only about 50 percent can do it successfully (Beilin, 1984; Beilin, Klein, & Whitehurst, 1982). They gradually develop a greater awareness of the type of differences between figures that are considered relevant and move from considering various parts of shapes to considering the spatial relationships of these parts (Vurpillot, 1976). Under the right conditions, preschoolers also can apply similarity transformations to shapes. For example, four-year-olds can identify similar shapes in some circumstances (Sophian & Crosby, 1998). An Australian study showed that most entering preschoolers understood the concept of "smaller," "more," "longest," and "shortest," but substantial proportions (more than one-third of children) could also answer far more complex items such as identifying "the shape that makes the side [sic] of the cube" (Thomson et al., 2005).

Angle is a difficult concept for any age student, but preschoolers use angles intuitively in their play, such as block building (Ginsburg, Inoue, & Seo, 1999). They can match angles in correspondence tasks (Beilin, 1984; Beilin et al., 1982) and perform turns if they have simple tasks and orientation cues (Rosser, Ensing, Glider, & Lane, 1984). Parallel and perpendicular lines are difficult concepts; however, children as young as three (Abravanel, 1977) and four years use parallelism in alignment tasks (Mitchelmore, 1992).

In summary, although data have not always been fully described and tasks, analyses, and reporting procedures have differed widely, the trend is that entering kindergarteners and preschoolers are acquiring mathematical knowledge approaching that of first graders of more than a half-century earlier. In the domain of numbers, present-day preschoolers appear to have slightly lower averages, or an acquisition of smaller numbers (e.g., in counting tasks) than kindergarteners, but they still approach those of first graders of 50 years earlier. In geometry, there is wide variance across studies on fewer tasks, but those limited data show entering preschoolers at the same level as previous studies of kindergarteners and first graders. Preschoolers also have some knowledge of congruence, transformations, turns, and angles.

Individual and Group Differences: The Equity Issue

Only a few of these studies measured effects of culture and socio-economic status (SES). As an example, Brownell (1941) reported that children from city areas generally outperformed those from rural areas by a small but consistent margin (e.g., 57 vs. 47 percent verbally counted to 20) and there are reports concluding that low-income children do not achieve as well as higher-income children (Ginsburg & Russell, 1981). Recent research confirms that culture and SES can be significant mediating factors. For example, some mathematical knowledge is more developed in East Asian children than in American children (Geary et al., 1993; Ginsburg, Choi, Lopez, Netley, & Chi, 1997; K. F. Miller, Smith, Zhu, & Zhang, 1995; Starkey et al., 1999) and some mathematical knowledge is more developed in children from middle-income, compared to lower-income, families (Griffin & Case, 1997; Jordan, Huttenlocher, & Levine, 1992; Kilpatrick et al., 2001; Saxe et al., 1987; Starkey & Klein, 1992).

Lower-income children show more varied math performance (Wright, 1991). This is an issue of major importance for early childhood educators. *Some children have acquired number knowledge before the age of four that other children will not acquire before the age of seven.* As an example, Peter was at the higher level of counting (beyond 120, can give the number word before or after any other). He could read three-digit numbers and count to solve a wide variety of addition and subtraction problems. In contrast, asked for the number after "six," Tom said "horse." He could not count beyond two. Both were beginning kindergarten (Wright, 1991).

We will return to equity issues repeatedly, but for now will briefly discuss two recent surveys of preschoolers' competencies. In an Australian study, there was a definite trend for students from lower SES backgrounds to perform at a lower level, and this was more apparent for the difficult items (Thomson et al., 2005; see also West, Denton, & Reaney, 2001). For example, for the task of counting eight objects, percentages were 52, 65, and 73 for low, middle, and upper SES children, respectively. For telling what number is "one less" than eight, the percentages were 15, 22, and 33.

In Study 1 of the second project (Sarama & Clements, 2008), only entering preschoolers from low-resource communities in New York and Texas were interviewed. About 68 percent could count verbally to five, 44 percent to 10 (Sarama & Clements, 2008). From 10 to 13 percent could start counting at four and continue to 10. Between 50 and 66 percent of the children could maintain correspondence and enumerate accurately to five. From 37 to 45 percent could count small groups of objects (two to seven). A somewhat lower proportion of children, 14 to 34 percent, could count eight objects in a scrambled arrangement or produce a collection of five objects. Only 5 to 15 percent could produce a group with the same number of objects as a given group of six. From 6 to 22 percent could identify object counting errors. Less than 3 percent could count 15 objects in a scrambled arrangement and less than 5 percent could count 30 objects in an array. In the realm of counting-based adding and subtracting, 2 to 16 percent of the children could perform various nonverbal addition and subtraction problems and 2 to 12 percent could solve verbal problems with sums of five or less. Similarly, children had limited competence recognizing the number in collections, with 0 to 14 percent successful with four and only a couple with higher numbers. Finally, from 2 to 10 percent recognized the numerals 1 to 5. Between 75 and 86 percent of the children could identify prototypical examples of squares, triangles, and rectangles. Fewer (39 to 74 percent) could identify palpable nonexemplars or categorize nonprototypical members and nonpalpable distractors (26 to 59 percent). These preschoolers had some competence in comparing shapes for congruence at a basic level (from 16 percent for difficult comparisons to 88 percent for congruent shapes that resemble real-world objects, with a mean above 50 percent). They are just beginning to learn to compose and decompose geometry shapes, with 16 to 34 percent operating at the first two levels and fewer operating at the succeeding two levels.

Study 2 compared lower- and higher-SES children. Children from pre-schools serving middle SES populations outperformed those serving low SES populations on the total number score and most individual subtests. The particular subtests that showed significant differences were, with few exceptions, those that measure more sophisticated mathematical concepts and skills. In number, there were no significant differences for simple verbal count-ing or recognition of small numbers (Clements & Sarama, 2004a; Sarama & Clements, 2008). There were significant differences on object counting and more sophisticated counting strategies, comparing numbers and sequencing, number composition, arithmetic, and matching numerals to dot cards. In geometry, there were no significant differences on the simple tasks involving shape and comparison of shapes. (The turns subtest was also relatively simple, but because it included only a single task, results should be interpreted with caution.) There were significant differences on representing shapes, composing shapes, and patterning. Measurement was an exception in that sophisticated concepts and skills were involved but no significant difference between the groups was found; development in this domain may be more dependent on school-based teaching.

Individual Differences: Psychometric Studies

Psychometric researchers are interested in individual differences on assess-ments and on figuring out whether people possess different *types* of cognitive abilities. As with studies of young children's competencies on school entry, psychometric research has a history stretching back more than 100 years. Using factor analysis, which helps groups ability tests into those that are related and probably share certain cognitive abilities, researchers have consistently found several areas of mathematical competence, such as numerical facility and mathematical reasoning (see Geary, 2006, for a review). The numerical facility is often composed of arithmetical computation and number relation-ships. The reasoning factor requires the ability to find, apply, and evaluate quantitative relationships. One study reported a numerical factor for kinder-garten children that included counting, simple arithmetic, working memory for number names, and general quantitative knowledge (Osborne & Lindsey, 1967). Reasoning is related to these numerical abilities in younger students and eventually, with schooling, emerges as a more distinct ability (Geary, 2006).

WHAT EDUCATORS KNOW ABOUT YOUNG CHILDREN'S MATHEMATICAL KNOWLEDGE

A recurrent theme in these research studies is that *young children's competencies were a surprise to most preschool educators* (Heuvel-Panhuizen, 1996; Thomson et al., 2005). *Why do we keep underestimating?* Past research such as Piaget's tended to emphasize broad cognitive foundations, and focused overmuch on conservation as a prerequisite to meaningful work. Also, throughout primary school, curricula and teachers continue to teach children concepts and skills they already know. Moreover, studies show that teachers recognize when tasks are too difficult, but tend to completely overlook tasks that provide no challenge to children—that do not demand enough (Heuvel-Panhuizen, 1996). Most children, especially those who have some number knowledge, learn little or nothing in kindergarten (Wright, 1991). All too often, children "busy at work" is interpreted as children working at an adequate level. Thus, it is essential that all educators learn more about children's learning (Thomson et al., 2005).

In summary, educators need to know where their children start mathematically and where they can go. This is one of the most important reasons we put *learning trajectories* front and center. Let us turn to this critical idea.

Learning Trajectories: Foundation for Effective, Research-based Education

Research suggests that foundational mathematical knowledge begins during infancy and undergoes extensive development over the first five years of life. It is just as natural for young children to think pre-mathematically and then mathematically as it is for them to use language, because "humans are born with a fundamental sense of quantity" (Geary, 1994, p. 1), as well as spatial sense, and a propensity to search for patterns.

Young children have the interests and ability to engage in significant mathematical thinking and learning. Their abilities extend beyond what is introduced in most programs (Aubrey, 1997; Clements, 1984b; Geary, 1994; Griffin & Case, 1997; Klein & Starkey, 2004). There are vast opportunities for early childhood educators to support this thinking, but also significant challenges. There are so many topics and so many different ways children think and act concerning those topics, that determining the content, structure, and pedagogical approach to early mathematics is a daunting task.

Big Ideas of Mathematics

We believe the research supports two related approaches. First, establishing a clear picture of the big ideas of mathematics for young children (Bowman et al., 2001; Clements, 2004; Fuson, 2004; Griffin et al., 1995; Tibbals, 2000; Weiss, 2002). Second, laying down paths for learning that help children develop those ideas. By the "big ideas of mathematics," we refer to overarching clusters and concepts and skills that are mathematically central and coherent, consistent with children's thinking, and generative of future learning (Clements & Conference Working Group, 2004; NCTM, 2006). This organization reflects the idea that children's early competencies are organized around several large conceptual domains.

An Introduction to Learning Trajectories

We have seen that even the youngest children possess powerful beginnings of mathematical ideas, and they use and develop these ideas to make sense of their everyday activities. However, their ideas and their interpretations of situations are particularly different from those of adults. Early childhood teachers must be particularly careful not to assume that children "see" situations, problems, or solutions as adults do. Therefore, teachers should interpret what the child is doing and thinking and attempt to see the situation from the child's point of view. Based on their interpretations, teachers conjecture what the child might be able to learn or abstract from potential educational experiences. Similarly, when they interact with the child, teachers also consider their own actions from the child's point of view. We believe that learning trajectories are the most powerful tool teachers can use to do this well.

In developing competencies with "big ideas," children often pass through a sequence of levels of thinking. These developmental progressions can underlie *hypothetical learning trajectories*, a pedagogical construct whose usefulness is supported by research (Bredekamp, 2004; Clements & Sarama, 2004b; Simon, 1995). Learning trajectories have three parts: a goal (that is, an aspect of a mathematical domain children should learn), a developmental progression, or learning path through which children move through levels of thinking, and instruction that helps them move along that path. Formally, learning trajectories are descriptions of children's thinking as they learn to achieve specific goals in a mathematical domain, and a related, conjectured route through a set of instructional tasks designed to engender those mental processes or actions hypothesized to move children through a developmental progression of levels of thinking (Clements & Sarama, 2004c).

Learning trajectories are useful pedagogical, as well as theoretical, constructs (Bredekamp, 2004; Clements & Sarama, 2004b; Simon, 1995; Smith, Wiser, Anderson, & Krajcik, 2006). Knowledge of developmental progressions—levels of understanding and skill, each more sophisticated than the last—is essential for high-quality teaching based on understanding both mathematics and children's thinking and learning. Early childhood teachers' knowledge of young children's mathematical development is related to their students' achievement (Carpenter, Fennema, Peterson, & Carey, 1988; Peterson, Carpenter, & Fennema, 1989). In another study, the few teachers that actually led in-depth discussions in reform mathematics classrooms saw themselves not as moving through a curriculum, but as helping students move through levels of understanding (Fuson, Carroll, & Drueck, 2000).

Further, researchers suggest that professional development focused on developmental progressions increases not only teachers' professional knowledge but also their students' motivation and achievement (B. A. Clarke, 2004; D. M. Clarke et al., 2001; D. M. Clarke et al., 2002; Fennema et al., 1996; Kühne, van den Heuvel-Panhulzen, & Ensor, 2005; G. Thomas & Ward, 2001; Wright, Martland, Stafford, & Stanger, 2002). Thus, learning trajectories can facilitate developmentally appropriate teaching and learning for all children (cf. M. Brown, Blondel, Simon, & Black, 1995). For these reasons, this review attempts to explicate the developmental progressions in each mathematical domain.

Just as important are the correlated instructional tasks. A description of children's development is essential, but is, alone, insufficient as it tells what types of thinking to look for and to facilitate, but not how to facilitate children's development of that "next level." The entire learning trajectory explains the levels of thinking, the mental ideas and actions that must be built, the processes that will engender those ideas and actions (e.g., promote learning) and specific instructional tasks and teaching strategies based on those processes. Tasks are often designed to present a problem that is just beyond the children's present level of operating, so they need to actively engage in reformulating the problem or their solution strategies, often with peers and teacher guidance. In reflecting on their activity, they see whether they have solved the original problem, or need to engage in more thinking. This cycle may continue until a new level of thinking is built. Exemplary series of lessons in Japan follow class based learning paths that are consistent with the notion of learning trajectories as described here (Murata & Fuson, 2006). Finally, a focus on both "big ideas" and the "conceptual storylines" of curricula in the form of hypothetical learning trajectories is supported by research on systemic reform initiatives (Heck, Weiss, Boyd, & Howard, 2002).

The learning trajectories we describe were developed as part of the *Building Blocks* project. Funded by the National Science Foundation (NSF)[3] to develop PreK to grade 2, software-enhanced, mathematics curricula, *Building Blocks* was a curriculum development and research project. Based on theory and research on early childhood learning and teaching (Bowman et al., 2001; Clements, 2001), we determined that *Building Blocks'* basic approach would be *finding the mathematics in, and developing mathematics from, children's activity*. To do so, all aspects of the *Building Blocks* project are based on learning trajectories. Most of the examples of learning trajectories emerged from our work developing, field testing, and evaluating curricula from that project (see Chapter 15 in the companion book for a description of the 10-phase Curriculum Research Framework model we created, and used, for *Building Blocks'* development).

Theoretical Frameworks

What theories are most useful in helping us understand and facilitate young children's mathematical thinking and learning? We will first briefly describe existing frameworks, then describe our own, a synthesis of the others we find particularly consistent with research evidence, and particularly useful for teaching.

Existing Frameworks

Three main theoretical frameworks for understanding young children's mathematical thinking are empiricism, (neo)nativism, and interactionalism. The introductory quote by Thorndike illustrates an *empiricist* framework. In traditional empiricism, the child is seen as a "blank slate," truth lies in correspondences between children's knowledge and reality, and knowledge is received by the learner via social transmission or abstracted from repeated experience with a separate ontological reality. An extension, traditional information processing theory, uses the computer as a metaphor for the mind and moves slightly toward an interactionalist perspective.

In contrast, *nativist* theories, in the tradition of philosophical rationalism (e.g., Plato and Kant), emphasize the inborn, or early developing, capabilities of the child. For example, quantitative or spatial cognitive structures present in infancy support the development of later mathematics, and thus innate structures are fundamental to mathematical development. Many theorists build on Gelman and Gallistel's "privileged domains hypothesis" (Rittle-Johnson & Siegler, 1998). In this view, a small number of innate and/or early-developing mathematical competencies are privileged and easy to learn. These are hypothesized to have evolutionary significance and be acquired or displayed by children in diverse cultures at approximately the same age. This is in contrast to other perspectives that would explain relative competence as resulting from frequency of experience. As we shall see in more detail, neither the empiricist nor nativist position fully explains children's learning and development. An intermediate position appears warranted, such as interactionalist theories that recognize the interacting roles of the nature and nurture (Newcombe, 2002).

In *interactionalist, constructivist* theories, children actively and recursively create knowledge. Structure and content of this knowledge are intertwined and each structure constitutes the organization and components from which the child builds the next, more sophisticated, structure. In comparison to nativism's initial representational cognition, children's early structures are prerepresentational.

Constructivist theories take several forms. In all, children are not passive receivers of knowledge, but active builders of their own intellects. In some forms, knowledge is seen as learning about an objective reality. In contrast, in others (sometimes called "radical constructivism"), cognition is adaptive and serves to help children organize their experiential world, rather than uncover or discover a separate, objective ontology. Such constructivism often uses an evolutionary view of cognitive development, in which the children generate cognitive schemes to solve perceived problems and test them to see how well they fit the experiential world. (A scheme is a cognitive unit with three components: a structure that recognizes a situation, a process that acts on that situations, and a result.) "Social constructivism," building on Vygotsky's seminal work, holds that individuals and the society are interconnected in fundamental ways; there is no isolated cognition.

Hierarchic Interactionalism: Our Theoretical Framework

We believe the research reviewed here supports a synthesis of aspects of previous theoretical frameworks that we call *hierarchic interactionalism*. The term indicates the influence and interaction of global and local (domain specific) cognitive levels and the interactions of innate competencies, internal resources, and experience (e.g., cultural tools and teaching). Mathematical ideas are represented intuitively, then with language, then metacognitively, with the last indicating that the child possesses an understanding of the topic and can access and operate on those understandings. The tenets of hierarchic interactionalism follow; research supporting these tenets will be developed throughout the book.

1. *Developmental progression.* Most content knowledge is acquired along developmental progressions of levels of thinking.[4] These progressions play a special role in children's cognition and learning because they are particularly consistent with children's intuitive knowledge and patterns of thinking and learning at various levels of development (at least in a particular culture, but guided in all cultures by "initial bootstraps"—see below), with each level characterized by specific mental objects (e.g., concepts) and actions (processes) (e.g., Clements, Wilson, & Sarama, 2004; Steffe & Cobb, 1988). These actions-on-objects are children's main way of operating on, knowing, and learning about, the world, including the world of mathematics.

2. *Domain specific progression.* These developmental progressions often are most propitiously characterized within a specific mathematical domain or topic (see also Dowker, 2005; Karmiloff-Smith, 1992; cf. Resnick's "conceptual rationalism," 1994; Van de Rijt & Van Luit, 1999). Children's knowledge, including the objects and actions they have developed in that domain, is the *main determinant of the thinking within each progression*, although hierarchic interactions occur at multiple levels within and between topics, as well as with general

cognitive processes (e.g., executive, or metacognitive processes, potentialities for general reasoning and learning-to-learn skills, and some other domain general developmental processes, see Chapter 13).

3. *Hierarchic development.* This key tenet contains two ideas. First, development is less about the emergence of entirely new processes and products and more an interactive interplay among specific existing components of knowledge and processes (both general and specific, often with the formation of an executive procedure controlling others) (Minsky, 1986; cf. Newcombe & Huttenlocher, 2000). Second, each level builds hierarchically on the concepts and processes of the previous levels (e.g., Goodson, 1982). In a related vein, developmental progressions within a domain can repeat themselves in new contexts (e.g., Siegler & Booth, 2004). Levels of thinking are coherent and often characterized by increased sophistication, complexity, abstraction, power, and generality. However, the learning process is more often incremental and gradually integrative than intermittent and tumultuous (i.e., occurring mainly between stable levels, although new experiences can engender rapid change to a new level). Various models and types of thinking grow in tandem to a degree, but a critical mass of ideas from each level must be constructed before thinking characteristic of the subsequent level becomes ascendant in the child's thinking and behavior (Clements, Battista, & Sarama, 2001). Successful application leads to the increasing use of a particular level. However, under conditions of increased task complexity, stress, or failure this probability level decreases and an earlier level serves as a fallback position (Hershkowitz & Dreyfus, 1991; Siegler & Alibali, 2005). No level of thinking is deleted from memory (Davis, 1984). That is, re-recording a mental representation at a more explicit level—an essential developmental process (of "Representational Redescription") does not erase the earlier representation (Karmiloff-Smith, 1992). (Indeed, replacing or deleting any successful representations would eliminate "fall-back" strategies that arguably are essential when new, untested knowledge is being formed, cf. Minsky, 1986; Vurpillot, 1976). The schemes that constitute the representation are instantiated dynamically (i.e., their form is interactively shaped by the situational context, including the task demands); and they can be modified at this time (or new schemes can be formed), although schemes that are basic subschemes of many other schemes become increasingly resistant to alteration because of the disruptive effect alteration would have on cognitive functioning. The continued existence of earlier levels, and the role of intentionality and social

influences in their instantiation, explains why in some contexts even adults fall back to earlier levels, for example, failing to conserve in certain situations.[5]

4. *Cyclic concretization.* Developmental progressions often proceed from sensory-concrete and implicit levels at which perceptual concrete supports are necessary and reasoning is restricted to limited cases (such as small numbers) to more explicit, verbally-based (or enhanced) generalizations and abstractions that are tenuous to integrated-concrete understandings relying on internalized mental representations that serve as mental models for operations and abstractions that are increasingly sophisticated and powerful. Again, such progressions can cycle within domains and contexts.

5. *Co-mutual development of concepts and skills.* Concepts constrain procedures, and concepts and skills develop in constant interaction (Baroody, Lai, & Mix, 2005; Greeno, Riley, & Gelman, 1984). In imbalanced cultural or educational environments, one of the two may take precedence, to an extent that can be harmful. Effective instruction often places initial priority on conceptual understanding, including children's creations of solution procedures (e.g., Carpenter, Franke, Jacobs, Fennema, & Empson, 1998), the importance of autonomy (Kamii & Housman, 1999), and mathematical dispositions and beliefs ("Once students have learned procedures without understanding, it can be difficult to get them to engage in activities to help them understand the reasons underlying the procedure," Kilpatrick et al., 2001, p. 122). The constructs of concepts and skills include symbolic representations, utilization competence (Greeno et al., 1984), and general cognitive skills.

6. *Initial bootstraps.* Children have important, but often inchoate, premathematical and general cognitive competencies and predispositions at birth or soon thereafter that support and constrain, but do not absolutely direct, subsequent development of mathematics knowledge. Some of these have been called "experience-expectant processes" (Greenough, Black, & Wallace, 1987), in which universal experiences lead to an interaction of inborn capabilities and environmental inputs that guide development in similar ways across cultures and individuals. They are not built-in representations or knowledge, but predispositions and pathways to guide the development of knowledge (cf. Karmiloff-Smith, 1992). Other general cognitive and metacognitive competencies make children—from birth— active participants in their learning and development (D. Tyler & McKenzie, 1990).

7. *Different developmental courses.* Different developmental courses are possible within those constraints, depending on individual,

environmental, and social confluences (Clements et al., 2001; Confrey & Kazak, 2006). Within any developmental course, at each level of development, children have a variety of cognitive tools—concepts, strategies, skills, utilization and situation knowledge—which coexist. The differences within and across individuals create variation that is the wellspring of invention and development. At a group level, however, these variations are not so wide as to vitiate the theoretical or practical usefulness of the tenet of developmental progressions; for example, in a class of 30, there may be only a handful of different solution strategies (Murata & Fuson, 2006), many of which represent different levels along the developmental progression.

8. *Progressive hierarchization.* Within and across developmental progressions, children gradually make connections between various mathematically relevant concepts and procedures, weaving ever more robust understandings that are hierarchical, in that they employ generalizations while maintaining differentiations. These generalizations and metacognitive abilities eventually connect to form logical-mathematical structures that virtually compel children toward decisions in certain domains, such as those on traditional Piagetian conservation of number tasks, that are resistant to confounding via misleading perceptual cues. Children provided with high-quality educational experiences build similar structures across a wide variety of mathematical domains (again, in contrast to instrumental knowledge, Skemp, 1976). (Maintaining such hierarchical cognitive structures makes more demands on the educational environment and the learner as mathematics becomes more complex, beyond the early childhood years.)

9. *Environment and culture.* Environment and culture affect the pace and direction of the developmental courses. For example, the degree of experience children have to observe and use number and other mathematical notions and to compare these uses will affect the rate and depth of their learning along the developmental progressions. The degree to which children learn mathematical words, exposure to which varies greatly across cultural groups (Hart & Risley, 1995), affects developmental courses. Words alert children to the class of related words to be learned and to specific mathematical properties, laying the foundation for learning mathematical concepts and language (cf. Sandhofer & Smith, 1999) by providing a nexus on which to build their nascent constructs (Vygotsky, 1934/1986). Because environment, culture, and education affect developmental progressions, there is no single or "ideal" developmental progression, nor learning trajectory. Universal developmental factors interact with culture and mathematical content, so the number of paths is not

unlimited. For example, educational innovations may establish new, potentially more advantageous, sequences.

10. *Consistency of developmental progressions and instruction.* Instruction based on learning consistent with natural developmental progressions is more effective, efficient, and generative for the child than learning that does not follow these paths.

11. *Learning trajectories.* An implication of the tenets to this point is that a particularly fruitful instructional approach is based on hypothetical learning trajectories (Clements & Sarama, 2004c). Based on the hypothesized, specific, mental constructions (mental actions-on-objects) and patterns of thinking that constitute children's thinking, curriculum developers design instructional tasks that include external objects and actions that mirror the hypothesized mathematical activity of children as closely as possible. These tasks are sequenced, with each corresponding to a level of the developmental progressions, to complete the hypothesized learning trajectory. Such tasks will theoretically constitute a particularly efficacious educational program; however, there is no implication that the task sequence is the only path for learning and teaching; only that it is hypothesized to be one fecund route. Tasks present a problem; people's actions and strategies to solve the problem are represented and discussed; reflection on whether the problem is solved or partially solved, leads to new understandings (mental actions and objects, organized into strategies and structures) and actions (the "cycle of constructive activity" that helps select viable ideas, Confrey & Kazak, 2006). *Specific learning trajectories are the main bridge that connects the "grand theory" of hierarchic interactionalism to particular theories and educational practice* (Confrey & Kazak, 2006).

12. *Instantiation of hypothetical learning trajectories.* Hypothetical learning trajectories must be interpreted by teachers and are only realized through the social interaction of teachers and children around instructional tasks. Societally-determined values and goals are substantive components of any curriculum (Confrey, 1996; Hiebert, 1999; Shavelson & Towne, 2002; R. W. Tyler, 1949); research cannot ignore or determine these components (cf. Lester & Wiliam, 2002). "There is no understanding without reflection, and reflection is an activity students have to carry out themselves. No one else can do it for them. Yet a teacher who has some inkling as to where a particular student is in his or her conceptual development has a better chance of fostering a further reflective abstraction than one who merely follows the sequence of a preestablished curriculum" (Glasersfeld, 1995, p. 382).

The Promise and the Broken Promises

Children have an impressive, often untapped, potential to learn mathematics. For many this has been a potential largely left unrealized. It is not their developmental limitation, but a limitation of the society and its schools. What has been said of learning in the sciences applies equally well to mathematics: "What children are capable of at a particular age is the result of a complex interplay among maturation, experience, and instruction. What is developmentally appropriate is not a simple function of age or grade, but rather is largely contingent on prior opportunities to learn" (Duschl, Schweingruber, & Shouse, 2007, p. 2).

Final Words

The research and theory described in this chapter indicated that learning trajectories can facilitate developmentally appropriate teaching and learning for all children. That is why we planned Chapters 2 to 12 to build learning trajectories for each critical topic in early mathematics. Part II introduces the essential topic of number and arithmetic.

Part II
Number and Quantitative Thinking

For early childhood, number and operations is arguably the most important area of mathematics learning. Fortunately, learning of this area also may be one of the best-developed domains in mathematics research, especially in the early primary grades (Baroody, 2004; Fuson, 2004; Kilpatrick et al., 2001; Steffe, 2004). Learning of number in preschool, although an emergent area, benefits from a wealth of psychological and early childhood studies.

In the chapters in Part II, we discuss children's numerical concepts and operations separately, although they and their components are highly inter-related. We do not limit "operations" to standard arithmetic operations of adding, subtracting, multiplying, and dividing, but include counting, comparing, unitizing, grouping, partitioning, and composing. The importance of these ideas is highlighted by their close correspondence to the components of *number sense*, including composing and decomposing numbers, recognizing the relative magnitude of numbers, dealing with the absolute magnitude of numbers, using benchmarks, linking representations, understanding the effects of arithmetic operations, inventing strategies, estimating, and possessing a disposition toward making sense of numbers (Sowder, 1992b). The competencies rest on early quantitative reasoning that begins to develop as early as the first two years of life. Preceding recent cognitive science by half a century, Vygotsky said, "The first stage is formed by the natural arithmetical endowment of the child, i.e., his operation of quantities before he knows how to count. We include here the immediate conception of quantity, the comparison of greater and smaller groups, the recognition of some quantitative group, the distribution into single objects where it is necessary to divide, etc." (Vygotsky, 1929/1994, p. 67).

2

Quantity, Number, and Subitizing

In 1917, Warren McCulloch's academic advisor asked him to describe his research interests. He replied, "What is number, that a man [*sic*] may know it, and a man that he may know number?" His advisor responded, "Friend, thee will be busy as long as thee lives" (McCulloch, 1963, p. 1).

We begin this chapter with a brief historical review of the early development of quantitative knowledge. For example, is it based in logic, in counting, or in some other process? As an example of the last, early sensitivity to number, and the ability the recognize or name a number without counting, has been called *subitizing*—the direct and rapid perceptual apprehension of the numerosity of a group, from the Latin "to arrive suddenly" (named by Kaufman, Lord, Reese, & Volkmann, 1949, who referred to verbal naming of the numerosity). We review research on subitizing in this chapter, and turn to counting in the next.

Introduction to the Early Development of Quantity

Over more than 100 years, research on early number knowledge has passed through four broad phases (cf. Clements, 1984b).[1] After a prescient analysis of early number by Dewey (1898), researchers studied subitizing, counting, and the relationship between subitizing and counting (e.g., Douglass, 1925; Freeman, 1912). (Mathematician Bertrand Russell, 1919, asserted that all traditional pure mathematics could be derived from the natural numbers.)

In the second phase, the wide influence of Piagetian theory redirected theoretical and empirical study, as it explained the development of number concepts based on underlying logical operations (Clements, 1984a, 1984c; Wright, Stanger, Stafford, & Martland, 2006).

> "Our hypothesis is that the construction of number goes hand-in-hand with the development of logic, and that a pre-numerical period corresponds with the pre-logical level. Our results do, in fact, show that number is organized, stage after stage, in close connection with the gradual elaboration of systems of inclusions (hierarchy of logical classes) and systems of asymmetrical relations (qualitative seriations), the sequence of numbers thus resulting from an operational synthesis of classification and seriation. In our view, logical and arithmetical operations therefore constitute a single system that is psychologically natural, the second resulting from generalization and fusion of the first,

under the two complementary headings of inclusion of classes and seriation of relations, quality being disregarded."

(Piaget & Szeminska, 1952, p. viii).

It may seem at first that this makes little sense—what does number have to do with a "hierarchy of logical classes"? An argument can be made that number and counting depend on such logical operations. For example, to understand counting, children must understand that each number *includes* those that came before. Figure 2.1 illustrates this notion.

Similarly, sequencing is an important aspect of meaningful counting. On the procedural side, children have to both properly produce number words in sequence and sequence the objects they count so that they count each object exactly once (no easy task for young children faced with a unorganized group). Conceptually, children have to understand this *and* that each counting number is *quantitatively* one more than the one before, illustrated in Figure 2.2.

The Piagetians viewed counting as ineffectual, with "no connection between the acquired ability to count and the actual operations of which the child is

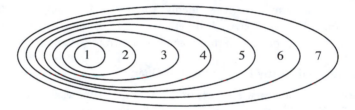

Figure 2.1 The hierarchical classification of numbers—each cardinal number includes those that came before.

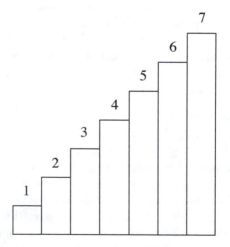

Figure 2.2 The seriation of numbers: Each comes after, and is one more than, the previous number.

capable" (p. 61), with the child *capable* of meaningful counting only upon reaching the level of reversible operation (p. 184). In support of this notion, they give examples of children who can count, but still fail the number conservation task. For example, although at a certain age they can make a set equal in number to an interviewer's set using matching, such as in Figure 2.3, when the interviewer spreads her or his objects out as in Figure 2.4, the child may claim that the interviewer now has more. Directly to the point, asking children to count the two sets, according to Piaget, did not help them determine the correct answer.

Based on such reasons, many studies in the Piagetian tradition tended to disregard subitizing as well as counting, which had been the major focus of earlier studies of number concepts. From this view, children do not acquire a notion of quantity and then conserve it; they discover true quantification only when they become capable of conservation. This develops in three stages: stage 1, gross quantity, in which children make global perceptual judgments without one-to-one correspondence; stage 2, intensive quantity, in which they can make one-to-one correspondences perceptually but cannot conserve (such as the example in Figures 2.3 and 2.4); and stage 3, in which they construct the notion of unit and numerical correspondence and they understand that length and density compensate each other and that changes are reversible. Spatial qualities no longer determine number. The elements become equivalent and interchangeable units (i.e., equivalent members of a class), differing only by their relative order (i.e., seriation). Each successive element creates a category containing all previous classes (i.e., hierarchical inclusion).

The result was a broad belief, in research and educational practice, that children could not reason logically about quantities until the early elementary school years. This view appeared to be supported by hundreds of investigations of the validity of the Piagetian stages. Studies generally supported the existence

Figure 2.3 Children may use 1-to-1 correspondence to build a row with the same number as another row.

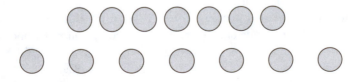

Figure 2.4 If one row is spread out, children who do *not* conserve believe that row has "more." Children who conserve number understand the rows still have the same number.

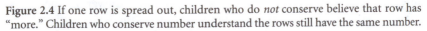

of the stages (Clements, 1984a). For example, children scoring lower on tests of conservation scored significantly lower on tests of problem solving (Harper & Steffe, 1968; Steffe, 1966).

The third phase began when new perspectives and research methodologies challenged critical aspects of the Piagetian view. Researchers questioned whether the Piagetian tasks measured number knowledge or other competencies, such as attending to relevant attributes (R. Gelman, 1969). Others doubted the Piaget position that without logical operations there is no possibility of meaningful quantitative reasoning, and, therefore, it makes no sense to attempt to develop children's number abilities, such as counting. Supporting the new perspective, seminal research showed numerical and arithmetic competencies in young children who were not operational in Piagetian assessments (R. Gelman, 1969; Harper & Steffe, 1968). For example, in Gelman and Gallistel's (1978) "magic" experiments, two plates where shown, one with, for example, two toy mice, called "the loser," and the other with three mice, called "the winner." After a series of identification tasks, the experimenter surreptitiously altered the winner, changing the spatial arrangement in some experiments (e.g., putting the three mice closer together or in a triangular arrangement rather than a line), altering the identity of the items or size of the collection in others (e.g., three smaller mice, or three toy dogs). The result we emphasize here is that children as young as three, and sometimes two and a half, years seem to know that transformations involving displacements do not change the numerical value of a display—an early form of conservation of number (R. Gelman & Gallistel, 1978). That is, they still called the plate with three "the winner." Children preferred to make such decisions based on equivalence or nonequivalence of verbal numbers, rather than on the one-to-one object correspondences emphasized in Piagetian studies. Such studies formed the basis for a *nativist* view of early number development.

Other researchers built number skills-integration models. Taking an information-processing approach, these empiricist-oriented models used task and scalogram analyses to describe sequences of learning numerals, counting and numeration of small before larger collections, and independence of counting and one-to-one correspondence (M. Wang, Resnick, & Boozer, 1971). Other models postulated hierarchic skills-integration sequences (Klahr & Wallace, 1976; Schaeffer, Eggleston, & Scott, 1974). Numerous studies supported the contention of a multidimensional concept of number in young children (Clements, 1984a).

The fourth and present phase is an extension of the third phase. Debates continue about the meaning of early (and lack of) competence (Baroody et al., 2006; Cordes & Gelman, 2005; Mix, Huttenlocher, & Levine, 2002; T. J. Simon, 1997; Spelke, 2003; Uller, Carey, Huntley-Fenner, & Klatt, 1999). Some researchers have attempted to synthesize components of the various theoretical perspectives or create intermediate positions. Nativist, empiricist, and interactionalist accounts have been evaluated both philosophically and empirically. Number knowledge similarly has been subjected to analysis, resulting in more sophisticated conceptualizations. For example, it appears that number and quantitative knowledge develops substantially earlier than Piagetian logical operations, but nonetheless appears to be built upon inchoate foundations, such as unitizing or creating an image of a collection of objects (classification) and tracking and ordering (seriation).

Issues concerning nativist, empiricist, and interactionalist accounts arise in this and most all remaining chapters. In the remainder of this section, we illustrate these issues by focusing on children's initial competence with number. For example, using new techniques, some researchers claimed that infants possessed understanding of cardinality. Many of these researchers built on Gelman and Gallistel's nativist position, including the privileged domains (see Chapter 1, p. 19) of whole-number counting and simple arithmetic, which necessitated an underlying foundation of both cardinality and ordinality. The hypothesis predicts that conceptual understanding precedes skilled execution of the relevant procedures in these domains (R. Gelman & Gallistel, 1978). In contrast, the empiricist skills-integration approach would predict that exposure frequency determines development, and thus procedural skill would emerge before conceptual development. The philosophical assumption appears to be that number is "out there."

Providing evidence for their position, nativists reported that babies in the first six months of life, and even in the first day of life, can discriminate one object from two, and two objects from three (Antell & Keating, 1983; Starkey, Spelke, & Gelman, 1990). This was determined via a *habituation* paradigm in which infants "lose interest" in a series of displays that differ in some ways, but have the same number of objects. For example, say that infants are shown a sequence of pictures that contain a small set of objects, such as two circular regions. The collections differ in attributes such as size, density, brightness, or color, but there are always two objects, such as those in the top row of Figure 2.5. The differences between successive pictures initially keep infants' attention—they continue to look at each picture in turn. Eventually, however, they *habituate* to the displays; for example, they begin to look at the screen less, and their eyes wander and their breathing becomes more relaxed. Then they are shown a collection of three circular regions that are similar in attributes to those they had previously seen, such as that in the bottom of Figure 2.5, and their eyes focus intently on this new collection and their breathing is more rapid. Such renewed interest when shown a display with a different number of objects provides evidence that they are sensitive to number (Wynn, Bloom, & Chiang, 2002). Thus, infants can discriminate among and match small configurations (one to three) of objects. The experiments also indicate that children's discrimination is limited to such small numbers. Children do not discriminate four objects from five or six until the age of three or four years

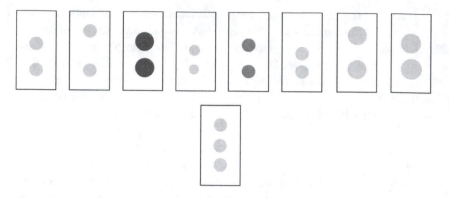

Figure 2.5 Collections of 2, and 3, that also vary in other attributes.

(Starkey & Cooper, 1980). Some researchers have therefore suggested that infants use an automatic perceptual process that people, including adults, can apply only to small collections up to around four objects (Chi & Klahr, 1975). (We return to the issue of subitizing as a construct in the next main section.) Children can also construct quantitative equivalence relations by six- to eight-months of age through exchange operations (substituting or commuting objects) (Langer, Rivera, Schlesinger, & Wakeley, 2003).

Some initial competence is generally accepted. What this competence *means,* however, remains in dispute. Some studies suggest that infants in "number" experiments may be responding to overall contour length, area, mass, or density, rather than discrete number (Feigenson, Carey, & Spelke, 2002; Tan & Bryant, 2000). In one study, infants dishabituated to changes in contour length when the number of objects was held constant, but they did not dishabituate to changes in number when contour length was held constant (Clearfield & Mix, 1999). To illustrate, the researchers showed six- to eight-month-old infants two squares with a total contour length of 16 in different spatial arrangements (i.e., the perimeter of each square was 8 cm in the original display, scaled in the top row of Fig. 2.6a). Once the child habituated on these, the researchers showed them one of two types of pictures. The first group contained the familiar contour length, but a different number. That is, the two pictures in Figure 2.6b have three squares, but the total contour length was 16. The second group contained the familiar number, but a different contour length. That is, the two pictures in Figure 2.6c have three squares, but the total contour length was 24—exactly what the contour would have been if a display had three squares like those of the top, habituation row (3 times 8). The results were that infants looked more often at the change in contour length, 2.6c, than they did to the change in number, Figure 2.6b. In another experiment, the researcher similarly changed area and number. Again, the infants noticed change in area, but not number.

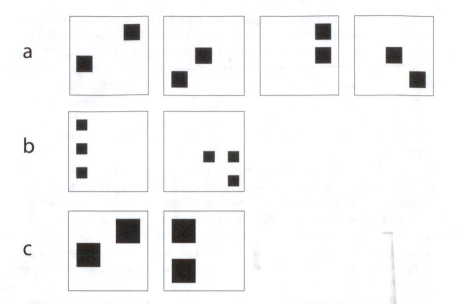

Figure 2.6 Collections that vary in either number or counter length and area.

Another theory is that infants create mental "object files" that store data on each object's properties. They can use these object files to respond differently to various situations. Thus, some situations can be addressed by using the objects' individuation or separateness as objects, and others can be addressed by using the analog properties of these objects, such as contour length (Feigenson, Carey, & Spelke, 2002). For example, children might use parallel-processed individuation for very small collections, but continuous extent used when storage for individuation is exceeded. Note that, from our perspective, even if such individuation is accepted as an early basis for number, it might not in itself constitute knowledge of *number* (cf. Gordon, 2004).

The strongest claim that infants are processing number, rather than perceptual information, is based on two types of evidence. First is the claim that infants discriminate not just collections of objects, but also temporal sequences such as sounds, or events such as puppet jumps, as early as six months of age (Wynn, 1998). Second is the claim that infants show cross-modal number abilities, that is, they can match visual representations of certain numbers and auditory sequences consisting of the same number of sounds (Starkey et al., 1990). For example, if six-month old infants are shown pictures with two dots, one dot and three dots, and then hear three drumbeats, they look more often at the picture with three dots.

Such evidence has led to strong nativist claims. More recent evidence, however, has called into question these results and claims. Even if children do sometimes make these connections, general, nonnumerical processes of comparing inputs from different modalities (e.g., from sounds and their locations) may be used (T. J. Simon, 1997). More important, one team found opposing results—either no effect of auditory information and merely a tendency to prefer the larger contour (consistent with several previous studies), or longer looking at *non*corresponding displays (Moore, Benenson, Reznick, Peterson, & Kagan, 1987). (R. Gelman, 1990a, points out they still appear to be responding to number, however, there is no theoretical reason to suspect a group would be predisposed to same vs. difference.) In another study, children as old as three years performed at chance on an auditory-visual equivalence test (Mix, Huttenlocher, & Levine, 1996). There is no theoretical reason to justify why children older than three years old would have difficulty with tasks with which neonates ostensibly show competence. Consistent with these findings, more recent data found no evidence that infants notice quantitative equivalence between auditory sequences and visual displays (Mix, Levine, & Huttenlocher, 1997). Thus, there is little reason to believe that infants have the ability to deal with cross-modal quantitative correspondence or even discrete quantity (i.e., number). Finally, some cultures without language for number words above two show low performance on most quantitative tasks (Gordon, 2004).

This is not to say that strict empiricist positions are supported either. Early quantitative competencies have been demonstrated. However, many, if not all, of the earliest competencies may be explicable through other frameworks than those that assume innate number knowledge. Further, researchers have not yet studied how infants may use a variety of processes and how they may be weighted or combined, as well as how they may be evoked differently in various situations (Baroody et al., 2005). We also need to learn more about what role such processes, even if they are numerical, play in children's early cognition or development of later numerical activity (Nunes & Bryant, 1996).

A good part of the problem is, of course, that, infant studies are particularly difficult to perform and interpret. For example, the frequently employed habituation methodology, while useful, was developed to study perceptual, not conceptual issues, leaving open the question of what results mean (Haith & Benson, 1998). Nevertheless, research suggests that children discriminate collections on some quantitative base(s) from birth. Furthermore, most accounts suggest that these limited capabilities, with as yet undetermined contributions of maturation and experience, form a foundation for later connection to culturally based cognitive tools such as number words and the number word sequence, so as to develop exact and extended concepts and skills in number. For example, neuroscience investigations using functional magnetic resonance imaging (fMRI, "brain scans") show that the intraparietal sulcus (IPS) responds selectively to number changes (Piazza, Izard, Pinel, Le Bihan, & Dehaene, 2004). Such findings suggest that humans, like other animal species, encode approximate number. The IPS coding for number in humans is compatible with that observed in macaque monkeys, suggesting an evolutionary basis for human elementary arithmetic (Piazza et al., 2004). Other fMRI studies show that adults showed a greater response in their IPS to visual arrays that change in the number of elements than to stimuli that change in shape (Cantlon, Brannon, Carter, & Pelphrey, 2006). Further, four-year-olds show the same pattern of responses. Deaf people who knew Japanese but not American Sign Language, showed no activation in regions associated with numerical processing when taught ASL for numerals (but only the signs, not the meanings). However, when told what the signs represented, they showed just such activation—even when they could not accurately code those signs (Masataka, Ohnishi, Imabayashi, Hirakata, & Matsuda, 2006). Thus, there is a special neural component of early numerical cognition present in the early years that may be the foundation for later symbolic numerical development. A language-independent ability to judge numerical values nonverbally appears to be an important evolutionary precursor to adult symbolic numerical abilities.

Early Work on Subitizing

In the first half of the twentieth century, researchers believed counting did not imply a true understanding of number, but subitizing did (e.g., Douglass, 1925). Many saw the role of subitizing as a developmental prerequisite to counting. Freeman (1912) suggested that whereas measurement focused on the whole and counting focused on the unit item, only subitizing focused on both the whole and the unit—thus, subitizing underlies number ideas. Carper (1942) agreed subitizing was more accurate than counting and more effective in abstract situations. (Recall that the term "subitizing" was not created until later, Kaufman et al., 1949.)

In the second half of the century, educators developed several models of subitizing and counting. Some models were based on the notion that subitizing was a more "basic" skill than counting (Klahr & Wallace, 1976; Schaeffer et al., 1974). One reason was that children can subitize directly through interactions with the environment, without social interactions. (Consistent with the inventor of the term, Kaufman et al., 1949, we prefer to restrict "subitizing" to the verbal naming of the numerosity. Not all researchers include this requirement.) Supporting this position, Fitzhugh (1978) found that some children could subitize sets of one or two, but were not able to count them. None of these very young children, however, were able to count any sets that they could not subitize. She concluded that subitizing is a necessary precursor to counting. Research with infants similarly suggested that young children possess and spontaneously use subitizing to represent the number contained in small sets, and that subitizing emerges before counting (A. Klein & Starkey, 1988). A longitudinal study showed early recognition of number before several counting competencies developed (Wagner & Walters, 1982).

As logical as this position seems, counterarguments exist. In 1924, Beckmann found that young children used counting rather than subitizing (cited in Solter, 1976). Others agreed that children develop subitizing later, as a shortcut to counting (Beckwith & Restle, 1966; Brownell, 1928; Silverman & Rose, 1980). In this view, subitizing is a form of rapid counting (R. Gelman & Gallistel, 1978).

Evidence for subitizing as a separate process from "fast counting" includes reaction time data showing that recognition of one to three objects is faster and more accurate than larger numerosities. Reaction times increase with the number of items in a set to be quantified; it takes adults about 250 to 350 msec longer to quantify a set of seven than six, or six than five. In contrast, the increase is slight when numbers are small: about 40 to 100 msec longer to respond to three than two, or two than one, and this may be response choice time rather than time to process the stimuli. At least some data indicate that adults can process three within the same exposure time as two or one (Trick & Pylyshyn, 1994).

Nature of the Subitizing Process and the Early Development of Quantity

Researchers still debate the basis for subitizing ability. Some claim that there are two distinct types of enumeration: numerical subitizing and nonnumerical (or figural) subitizing. In addition, some models assume that subitizing is possible only for sets that are simultaneously displayed, whereas others allow for sequential enumeration (Canfield & Smith, 1996).

Recognition of spatial patterns, such as triangular arrays, and attentional mechanisms are the main explanations for those who assume an underlying *non*numerical process (Chi & Klahr, 1975; Glasersfeld, 1982; Klahr & Wallace, 1976; Mandler & Shebo, 1982). For Mandler and Shebo, these abstract geometric patterns are mapped to specific numerosities using processes like those for recognizing colors.

For Glasersfeld, the patterns are empirical abstractions, or figural patterns generated from sensory-motor experience. These occur when the child attends not to specific sensory content (e.g., three yellow plates), but to the operations that combine perceptual elements into stable patterns. Patterns are constituted by motion, either physical or attentional, forming scan-paths. It is motion, not the specific sensory material used, that determines the patterns' character. For example, scanning from one yellow plate to the next and then to the last is recognized as a similar pattern of moving one's eyes and focusing one's eyes and one's attention as scanning other groups of three objects. See the "scan-paths" column in Figure 2.7 for an illustration of this hypothesized way to subitize. All patterns are taken as figural wholes, not composites of units. Numerical subitizing requires a subsequent reflective abstraction, which occurs when the experiencing subject abstracts the mental from the sensory-motor contexts. Such empirical abstractions can also be temporal and rhythmic

(Glasersfeld, 1982). They become numerical after reflective abstraction that focuses attention on their iterative structure raises them to "pure" abstraction characteristic of the conception of number. In another model, objects are first individuated by a limited, but parallel, preattentive mechanism associated with object tracking and then markers are enumerated in a serial process (Trick & Pylyshyn, 1994). There is a neural mechanism that distinguishes single, dual, or triple incidences of a given evident, based on inherent temporal parameters.

Other models consider subitizing to be a numerical process. In the Meck and Church model (1983), subitizing is a numerical process enabled by the availability of the functional equivalent of a number line (see Chapter 4 for a mathematical discussion of number lines and a warning that mental constructs are not the same as "number line models") in the brain that operates on both simultaneous and sequential items (cf. Huntley-Fenner, 2001a). There is a pacemaker that emits equivalent pulses at a constant rate. When a unitized item (e.g., a yellow plate taken as "one") is encountered, a pulse is allowed to pass through a gate, entering an *accumulator*—think of a squirt of water entering a tall glass. The gradations on the accumulator estimate the number in the collection of units, similar to height indicating the numerosity of squirts in the glass. This is illustrated in the "accumulator" column of Figure 2.7.

An alternative model postulates an evolutionarily based, abstract *module*. A module is a distinct mental component that is dedicated to a particular process or task and is unavailable for general processing. A number perception module would perceive numbers directly (Dehaene, 1997). This counting-like process is hypothesized to guide the development of whole number counting,

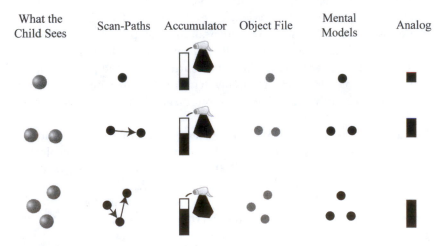

Figure 2.7 Simplified illustrations of different models of subitizing.

hypothesized to be a privileged domain (see Chapter 1, p. 40). Researchers use findings from both humans and non-human animals to support this position (Gallistel & Gelman, 2005).

Research using different methodologies suggests that infants can rapidly recognize and use the number of sequentially presented pictures to predict the location of the next picture in the sequence (Canfield & Smith, 1996). That is, the infants that repeatedly saw pictures appear in a left-left-left-right pattern were thereafter less likely to look to the right side after the first or second picture appears on the left. They were more likely to look to the right, anticipating a picture appearing there, after the third picture was presented on the right. There was no evidence they had to reaccumulate items by scanning working memory, supporting subitizing rather than fast counting, models. (G. A. Miller, 1956, agreed that his famous working-memory limit was not related to human subitizing limits.) Thus, the researchers (Canfield & Smith, 1996) judged the Meck and Church accumulator model (1983) most consistent with their results. Because infants never saw more than a single stimulus at any moment during the session and the items were presented in a manner that was neither rhythmic nor temporally predictable, the process of combining sequential events was viewed as numerical.

The Meck and Church model does *not* require that the accumulator has an *exact* representation of number (see also Feigenson, Dehaene, & Spelke, 2004). The "squirts" and the amount in the "glass" are approximate. Recent reviews (Baroody et al., 2005; Mix et al., 2002) agree that children younger than three years tend not to represent any numbers except one and two precisely. For example, three-day-old to five-month-old infants could discriminate between collections of one and two, two and three but not between collections of three and four (Antell & Keating, 1983), and 10- to 16-month-olds successfully discriminated between two and three but not between three and four or even two and four or three and six (Feigenson, Carey, & Hauser, 2002). Even in studies that did show success, results are equivocal; for example, 10–12-month-olds could discriminate between two and three items, but not four and five, with mixed results for three vs. four (Strauss & Curtis, 1984); and performance of even two-year-olds drops off on tasks involving three items, with above-chance levels not necessarily indicating exact representations (Starkey & Cooper, 1995).

There may be developmental differences in the processes that underlie subitizing (cf. Resnick & Singer, 1993). The mental models view (Huttenlocher, Jordan, & Levine, 1994; Mix et al., 2002) postulates that children represent numbers nonverbally and approximately, then nonverbally but exactly, and eventually via verbal, counting-based processes. (This in contrast to the accumulator model, which the researchers criticize as unable to account for the greater difficulty of sequential presentations, use of overall amount, such as contour length, in early quantification, and representation of cardinality, Mix et al., 2002.) In the mental models view, children cannot initially differentiate between discrete and continuous quantities, but represent both approximately using one or more perceptual cues such as contour length (Mix et al., 2002). Children develop the ability to individuate objects, providing the ability to build notions of discrete number. About the age of two years, they develop representational, or symbolic, competence (such as shown in symbolic play), allowing them to create mental models of collections, which they can retain, manipulate (move), add to or subtract from, and so forth (although the model does not adequately describe how cardinality is ultimately cognized and how comparisons are made). (This symbolization differentiates this view from the related "object files" theory, although the symbols in the mental models view are grounded in object individuation. See the "object files" column of Figure 2.7 and compare it to the "mental models" column.) Early nonverbal capabilities then provide a basis for the development of verbally-based numerical and arithmetic knowledge (young children are more successful on nonverbal than verbal versions of number and arithmetic tasks: Huttenlocher, Jordan et al., 1994; Jordan, Hanich, & Uberti, 2003; Jordan et al., 1992; Jordan, Huttenlocher, & Levine, 1994; Levine, Jordan, & Huttenlocher, 1992). (One difficulty with this argument is that calling both "arithmetic tasks" may unintentionally hide potential differences in children's schemes.) In this view, there is no reason to consider early quantitative development solely a number competence, much less assume that number is a privileged domain (Mix et al., 2002).

A recent version of this theory (Baroody et al., 2005) suggests that at the same time children are gaining representational precision, they are also moving toward more generalized but deeper (more interconnected) concepts. Approximate mental models serve as a transition between number based on perceptual cues and one based on an exact, abstract, mental model. Implicit distinctions between discrete and continuous quantities lie on a continuum from clearly distinct for collections of one to indistinct in the case of "many"— more than three or four. Meaningful learning of number words (in contrast to symbolic ability) causes the transition to exact numerical representations. Such development may apply to certain numbers at different times, even among very small numbers. The child can then begin to verbally represent numbers (beyond one and two, which may be represented nonverbally and exactly and verbally at about the same time). This may provide the basis for understanding cardinality and other counting principles, as well as arithmetic ideas (Baroody et al., 2006). Anywhere from three to six years, depending on the home and preschool environments, children also make the transition to using written representations, which helps them develop numerical or abstract reasoning.

The model that we believe is most consistent with the research is similar, with a few modifications. What infants quantify are collections of rigid objects; that is, sequences of sounds and events, or materials that are non-rigid and non-cohesive (e.g., water), are not quantified (Huntley-Fenner, Carey, & Solimando, 2002). (Quantification of rigid linear extent develops early, but not necessarily in the first few months of life, as discussed in the chapter on measurement.) Such quantifications, including number, begin as an un-differentiated, innate notion of amount of objects. Object individuation, which occurs early in preattentive processing (and is a general, not numerical, process), helps lay the groundwork for differentiating discrete from continuous quantity. Multiple systems are employed, including an object file system that stores information about the objects (the "object file" column of Figure 2.7), some or all of which is used depending on the situation, and an estimator (accumulator-type—see that column in Figure 2.7) mechanism that stores analog quantitative information only (Feigenson, Carey, & Spelke, 2002; Gordon, 2004; Johnson-Pynn, Ready, & Beran, 2005). This estimator may also include a set of number filters (a cognitive scheme detects the numerosity of a group), each tuned to an approximate number of objects (e.g., three), but overlapping (Nieder, Freedman, & Miller, 2002), that apply to very small numbers. The child encountering small sets opens object files for each in parallel. If the situation elicits quantitative comparisons, continuous extent is retrieved and used except in extreme circumstances. For example, by about a half-year of age, infants may represent very small numbers (one or two) as individuated objects (close to the "mental models" column of Figure 2.7, but only for one or two). Conversely, large numbers in which continuous extent varies or is otherwise not reliable (McCrink & Wynn, 2004) may be processed by the analog estimator as a collection of binary impulses (as are event sequences later in development, see the "analog" column of Figure 2.7), but not by exact enumeration (Shuman & Spelke, 2005), but rather by a brain region that processes quantity (size and number, undifferentiated, Pinel, Piazza, Le Bihan, & Dehaene, 2004). Without language support, these are inaccurate processes for numbers above two (Gordon, 2004).

To compare quantities, correspondences are processed. Initially, these are inexact estimates comparing the results of two estimators, depending on the ratio between the sets (Johnson-Pynn et al., 2005). Once the child can represent objects mentally, they can also make exact correspondences between these nonverbal representations, and eventually develop a quantitative notion of that comparison (e.g., not just that ••• is more than ••, but also that it contains one more •; Baroody et al., 2005).

Even these correspondences, however, do not imply a cardinal representa-tion of the collection (a representation of the collection *qua* a *numerosity* of a *group* of items). That is, we still must distinguish between noncardinal repre-sentations of a collection and *explicit* cardinal representations. Indeed, a neuroimaging study found that brain regions that represent numerical magni-tude also represent spatial magnitude, such as the relations between sizes of objects, and thus may not be numerical in function (Pinel et al., 2004). Only for the latter does the individual apply an integration operation to create a composite with some numerical index. Some claim that the accumulator yields a cardinal output; however, it may be quantitative, and even numerical in some situations, but constituted as an indexing of a collection using an abstract, cross-modality system for numerical magnitude (Shuman & Spelke, 2005) without an explicit cardinality. This system would not necessarily differentiate between ordinal and cardinal interpretations. Comparisons, such as correspondence mapping, might still be performed, but only at an implicit level (cf. Sandhofer & Smith, 1999). (Anticipating a discussion of cardinality in the succeeding section on counting, it is possible to connect such an indexing to a numerical label without attributing explicit cardinality. For example, lower animal species seem to have some perceptual number abilities, but only birds and primates also have shown the ability to connect a subitized number with a written mark or auditory label, Davis & Perusse, 1988). In this view, only with experience representing and naming collections is an explicit cardinal representation created. This is a prolonged process. Children may initially make word-word mappings between requests for counting or numbers (e.g., "how many?") to number words until they have learned several (Sandhofer & Smith, 1999). Then they label some (small number) cardinal situations with the corresponding number word, that is, map the number word to the numerosity property of the collection. They begin this phase even before two years of age, but for some time, this applies mainly to the word "two," a bit less to "one," and with considerable lower frequency, "three" and "four" (Fuson, 1992a; Wagner & Walters, 1982). Only after many such experiences do children abstract the numerosities from the specific situations and begin to understand that the situations named by "three" correspond; that is, they begin to establish what adults would term a numerical equivalence class. Counting-based verbal systems are then more heavily used and integrated, as described in the following section, eventually leading to explicit, verbal, mathematical abstractions. The construction of such schemes probably depend on guiding frameworks and principles developed from interactions with others, especially parents, teachers, and other knowledgeable people. Our model is supported by research on speakers of Mundurukú in the Amazon, who lack number words for numbers above five. They can compare and add large approximate numbers, but fail in exact arithmetic (Pica, Lemer, Izard, & Dehaene, 2004).

In summary, early quantitative abilities exist, but they may not initially constitute systems that can be said to have an explicit number concept. Instead, they may be pre-mathematical, foundational abilities (cf. Clements, Sarama et al., 2004) that develop and integrate slowly, in a piecemeal fashion (Baroody, Benson, & Lai, 2003). For example, object individuation must be stripped of perceptual characteristics and understood as a perceptual unit item through abstracting and unitizing to be mathematical (Steffe & Cobb, 1988), and these items must be considered simultaneously as individual units and members of a collection whose numerosity has a cardinal representation to be numerical, even at the lowest levels. The explicit, cultural, numeral-based sense of number develops in interaction with, but does not replace (indeed, may always be based on, Gallistel & Gelman, 2005), the analog sense of number. Regardless of its origins in continuous or discontinuous processing, number rather than amount of substances does achieve a core status in quantitative reasoning for preschoolers to adults (K. F. Miller, 1995). The human facility with language probably plays a central role in linking relations between different representations and thus making early pre-mathematical cognition numeric (cf. Gordon, 2004; Wiese, 2003a). Some have claimed that linguistic factors play an important *bootstrapping* role. That is, grammatical structures for plurals ("dogs") and quantifiers ("some," "all," and "a") provide a framework that allows quantitative ideas to develop (Carey, 2004).

Types of Subitizing

Regardless of the precise mental processes, subitizing appears to be phenomenologically distinct from counting and other means of quantification and deserves differentiated educational consideration. Supporting this assertion is evidence that there is little or no relationship between children's performance on counting and subitizing tasks (Pepper & Hunting, 1998). Further, subitizing ability is not merely a low-level, innate process. As stated previously, in contrast to what might be expected from a view of innate ability, subitizing *develops* considerably and combines with other mental processes. *Perceptual subitizing* (Clements, 1999b; see also a theoretical justification in Karmiloff-Smith, 1992) is closest to the original definition of subitizing: recognizing a number without consciously using other mental or mathematical processes and then naming it.

Perceptual subitizing employs a pre-attentional quantitative process but adds an intentional numerical process; that is, infant sensitivity to number is not (yet) perceptual subitizing. The term "perceptual" applies only to the quantification mechanism as phenomenologically experienced by the person; the intentional numerical labeling, of course, makes the complete cognitive act conceptual.

Perceptual subitizing also plays the primitive role of *unitizing*, or making single "things" to count out of the stream of perceptual sensations (Glasersfeld, 1995). "Cutting out" pieces of experience, keeping them separate, and eventually coordinating them with number words are not trivial tasks for young children. For example, a toddler, to recognize the existence of a plurality, must focus on the items such as apples and repeatedly apply a template for an apple *and* attend to the *repetition* of the template application.

A second type of subitizing (a distinction for which there is empirical evidence, Trick & Pylyshyn, 1994), *conceptual subitizing* (Clements, 1999b) plays an advanced organizing role, as seeing "10" on a pair of dice by recognizing the two collections (via perceptual subitizing) and composing them as units of units (Steffe & Cobb, 1988). Some research suggests that only the smallest numbers, perhaps up to three, are actually perceptually recognized; thus, sets of one to three may be perceptually recognized, sets of three to about six may be decomposed and recomposed without the person being aware of the process. Conceptual subitizing as we use the term refers to recognition in which the person *consciously* uses such partitioning strategies. Because conceptual subitizing is a composing/decomposing approach to addition and subtraction, we discuss it more fully in Chapter 6.

Factors Affecting Difficulty of Subitizing Tasks

Subitizing ability develops in a stepwise fashion. That is, in laboratory settings, children can initially differentiate one from "more than one" at about 33 months of age (Wynn, 1992b). Between 35 and 37 months, they differentiate between one and two, but not larger numbers. A few months later, at 38 to 40 months, they identify three as well. After about 42 months, they can identify all numbers that they can count, four and higher, at about the same time. However, research in natural, child-initiated settings shows that the development of these abilities can occur much earlier, with children working on one and two around their second birthdays or earlier (Mix, Sandhofer, & Baroody, 2005). Further, some children may begin with "two" rather than "one." These studies suggest that language and social interactions interact with internal factors in development, as well as showing that number knowledge develops in levels, over time (see also Gordon, 2004). Most studies suggest that children begin recognizing "one," then "one" and "two," then "three" and then "four," whereupon they learn to count and know other numbers (see R. Gelman & Butterworth, 2005, for an opposing view concerning the role of language; Le Corre, Van de Walle, Brannon, & Carey, 2006).

The spatial arrangement of sets also influences how difficult they are to subitize. Children usually find rectangular arrangements easiest, followed by linear, circular, and scrambled arrangements (Beckwith & Restle, 1966; M. Wang et al., 1971). This is true for students from the primary grades to college in most cases. The only change across these ages is rectangular arrangements were much faster for the oldest students, who could multiply.

Certain arrangements are easier for specific numbers. Arrangements yielding a better "fit" for a given number are easier (Brownell, 1928). Children make fewer errors for ten dots than for eight with the "domino five" arrangement, but fewer errors for eight dots for the "domino four" arrangement.

For young children, however, neither of these arrangements is easier for any number of dots. Indeed, children two to four years old show no differences between any arrangements of four or fewer items (Potter & Levy, 1968). For larger numbers, the linear arrangements are easier than rectangular arrangements. It may be that many preschool children do not use decomposing (conceptual subitizing). They can learn to conceptually subitize, though older research indicated that first graders' limit for subitizing scrambled arrangements is about four or five (Dawson, 1953). If the arrangement does not lend itself to grouping, people of any age have more difficulty with larger sets (Brownell, 1928). They also take more time with larger sets (Beckwith & Restle, 1966).

What skill level do children achieve? Recall from Table 1.1, most Kindergarteners appear to have good competence recognizing two and three, with most recognizing four and some recognizing higher numbers (note that different tasks were used, some of which did not limit time, so wide ranges are expected). A recent study of low-income children beginning pre-K, using a short-exposure subitizing task, report 2 percent to 14 percent accuracy for three, 0 percent to 5 percent for four, and virtually no competence with five, eight, or 10 (Sarama & Clements, 2008). Thus, children appear to be most confident with very small numbers, but those from less advantaged environments may not achieve the same skills levels as their more advantaged peers. Some special populations find subitizing particularly difficult. Only a minority (31 percent) of children with moderate mental handicaps (chronological ages six to 14 years) and a slight majority (59 percent) of children with mild mental handicaps (ages six to 13) successfully subitize sets of three and four (Baroody, 1986). Some children with learning disabilities could not subitize even at 10 years of age (Koontz & Berch, 1996).

Role of Spontaneous Subitizing in Early Mathematics Development

A series of five studies indicated that the child's tendency to spontaneously focus on numerosity is a distinct, mathematically significant process (Hannula, 2005). Such a tendency at three years predicted development of cardinality knowledge a year later. Focusing on numerosity was also related to counting and arithmetic skills, even when nonverbal IQ and verbal comprehension were controlled. Some children's failure to focus on numerosity is not due to their lack of cognitive requirements of the task (Lehtinen & Hannula, 2006). They just have not developed the habit of focusing on numerosity. Results suggested that spontaneous focus builds subitizing ability, which in turn supported the development of counting and arithmetic skills. Thus, children low in the tendency to spontaneously focus on numerosity in the early years are at risk for later mathematical failure (Hannula, 2005). Subitizing small numbers appears to precede and support the development of counting ability (Le Corre et al., 2006). To the extent that this is true, subitizing forms a foundation for all learning of number.

Supporting and extending these findings, spontaneous focus on numerosity in four-year-olds was shown to be related to verbal counting ability a year later, but the relationship of focus on numerosity and object counting was mediated by subitizing (Hannula, Räsänen, & Lehtinen, 2007). Although not causal, these findings suggest that spontaneous focus on numerosity promotes interest in numbers that supports children's development of verbal counting. It also supports the development of subitizing skill, which in turn supports the cardinal aspect of object counting. Finally, better enumeration may increase children's interest in using all their quantitative skills, thus increase subitizing ability as well.

Across development, numerical knowledge initially develops qualitatively and becomes increasingly mathematical. In subitizing, children's ability to "see small collections" grows from preattentive but quantitative, to attentive perceptual subitizing, to imagery-based subitizing, to conceptual subitizing (Clements, 1999b; Steffe, 1992). Perceptual patterns are those the child can, and must, immediately see or hear, such as domino patterns, finger patterns, or auditory patterns (e.g., three beats). A significant advance is a child's focusing on the exact number in these patterns, attending to the cardinality. Finally, children develop conceptual patterns, which they can operate on, as when they can mentally decompose a five pattern into two and three and then put them back together to make five again. These types of patterns may "look the same" on the surface, but are qualitatively different. All can support mathematical growth and thinking, but conceptual patterns are the most powerful.

Experience and Education

A quasi-experimental study (Hannula, 2005) showed that it is possible to enhance three-year-old children's spontaneous focusing on numerosity, and thus catalyze children's deliberate practice in numerical skills (cf. Ericsson, Krampe, & Tesch-Römer, 1993). Children in the treatment group showed increased tendency to focus on numerosity and develop cardinality competencies on a delayed posttest compared to children in the comparison group. It is not just the subitizing ability that is developed in such programs, but the habits of mind, such as the predisposition to *direct attention to number* (Lehtinen & Hannula, 2006). These habits of mind generate further development of specific mathematical knowledge *and* the ability to direct attention to mathematics in situations in which it is relevant; that is, they *generalize* and *transfer* knowledge to new situations.

Most implications for educational practice are detailed in the companion book, *Learning and Teaching Early Math: The Learning Trajectories Approach* (Clements & Sarama, 2009). This includes research indicating that textbooks often discourage subitizing (Carper, 1942; Dawson, 1953), and that teachers often do not do sufficient subitizing work, leading to their students *regressing* in subitizing from the beginning to the end of kindergarten (Wright, Stanger, Cowper, & Dyson, 1994), along with a complete learning trajectory with multiple activities for each level.

Learning Trajectory for Recognition of Number and Subitizing

Accepting that the *goal* of this learning trajectory is sophisticated conceptual subitizing, this book provides the second component, the *developmental progression*. Here we omit the third component, the *instructional tasks*, because they are described in detail in the companion book. We do include our hypothesized *mental actions on objects* for each level of the developmental progression (Table 2.1). The ages are estimates based on extant research and are provided only as a general guide—actual age levels are strongly dependent on experience.

Table 2.1 A Developmental Progression for Recognition of Number and Subitizing

Age	Developmental Progression	Actions on Objects
0–1	**Pre-Explicit Number** Within the first year, dishabituates to number, but does not have explicit, intentional knowledge of number. For infants, this may include very small collections of rigid objects.	An initial bootstrap: Implicit sensitivity to quantity with perceptual input. An object file system stores information about the objects (some or all of which is used depending on the situation). An estimator (accumulator-type) mechanism stores analog quantitative information. If the situation elicits quantitative comparisons, continuous extent is retrieved and used except in extreme circumstances (e.g., one and maybe two are processed as individuated objects; numbers in which continuous extent varies or is otherwise not reliable are processed by the analog estimator as a collection of binary impulses). To compare, bootstrap processes make a correspondence between estimators.
1–2	**Small Collection Namer** Names groups of one to two, sometimes three. Shown a pair of shoes, says, "Two shoes."	Mental schemes (number filters) act on perceptions of collections of one to three. Eventually, mental, nonverbal representations are developed of each object in such collections. They become exact and associated with the verbal labels ("two" then "one" then "three," etc.). To compare, two such representations can be placed in mental correspondence.

Age	Developmental Progression	Actions on Objects
3	**Maker of Small Collections** Nonverbally makes a small collection (no more than four, usually one–three) with the same number another collection (via mental model; i.e., not necessarily by matching—for that process, see Compare Number). Might also be verbal. When shown a collection of three, makes another collection of three.	Mental representations can be maintained and direct physical actions so that one perceived object corresponds to each represented object.
4	**Perceptual Subitizer to Four** Instantly recognizes collections up to four briefly shown and verbally names the number of items. When shown four objects briefly, says "Four."	Schemes act on perceptual input (including collections, but also sounds, etc.) to identify sets of zero to four (schemes may use lower-level schemes for one-three and combine them to recognize four), each of which is associated with the verbal number name.
5	**Perceptual Subitizer to Five** Instantly recognizes briefly shown collections up to five and verbally names the number of items. Shown five objects briefly, says "Five."	Schemes act on perceptual input (including collections, but also sounds, etc.) to identify sets of zero to five (schemes may use lower-level schemes for one-three and combine them to recognize four; note that visual patterns used in the following levels are beginning to be constructed), each of which is associated with the verbal number name.
	Conceptual Subitizer to Five Verbally labels all arrangements to about five, when shown only briefly. "Five! Why? I saw three and two and so I said five."	An executive process determines whether an existing scheme can quantify the perceptual input; if so, that is used. If not, gestalt visual principles (for visual collections; see the geometry chapter) are used to partition the collection to identify two or more sets that existing schemes can quantify; the results of these are combined with pattern matching to known compositions.

Continued Overleaf

Age	Developmental Progression	Actions on Objects
	Conceptual Subitizer to 10 Verbally labels most briefly shown arrangements to six, then up to 10, using groups. "In my mind, I made two groups of three and one more, so seven."	As in the previous level, with the addition of other compositions.
6	**Conceptual Subitizer to 20** Verbally labels structured arrangements up to 20, shown only briefly, using groups. "I saw three fives, so five, 10, 15."	As in the previous level, with the addition of other compositions and explicit knowledge of teens as ten and some number more.
7	**Conceptual Subitizer with Place Value and Skip Counting** Verbally labels structured arrangements shown only briefly, using groups, skip counting, and place value. "I saw groups of tens and twos, so 10, 20, 30, 40, 42, 44, 46 . . . 46!"	As in the previous level, with the addition of other compositions and explicit place value knowledge.
8	**Conceptual Subitizer with Place Value and Multiplication** Verbally labels structured arrangements shown only briefly, using groups, multiplication, and place value. "I saw groups of tens and threes, so I thought, five tens is 50 and four threes is 12, so 62 in all."	As in the previous level, with the addition of other compositions and explicit knowledge of multiplication and place value.

Final Words

Subitizing small numbers appears to precede and support the development of counting ability (Le Corre et al., 2006). Thus, it appear to form a foundation for all learning of number. Indeed, a language-independent ability to judge numerical values nonverbally appears to be an important evolutionary precursor to adult symbolic numerical abilities. Across development, numerical knowledge initially develops qualitatively and becomes increasingly mathematical. In subitizing, children's ability to "see small collections" grows from preattentive but quantitative, to attentive perceptual subitizing, to imagery-based subitizing, to conceptual subitizing (Clements, 1999b; Steffe, 1992). Perceptual patterns are those the child can, and must, immediately see or hear, such as domino patterns, finger patterns, or auditory patterns (e.g., three beats). A significant advance is a child's focusing on the exact number in these patterns, attending to the cardinality. Finally, children develop conceptual patterns, which they can operate on, as when they can mentally decompose a five pattern into two and three and then put them back together to make five again. These types of patterns may "look the same" on the surface, but are qualitatively different. All can support mathematical growth and thinking, but conceptual patterns are the most powerful.

Children can use subitizing to discover critical properties of number, such as conservation and compensation. They can develop capabilities such as unitizing as well as arithmetic capabilities. Thus, subitizing is a critical competence in number, but it is not the only way children think and learn about number. *Counting* is ultimately a more general and powerful method, and we turn to this topic in Chapter 3.

3

Verbal and Object Counting

Verbal Counting

As described in Chapter 2, historically some (Dewey, 1898; Thorndike, 1922) argued that initial mathematics education should emphasize counting, whereas others (e.g., Piaget et al., 1960; Piaget & Szeminska, 1952; B. Russell, 1919) contended that counting was a rote skill until logical foundations were acquired (for discussions, see Clements, 1984a; Clements, 1984c; Wright et al., 2006). Even recent accounts treated counting, at least verbal counting, as a rote skill (Fuson, 1992a; H. P. Ginsburg, 1977). However, number words can be meaningful in some contexts and can orient children to numerical meanings (Mix et al., 2002). Further, without language, development of number appears to be severely restricted. For example, members of a tribe with only a "one-two-many" system of counting had remarkably poor performance on number tasks above two or three (Gordon, 2004). Even with language, without a verbal counting system, exact naming of and operations on number does not appear (Pica et al., 2004). Finally, counting skills and the logical foundations seem to be separate competencies (Aunio et al., 2004; Aunio et al., 2006), which become more integrated with learning (Case & Okamoto, 1996). Language is necessary for a systematic conception of number (Wiese, 2003b).

Children's Development of Verbal Counting

By 24 months of age, many toddlers have learned their first number word (typically "two"). Words for larger collections usually appear after children use verbal counting. Depending on their early environment, children begin to try to count using verbal number names at age two or three years. Important developments in counting continue during the preschool years. Children from ages two to five years learn more of the system of number words ("one, two, three, . . .") due to a desire to count larger collections and a curiosity about the number word system itself (Baroody, 2004; Fuson, 1988, 2004; Griffin, 2004; Steffe, 2004).

We do not use the common phrase "rote counting" for verbal counting, because children have to learn the principles and patterns in the number system as coded in their natural language, at least for number words above twenty (Baroody, 1987a; Fuson, 1992a). Supporting evidence for this position is that children who could count when given a new point from which to start performed better on all numerical tasks, suggesting that fluent verbal counting does not depend primarily on rote factors, but rather on the recognition that the system is rule-governed (Pollio & Whitacre, 1970).

Further, cross-cultural studies indicate that learning of counting varies with the language in which the number system is learned (H. P. Ginsburg et al., 1997; Han & Ginsburg, 2001; K. F. Miller, Major, Shu, & Zhang, 2000; K. F. Miller et al., 1995). For example, Chinese, like many East Asian languages, has a more regular sequence of number words than does English. In both English and Chinese, the numbers one through 10 are arbitrary and the numbers after 20 follow a regular pattern of naming the decade name and then the digit name (e.g., "twenty-one"). However, in Chinese (and in many Asian languages rooted in ancient Chinese), there are two important characteristics. The tens numbers directly mirror the single digit number names ("two-tens" rather than "twenty; "three-tens" rather than "thirty") and the numbers from 11 to 20 also follow a regular pattern (comparable to "ten-one," "ten-two," etc.) instead of the obscure "eleven, twelve. . .". Languages in Mozambique have a fives-and-tens structure, so that six is called "five-and-one" and 74 is called "five-and-two tens, and four" (Draisma, 2000). Through three years of age, children in the various cultures learn one through 10 similarly; however, those learning English learn the "teens" more slowly and with more errors. The greatest number of errors are made on 13 and 15 (Baroody, 1996). Further, Asian number words can be pronounced more quickly, providing another significant cognitive advantage (Geary & Liu, 1996). German (and Dutch) children are one group that has it even more difficult than English children: Their "twenty-two" is translated to "two and twenty," putting the ones first through the number sequence.

Overall, children learning Asian languages show a substantial advantage in learning verbal counting (Aunio et al., 2004; Aunio et al., 2006). Support for the notion that this advantage is a direct consequence of language is provided by parallel findings that Asian children do *not* differ in other aspects of number knowledge, including counting small sets and solving simple numerical problems (Fuson, 1992a; K. F. Miller et al., 2000). One group of researchers abandoned studying U.S. kindergarteners because they could not count consistently and accurately from one to 50, but Korean kindergarteners had no such problems (Miura & Okamoto, 2003). Only U.S. children made errors such as "twenty-nine, twenty-ten, twenty-eleven. . ."; Chinese children do not make that kind of mistake (K. F. Miller et al., 2000). Although all children tend to make more mistakes at decade boundaries, for Chinese-speaking children, these are largely limited to infrequent mistakes with numbers above 60. Conclusions must be made with caution, however, as other cultural factors, such as Asian parents' emphasis on counting in the early years, may affect these results (Towse & Saxton, 1998; J. Wang & Lin, 2005). Still striking is research indicating that it is not until 1st grade that many U.S. children recognize that the decades sequence mirrors the single-digit sequence and know the decade transitions (Baroody, 1996).

The deleterious effects of less mathematically coherent languages are not limited to counting larger numbers, but hamper children's development of place value, multidigit arithmetic, and other concepts (Fuson, 1992a; Miura, Kim, Chang, & Okamoto, 1988). The effects are detrimental in surprising ways: Even the counting words from one to nine are learned better by Chinese children, because they practice these exact numbers when learning to count from 11 to 19 (Miura & Okamoto, 2003).

Fuson and colleagues traced the development of the number word sequence from its beginnings at age two to its general extension to the notion of base 10 systems at about the age of eight (Fuson & Hall, 1982; Fuson, Richards, & Briars, 1982). Most middle-class children less than three and a half years of age are working on learning the sequence to 10 (Fuson, 1992a; Saxe et al., 1987). For the next year, they develop the sequence from 10 to 20. From four and a half to six years, they still make errors in the teens, but most also develop the decades to 70, although a substantial number count to 100 and higher (Bell & Bell, 1988; Fuson et al., 1982).

Fuson and colleagues also reported two distinct, overlapping phases: an acquisition phase of learning the conventional sequence of the number words, and an elaboration phase, during which this sequence is decomposed into separate words and relations upon these words are established. During the first phase the sequence is a single, connected serial whole from which interior words cannot be produced singly. The most common overall structure of the sequences is: (a) stable conventional, an initial group that is the beginning of the conventional sequence; (b) stable nonconventional, a group that deviates from convention but is produced with some consistency, and (c) nonstable, a final group with little consistency. The acquisition of longer sequences consists of the extension of the sequence and the consolidation of the extension so that it is produced reliably.

The sequence itself develops. Five levels were differentiated and empirically supported (Fuson & Hall, 1982; Fuson et al., 1982): (a) string level—words are not distinct nor objects of thought; (b) unbreakable list level—words separate and become objects of thought; (C) breakable chain level—parts of the chain can be produced starting from an arbitrary number (enabling certain counting on strategies); (d) numerical chain level—words become units that themselves can be counted; and (e) bidirectional chain level—words can be produced in either direction and the unitized embedded numerical sequence allows part-whole relations (including Piagetian class inclusion—recall the discussion in Chapter 2 and accompanying Figure 2.1) and a variety of flexible strategies to be employed. These developments precede and enable changes in addition and subtraction solution strategies (Fuson, 1992a).

The ability at the breakable chain level to start from an arbitrary number is often underappreciated. It may be a prerequisite skill both for counting on (Chapter 5) and for number composition (Chapter 6) (Martins-Mourão & Cowan, 1998).

Fuson and colleagues (1982) also claimed that backward verbal counting is learned in a slow and laborious manner, based on an already-mastered forward sequence. However, specific instruction may enable children to develop backward counting almost to the same extent as forward counting (Wright, 1991).

A descriptive study of children's external representations of the numbers one to 100 suggested that these representations develop in structure from grades K to 6 (N. D. Thomas, Mulligan, & Goldin, 2002). Initially, children assign imagistic meanings to mathematical words and symbols, such as a dinosaur with the numeral 100 on it. Then they develop structure associated with sequences of numbers (e.g., in a sequence along a spiral) and, eventually, groupings into tens. Later, they make autonomous inscriptions in which insightful, mathematical meanings are freely and flexibly found in new contexts, distinct from those used in representing the number system. For example, one girl drew an array with the number sequence in rows of 10, each one moved slightly to the right.

Fuson links verbal to object counting by positing six types of changes in the counting word sequence that facilitate its development from initial use in the counting of objects to later use as objects which can themselves be counted. These included acquisition of: increased speed of production, relations between the counting words, sequence meanings for the words, ordinal and cardinal meanings for the words, symbolic and written form of the words, and linkage of sequence to cardinal or ordinal meanings. Increased production speed may increase the available M-space (cognitive "space" or capacity in working memory), allowing the child to do something else; for example, remember sets already counted, notice relationships, or count the words produced. Relations between the words can be derived and stored as facts. The child becomes capable of producing parts of the sequence and of finding the number that comes "just before N" or just after another. These sequence relations produce sequence meanings that become associated with the counting words. Ordinal and cardinal meanings arising outside of the counting act become associated with particular words. By juxtaposing different types of meanings in time, links become established. In summary, the child first learns the number word as several different context-dependent words that later become interrelated, finally resulting in a mature set of meanings for that word (Fuson & Hall, 1982).

Object Counting[1]

To count a set of objects, children learn to coordinate the production of counting words—verbal counting—with indicator actions, such as pointing to or moving objects (Dewey, 1898; Fuson, 1988; H. P. Ginsburg, 1977; Judd, 1927). The counting word associated with the last object names the cardinality of the set. Cognitively, a fully developed object counting scheme has four components. First, there is a situation that is recognized, say a collection of countable items. Second is a goal, to find out how many. Third is an activity, counting, and fourth, the result, a unitary whole of counted items (Steffe & Cobb, 1988).

How does counting develop? Gelman and Gallistel (1978) hypothesized that the ease and rapidity that even very young children display in learning to count indicated that such development was guided by knowledge of counting principles. In particular, they hypothesized that young children know five principles. The three how-to-count principles included the stable order principle (always assign the numbers in the same order), one-one principle (assign one and only one number word to each object), and cardinal principle (the last count indicates the number of objects in the set). The two what-to-count principles were the order irrelevance principle (the order in which objects are counted is irrelevant) and the abstraction principle (all the other principles can apply to any collection of objects). The researchers presented evidence indicating that children understand—explicitly or implicitly—all these principles by age five, and many by age three years. For example, in the "magic" experiments described previously, all three how-to-count principles were followed (not perfectly, as the question was competence, not perform-ance) by children as young as two and a half years, at least with homogeneous, linearly arranged collections of no more than five items (R. Gelman & Gallistel, 1978). The one-one errors tended to be over- or undercounting on all set sizes, or skipping or double counting on the larger of the set sizes. Almost no children even used the same number word more than once.

As another example, even when children make mistakes, they show knowledge of the principle. For example, if they do not know the standard order of number words, the idiosyncratic order they *do* use is usually stable. Or, they may make mistakes in executing the one-one rule (Fuson, 1988), but nevertheless assign exactly one number word to most of the objects (about 75 percent of the objects even for two- and three-year-olds). Thus, these might reflect performance errors, not conceptual limitations. Preschoolers give evidence of using the cardinal principle by repeating or emphasizing the last number. They count events, collections that include different categories of objects, and even "missing" objects (e.g., eggs not in a carton). The order irrelevance principle is not demonstrated as widely, but most five-year-olds will start counting in the middle of a row of objects and count each object.

The principles were expanded and implemented within a computational model in which it was assumed that implicit understanding of principles was characterized as conceptual competence, hypothesized to be a set of action schemata corresponding to those principles (Greeno et al., 1984).

Theoretically, a main thrust of the nativist argument is that such principles guide children's acquisition of counting skills and understandings. This was in contrast to Piagetians (e.g., Elkind, 1964; Kamii & DeVries, 1993) who maintained that counting errors occurred because the child lacked fundamental understandings; for example, recognizing the logical need to order objects.

Other researchers gave more importance to repeated, often massive, experience and demonstrations, modeling, or scaffolding from adults in learning counting competencies (e.g., Fuson, 1988). Supporting this view are findings that suggest children count skillfully before they understand the principles that underlie counting (Bermejo, 1996; Briars & Siegler, 1984; Frye, Braisby, Lowe, Maroudas, & Nicholls, 1989; Wynn, 1992b). From this perspective, children may abstract features that are common to all acts of counting (e.g., counting each object exactly once) and distinguish them from those that are incidental (e.g., starting at the end of a row). Another possibility is that children build on their verbal number recognition (subitizing) skill to abstract the counting principles from their own counting experience (Le Corre et al., 2006) or to make sense of adult efforts to model counting procedures (Baroody et al., 2006). Specifically, subitizing predicts knowledge of cardinality in counting (Eimeren, MacMillan, & Ansari, 2007).

Additional research has clarified these issues, especially the main principles. Fuson and colleagues doubted the validity of the "stable order principle," preferring a probabilistic model (Fuson & Hall, 1982; Fuson et al., 1982). Similarly, other researchers found that children had only limited success recognizing procedures that violated the stable order of count words or violated the one-one correspondence, or found no evidence of stable-order use on non-standard sequences (Wagner & Walters, 1982). They lacked understanding of the order irrelevance in that they judged valid, nonstandard counting orders as incorrect.

Regarding the one-one principle, researchers agree that early counting does usually display one-to-one correspondences. About the age 1-8, children first make one-to-many correspondences, such as applying number words repeatedly to a collection, "one, two, one, two" (Wagner & Walters, 1982). About age 2-2, they mix one-one and many-one (sometimes one-many) correspondences. About age 2-6, they display a rigid one-one correspondence in which every element in one set must match an element in the second set. In counting, for example, if they know more counting words than the number of objects, they may produce the "extra" words quickly at the end of counting. If on the other hand there are more objects, children "recycle" number words. This reflects on inflexible list-exhaustion scheme, with a goal of processing every element of both sets (Wagner & Walters, 1982). With only a few number words, children must recycle them. Children's use of "two," and later, "three," to mean "many," and then using them for only sets of two and three, respectively, may interrupt the list-exhaustion scheme and allow for the creation of a stop rule in counting.

As young as three years of age, children can accurately enumerate small collections arranged in a straight line (Fuson, 1988). However, they do not do so in all situations. Although it is common to speak of "one to one correspondence," there are actually related but distinct competencies, including coordinating number words with objects and keeping track of counted objects (Alibali & DiRusso, 1999). Even five-year-olds show difficulty sequencing large disorganized collections. Further, coordination of words with objects actually involves a chain of two types of correspondence, that between the production of a number word and an indicating act such as pointing, and another between that act and each item to be counted. At age three or four, children violate the first type of correspondence in two main ways, by pointing to an object without saying a word and by pointing to an object and saying more than one number word. They violate the second by skipping over objects or by double-counting (see Fuson, 1988, for an elaboration of many less frequent errors). Gesturing helps children maintain both types of correspondences, keeping track and coordinating number words with objects (Alibali & DiRusso, 1999). The rhythmic, physical motions may focus children's attention on the individual items, aiding segmentation. Further, the use of touching may lessen the working memory demands of counting by externally representing some of the contents of working memory, such as marking the child's place in the set of objects.

By five years, most children can count up to 20 to 30 objects, although their accuracy is affected by their degree of focus and effort. Further, the number of objects affects different kinds of errors in different ways. Similarly, the type of counting situation affects errors. Counting as one moves objects, for example, can engender additional types of errors, such as stopping the production of number words altogether due to a focus on building something with the moved objects, or moving more than one object with each counting word. Because such errors are not seen in pointing situations, Fuson (1988) cautioned that assessments using point situations may overestimate children's competence. Skim errors, in which the finger skims over objects with no specific pointing acts and words are uttered in a stream having no apparent connection with the objects, had previously been considered an early stage. Evidence showed that, because each child who made such errors pointed at distinct objects on at least one trial, this was not a stage, but just a degenerate form of counting.

Evidence regarding the cardinality principle is perhaps most inconsistent with a strong nativist view. Cardinality does not appear to be a component of many children's early counting in most situations, especially with numbers larger than those they can subitize (Fuson, 1988; H. P. Ginsburg & Russell, 1981; Le Corre et al., 2006; Linnell & Fluck, 2001; Schaeffer et al., 1974). As previously stated, to these children, the purpose of counting is the action of enumeration (Fluck, 1995; Fluck & Henderson, 1996). Showing an even more limited understanding, some children, when asked why they count, seem perplexed by the notion of counting as a purposeful activity (Munn, 1994; 1997). Children 51–64 months of age answered in four categories: no interpretable responses or to please myself (74 percent), to conform to others' expectations (4 percent), to learn (13 percent) and to know how many (9 percent). After school entry, many, but not all, moved to more sophisticated responses. Caveats include a high percentage of uncoded responses, children's interpretation of the question, and considerations of implicit and explicit knowledge, but such results at least highlight the need to be aware of children's conceptualizations. Fuson and colleagues also posited that repeating the last number of a counting act is initially merely the last step in a chain of responses that children learn to meet adult requests (Fuson & Hall, 1982; Fuson et al., 1982). There is evidence that even when children respond correct to the cardinality question, they may not fully understand it (Sophian, 1988). For example, asked to indicate which object(s) to which their last-number-word response referred, children often indicate only the last object. As another example, children give the last-number-word responses even when it is incorrect (e.g., when they were asked to begin counting with a number other than one, Bermejo, 1996).

One position is that children have to represent, or "redescribe," the final number word at an explicit level before it is available to serve the purpose of establishing a relationship between the counting act and cardinality (Karmiloff-Smith, 1992). Before that, even when they give a last-number-word response, they may just "run" the entire counting procedure without thinking about the individual components of the procedures, such as the "How many" component (much less each object counted, the cardinality of the whole, and how they relate). This theory emphasizes internal processes, including visuo-spatial ability, which plays a greater role than language ability in the development of cardinality in normally developing young children (although the reverse is true for children with Williams Syndrome, for whom visuo-spatial and problem solving abilities are impaired, Ansari et al., 2003). However, social interaction probably aids this development (Linnell & Fluck, 2001).

This does not mean that cardinality is not understood, only that it is not an innate notion within the context of counting. Instead, young children's earliest notion of the meaning of number words appear to be rooted in subitizing (Le Corre et al., 2006). This may be generalized to counting with much experience counting small numbers between the ages of two and three years, so that by three and a half years, many children begin to use and understand the cardinal notion in counting (Wynn, 1990, 1995), at least for small numbers, and most five-year-olds do so consistently in simple counting situations. Examples of children who modify their number word sequences or 1-1 correspondence procedures to have the last object be assigned the number word that they predicted or desired the collection to have (Wagner & Walters, 1982) suggest that early concepts of cardinality and counting procedures can operate in conflict. This is consistent with the *hierarchic development* tenet of hierarchic interactionalism, revealing that interacting components (or agents, Minsky, 1986) interact and vie to meet their goals, creating the need for a hierarchically-higher integrative scheme or agent.

Moreover, knowledge of the cardinality notion develops. For example, younger children may not maintain cardinal and ordinal meanings in Piagetian conservation of number tasks in which the child builds a row of objects equivalent to a given row of objects. Most four-year-olds can do so, and will judge the two rows to be equal in number. However, when one row is spread out, they may judge the transformed row to have more objects (less frequently, to be less dense and thus have fewer). Children who conserve maintain that the number remains the same, and often respond even without counting. Some five-year-olds, many six-year-olds, and most seven-year-olds conserve in this way. Piaget and Szeminska (1952) discounted the role of counting, and there are children in transition who will not conserve even after counting both rows before and again after the transformation. However, alterations of the tasks reveal greater competence. Many preschoolers, told the cardinal value of each of two sets, can determine whether the items would be put in one-to-one correspondence (and the inverse), providing evidence that they understand the relation between the number words and quantity and can use number words to reason numerically about one-to-one correspondences that are not perceptually available (Becker, 1989; Sophian, 1988). This provides evidence that preschoolers have at least initial integration of the cardinality of the collection as a whole and the individual items in the collection. If asked to count, many transitional five-year-olds will count and use that information to correctly judge equivalence, and older five-year-olds do so spontaneously (Fuson, 1988; Fuson, Secada, & Hall, 1983). Many four-year-olds will similarly use their counting skills effectively if provided a visual display of numbers (numerals and dot patterns), and more so when conflicting perceptual cues are not present (Michie, 1984a). Counting increases when children are given feedback as to the correctness of their previous judgments, showing them that relying on counting was valid, but using length or density was not. Along with evidence on object counting and addition and subtraction (e.g., Frontera, 1994), this indicates that counting can be a meaningful quantifier for children before they reach the Piagetian levels of operational thought about number conservation.

From a consideration of the abstraction principle emerges the question of what units children can count. Research indicates that another significant development is to understand fully the unit that one is counting and its role in fulfilling the purpose of a counting act, such as in measurement (Miller, 1989, to be discussed in a later section). This is an issue even when counting discrete objects. Asked to count whole forks when shown some intact forks and some broken in half, children four to five years of age were reluctant to count two halves as a single item (Shipley & Shepperson, 1990). Their counts of classes were more accurate in the absence of objects, or in the presence of a single member of each class, than in the presence of several members of each class. Young children's bias to process discrete physical objects precedes learning to count. There was a palpable division between five-year-olds, some of whom could solve the task, and four-year-olds, who could not (Shipley & Shepperson, 1990). Results were generally confirmed even as language was changed to highlight classes and more familiar materials that separated into halves (plastic eggs) were used (Sophian & Kailihiwa, 1998). Some children counted physically discrete items, some only wholes, some only halves. Some also counted wholes or parts and included, for example, wholes that were separated into halves, but where children, especially four-year-olds, had difficulty was in switching units and in counting the unit they were instructed to count. Although performance improved from four to seven years, a substantial portion of each age had such difficulties. Thus, the abstraction principle appears only partially valid. Children as young as four to five years of age can count in many-to-one situations, such as two stickers to each doll (Becker, 1993), so the difficulty is not simply that children must apply one counting word to each discrete object or that children have only one skill but little understanding of counting.

A review of research discussed seven types of evidence that might be used comparing the two broad perspectives, one of which postulates that competence with principles precedes competence with skills, the other the opposite. Studies with findings in four of these types generally substantiated the skills-before-concepts position (Rittle-Johnson & Siegler, 1998). Thus, the evidence favors this position, with three caveats. First, there is little or no evidence of the three strongest types. Second, Rittle-Johnson and Siegler tend to define a "skill" as application in a narrow domain and every novel application as requiring concepts (instead of a generalized skill). That is, concept measures tend to involve far, and skill measure near, transfer. Third, as the authors discuss, early mathematics teaching in U.S. homes and schools often can not be characterized as conceptual instruction, and weak teaching of mostly skills may result in skills appearing in relative isolation from concepts (cf. multidigit computation, in which children who used a correct procedure first were likely to have received conventional, skills-based instruction). Thus, the argument and evidence against a nativist (privileged domains) position is more compelling than for the skills-before-concepts position. This is not to say the concepts-before-skills position is supported, but rather that the evidence reviewed may provide the most support for an interactive position, in which growth in each of the concepts and skills supports growth in the other (Baroody, 1992; Fuson, 1988). For example, a skills-first perspective may suggest that very early use of number or counting is mathematically meaningless (H. P. Ginsburg, 1977; Glasersfeld, 1982); however, early developing quantitative and numerical concepts may imbue these words and procedures with meaning (Baroody et al., 2005;

Baroody & Tiilikainen, 2003), and the words may help explicate and differentiate the initially syncretic quantities (Clements, Battista et al., 2001b). Further, humans are sufficiently flexible to permit different paths to learning (e.g., mostly skills or concepts first), even if they are differentially generative of future learning (cf. Clements, Battista et al., 2001b). Finally, the extant literature offers many cases in which conceptual knowledge leads to construction of procedures (i.e., concepts result in skills). In one illustrative study primary grade students' conceptual knowledge relevant to arithmetic predicted not only their concurrent, but *future* procedural skill (Hiebert & Wearne, 1996), Moreover, that literature often does not examine the types of experiences that have been offered to children; we contend that especially in school, but also at home, simplistic and reductionistic views of mathematics and mathematics learning have biased research examining relationships between concepts and skills. We need better evidence, including solid causal evidence (Rittle-Johnson & Siegler, 1998), on these issues.

Even researchers supporting a skills-first perspective emphasize that young children's knowledge is not limited to the standard counting procedures (Briars & Siegler, 1984). It is likely that children learn gradually which typical procedures are essential and which are optional, generalizing from more experiences and learning from direct feedback. However, there is also reason to believe that their conceptual knowledge and inquiry guides such learning (e.g., Baroody et al., 2005; Briars & Siegler, 1984; Clements & Conference Working Group, 2004). Even more important, evidence of early learning indicates the existence of initial predispositions and attentional guides that direct children to be sensitive to number and number words. Initial evidence indicates that if such innately-determined ("bootstrap-based") principles for counting and number are not put in use early, they may decay (Karmiloff-Smith, 1992). Put into use, they appear to direct children's development in ways that indicate foundational conceptual structures. For example, when Abby was three years old, her articulations of "th-" and "r" were inaccurate. When she learned the teen numbers, she said, "ten, eleven, twelve, fifteen, forteen, fifteen . . ." but the fourth and fifth pronunciation, representing 13 and 14, were even closer to the same pronunciation than the spelling indicates. After a period of being given models for these, she practiced on her own, *and eventually omitted one of the "duplicate" pair.* To Abby, the concept that counting words should not be repeated (probably abstracted from observations of others' counting) was more important than the adult model. Once her articulation improved, and with further adult feedback, she added "thirteen" and "fourteen" as separate counting words.

Children also develop a wider utilization competence—knowledge and propensity to *use* counting in different situations. For example, presented with three situations, asked (a) "how many?" (b) put *n* objects, and (c) make two groups equal, three-year-olds often used counting only in the "how many" situation (Sophian, 1998). Children were next most likely to use counting on "put *n* objects" problems. The four-year-olds were most likely to count on all three types. Again, it is likely that both goals of counting, which help structure the counting process (e.g., "goal sketches," Siegler & Booth, 2004), and the principles/procedures of counting, are heavily influenced by social interaction (Saxe, 1991; Sophian, 1998) and are themselves mutually reinforcing and generative.

Up to this point, we have dealt with children's counting of immediately perceivable objects. As children progress, they become increasingly able to count things they cannot see or hear (Davydov, 1975), including more abstract units. This progression not only increases the range of counting situations that can be addressed, but also supports the understanding of units and composite units in other domains, such as arithmetic, measurement, and fractions.

Researcher Les Steffe was working with five-year-old Brenda. He showed her three squares and told her four more were covered under a cloth. He asked her how many squares there were in all. Brenda tried to raise the cloth. Steffe stopped her. She counted the three visible squares.

B: One, two, three. [Touches each visible item in turn.]

LS: There's four here. [Tapping the cloth.]

B: [Lifts the cloth, revealing two squares] four, five. [Touches each and puts cloth back.]

LS: OK, I'll show you two of them [shows two]. There's four here, you count them.

B: 1, 2 [then counts each visible]: three, four, five.

LS: There's two more here [taps the cloth].

B: [Attempts to lift the cloth.]

LS: [Pulls back the cloth.]

B: Six, seven [touches the last two squares].

Brenda's attempt to lift the cloth indicates that she was aware of the hidden squares and intended to count the collection. But this did not lead to counting because she was yet to coordinate the utterance of a number word sequence with the sequential production of figural items. She could take *perceived* items as being countable, but could not imagine items. Later, she counted the interviewer's fingers instead of six items he was hiding. When he pointed out he had six marbles hidden, Brenda said, "I don't see no six!"

This episode comes from an interdisciplinary research program with a bond of shared constructivist philosophy (Steffe, Thompson, & Richards, 1982). Their model views number as a conceptual creation, a double act of abstraction. Because children usually develop the higher levels only after kindergarten, this model is described briefly. Levels are distinguished by the type of unit the child can count. Perceptual unit items are sensory-motor signals that are abstracted and separated out as experientially separate items.

Counters of perceptual unit items need a collection of objects, such as marbles, beads, or fingers, to count. When these items can be re-presented by the child—that is, reconstructed mentally without actual material, like a "playback"—the unit is a figural unit item. Counters of motor unit items might use the motor act (e.g., pointing or putting up fingers), and counters of verbal unit items an utterance of a number word, as a substitute for a perceptual object or its figural representation. They can count two collections, even if hidden, by performing a single sequence of counting acts (i.e., early counting on). However, they do not make an initial plan; instead, they re-present a particular pattern after they count the first collection. They usually have to start counting from "one." Up to this point, uttering the number words implied the presence of accompanying tangible items for children. That is, the children use their object concepts to produce more than one countable item in visualized imagination, but they still need to actually count as counting is still a sensory motor activity.

At the next, abstract, stage, they could take any items as the units to be counted. For example, with eight visible, four screened, and told how many in all, Merrill counted, "Nine, 10, 11, 12," and said, "Let's see, nine is one, 10 is two . . . . four!" She "stepped back" and took each counting act as a countable unit itself. She also reflected on potential counting activity and separated it into two parts, which necessitated the use of the integration operationally uniting that which can also be viewed as distinct units. Finally, she intended to count how many counting acts she would perform before beginning to count (i.e., she anticipated). At that point, she was said to possess an abstract conception of number. Thus, whereas re-presentation and substitution of units to be counted were previously essential constructions, integrations and anticipations engendered progression to the abstract stage. At this stage, children have constructed arithmetical units. That is, counting is an operation in that the child can imagine counting up to six, without actually engaging in the activity. The countable items are still visualized images of hidden items, but the visualized images change in nature from figurative to operative images. The children can posit collections willfully rather than simply imagine a collection that is hidden from view, allowing them to imagine counting the posited collection.

The advent of the three abstract stages marks the completion of the construction of the initial number sequence (via the integration operation), and the beginning of the construction of part-whole operations. In the first stage, sequential integration operations, children might apply the integration operation twice in succession (e.g., Merrill's aforementioned solution). In the next stage, progressive integration operations, children might count to 10, take that result as "one ten," and then proceed to count four more times. Here, the integration operation is applied to the composite (pattern) of 10 units that was itself constructed by applying the integration operation. The child is now aware of this composite unit qua unit. "Fourteen" is seen as "one 10 and four more ones." Finally, in the stage of part-whole operations, children can apply the integration operation to the two component units, one of numerosity 10 and one of four. Thus, they apply the integration operation a third time to the results of a progressive integration operation. The composite unit can be viewed simultaneously as a separate unit and as a part of another unit. This permits additional flexibility and anticipatory planning of solutions.

These developments support the children's ability to subitize and create mental images (visualized, operative images) of certain quantities and numbers that support more sophisticated and efficient strategies. We discuss these strategies at more length in a following section.

Zero and Infinity

Situations similar to those that engender counting may also lead to children's initial encounter with the mathematical notions of zero and infinity. Pre-schoolers often have a limited understanding of both (Evans, 1983; R. Gelman & Meck, 1983). However, even three-year-olds represent zero as the absences of objects more than half the time, and by four years, children did as well with zero as with small whole numbers (Bialystok & Codd, 2000; similar results are reported by Hughes, 1986).

Because touching objects is important to young children's initial counting, zero is often not encountered in the act of counting. (Resistance to the ideas of zero and infinity is not merely a developmental limitation, of course. His-torically, societies have taken considerable time to confront, represent, and incorporate these ideas.) In comparison, older children and adults judge numbers zero to nine to be similar based on "counting distances." Kindergar-teners solve problems with zero well, although there is a separation between their knowledge of zero and their knowledge of the counting numbers. In one study, for example, they showed no evidence of applying counting strategies to zero problems, and performed better on zero problems than on problems involving one or two, suggesting that such problems were solved differently (Evans, 1983).

Another study (Wellman & Miller, 1986) confirmed that zero was a special number, difficult to learn but generative of deeper reasoning. That is, the developmental sequence for all children included three levels. First, children acquire familiarity with the name "zero" and the symbol "0." Second, they learn that zero refers to a unique numerical quantity, none or nothing. Third, children relate zero to the small counting numbers. They learn to compare zero to those numbers and, lastly, learn that zero is the smallest whole number. Before reaching this third level, children know that zero denotes nothing, and is smaller than most other numbers, but still insist that "one" is the smallest number. Children followed this developmental progression despite experiencing several different curricula, so it appears to not merely reflect a curriculum sequence. Preschool education did, however, increase the development of these levels by a full year.

However, probably because zero is difficult to understand and operate on originally, children develop special rules for its use, and the understandings and rules they learn provide a first step towards more general algebraic rules and towards an expanded conception of number and mathematics. Even children as young as kindergarten could respond to tasks involving zero and "hidden numbers," exhibiting nascent knowledge of algebraic rules, such as a + 0 = a. (About a third responded correctly.) First to third graders showed increased accuracy. In addition, although younger children's justifications exhibited "rule denial" (refusal to respond because exact numbers were not know), this declined substantially over the early childhood years.

In summary, children think about zero in different ways. Children build special rules to account for this exceptional number.

Preschoolers often have a more limited understanding of infinity (Evans, 1983; R. Gelman & Meck, 1983). Piaget and Inhelder's early research focused on subdividing a geometrical figure (including a line segment) as many times as possible. Pre-operational children (before about seven years of age in Piagetian theory) could not continue such subdivision far. Concrete operational children could continue, creating a large, but not infinite number of subdivisions. Only in the period of formal operations (more than 12 years of age, approximately) could children understand that such a process could be continued indefinitely. Different tasks reveal different notions. Asking children to extend a repeating sequential pattern of shapes on a sheet of blank paper revealed that some grade K-2 children believed that space is unbounded, but others belief it to be bounded (Marchini, 2005).

In a game context (e.g., "Each of us say a number. The one whose number is larger wins. Would you like to be first or second?"), most six- to seven-year-old children did not show understanding of the boundlessness of integers (Falk, Gassner, Ben Zoor, & Ben Simon, 1986). Only for students toward 12 years of age could the majority explain why you should play second. More difficult were the similar games for negative integers and infinitesimals (i.e., very small fractions; numbers nearing zero as the limit). Such ideas are not understood in clear and complete ways at any point in development. For example, one five-year-old said there were more numbers than grains of sand in the world because numbers never end, but the grains of sand stay as they are. However, she chose to go first in the game. Others thought that naming the numbers was important, that no one could know the largest number.

Counting may play an even larger role in children's early ideas related to infinity than it does for zero (Evans, 1983). Children reasoning at what the researchers called "level 1" showed little or no knowledge of numbers greater than one hundred, and their answers reflected only limited knowledge of the structure of the counting sequence. Children at level 2 showed knowledge of this structure, including for generating new, larger numbers. Children reasoning at level 3 had a stable understanding that there was no greatest number because it was always possible to create a larger number. Most children were able to give sensible answers about infinite space, time, or number, usually based on their reasoning that one is always able to add one more. Although language, and its recursive nature, has been claimed as the *root* of children's initial ideas of infinity, others say that the concept can be shown to develop before language (R. Gelman & Butterworth, 2005). For example, a child of age 5-9 did not have language for such numbers, but claimed that adding one more would always result in a larger number ("You still put one and they get real higher," p. 9). The fast adoption of English counting words by speakers of languages with restricted number terms was considered another counter-example to the foundational role of language (R. Gelman & Butterworth, 2005).

Language, Numerals, and Other Symbols

As the brief history of research on early number knowledge suggested, the hypothesized role of language has changed through the four historical phases described in Chapter 2. In the first phase, counting and number words played a definite, if underspecified, role. The second, Piagetian, phase severely limited the role of language. In the theories of the nativists and skills-integration theorists of the third phase, language was important in building more sophisticated number concepts, but was not central to development per se, especially in its earliest foundations. However, it was noted that nativist principles explained very young children's separation of object labels from number words (Gelman, 1990a, 1990b; Karmiloff-Smith, 1992). In the fourth phase, several theorists proposed that language plays a critical role in developing the concept of cardinal numbers. For example, they claimed that language sensitizes children to cardinality and helps them move from approximate to exact representations of number (Spelke, 2002; Van de Walle, Carey, & Prevor, 2000). That is, the word "three" may enable children to create an explicitly cardinal representation that applies to various triads of objects (Baroody et al., 2006). One study even provides support for a strong version of the Whorfian hypothesis (Gordon, 2004). The Pirahã, who live along in the Amazonia region of Brazil, have words only for "one," "two," and many. Moreover, their word for one, "hòi," also means small, suggesting there may be little differentiation between discrete and continuous quantities. and no unique grammar for singletons. They have little or no ability to enumerate exact quantities when the set sizes exceeded two or three (they do appear to use analog estimation processes, supporting early conclusions about subitizing and estimating mechanisms, but their accuracy is low).

However, language and culture are intricately interwoven (Vygotsky, 1929/

1994, 1934/1986), and cultural practices in which children and adults are or are not engaged affect both language and the understanding and employment of mathematics (Saxe, 1991). Thus, it is not just "words" that are important, but the language that is used in learning and engaging in cultural practices that involve mathematics. Language supports, but does not alone account for, thinking and learning about mathematics.

Empirical evidence indicates that basic verbal number competencies precede some nonverbal tasks, contrary to the mental models view (Baroody, Benson et al., 2003). This supports the view that learning number words facilitates the development of exact representations. Thus, as stated previously, human language plays an important role in connecting different representations, helping to make early pre-mathematical cognition numeric (Wiese, 2003a). Much of the research in this section supports this view, as does research on learning other concepts, such as color words (Sandhofer & Smith, 1999). Not all language involves the mathematical term for the concept. Often introduction of such sophisticated terms is better delayed until concepts are developed with informal language and experiences (Lansdell, 1999). Further, there is still an open debate about the exact role of language, with some arguing that it is critical for the development of number concepts above four, and others citing evidence of competence in cultures with limited counting words and other evidence that language is not the cause of the development of these concepts (R. Gelman & Butterworth, 2005). For example, there is evidence that when verbal counting is too slow to satisfy time constraints, nonverbal mental magnitudes mediate the production of a number word that approximates that numerosity of a set. It also mediates the ordering of symbolic numbers (Gallistel & Gelman, 2005). In general, research indicates that the interactions between language on the one hand, and number concepts and skills on the other, are more bidirectional, fluid, and interactive than previous accounts allowed (Mix et al., 2005). For example, one study shows that pre-school children's early storytelling abilities are predictive of their mathematical ability two years later (O'Neill, Pearce, & Pick, 2004). Specifically, it was only children's ability to relate all the different events in the story, to shift clearly from the actions of one character to another, and to adopt the perspective of different characters and talk about what they were feeling or thinking (aspects such as mean length of utterance and vocabulary were not predictive). Thus, both abilities may be related to reasoning about relations. This study is correlational, so there is no evidence that building storytelling will affect mathematics learning, but it does connect general language and mathematics competencies.

Children enter elementary school, and often pre-K, with initial knowledge of reading and even writing numerals (Bell & Bell, 1988; Bialystok & Codd, 2000; Fuson, 1992a); indeed, very young children differentiate written numerals and letters before they can read (Karmiloff-Smith, 1992). For example, kindergarteners from a range of populations were generally competent with the numerals from 1 to 20, and many from 1 to 100. The early autumn percentages for reading and writing were: "3," reading, 95 percent, writing, 80 percent; "9," 74 percent, 53 percent; "17," 54 percent, 21 percent; "57," 26 percent, 21 percent; "100," 41 percent, 31 percent. By the end of the year, the percentages for numerals 3 and 9 for both reading and writing were above 93 percent and for the others between 55 percent and 80 percent. Reversing the digits for numbers in the teens was a frequent error, due to the reversal in English pronunciation. (Reversals in writing digits, e.g., writing numeral 3 "backwards," were ignored in scoring as common errors that children outgrow.)

Children's ability to read or produce numerals or other representations does not imply a commensurate understanding of what they represent (Bialystok & Codd, 2000). In one study, about a fourth of the children entering school were not aware of the function of numerals (Munn, 1998). When asked to represent how many objects there were, children might produce idiosyncratic, pictographic (representing the appearance of objects as well as their numerosity), iconic (one-to-one correspondence between objects and marks), or symbolic (numerals) responses (Ewers-Rogers & Cowan, 1996; Hughes, 1986; Munn, 1998). Similarly, in other studies, preschoolers showed an understanding that written marks on paper can preserve and communicate information about quantity (Ewers-Rogers & Cowan). For example, three- and four-year-olds invent informal marks on paper, such as tally marks and diagrams, to show how many objects are in a set (Allardice, White, & Daugherty, 1977). However, children this age did not notice when numerals were missing from pictures of such objects and rarely said number words in giving fast-food orders; thus, understanding preceded use of numerals (Ewers-Rogers & Cowan, 1996).

However, there is evidence that the development of mathematics concepts on one hand and notational systems on the other interact, each supporting the other (Brizuela, 2004). So too do invented and conventional mathematical notions; thus, children's inventions or reinventions of notations may be important to their mathematical development, as are their reinventions of mathematical concepts. Children spontaneously and without hesitation invent symbols for numbers above 10, such as representing 13 as "03," "103," and "31" (Zhou & Wang, 2004). Similarly, a kindergartener represented 17 as "70", saying "there's the seven (pointing to 7) and there's the teen (pointing at the zero) (Brizuela, 2004, p. 11). Another kindergartner made sense of place value notion by saying the first 3 in 33 a "capital number", having greater significance.

When asked to distribute a quantity, create a representation, then recall it (soon, or three weeks thereafter), children's productions were global (idiosyncratic or pictographic), analogue (iconic), and symbolic (Bialystok & Codd,

2000). Children could represent, and later read their representations of zero and small whole numbers almost as accurately as they could produce them, but only seven-year-olds could represent fractions. Global representations were not well understood; of the others, three- to four-year-olds tended to choose analogue representations, six- to seven-year-olds numerals, and five-year-olds used both. Numerals were read correctly far better than other representations; even accurate analogues may not have functioned as symbols for the children. Thus, children understood quantities before they could represent them, and produce representations that they were unable to read later, although they understood the purpose of the representations.

Just as important as learning to read and write representations of number is learning to use such representations functionally. Except for the idiosyncratic representations, children use their symbols to remember the amount in collections, one level of functional use. Children continue to develop competence in functional use of numerals. For example, children were shown several collections labeled with symbols. They were told a teddy bear added one object to only one collection and asked to figure out which one had the extra object. Only some young children could use the symbol to complete the task (Munn, 1998). Functional use is more likely when children use numerals rather than pictographic or iconic representations, and nonconventional representations may not be important precursors to conventional symbol use. However, even cultures without numeric notional systems use number computations successfully, so external number notational systems are not universal, and thus not requisite to calculation (Karmiloff-Smith, 1992). Children who learn, appropriate, and invent notational systems do have a powerful tool for mathematical reflection at their disposal (Brizuela, 2004).

Similar to other domains, there are cultural differences in knowledge of numerals. In different countries, low-income children exhibit less knowledge than those from more advantaged backgrounds (Hughes, 1998; Zhou & Wang, 2004). Differences are also found between countries. Whereas 30 percent of British five-year-olds represented numbers one to six with numerals (Hughes, 1998), 40 percent of Chinese four-year-olds could represent numbers one to 20 (Zhou & Wang, 2004). Whereas 50 percent of British six- to seven-year-olds represented the numbers one to six with numerals, 85 percent of Chinese five-year-olds could represent 20 numbers.

In our development of the *Building Blocks* curriculum and subsequent summative evaluations, several developmental psychologists questioned our introduction to numerals in the preschool years as "developmentally inappropriate." The evidence reviewed here suggests that, as with many topics, there is little chance of harm, and much to gain, by introducing and using numerals functionally in preschool. Such use is related to cardinal understandings (Zhou & Wang, 2004) and is consistent with children's capabilities and interests. Such functional use, in line with children's interests, is not rote practice, but rather use of numerals to represent ideas that children find meaningful and motivating.

A simple learning trajectory suggests that children first learn that written numerals are distinct from other symbols. Written numerals are then recognized without a full functional understanding. Later, children come to match numerals to quantities, and then to represent quantities with numerals they produce.

Young children are less able to represent changes in sets or relationships, in part because they fail to realize that the order of their actions is not automatically preserved on paper (Allardice et al., 1977). One study indicated that children needed numbers to refer to certain objects to do well in arithmetic (Hughes, 1986). Children as old as seven years had a difficult time representing the actions of +/− in very simple situations—two bricks and two more bricks—with written symbols. Instead, they represent only the result.

Summary

That meaningful counting is not dependent upon concrete operations, but is nonetheless closely related to incipient classification and seriation abilities was anticipated by Dewey's (1898; see also Judd, 1927) formulation that counting involves both order and cardinal ideas. Dewey postulated that difficulties in counting are with successive ordering of units in a series and that children are first interested in such series when motor recitations break up a sensory blur into definite states. The continuity of motor adjustments arranges these states into a series, which become numerical when their parts are ordered with reference to place and value in constituting the whole group. In parallel is a developing recognition of "muchness," made definite through counting.

Accurate, effortless, meaningful, and strategic counting is an essential early numerical competence. Initial level of achievement and subsequent growth in number and arithmetic from preschool into the elementary years are both predicted better by early counting ability than by other abilities, such as visual attention, metacognitive knowledge, and listening comprehension (Aunola, Leskinen, Lerkkanen, & Nurmi, 2004).

Experience and Education

Studies have disproved the Piagetian notion that counting is meaningless until children achieve logical operations in classification, seriation, and conservation. Piagetian classification and seriation are not prerequisite for learning counting; the domains of classes, series, and number appear to be interdependent but experiences in number have priority (Clements, 1984c; Fuson, 1988; Fuson et al., 1983; Lesh, 1972; Steffe & Cobb, 1988).

As a reminder, most implications for education are detailed in the companion book, *Learning and Teaching Early Math: The Learning Trajectories*

Approach (Clements & Sarama, 2009). This includes research indicating that kindergarten and first grade teachers often do far too little to develop counting skills, with many children learning little or nothing during the entire period (Wright et al., 1994). In a similar vein, too frequently textbooks wait until the primary grades to "introduce" counting skills that children already possess or are developing in pre-K and kindergarten (Fuson, 1992a).

Learning Trajectory for Counting

Accepting that the *goal* of this learning trajectory is sophisticated counting, this book provides the second component, the *developmental progression*. Here we omit the third component, the instructional tasks, because they are described in detail in the companion book. We do include our hypothesized *mental actions on objects* for each level of the developmental progression (Table 3.1). Recall that the ages are estimates based on extant research and are provided only as a general guide—age levels are strongly dependent on experience.

Table 3.1 A Developmental Progression for Counting

Age (years)	Developmental Progression	Actions on Objects
1	**Pre-Counter** *Verbal* No verbal counting.	Initial (bootstrap) sensitivity to quantity supports the implicit categorization of words into quantity/number relevant vs. irrelevant.
	Names some number words with no sequence.	
	Chanter *Verbal* Chants "sing-song" or sometimes-indistinguishable number words.	A verbal list composed of a string of paired associates of sounds/syllables is available (and increasingly expanded and differentiated). It can be produced at will.
2	**Reciter** *Verbal* Verbally counts with separate words, not necessarily in the correct order above "five."	The verbal list is differentiated into distinct numbers words associated with the term "counting" and the notion of quantifying (at least in the aspect of sequencing).
	"one, two, three, four, five, seven."	
	Puts objects, actions, and words in many-to-one (age 1–8) or overly rigid one-to-one (age one; correspondence (age 2–6)	Counting is intuitively connected to analog estimators of quantity (see Chapter 2).
	Counts two objects "two, two, two."	
	If knows more number words than number of objects, rattles them off quickly at the end. If more objects, "recycles" number words (inflexible list-exhaustion).	

Continued Overleaf

Age (years)	Developmental Progression	Actions on Objects
3	**Reciter (10)** *Verbal* Verbally counts to ten, with *some* correspondence with objects, but may either continue an overly rigid correspondence, or performance errors (e.g., skipping, double-counting). Producing, may give desired number. "one [points to first], two [points to second], three [starts to point], four [finishes pointing, but is now still pointing to third object], five, . . . nine, ten, eleven, twelve, 'firteen,' fifteen . . ." Asked for five, counts out three, saying "one, two, *five*."	The verbal list is produced reliably from one to ten; after ten, increasing amounts of the list, sometimes with omissions or other errors, can be produced. The procedure to produce the list is, with more or less strength, associated with "indicator" acts (frequently pointing), using an initial bootstrap process (probably linked to naming objects and rhythm) to produce a correspondence (also with more or less strength to be a one-to-one correspondence) between the two.
	Corresponder Keeps one-to-one correspondence between counting words and objects (one word for each object), at least for small groups of objects laid in a line. ☐ ☐ ☐ ☐ "One, two, three, four." May answer a "how many?" question by recounting the objects, or violate one-to-one or word order to make the last number word be the desired or predicted word.	The counting procedure is further constrained in producing a correspondence, both in the development of the initial bootstrap process and by developing conceptual constraints (i.e., the idea to "count each object once and only once") so one-to-one correspondence is maintained in simple contexts (and is strove for in most contexts, until other mental demands, especially fatigue, achieve prominence).
4	**Counter (Small Numbers)** Accurately counts objects in a line to five and answers the "how many" question with the last number counted. When objects are visible, and especially with small numbers, begins to understand cardinality. ☐ ☐ ☐ ☐ "One, two, three, four . . . *four!*"	Connection is made between the output of subitizing processes (see Chapter 2) and counting process. During object counting (which can apply to any set of "objects," including events, etc.), a procedure applies to the final counting word makes a count-to-cardinal transition, producing a cardinal value that is associated with the set.
	Counter (10) Counts arrangements of objects to 10. May be able to write numerals to represent one to 10. Accurately counts a line of 9 blocks and says there are nine.	Processes developed in previous levels extended to sets of 10 (and verbal skills to 20) and tracking-of-what-objects-have-been-counted procedures extended to structured arrangements other than lines (e.g., without moving objects using nascent spatial

Age (years)	Developmental Progression	Actions on Objects
	May be able to tell the number just after or just before another number, but only by counting up from one.	structuring, see Chapters 8 and especially 12; or using a move-and-count procedure).
	What comes after four? "One, two, three, four, five. *Five!*"	If learned motor schemes to produce written numerals, can use these to represent a quantity.
	Verbal counting to 20 is developing.	
	Producer (Small Numbers) Counts out objects to five. Recognizes that counting is relevant to situations in which a certain number must be placed.	Using the goal structure developed in "Maker of Small Collections" (see Chapter 2), a new executive control procedure monitors the move-and-count procedure from the "Counter (10)" level to check, at the production of each count word, if that word matches the goal number; if so, stops the move-and-count procedure.
	Produces a group of four objects.	
5	**Counter and Producer (10+)** Counts and counts out objects accurately to 10, then beyond (to about 30). Has explicit understanding of cardinality (how numbers tell how many). Keeps track of objects that have and have not been counted, even in different arrangements. Writes or draws to represent one to 10 (then, 20, then 30). Gives next number (usually to 20s or 30s). Separates the decade and the ones part of a number word, and begins to relate each part of a number word/numeral to the quantity to which it refers.	Processes developed in previous levels extended to sets of 30 and more, including tracking-of-what-objects-have-been-counted procedures to any arrangement (using a move-and-count procedure or a systematic spatial plan). Re-representation of the chain of number words has allowed the production of the next (forward) number in the counting sequence. Count-to-cardinal transition is procedurally automatic and conscious (re-represented at an explicit level).
	Recognizes errors in others' counting *and* can eliminate most errors in own counting (point-object) if asked to try hard.	Similarly, the combination of automaticity for the counting algorithm and the re-representation of it to an explicit level has generated an executive process that monitors counting of others and self, detecting and identifying errors.
	Counts a scattered group of 19 chips, keeping track by moving each one as they are counted.	
	Counter Backward from 10 *Verbal and Object*	Production of the number word sequence is reversed, allowing backwards counting.
	Counts backward from 10 to one, verbally, or when removing objects from a group.	
	"10, 9, 8, 7, 6, 5, 4, 3, 2, 1!"	

Continued Overleaf

Age (years)	Developmental Progression	Actions on Objects
6	**Counter from N** (N+1, N−1) *Verbal and Object* Counts verbally and with objects from numbers other than 1 (but does not yet keep track of the *number* of counts). Asked to "count from five to eight," counts "five, six, seven, eight!" Determines numbers just after or just before immediately. Asked, "What comes just before seven?" says, "Six!"	The procedure to produce number words is developed to allow a "break" in the chain of numbers at any point in the known verbal counting sequence to procedure from that point forward or backward. Understands that each number is one more than the one before and one less than the other after (begins to build a mental model such as illustrated, but may be constrained to "next to" relations—immediately before or after). 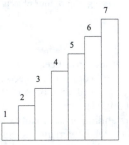 May develop the level of thinking in "Counter On Using Patterns" in constrained situations of plus and minus one and possibly two with external support and/or guidance.
	Skip Counter by 10s to 100. *Verbal and Object* Skip counts by 10s up to 100 or beyond with understanding; e.g., "sees" groups of ten within a quantity and counts those groups by 10 (this relates to multiplication and algebraic thinking; see chapters 7 and 13). "10, 20, 30 . . . 100."	The verbal sequence consisting of multiples of tens is stored and can be retrieved. Cardinality concepts are extended (here, in the limited context of tens) to recognize that a group of objects can be named by a number (without needing to count every object to produce that cardinality). These two concepts are combined by an executive "skip-counting" procedure that counts groups believed to each contain ten by tens.
	Counter to 100 *Verbal* Counts to 100. Makes decade transitions (e.g., from 29 to 30) starting at any number. ". . . 78, 79 . . . 80, 81 . . ."	Previous verbal counting skills are extended to 100 relying on a bootstrap pattern recognizer; verbal counting by tens supports the procedure of the next decade in the counting algorithm.

Age (years)	Developmental Progression	Actions on Objects

Counter On Using Patterns
Strategy Keeps track of a few counting acts, but only by using numerical pattern (spatial, auditory or rhythmic).

> "How much is three more than five?" Child feels five "beats" as counts, "five . . . *six, seven, eight!*"

The concept that each number in the counting sequence includes the number before, hierarchically—nascent and implicit at the "Counter (Small Numbers)" level—is at least a theorem-in-action (Vergnaud, 1982) and is evoked explicitly in some contexts.

This concept supports the use of the previously-acquired skill of "Counter from N (N + 1, N − 1)", and the knowledge of rhythmic subitizing (see Chapter 2) in adding a small number of objects to an existing set.

Skip Counter *Verbal and Object* Counts by fives and twos with understanding.

> Child counts objects, "Two, four, six, eight . . . 30."

Previous skills from the "Skip Counter by 10s to 100" level are extended to include groups of fives and twos.

Counter of Imagined Items:
Strategy Counts mental images of hidden objects.

> Asked, "There are five chips here and five under the napkin, how many in all?" says fiiiiive . . . then points to the napkin in four distinct points, [corners of an imagined square] saying, "Six, seven, eight, nine."

Bootstrap abilities to represent objects as mental objects (see Chapter 2), re-represented components of counting and cardinality, and an implicit part-part-whole scheme (see Chapters 5 and 6) support the production of an intended set of a given numerosity, which can be produced with perceptual support, such as a known spatial pattern (e.g., "corners of square" for four) as a part added on to another part to determine the whole.

Counter On Keeping Track
Strategy Keeps track of counting acts numerically, first with objects, then by "counting counts." Counts up one to four *more* from a given number.

> How many is three more than six? "Six . . . seven [puts up a finger], eight [puts up another finger], nine [puts up third finger]. *Nine.*"

> What is eight take away two? "Eight . . . seven is one, and six is two. *Six.*"

Competencies from the previous level are extended to explicitly represent the cardinality of an intended set (of objects, numbers/counting acts) and keep track of the number in that set, even without perceptual support. Thus, a subgoal of explicitly quantifying that set is established and establishes the structure of the counting on procedure.

Continued Overleaf

Age (years)	Developmental Progression	Actions on Objects
	Counter of Quantitative Units/ Place Value Understands the base-ten numeration system and place-value concepts, including ideas of counting in units and multiples of hundreds, tens, and ones. When counting groups of ten, can decompose into 10 ones if that is useful.	A relationship between single digitals and tens place names is established (e.g., "fifty" is five tens). The counting procedure is reorganized to include an explicit re-representation of the hierarchical structuring of number (see "Counter On Using Patterns"), allowing numbers to be understood as embedded within other numbers.
	Understands value of a digit according to the place of the digit within a number.	
	Counts by tens and one to determine.	
	Counts unusual units, such as "wholes" when shown combinations of wholes and parts.	
	Shown three whole plastic eggs and four halves, counts and says there are five whole eggs.	
	Counter to 200 *Verbal and Object* Counts accurately to 200 and beyond, recognizing the patterns of ones, tens, and hundreds.	Previous verbal counting skills are extended beyond 200, the bootstrap pattern recognizer is re-applied to counting above 100.
	"After 159 comes 160 because after five tens comes six tens."	
7	**Number Conserver** Consistently conserves number (i.e., believes number has been unchanged) even in face of perceptual distractions such as spreading out objects of a collection.	Connections among concepts and skills, including the counting algorithms, cardinality, ordinality (see also Chapter 4), and subitizing (see Chapter 2), and explicit representation of the hierarchical structuring of number (see "Counter of Quantitative Units/Place Value").
	Counts two rows that are laid out across from each other and says they are the same. Adult spreads out one row. Says, "Both still have the same number, one's just longer."	
	Counter Forward and Back *Strategy* Counts "counting words" (single sequence or skip counts) in either direction. Recognizes that decades sequence mirrors single-digit sequence.	Integration of all previous concepts and skills allow numerical counting with embedding. Multiple part-part-whole schemes can be held in memory and related.

Age (years)	Developmental Progression	Actions on Objects
	What's four less than 63? "62 is one, 61 is two, 60 is three, 59 is four, so 59."	
	What is 15 more than 28? "Two tens and one ten is three tens. 38, 39, 40, and there's three more, 43."	
	Switches between sequence and composition views of multidigit numbers easily.	
	Counts backward from 20 and higher with meaning.	

Final Words

Subitizing and counting are children's main strategies for quantification. In many situations, this is only a step in the problem-solving process. Often, what we wish to do is compare two numbers or sequence several numbers. This is the topic of the following chapter.

4
Comparing, Ordering, and Estimating

In this chapter, we discuss comparing, ordering, and estimating quantities, with an emphasis on discrete quantity (Chapters 11 and 12 in Part IV discuss continuous quantity).

Comparing and Equivalence

Infants begin to construct equivalence relations between sets, possibly by intuitively establishing correspondences (spatial, temporal, or numerical), as early as 10 months (Brannon, 2002) and at most by 24 months of age (Langer, Rivera et al., 2003), although the ability continues to develop (Wagner & Walters, 1982). Studies of early discrimination and conservation of number (see Chapter 2), also address children's initial abilities to compare quantities. To briefly highlight relevant findings, children may base comparisons on number and may use nonverbal representations of cardinality (Mix et al., 2002). For example, they may share with monkeys a set of mental filters, each tuned to an approximate number of objects (e.g., two), but overlapping with adjacent filters (e.g., those that detect one or three also sensitive to two, but less so than the "two filter"), which explains why discrimination improves with greater numerical distance (Nieder et al., 2002). At three years of age, children can identify as equivalent or nonequivalent static (simultaneously presented) collections consisting of a few (one to about four) highly similar items (e.g., Huttenlocher, Jordan et al., 1994; Mix, 1999). For instance, they can identify ••• and •‌•‌• as equal and different from •• or •‌• (the researchers describe this as a nonverbal competence, but children may have subitized the arrays). At three and a half years, they can match different homogeneous visual sets and match sequential and static sets that contain highly similar items. At four and a half, they can nonverbally match equivalent collections of random objects and dots—a heterogeneous collection and a collection of dissimilar items.

Not all comparisons, however, use regions of the brain tuned to number. A neuroimaging study found that brain regions that represent numerical magnitude also represent spatial magnitude, such as the relations between sizes of objects, and thus may not be numerical in function (Pinel et al., 2004). Judgments of number and size engaged a common parietal spatial code. No region was specific to judgments for number, size, or luminance, nor was there one generic "comparison" region, but rather these functions are distributed across several regions that overlap.

Another neuroimaging study found both commonalities and differences in the children's and adults' judgments of relative magnitude between two numerals (Ansari, Garcia, Lucas, Hamon, & Dhital, 2005). They used the well-known "distance effect"—the more distance between two numbers, the faster and more accurate are people's judgments (e.g., of "which is larger"). Children showed more activation in the right frontal regions that control attention, working memory, and executive functions, whereas adults show more engagement of intraparietal and posterior parietal regions, which may indicate increasingly strong and flexible mappings from numerals to the numerical quantities they represent, as well as more specialization in these regions.

Similarly, a study of three-year-olds found no evidence that preschoolers use either an analog number magnitude or an object-file mechanism to compare numerosities. They were unable to compare sets controlled for surface area, suggesting that they rely on perceptual cues. Their development of numerosity-based representations seems to be related to some understanding of cardinality (Rousselle, Palmers, & Noel, 2004).

Children's success with sequentially-presented objects emerges later than with simultaneously-presented objects, and sequential events are the most difficult (Mix, 1999). These abilities seem to depend on counting abilities, with sequential events requiring a mastery of counting. Thus, children appear to use conventional, or some form of, counting to solve these tasks.

Both infants (R. G. Cooper, Jr., 1984) and preschoolers (Sophian, 1988) do better comparing sets of equal, rather than unequal, number, presumably because there are many ways for collections to be unequal (difficulty is also increased if the task demands unequal collections be ordered in size, as is discussed in the following section). (Although in an early study, high, but not low, conservers scored higher on the equivalence than the order relations on a transitivity test, D. T. Owens & Steffe, 1972.) In brief, children show competence in explicitly comparing simultaneously present, equivalent collections as early as two or three years of age in everyday, spontaneous, situations, but show only the beginnings of such competence on clinical tasks at two and a half to three and a half years of age, with success across a wide range of tasks only appearing at ages suggested by Piaget (Baroody et al., 2005; Mix et al., 2002).

Clinical studies of equivalence also highlight specific difficulties children have in number comparison tasks. For example, some children will count the sets, recognize the number is the same, but still maintain that one set has more (Piaget & Szeminska, 1952). Children from four to five years of age do compare set sizes on the basis of misleading length cues, even when the situation is set up to encourage counting (Fuson, 1988).

Conversely, children cannot always infer number from that of an equivalent set. In one study, fair sharing was established by dealing out items to two puppets, and the experimenter counted one set out loud and asked children how many the other puppet had. No four-year-old children made the correct inference that the number was the same; instead, they tried to count the second set. The experimenter stopped them and asked again, but less than half made the correct inference (Frydman & Bryant, 1988).

Information-processing demands may help explain why. For example, to compare the number in two sets, children must count each set, keeping track of the two numbers, and then compare these numbers' ordinal values. This may exceed young children's information-processing capabilities (e.g., their working memory). For example, in one study, children were asked two types of questions about toy animals, one was "Can every big horse have its own baby horse?" and the other was, "How many animals are there all together?" A puppet either counted all the animals or the two subsets separately. Both three- and four-year-olds preferred the puppet to count all the animals on the "how many in all" task. However, on the comparison tasks, three-year-olds accepted both types of counting, whereas four-year-olds still preferred counting all the animals. Thus, neither age group was as knowledgeable about using counting to compare sets as they were about using counting to find a total amount (Sophian, 1998). The additional information-processing load may be part of the limitation, but knowledge about the relevance of counting may also be lacking. This is illustrated in another study, in which two sets were placed in one-to-one correspondence, and then one was hidden. Children in one condition were told to count the visible set before being asked how many in the hidden set. In the other condition, they were asked to move the still-visible set, emphasizing each item, but not the numerosity. Even three-year-olds, when told to count, made appropriate inferences. Most children in the "move" condition did not make appropriate inferences, even though the objects were right there to count. They did not understand the relevance of counting.

Different researchers have given several additional explanations for preschoolers' reluctance or inability to use counting (Curtis, Okamoto, & Weckbacher, 2005). Several agree with the explanation of available memory resources (Pascual-Leone, 1976). For example, one theory is that children have two conceptual structures that are initially separate and only later become integrated. The first, a quantity comparison structure, allows young children to compare two set sizes intuitively (see Chapter 2). The second, the early enumeration structure, allows them to count small sets (see Chapter 3). They do not use this counting structure to compare sets. After six years of age, their ability to hold these two structures simultaneously in memory allows them to integrate them, and thus use counting to compare sets (Case & Okamoto, 1996).

Other researchers state that children believe that counting-based strategies are too difficult or unreliable (Cowan, 1987; Michie, 1984b; Siegler, 1995; Sophian, 1988). Finally, others say that counting is an activity, embedded in situated tasks, and that use of it in other tasks develops only over time (Nunes & Bryant, 1996; Steffe, Cobb, Glasersfeld, & Richards, 1983), as children come to trust the results of counting (e.g., relative to conflicting perceptions of length, Cowan & Daniel, 1989). Most agree that preschoolers do not often use counting to compare numerosities of collections.

However, presented different tasks, preschoolers can perform such inferences, such as from matching-based to counting-based equivalence. Recall studies showing that, told the cardinal value of each of two sets, preschoolers determined whether the items would be put in one-to-one correspondence and the inverse (Becker, 1989; Sophian, 1988). Thus, success is dependent on the task, with success appearing first when one-to-one correspondence (rather than sharing) is used to establish equivalence. Between the ages of three and five children develop from counting only single collections to being able to use counting to compare the results of counting two collections (Saxe et al., 1987) and reason about these comparisons across different situations.

Further, counting is not without positive influence. Even when children use misleading length cues, from 70 to 80 percent turned to counting when asked to "do something" to justify their response (Fuson, 1988). Further, while encouraging four and a half to five-year-old children to match and count increases their correct judgments of equivalence, children only spontaneously adopt counting for subsequent problems of the same type (Fuson et al., 1983). When the counting is performed for them, preschoolers are more likely to base their comparison decisions on the results of counting (Curtis et al., 2005), which may imply that counting imposes a large processing load on children of this age, or that they are uncertain of the reliability of their own counting or did not initially appreciate the relevance of the counting strategy.

Taken together, research seems to indicate multiple factors that influence children's use of counting to compare collections. They do need to develop sufficient working memory to make a plan to compare, count two collections, keep the results in mind, relate these results, and draw conclusions about the two collections. To do so, their counting scheme itself first must be developed to a particular level. Consistent with the hierarchic development tenet of our hierarchic interactionalism theory, counting is at first a procedure to be mastered, not an object from which the child can "step back" and about which they can think explicitly. Once repeated experience causes the components of counting to be "representationally redescribed" and thus available to other mental processes, it can serve that purpose (Karmiloff-Smith, 1992).

At that point, another aspect of the tenet of hierarchic development operates (showing that development is less about the creation of entirely new procedures and more the interplay among existing components of knowledge and processes); that is, counting can be used in quantitative comparison because a new mental executive can be formed linking the results of counting to the requirement for quantification of two collections that are to be compared. To do so accurately, children also have to learn that the same number implies the same numerosity and that different numbers imply (and necessitate) different numerosities (Cowan, 1987). That is, many children (some as old as first graders) need to learn about the significance of the results of counting in different situations, such as comparing sets or producing equivalent sets (Nunes & Bryant, 1996). Finally, they may need to have a concept of space that is sufficiently articulated and unitized to reconcile the perceptual evidence and numerical interpretation of the situation (Becker, 1989). If all these are in place, children's utilization competence is expanded; they know more situations in which counting can be profitably used.

Thus, as we previously concluded, counting can be a meaningful quantifier for children before they reach the Piagetian levels of operational thought about number conservation. However, children's ability to solve problems using counting develops slowly, as they learn counting skills and about the application of counting to various tasks.

Ordering and Ordinal Numbers

Ordering numbers is the process of determining which of two numbers is "larger than" the other. When whole numbers are used to put items in order, or in a sequence, they are *ordinal numbers*. When the topic of "ordinality" is discussed, even by some researchers, it is often assumed that all ordinal notions must involve the terms "first, second, third . . ." and so forth. This is a limited view. As was previously discussed, numbers have an ordinal property in that they are sequenced. A number may be first or second in an order without considering cardinality, or it may be considered to have a greater or lesser magnitude than another number. A person who is "number 5" in a line is labeled by a word that is no less ordinal in its meaning because it is not expressed as "fifth." We first address young children's ability to order collections by number, then their ability to deal explicitly with traditional ordinal numbers.

Ordering Numbers

Given that chimpanzees can order numbers (Kawai & Matsuzawa, 2000), this ability is probably supported by "bootstrapped" abilities. Children can learn such ordering with high-quality experiences. In most studies of conservation discussed previously, children needed only to decide whether collections were equivalent or not, but not to explicitly order them (even determining which contained more). Evidence indicates that human beings can make perceptual judgments of relative quantities early, but somewhat later than they evince other quantitative abilities. As an example, 16- to 18-month-olds were reinforced for selecting a square containing two dots but not another square containing one dot, regardless of which side it was on and regardless how big or bright the dots were (Strauss & Curtis, 1984). Then, presented two new squares with three and four dots, respectively, the infants more often chose the square with more dots, indicating sensitivity to the ordinal concept of "more numerous." Other studies confirm that children differentiate between "less than" and "greater than" relations by 14 months of age (R. G. Cooper, Jr., 1984; Feigenson, 1999; Haith & Benson, 1998), and possibly earlier, at least with collections no larger than two (Sophian & Adams, 1987). Even 11-, but not nine-month-olds, can distinguish between ascending and descending sequences of quantities (Brannon, 2002). That is, following habituation to three-item sequences of decreasing numerical displays, in which area was not confounded with number, only 11-month-olds could then distinguish between new displays of decreasing vs. increasing sequences.

Seminal research on equivalence, Gelman's "magic experiments," showed that children explicitly recognized which of two sets was the "winner" even if the length, density, or even properties (color) of one set were altered. However, when the change involved an addition or subtraction that created equivalent sets, children correctly responded that there was no winner (R. Gelman & Gallistel, 1978). These experiments also revealed that children about three years of age are sensitive to ordinal relations. Shown that two was the winner compared to one, children selected four as the winner compared to three. In both experiments, this competence was just emerging at two to three years of age. By three years of age, children show knowledge of order in comparing collections, separate from their counting skills (Huntley-Fenner & Cannon, 2000; Mix et al., 2002).

As with cardinal number, children develop the ability to order numbers over several years by learning the cultural tools of subitizing (Baroody et al., 2006), matching, and counting (Fuson et al., 1983). For example, children can answer questions such as "which is more, six or four?" only by age four or five years (Siegler & Robinson, 1982). Tasks involving smaller numbers and numbers farther apart are easier (Cowan & Daniel, 1989), suggesting that counting skills are relevant with numbers larger than four. Unlike middle-income children, low-income five- and six-year-olds were unable to tell which of two numbers, such as six or eight, is bigger, or which number, six or two, is closer to five (Griffin et al., 1994). They may not have developed the "mental number line" representation of numbers as well as their more advantaged peers. This mental number line—grounded in *spatial* representations of numbers—may be the most direct neural representation of number (Zorzi, Priftis, & Umiltà, 2002). These representations have several aspects, such as two additional principles of counting. The "plus and minus one" principle involves understanding the generative pattern that relates adjacent numerical values (e.g., a collection of four is a collection of three with one added). The related comparison principle involves understanding the consequences of each successive number representing a collection that contains more objects (Griffin et al., 1994). Children who use and understand these principles can reason that if the counts of two collections are nine and seven, the collection with nine has more because nine comes later in the counting sequence than seven.

Ordinal Numbers

Of children entering their first year of school in Australia, 29 and 20 percent respectively could identify the third and fifth items in a series (B. A. Clarke, Clarke, & Cheeseman, 2006). In the U.S., performance for "first" was 60 and 72 percent, and for "third," was 9 and 13 percent for low- and middle-income preschoolers, respectively (Sarama & Clements, 2008). As in other areas, different languages differentially affect children's acquisition and use of ordinal words. Differences in ordinal words are even more distinct across languages. Beginning right with "first" and "second" compared to "one" and "two," English ordinal and counting words often have little or no relation. In comparison, Chinese speakers form ordinal words simply by adding a predicate (di) to the cardinal number name. English-, compared to Chinese-, speaking children show dramatically lower performance on naming ordinal words from the first words and from the earliest ages, persisting into elementary school (K. F. Miller et al., 2000). There is a precipitous decline between 19th and 21st, with only 30 percent of the English-speaking sample counting to 21st, vs. nearly perfect performance in Chinese-speaking children. However, this research also reveals complexities in the relationships between concepts and language. Although few children understood the unique features of ordinal numbers, English speakers appear to understand the distinctions between ordinal and cardinal number concepts sooner, perhaps because struggles with the different names engendered reflection on these differences (K. F. Miller et al., 2000).

Estimation

Estimation is a process of solving a problem that calls for a rough or tentative evaluation of a quantity. There are many types of estimation, including measurement, numerosity, and computational estimation (Sowder, 1992a). Measurement estimation will be addressed in Chapters 11 and 12. Computational estimation has been most widely researched (see Chapter 6). A hybrid, "number line estimation," such as the ability to place numbers on a number line of arbitrary length, appears particularly important for young children, so we begin there.

Number Line Estimation

Research on assessments of multiple mathematical areas identifying the ability to quickly tell which of two numerals, 0 to 20, represented the larger number as one of the only three that predicted later mathematics achievement (Chard et al., 2005). After learning a mental number *list* children can learn to form a linear representation of numbers. That is, in many situations, people represent numbers logarithmically, rather than linearly (Dehaene, 1997; Siegler & Booth, 2004). That is, they tend to exaggerate the distances between numbers at the lower end of a given number line and underestimate the distances between numbers at the high end. This tendency has been found in all types of estimation tasks, number line, numerosity, and measurement (Siegler & Ramani, in press). For example, given a line segment is labeled with 0 at one end and 100 at the other, kindergarteners may guess "32" for a position that should be labeled 11, and guess a number such as "65" for positions from 50 to 100.

Some researchers (e.g., Dehaene, 1997) have postulated that people's mental processes *are* logarithmic ruler representations. Others suggest the accumulator model (see Chapter 2) that yields similar estimates and still others that different representations are used by children of different ages.

Siegler and Booth (2004) proposed that there are multiple representations of number and that contextual variables influence which representation is chosen in a given situation. Experience with formal number systems in counting, arithmetic, and other contexts leads children to add linear representations, as well as such categorical representations as even/odd. Different representations are used in different contexts (again, consistent with the context-variable nature of the tenet of hierarchic development). These can be developmentally adaptive; for example, an early logarithmic representation may enhance discrimination among the magnitudes of the small numbers being learned. Evidence supported this proposal: young children have such a logarithmic representation for 0–10; kindergarteners tend to have a more linear representation of 0–10, but are logarithmic for 0 to 100; and elementary-school children are linear for 0–100 and only gradually move to linear representations for 0 to 1000 or 10,000 (Siegler & Booth, 2004). Thus, people's refining of number line estimation is begun with smaller ranges and then repeated with larger numbers (the tenet of hierarchic development). Further, this development occurs at the same ages for numerosity estimation and measurement estimation. Finally, it correlates with magnitude comparison (e.g., which is bigger, seven or nine?), learning of unfamiliar addition problems, and overall mathematics achievement. This learning reflects developing knowledge of numbers in the given range, rather than simple abstract learning about place value and the base-ten numeration system (J. L. Booth & Siegler, 2006).

Improving children's number line estimation may have a broad beneficial effect on their representation, and therefore knowledge, of numbers (Siegler & Booth, 2004, although most evidence is not yet causal). Estimates of many children from low-income backgrounds did not even reveal knowledge of the ordering of the numbers' magnitudes; 60 percent of children correctly ordered fewer than 60 percent of the magnitudes of these single digit numbers (Siegler & Ramani, in press).

Estimation of Numerosities

Given children's early competence in subitizing (Chapter 2) and counting (Chapter 3), it is reasonable to assume that their ability to estimate the number of objects in a collection would also be an early developing skill. However, empirical evidence reveals this type of estimating to be challenging for young children.

Early research indicated that children from five to eight years of age could operate at a better than chance level in numerosity estimation tasks, and that this age range represented a period of development of these abilities, although only slowly at the earlier ages (Hecox & Hagen, 1971). A later series of studies examined people's ability to determine the numerosity of colored squares within square grids. In the first study, researchers used a 10 by 10 grid and reported that the use of the simplest, addition strategy (count and/or subitize blocks and add them) decreased with age from second grade to sixth grade to university students, with a corresponding increase in the use of subtraction strategy (subtract the number of empty squares from 100 when most squares were colored) (Verschaffel, De Corte, Lamote, & Dhert, 1998). Also, the combined and adaptive use of both strategies correlated with higher performance on the task, but only for sixth graders and university students.

Building on this work, a related team of researchers (Luwel, Verschaffel, Onghena, & De Corte, 2000) used grids that were hypothesized not to provide as much support for subtraction strategies: seven by seven, eight by eight, and nine by nine grids. "Experts" were expected to apply the addition strategy for trials with few blocks (the left-most grid in Figure 4.1) and subtraction strategy for trials with many blocks (the right most figure). In the middle region, they were expected apply a subitize-and-accumulate estimation strategy. "Novices" were expected to apply the addition strategy for trials with small numerosities, and otherwise use a cognitively less-demanding estimation strategy, even when the grid was almost filled with blocks.

Second and sixth graders did not differ from sixth graders on the use of the more sophisticated subtraction strategy, but they did not use it as well. For example, many second graders, probably due to their use of 100s charts, took

Figure 4.1 Three 8-by-8 grids with different numbers of squares colored gray.

the total of all grids to be 100. To check this hypothesis, the same researchers presented second graders with explicit information about the grid size (Luwel, Verschaffel, Onghena, & De Corte, 2001). This increased children's accuracy, as well as the number of tasks to which they applied the subtraction strategy. They needed to use an estimation strategy for a larger middle region than sixth graders, who could still solve these problems with arithmetic strategies for all but the largest grid sizes.

In summary, students from second grade on used similar strategies. However, there may not be a single estimation strategy, but distinct strategies whose details are as yet unknown. With increasing age, students rely more on accurate (here, arithmetic) strategies. It could not be determined if older students were more adaptive in their strategy choice. A final follow-up study with older students indicated that the first source of improvement is an increasing reliance on the subtraction strategy when this is appropriate (probably due to the greater difficulty younger, third-grader, students had subtracting, Luwel, Lemaire, & Verschaffel, 2005). The second source was improved strategy proficiency, with younger students executing subtraction more slowly. The third source was increasing adaptiveness of strategy choices with age. That is, older students more frequently used strategies that worked best for them.

Another early study reported that the type of strategy use was not related to accuracy in one early study of students in grades two to eight and adults (A. W. Siegel, Goldsmith, & Madson, 1982). Younger children used perceptually-based strategies most of the time. The size of the to-be-estimated collection (TBE), and the available benchmarks, influenced students' behaviors; for example, if the TBE number was large, students who could tried decomposition strategies, or just "bailed out" and used perceptually based strategies. This was reported as more of an affective than a cognitive decision.

A group of high-achieving (potentially mathematically gifted) kindergar-teners were able to estimate sets of eight between five and 10 reliably, but they were less accurate with sets of 15 and not competent with sets of 35 (Baroody, 1991). The results suggest that the children had not constructed accurate per-ceptual anchors, or benchmarks, and may have an exaggerated mental image of benchmarks such as five, 10, and 20.

Based on the available research, we, along with Gail Brade, produced a developmental progression as the basis for a learning trajectory for numerosity estimation. Early, "pre-estimation" developmental levels included "Counting" (refusing to estimate without counting), "Wild Guessing," and "Transition to Spatial Extent" (not wild guesses, usually some counting, followed by an esti-mate that does not demonstrate evidence of a distinction between small and large numbers). The remainder of the levels includes increasingly sophisticated strategies and has been incorporated into the learning trajectory in Figure 4.1. Brade used it in a study presenting numerosity tasks to children in grades K to 2

(Brade, 2003). There was a positive and significant correlation between learning trajectory (strategy) level used and accuracy, but children's competence with a strategy at any level was also important in determining estimation accuracy. Kindergarteners could estimate collections of eight, but not larger numbers, consistent with earlier research (Baroody, 1991). First graders also had some success estimating collections of 15 and 25.

Numerosity estimation may depend on highly developed number skills such as subitizing and counting, and the mental images their execution creates. Preschool and kindergarten children who cannot count beyond 60 fail the estimation and ordering tasks for number words larger than 60. Adults and children who can count reliably to 100 succeed on all these tasks. Unskilled counters failed even to correctly order large number words differing by a 2:1 ratio, whereas they performed well on this task with smaller numbers, and performed well on a nonsymbolic ordering task with the same numerosities. All children could succeed at those tasks—they showed a linear relationship between number words and numerosities—when tested with number words *within their counting range* (Lipton & Spelke, 2005). Therefore, children appear to quickly learn to map the words in their counting sequence to nonsymbolic numerosities. That is, children quickly connect number words to approximate numerosity representations about the time they learn to count to those words well. Learning to count accurately and farther along the number word sequence appears to support a variety of mathematical skills.

Computational Estimation

Estimation of the answers of arithmetic problems is probably related to other types of estimation—number line, numerosity, and measurement—but also depends on specific knowledge of arithmetic combinations and procedures (J. L. Booth & Siegler, 2006). There are few studies on computational estimation of young children. One reported that six of 17 kindergarteners used mechanical rules to estimate single-digit addition sums (Baroody, 1989a). Two each stated one of the addends, added one to an addend and constructed a teen answer from one of the addends. Five other children appeared to use more genuine estimation strategies, such as estimating in the range of two more than the larger addend but not more than 19. Previous practice (forming associations) would not have led to such estimates; it is more likely that they used knowledge of numbers. Another study categorized five- to nine-year-olds into four levels of computational estimation competence (Dowker, 1989, as reported in Sowder, 1992a). Children at the lowest level, even though they were given the easiest problems, such as 5 + 2, performed the worst. Many of their estimates were less than one of the addends or more than double the actual sum.

It would appear that computational estimation develops slowly, and teaching it to young children before they have developed a firm grasp of concepts, skills, strategies, and knowledge of combinations may not be effective or efficient. Given this assumption, and given that most research, and most recommendations to teach, computational estimation involve students at higher grade levels, we will not discuss this type further here (see Sowder, 1992a, for a comprehensive review).

Experience and Education

Comparing Numbers

Research has identified some aspects of effective educational interventions for comparing numbers. One main implication is that young children need to learn about the significance of the results of counting in comparison situations (Fuson, 1988).

Just as important is asking children why and how counting is relevant. Children in the Yemen, five and a half to seven and a half years of age, who were given experiences comparing sets improved, but those who had the additional experience of verifying that counting led to correct judgments improved the most, with the majority of children counting on every trial (Cowan, Foster, & Al-Zubaidi, 1993). The emphasis should be on counting as a tool for thinking and solving problems. Teachers should help young children learn which strategies (counting, comparing length, etc.) are reliable and accurate in which situations (Michie, 1984a). They might compare amounts counting them into boxes or piggy banks first (so there are no confusing perceptual cues) and then into lines. A reminder or meaningful record of each count might also be helpful. The situational language in comparing situations is complex and children need considerable experience solving comparing problems and hearing and telling comparing stories.

Number Line Estimation

Number line estimation is clearly an important competence. It correlates with other types of estimation and general mathematics achievement (Siegler & Ramani, in press). It is a core competence and, as we shall see in the following section, probably a good educational place to begin to develop estimation skills. Numerosity estimation may build upon number line estimation.

One approach to teaching this skill, having children place numerals on a number line (Siegler & Booth, 2004), was confusing for kindergartners, but helpful for first and second graders. Another approach, playing line "race" games, was successful for very young children, having a significant effect in only four 15-minute sessions (Siegler & Ramani, in press). Preschoolers' numerical estimates became more linear and accurate. They also increased their ability to order magnitudes, count, and recognize numerals. These low-income children were then indistinguishable in these domains from their middle-class peers. Both three- and four-year-olds benefited. In a connected study, the researchers confirmed that the more board games the children played at home, the greater was their competence in number line estimation (Siegler & Ramani, in press). Connections between the numerical magnitudes and all the visual-spatial, kinesthetic, auditory, and temporal cues in the games (i.e., all magnitudes increase together: numerals, distance moved, number of moves, number of counting words, etc.) may provide a rich mental model for a mental number line.

Estimation of Numerosities

There are wide disagreements on when numerosity estimation should be taught, ranging from early childhood to junior high school. Instructional activities (admittedly short in duration) did not substantially improve the estimation skills of K–grade 2 children in one study (Brade, 2003).[1] Kindergarteners showed the most improvement on a set size of eight; first graders and second graders on 15 (the instructional treatment affecting first graders' estimate of 15 the most), 25, and 35, but not 83. There was a positive and significant correlation between learning trajectory (strategy) level used and accuracy, but children's competence with a strategy at any level was also important in determining estimation accuracy. There was limited movement along the learning trajectory; however, those who did change moved to adjacent levels, providing some support for the trajectory.

Math for a Purpose

Across these topics, a pattern similar to previous chapters emerges: effective learning takes place in situations with meaningful contexts and goals. Those activities that make sense to children, and in which they make sense of the mathematical structures of the activities, build solid conceptual understandings and skills.

Learning Trajectories for Comparing, Ordering, and Estimating Numbers

As we have in previous chapters, we present the research-based developmental progressions for these learning trajectories, and the hypothesized *mental actions on objects* for each level of each developmental progression, in Table 4.1.

Table 4.1 A Development Progression for Comparing, Ordering, and Estimating Numbers

Age (years)	Developmental Progression	Actions on Objects
0–1	**Many-to-One Corresponder** *Comparing* Puts objects, words, or actions in one-to-one or many-to-one correspondence or a mixture. Puts several blocks in each muffin tin.	(See Chapter 2's learning trajectory for underlying cognitive mechanisms.)

Continued Overleaf

Age (years)	Developmental Progression	Actions on Objects
2	**One-to-One Corresponder** *Comparing* Puts objects in rigid one-to-one correspondence (age 2–0). Uses words to include "more," "less," or "same."	Underlying mental correspondence mechanism (see Chapter 2's learning trajectory) directs perceptually-guided physical activity of matching object in one group to an object in the other. Innate, inflexible list-exhaustion scheme motivates matching *each* object in each group.
	Puts one block in each muffin tin, but is disturbed that some blocks left so finds more tins to put every last block in something.	
	Implicitly sensitive to the relation of "more than/less than" involving very small numbers (from one to two years of age).	Objects that cannot be matched intuitively indicate "more" of that group to the system.
	Object Corresponder *Comparing* Puts objects into one-to-one correspondence, although may not fully understand that this creates equal groups (age 2–8).	As above, with explicit representation that extra objects following matching indicate a greater number of that group. Equality of sets of matched objects is established at an implicit level, but is not yet explicitly represented as the "same number" (and not connected to number as constructed by the subitizing or counting operations).
	Put a straw in each carton (doesn't worry if extra straws are left), but doesn't necessarily know there are the same numbers of straws and cartons.	
	Perceptual Comparer *Comparing* Compares collections that are quite different in size (e.g., one is at least twice the other).	Cognitive mechanisms (see Chapter 2) make comparisons. Larger collections different in size are processed by an analog estimator as a collection of binary impulses by a brain region that processes quantity (e.g., bilateral horizontal segment of the intraparietal sulcus). These are then compared.
	Shown 10 blocks and 25 blocks, points to the 25 as having more.	
	If the collections are similar, compares very small numbers. Compares collections using number words "one" and "two" (age 2–8).	For similar small numbers, object files are established for each object in each collection and continuous extent for each retrieved unless the numbers are very small or able to be subitized, in which case exact discrete quantities are compared by mental correspondence (see Chapter 2).
	Shown groups of two and four, points to the group of four as having more.	

Age (years)	Developmental Progression	Actions on Objects
3	**First-Second Ordinal Counter** *Ordinal Number* Identifies the "first" and often "second" objects in a sequence.	The verbal list containing, initially, "first" and "second," is connected to innate notions of positions and event relations/sequences, with first connected to the initial event/object, and second to the next (initially loosely, so that other succeeding event/objects may also be so labeled).
	Nonverbal Comparer of Similar Items. (one–four items) *Comparing* Compares collections of one–four items verbally or nonverbally ("just by looking"). The items must be the same. May compare the smallest collections using number words "two" and "three" (age 3–2), and "three" and others (age 3–6) Can transfer a ordering relation from one pair of collections to another.	Quantification procedures produce nonverbal representations of each collection, which are placed in mental correspondence; if correspondence is one-to-one, the notion of "same" is activated. If there are items in a group not matched, the notion of "more" is activated.
	Identifies ••• and •‧• as equal and different from •• or ‧•.	
4	**Nonverbal Comparer of Dissimilar Items** *Comparing* Matches small, equal collections, showing that they are the same number.	Similar quantification procedures are extended to apply to dissimilar items.
	Matches collections of three shells and three dots, then declares that they "have the same number."	
	Matching Comparer *Comparing* Compares groups of one to six by matching.	Implicit scheme that any two collections can be compared by matching, with the result of "same number" if there are no unmatched items and "more" for any collected with unmatched items guides explicit matching of collections (at least up to size six; information-processing and attentional limitations may negatively affect the accuracy of the procedure for larger collections).
	Gives one toy bone to every dog and says there are the same number of dogs and bones.	
	Counting Comparer (Same Size) *Comparing* Accurate comparison via counting, but only when objects are about the same size and groups are small (about one to five).	Count-to-compare (executive) scheme holds results of two (redescribed) counting acts in (expanded) working memory and compares them for which occurs first in the counting word list (the "mental number list"), based on

Continued Overleaf

Age (years)	Developmental Progression	Actions on Objects

Counts two piles of five blocks each, and says they are the same.

Not always accurate when larger collection's objects are smaller in size than the objects in the smaller collection.

> Accurately counts two equal collections, but when asked, says the collection of larger blocks has more.

conceptual knowledge that a later-occurring count word implies a more numerous collection. However, the strength of this result can be overwhelmed by automatic scanning processes for continuous quantity (see Chapters 2, 11, and 12) when the count-to-scheme is nascent, when the difference in volume is large (and counter to the numerosity judgment), and/or when a question (often repeated) creates doubt in the correctness of the outcome (attributed to the questioner).

Mental Number Line to Five
Number Line Estimation Uses knowledge of counting number relationships to determine relative size and position when given perceptual support.

> Shown a zero at one end of a line segment and five at the other, places a "three" approximately in the middle.

Number word list is connected to several or all of distinct quantification schemes, e.g., for discrete number (subitizing and counting based), duration, and length, so as to form a mental image with properties analogous to a number line (i.e., ruler), in which distance between numbers is increasingly in proportion to their separation in the list.

5   **Counting Comparer (Five)**
Comparing Compares with counting, even when larger collection's objects are smaller. Later, figures out *how many* more or less.

> Accurately counts two equal collections, and says they have the same number, even if one collection has larger blocks.

Strengthening of count-to-compare (executive) scheme (see above; strengthening in use of the scheme and confidence in the reliability of counting procedure) and explicit conceptualization of differentiation between discrete ("counted") and continuous (measurable; "how much stuff") quantities allows count-to-compare to operate accurately even when the volume or mass of the less numerous collection is far greater than that of other collection.

Ordinal Counter *Ordinal Number* Identifies and uses ordinal numbers from "first" to "tenth."

> Can identify who is "third in line."

Extension of actions on objects for **First-Second Ordinal Counter**, above, including additions to the verbal list and explicit distinction between cardinal and ordinal notions.

Age (years)	Developmental Progression	Actions on Objects
	Spatial Extent Estimator—Small/Big *Numerosity Estimation* Names a "small number" (e.g., one–four) for sets that cover little space and a "big number" (10 to 20 or more; children classify numbers "little/big" idiosyncratically, and this may change with the size of the to-be-estimated collection, or TBE).	A fast intuitive scanning process (Joram, Subrahmanyam, & Gelman, 1998, see also Chapter 2) yields an accumulator-like record which is implicitly sorted into a range of "small" or "large" numbers, one of which is named.
	Shown nine objects spread out for one second and asked "How many?" responds "Fifty!"	
	Counting Comparer (10) *Comparing* Compares with counting, even when larger collection's objects are smaller, up to 10.	Strengthening of count-to-compare scheme (see above) and attentional resources extend the scheme to accurately apply to situations with larger numbers.
	Accurately counts two collections of nine each, and says they have the same number, even if one collection has larger blocks.	
6	**Mental Number Line to 10** *Number Line Estimation* Uses internal images and knowledge of number relationships to determine relative size and position.	Mental number line (see above) is strengthened and extended.
	Which number is closer to six, four or nine?	
	Serial Orderer to Six + *Comparing/Ordering* Orders numerals, and collection (small numbers first)	Available comparison and mental number line and expansion of working memory resources form an anticipatory scheme in which multiple objects (collections, lengths) are placed in order of size, with the recognition (initially implicit) that each subsequent item in the series is more than the item before and less than the item after.
	Given cards with one to five dots on them, puts in order.	
	Orders lengths marked into units.	
	Given towers of cubes, puts in order, one to 10.	
	Spatial Extent Estimator *Numerosity Estimation* Extends sets and number categories to include "small numbers" which are usually subitized, not estimated, "middle-size numbers" (e.g., 10–20) and "large numbers." The arrangement of the TBE affects the difficulty.	Executive process determines if number is subitizable; if so, that is the result. If not, a fast intuitive scanning process yields an accumulator-like record which is implicitly sorted into a range of "small," "middle-size," or "large" numbers, one of which within that category is named.

Continued Overleaf

Age (years)	Developmental Progression	Actions on Objects
	Shown nine objects spread out for one second and asked "How many?" responds "Fifteen."	
7	**Place Value Comparer** *Comparing* Compares numbers with place value understandings. "63 is more than 59 because six tens is more than five tens even if there are more than three ones."	Mental number line and embedded number/place value concepts (see Chapters 3 and 6) are applied to order based on larger place value quantities that differ.
	Mental Number Line to 100 *Number Line Estimation* Uses internal images and knowledge of number relationships, including ones embedded in tens, to determine relative size and position. Asked, "Which is closer to 45, 30 or 50?"says "45 is right next to 50, but fives, but 30 isn't."	Mental number line (see above) is extended with embedded number (both in the number word sequence pattern and in place value quantity) up to 100.
	Scanning with Intuitive Quantification Estimator *Numerosity Estimation* Shown 40 objects spread out for one second and asked "How many?" responds "About thirty."	Fast intuitive scanning process yields an estimate based on connection between nonverbal magnitudes and mental number line.
8	**Mental Number Line to 1000s** *Number Line Estimation* Uses internal images and knowledge of number relationships, including place value, to determine relative size and position. Asked, "Which is closer to 3500, 2000 or 7000?"says "70 is double 35, but 20 is only 15 from 35, so 20 hundreds, 2000, is closer."	Mental number line (see above) is extended to place vs. value up to 1000 or more.
	Benchmarks Estimator *Numerosity Estimation* Initially, a portion of the TBE is counted; this is used as a benchmark from which an estimate is made. Later, scanning can be linked to recalled benchmarks.	An initial count is performed of a visually salient, intuitively determined "manageable" proper subject of the objects. This is used as a benchmark. Or, the fast scanning process yields an estimate based on connection to mental number line, supplemented with benchmarks (e.g., images of collections

Age (years)	Developmental Progression	Actions on Objects
	Shown 11, says "It looked closer to 10 than 20, so I guess 12." Shown 45 objects spread out for one second and asked "How many?" responds "About five tens—fifty."	of 10) that are linked to that number line and to mental images of collections of that size. This develops from an ability to tell if the TBE is close to, more, or less than the benchmark to estimates of the TBE's own numerosity.
	Composition Estimator *Numerosity Estimation* Initially for regular arrangements, subitizing is used to quantify a subset and repeated addition or multiplication used to produce an estimate. Later, the process is extended to include irregular arrangements. Finally, it includes the ability to *decompose* or *partition* the TBE into convenient subset sizes, then recompose the numerosity based on multiplication. Shown 87 objects spread out and asked for an estimate responds, "That's about 20—so, 20, 40, 60, 80. Eighty!"	Subitizing (often conceptual subitizing) is performed to yield a number. An iterative process is used to determine the number of such groups and multiplication is applied to yield an estimate. Alternatively, the TBE is partitioned, one unit is subitized, counted, or estimated, and multiplication again applied.

Final Words

Many mathematical situations involve comparing, sequencing, and/or estimating number. Another common type of situation involves incrementing/decrementing numbers. We begin the discussion of the operations of arithmetic in Chapter 5.

5
Arithmetic
Early Addition and Subtraction and Counting Strategies

For most people in the U.S., arithmetic is arguably the most salient topic in elementary mathematics education. However, most people would also argue that this would be an inappropriate topic in preprimary education. We begin our discussion considering research on the age at which knowledge of and skills in arithmetic appear to emerge.

The Earliest Arithmetic

Educational practice, past and present, often takes a skills hierarchy view that arithmetic follows counting and other simple work with number and therefore is beyond children's grasp until about first grade. However, decades ago, researchers illustrated the possibility of arithmetic competence in children before kindergarten (R. Gelman & Gallistel, 1978; Groen & Resnick, 1977; Hughes, 1981).

More recently, nativist researchers claimed that even infants have knowledge of simple arithmetic. Consider evidence that infants and toddlers notice the effects of increasing or decreasing small collections by one item. For example, after seeing (a) a hand place one or two dolls on a stage, (b) a screen raised, (c) a hand place another doll behind the screen, and (d) the screen retracted, five-month-olds look longer when an incorrect, rather than a correct, result is revealed (a violation-of-expectations procedure, Wynn, 1992a, see the illustration in the companion book).

In another study, children placed balls in a box placed high enough that they could not see into the box. They then watched as balls were added or removed (Starkey, 1992). Finally, they were asked to remove all the balls. The question was whether the number of times children reached was the same as the number of balls they placed. To prevent children from feeling whether or not any remained in the box, the balls were secretly removed and replaced one-by-one before each reach. Children did reach the same number of times above chance. However, a flaw in the design was that these removals might have inadvertently kept children from reaching in again when they would have (mistakenly) done so (Mix et al., 2002). This would favor tasks with an answer of one. Note that children were evaluated as correct on 64 percent of the 4 − 3 trials but only

14 percent on the 4 − 1 trials, even though the latter would be considered the easier of the two tasks.

Despite such limitations of the research designs, authors of the original studies have made strong nativist claims, such as "infants can discriminate between different small numbers . . . determine numerical equivalence across perceptual modalities," and "calculate the results of simple arithmetical operations on small numbers," all of which indicates that they "possess true numerical concepts, and suggests that humans are innately endowed with arithmetic abilities" (Wynn, 1992a, p. 749). They have "access to the ordering of and numerical relationships between small numbers, and can manipulate these concepts in numerically meaningful ways" (p. 750). As one example, five-month-olds added one object and one tone or one object and two tones (Kobayashi, Hiraki, Mugitani, & Hasegawa, 2004). A recent study grounded in that perspective suggested that very young children, viewing dots representing 5 + 5 and 10 − 5 (controlled for area and contour length), could discriminate between outcomes of 5 and 10 (McCrink & Wynn, 2004).

Possible alternative explanations have been addressed and proposed that do *not* imply arithmetic competence. For example, it is possible that infants merely track locations, but evidence indicates they can track objects or number of objects (Koechlin, Dehaene, & Mehler, 1997). A different possible confound is that every outcome in Wynn's work that was arithmetically impossible was also physically impossible; however, evidence indicated that three- to five-month old babies were more upset if an arithmetically impossible result occurred than if one doll changed to another (T. J. Simon, Hespos, & Rochat, 1995). Others say that attentional preference for an optimal mix of familiarity and complexity explain Wynn's and others' findings (L. B. Cohen & Marks, 2002). For example, the unexpected "1" following a "1 + 1" condition is also *familiar*, as it was the starting situation.

Other concerns have been raised. In some studies, using standardized procedures, infants were *not* found to discriminate between correct and incorrect results of addition and subtraction (Wakeley, Rivera, & Langer, 2000). Multiple studies have found that three- but not two-year-olds are successful on nonverbal addition and subtraction tasks (Houdé, 1997; Huttenlocher, Jordan et al., 1994). If toddlers do not have the ability, it may be unreasonable to suggest that infants do (see Huttenlocher, Jordan et al., 1994, for a discussion of these and other problems with research claiming that infants perform exact arithmetic).

Further, early behaviors often are explicable through other frameworks (Haith & Benson, 1998). For example, the children might be processing continuous amounts. Using Wynn's tasks but different size puppets, infants were more likely to attend to the display with the unexpected change in amount and the expected number than the opposite (Feigenson, Carey, & Spelke, 2002; Mix et al., 2002). Children's success with larger-number arithmetic (e.g., 10 − 5, McCrink & Wynn, 2004) may involve their use of an estimator such as in the "large number exception" situation discussed in Chapter 2 on subitizing. This is supported by cultures that have number words only up to five, but can compare and add large *approximate* numbers beyond that range (Pica et al., 2004). It is also consistent with the view that infants represent small collections as individual objects but not as groups and large numbers as groups but not as individual objects (Spelke, 2003). Thus, analogue estimators may be innate or early developing, and may mediate (Gallistel & Gelman, 2005), but not directly determine, later-developing explicit, accurate arithmetic.

Another possible framework for smaller-number problems postulates that infants are tracking objects via "mental tokens" using general processes of simple categorization (an early "object concept") and comparison (Koechlin et al., 1997; T. J. Simon, 1997; T. J. Simon et al., 1995). Children may possess neural traces of visual information that are not consistent with the final display, and thus their "representations" could be literal and knowledge-based. That is, these babies may not be *quantifying* a *collection* of objects, but instead individuating and tracking separate objects, reacting if one disappears or appears mysteriously (Koechlin et al., 1997; Sophian, 1998). For example, infants' surprising greater sensitivity to subtraction than addition across multiple studies (Koechlin et al., 1997; Wynn, 1992a, 1995) may indicate that the smaller the result, the more likely the child will track accurately. Further, experiments directly comparing two models, numeric/symbolic and object file, were consistent with the object file model's predictions (Uller et al., 1999). For example, infants are much more likely to succeed if the first object in a $1 + 1$ task is seen on the floor before the screen is introduced, compared to tasks in which the screen is introduced first and thus the objects must be imagined there (Uller et al., 1999). Consistent results from other experiments (Uller et al., 1999) and the mixed results of various researchers, imply that adults should remain aware that we often attribute numerosity and arithmetic operations to reactions to changes in number, but that may be our inability to decenter and understand this is our projection of number onto the situation, deeply embedded in our adult cognition (cf. Glasersfeld, 1982).

This does not mean competencies do not exist, or that they are irrelevant to the foundations of numbers development; in contrast, relevant competencies are supported in most studies. However, even comparing via an early version of one-to-one correspondence may be at the service of general goals and *not be numerical for the infant in the sense that it would be for adults*. Probably the most we can confidently say is that infants react to situations that older children and adults would experience as arithmetical.

Semantic analysis is consistent with this latter interpretation (Glasersfeld, 1982). For example, children may discover, perhaps by putting up two fingers on each hand, that they can make a configuration of four fingers, but perhaps only at the sensory-motor level. Through application of subitizing or counting and reflective abstraction on the attentional patterns whose unconscious "automatic" application to sensory material made the figurative compositions possible, children eventually rebuild these experiences as arithmetical relationships.

Supporting this constructivist approach is evidence that young children's active sensori-motor production may develop before their reactive perceptual discrimination of adding and subtracting. For example, when exposed to a standardized violation-of-expectations procedure (Wynn's were not standardized), 11, 16, and 21-month-olds did not look longer at results for $1 + 1$ or $2 - 1$ that were incorrect than those that were correct (Langer, Gillette, & Arriaga, 2003). However, 21-month-olds did reach into a box correctly in about three-fourths of the trials. Thus, pragmatic knowledge of what "works" with objects may precede "understanding how" or "what."

Similarly, children discriminate situations of adding or subtracting two to three objects between ages two and a half to three and a half years (note that the authors' conclusions on chance levels appear to be incorrect, see Bisanz, Sherman, Rasmussen, & Ho, 2005; Houdé, 1997; Vilette, 2002). Wynn reported no difference on her oculomotor tasks for the impossible situations of $1 + 1 = 1$ and $1 + 1 = 3$ and used this result to argue against a global perceptual processing interpretation and for exact calculation. However, on verbal versions of those tasks, two- to three-year-olds succeed on $1 + 1 = 1$ before they succeed on $1 + 1 = 3$ (Houdé, 1997). Such discrepancies appear to require either complex phrases of redescription (Karmiloff-Smith, 1990) or simpler nonnumerical interpretations of infant processing. Training studies support the latter (Vilette, 2002).

When do children explicitly understand the order relations in arithmetic? An early study showed that children from three to six years show sensitivity to the effects of adding or subtracting one or two marbles to one or more containers, initially established to hold an equal (but uncounted) number of marbles, when exact computations were not required (Brush, 1978). Children 14 to 28 months showed similar sensitivity to insertions and deletions from hidden sets of numerosity no more than two, with a caveat that results are affected by children's bias toward choosing the transformed set (Sophian & Adams, 1987). Thus, as early as 14 to 24 months of age, children appear to understand some sense of addition increasing, and subtraction decreasing, the size of collections, before their counting skills are well established (Bisanz et al., 2005; Cowan, 2003; Mix et al., 2002).

Preschoolers develop in reasoning about the effects of increasing or decreasing the items of two collections of objects. Consider preschoolers watching an adult create two collections created simultaneously by placing items one-for-one in separate locations. Many preschoolers will correctly judge that the items in the two collections are equal, even though they do not know exactly how many objects are in the collections. If items of one collection are then increased or decreased, children as young as age three correctly judge that the collection added to contains more or the collection subtracted from contains fewer than the collection that was not changed. However, problems involving two collections that are initially unequal present a difficulty for three-year-olds. For example, if two collections initially differ by two objects, and one object is added to the smaller collection, many three-year-olds will incorrectly say that the collection to which the object was added has more. In contrast, some five-year-olds know that this collection still has fewer. They know that both the addition and the initial inequality must be taken into account in reasoning about the effect of the addition on the collection (R. G. Cooper, Jr., 1984).

Further, children's intuitive, approximate arithmetic continues to develop and may facilitate the development of explicit, exact arithmetic with larger numbers. A series of studies showed that five-year-olds could mentally combine two successively-presented arrangements of dots and compare them to a third arrangement (see Figure 5.1, where the arrows indicate the movement of the dots onto the screen).

Further, children could also compare the dot total to a sequence of *sounds*. Two screens were shown, the white dots entered as Figure 5.1, children were told, "Now you'll *hear* the black dots" and then the children heard a sequence of sounds. Children were successful with this task as well. Because children could add within a single visual-spatial modality (dots) and across two modalities and formats (dots and sequences of tones), children's intuitive, approximate arithmetic appears to be abstract and may guide the development of later language-based arithmetic.

Children's accuracy for exact arithmetic is limited until about three years of age. Children are initially more accurate with small numbers (operands from one to three) and nonverbal problems (Hughes, 1981; see also Huttenlocher, Jordan et al., 1994). For example, children solve nonverbal arithmetic problems at about three years of age. In such tasks, the experimenter might show a number of disks, move them behind a screen, add more disks to the now-hidden collection, and ask the child to make a collection showing the number

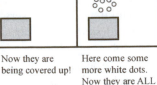

| Look, here come some white dots! | Now they are being covered up! | Here come some more white dots. Now they are ALL back there! | And here come some black dots! | Are there more white dots or more black dots? |

Figure 5.1 Approximate addition of larger numbers.

hidden (Huttenlocher, Jordan et al., 1994). Even when preschoolers develop this ability, their competencies are approximate and are strongly related to their general intellectual competence. This is inconsistent with a perspective that such arithmetical competence is innate. Addition is easier than subtraction for larger problems (operands five to eight) (Hughes, 1981). Verbal-based addition develops later, as counting becomes the key basis for understanding verbal computation above small numbers (Cowan, 2003).

Thus, most agree that children have built an initial, explicit understanding of addition and subtraction situations by about three years of age. However, it is not until four years of age that most children can solve addition problems involving even slightly larger numbers with accuracy (Huttenlocher, Jordan et al., 1994).

Most children do not solve larger-number problems without the support of concrete objects until five and a half years of age (Levine et al., 1992). They have, apparently, not only learned the counting sequence and the cardinal principle (usually about three and a half years), but also have developed the ability to convert verbal number words to quantitative meaning (cf. the ordinal-to-cardinal shift in Fuson, 1992a). However, the need for concrete materials is probably not so much a developmental, as an experiential, limitation. With experience, preschoolers and kindergartners can learn "counting-all" and even beginning "counting-on" strategies (Clements & Sarama, 2007c; Groen & Resnick, 1977; Hughes, 1986), a point to which we will return.

Addition and Subtraction Problem Structures (and other factors that affect difficulty)

Unsurprisingly, the larger the numbers the more difficult the single-digit problem, due at least in part to the frequency one has experienced in the arithmetic computations and the strategies one must use (Ashcraft, 2006). Children use a more sophisticated strategy to solve subtraction combinations whose minuends (the "wholes" from which a part is subtracted) are larger than 10 than for those that are smaller than 10.

Once children show dependable signs of understanding addition and subtraction tasks, they also show a range of strategies for solving them. Research has shown that categorization of these problems according to their main semantic structure helps explain to a large extent the level of difficulty, children's solutions strategies, and children's errors (Verschaffel, Greer, & Torbeyns, 2006). Therefore, this section describes these structures, which will be discussed through this and the following chapters (Carpenter, Ansell, Franke, Fennema, & Weisbeck, 1993; Carpenter, Fennema, Franke, Levi, & Empson, 1999; Fuson, 1992b; Kilpatrick et al., 2001). This categorization is not exhaustive and only includes simple one-step problems. More complex situations, such as those involving two or more steps, are important, especially for primary grade and older students, but these structures will be adequate for our needs (see Verschaffel, Greer, & De Corte, 2007, for an extended discussion).

Semantic structures describe different problem situations. As shown in Table 5.1, the categories include Join, Separate, Part-Part-Whole, and Compare (the names in quotation marks are those considered most useful by teachers and students, as reported in Fuson & Abrahamson, in press). For each category, there are three quantities that play different roles in the problem, any one of which could be the unknown. The specific semantic structure is given by specifying the category and the unknown. For example, the most typical

Table 5.1 Addition and Subtraction Problem Types

Category	Start/Part Unknown	Change/Difference Unknown	Result/Whole Unknown
Join ("Change Plus")	*start unknown* $\Box + 6 = 11$ Al had some balls. Then he got 6 more. Now he has 11 balls. How many did he start with?	*change unknown* $5 + \Box = 11$ Al had 5 balls. He bought some more. Now he has 11. How many did he buy?	*result unknown* $5 + 6 = \Box$ Al had 5 balls and gets 6 more. How many does he have in all?
Separate ("Change Minus")	*start unknown* $\Box - 5 = 4$ Al had some balls. He gave 5 to Barb. Now he has 4. How many did he have to start with?	*change unknown* $9 - \Box = 4$ Al had 9 balls. He gave some to Barb. Now he has 4. How many did he give to Barb?	*result unknown* $9 - 5 = \Box$ Al had 9 balls and gave 5 to Barb. How many does he have left?
Part-Part-Whole ("Collection")	*part ("partner") unknown* Al has 10 balls. Some are blue, 6 are red. How many are blue?	*part ("partner") unknown* Al has 10 balls; 4 are blue, the rest are red. How many are red?	*whole ("total") unknown* Al has 4 red balls and 6 blue balls. How many balls does he have in all?
Compare	*smaller unknown* Al had 7 balls. Barb has 2 fewer balls than Al. How many balls does Barb have?	*difference unknown* "Won't get". Al has 7 dogs and 5 bones. How many dogs won't get a bone? Al has 6 balls. Barb has 4. How many more does Al have than Barb?	*larger unknown* Al has 5 marbles. Barb has 2 more than Al. How many balls does Barb have?

problem in U.S. curricula is the "Join, result unknown" problem, such as "Alissa has three apples, then gets two more. How many does she have now?" There is a dynamic action of joining, and the problem is to find the resulting whole, five apples.

In some cases, such as the unknown parts of Part-Part-Whole problems, there is no real difference between the roles, so this does not affect the difficulty of the problem. In others, such as the result unknown, change unknown, or start unknown of Join problems, the differences in difficulty are large. Result unknown problems are easy, change unknown problems are moderately difficult, and start unknown are the most difficult. Differences in the size of the numbers also affects problem difficulty, as does the language and contexts of the problems. As we shall see, these difficulties are related to strategies children can use. For example, the three Join problems become increasingly difficult to model, or "act out," directly with concrete objects.

There also are other non-semantic variables that also contribute to the difficulty of problems, such as the presence of particular lexical items (e.g., "more" or "both"), the order of the different information elements and the chronology of events in the situations, and the clarity with which the semantic elements and relations are stated in the text (Vergnaud, 1982; Verschaffel et al., 2006). Understanding the language of word problems is no simple task for young children. In one study, children sort "add," "more," and "how many more" together (Warren, 2003). They similarly thought other terms, such as "difference" and "different" shared a meaning. They sorted "altogether," "equal," and "many left" together because "they come at the end" of word problems or expressions (e.g., 3 + 4 =). Many children described compare as "comparing two groups. . .like adding them together" or said "compare" is like "plus" because "when you compare a number it has more." Such tenuous understandings of the language used could cause serious difficulties.

Arithmetic Counting Strategies

As stated, children develop a range of strategies for solving additional and subtraction tasks (for a thorough review, see Fuson, 1992a; Verschaffel et al., 2007). Most people of any age can show diversity in solution strategies, as was recognized for young children more than 50 years ago (Ilg & Ames, 1951). Strategies of children as young as preschool (perhaps because school has not yet negatively affected them, cf. Kamii & Lewis, 1993) are notably creative and diverse (Bisanz et al., 2005; Geary et al., 1993). For example, preschool to first-grade children use a variety of covert and overt strategies, including counting fingers, finger patterns (via conceptual subitizing), verbal counting, retrieval, derived combinations, and covert strategies, some slower and some faster (Siegler & Jenkins, 1989; Siegler & Shrager, 1984; Steffe, 1983). Children are flexible strategists; using different strategies on problems they perceive to be easier or harder. Preschoolers can invent surprisingly sophisticated arithmetic strategies without instruction (Groen & Resnick, 1977).

Modeling and the Birth of Strategies

Strategies usually emerge from children's modeling the problem situation. Kindergartners can solve a wide range of addition and subtraction problem types when they represent the objects, actions, and relationships in the situations (Carpenter et al., 1993). About 90 percent used a valid strategy even for the basic subtraction and multiplication problems, with half the children using a valid strategy on every problem. About 62 percent solved more than three-fourths of the problems accurately.

In another study, four-year-olds solved 91 percent of arithmetic problems by modeling, 9 percent by counting, and none with number combinations. Children improved through the grades (Frontera, 1994).

Strategies of Different Groups of Children

Although it is not always possible to ascertain their strategies, children from all income levels are first able to respond to the simplest tasks, nonverbal addition and subtraction problems with small numbers (no number greater than four) (Huttenlocher, Jordan et al., 1994; Jordan et al., 1994). Middle-income children can also respond verbally to these problems; low-income children find this, and conventional skills such as counting, more difficult. Thus, early solutions may use manipulation of nonverbal images when possible, and conventional skills may be requisite for wider types of response types and solution procedures, especially for problems that involve larger numbers. Automatic (fast and accurate) counting skills, such as naming the counting number immediately after a given number, predicts accuracy of arithmetic performance, which predicts overall mathematics achievement for kindergartners (Penner-Wilger et al., 2005). An open question is whether the distinction between nonverbal and verbal responses is mainly a difference in language competencies or also includes the children's possession of a mental figural collection (which may not have a cardinal representation) versus numerosity (Steffe & Cobb, 1988).

Confirming cultural or experiential influences, Chinese kindergartners answer three times as many addition problems as U.S. children in a given period of time (Geary et al., 1993). Language, again, appears to be a substantial factor. Quicker pronunciation of Chinese number words allows a greater memory span for numbers which in turn supports more sophisticated verbal strategies (compared to use of fingers) which in turn support learning number combinations (because addends and sum are simultaneously in working memory).

The structure and abstruseness of English (compared to East Asian) counting words slows early learning of counting, as we saw (Chapter 3). Given the importance of counting in learning subsequent skills such as addition and subtraction, the complexity of the number system may slow learning in those areas as well (Fuson, 1992a; K. F. Miller et al., 1995). Further, languages such as Japanese add coherence to problem statements by integrating items into a set using numeral classifiers (Miura & Okamoto, 2003). A word problem such as "Joe has six marbles, two more than Tom. How many does Tom have?" in Japanese, would be "Joe has six-round-small-things, two-round-small-things more than Tom. How many round-small-things does Tom have?" This may help children build images and keep the notion of the sets of objects explicit.

Also, some studies have reported that Japanese children move from early, more primitive counting strategies, to more sophisticated strategies such as using composition and decomposition of numbers (see Chapter 6) without progressing through a long use of counting strategies, as described in the following section. This may have to do with the language and a variety of cultural and instructional supports for using five as an intermediate anchor (Verschaffel et al., 2007). These findings may serve as an important counterpoint to primarily English-based research on children's development of arithmetic counting strategies, and as a caution as we draw implications for teaching.

The learning of arithmetic is a key issue for those working with children with mathematical learning disabilities or mathematical difficulties. This and related issues are discussed at length in Chapters 15 and 16.

Counting Strategies

Even preschoolers show remarkable competence in relating counting and arithmetic. For example, they can make reasonable predictions about addition and subtraction problems and count to check those predictions accurately (Zur & Gelman, 2004). Other studies have also shown that average four-year-olds in the U.S. integrate counting with their arithmetic knowledge and, in doing so, invent counting strategies to compute the effects of addition and subtraction operations on sets of objects. Most initially use a counting-all procedure. (This may indicate they are counters of perceptual unit items, see Chapter 3 and Steffe et al., 1982.) For example, given a problem involving adding five and two, they count out a set of five items, then count out two more items, and then count all those and—if they made no counting errors—report "seven." These children naturally use such counting methods to solve story situations as long as they understand the language in the story.

After children develop such methods, they eventually curtail them (Fuson, 1992a). (This may indicate that they are counters of figural unit items if they count-up using manipulatives, or abstract unit items for more sophisticated strategies.) In an early study, researchers were surprised that, given only practice on addition problems and demonstrations of the counting-all strategy, about half of the five-year-olds moved from a counting-all strategy to a counting-on-from-larger strategy (also called "min") by themselves (Groen & Resnick, 1977). That is, given 2 + 4, they might start with four (possibly showing four fingers) and count two more: "Four ... five, six. Six!" This illustrates that young children can invent efficient strategies without direct instruction, or even despite being taught alternative methods (see also J. Cooper & Gelman, 2007; Siegler & Jenkins, 1989).

Considerable numerical competence underlies such abilities. The child must possess a meaning for "four" that is more sophisticated than four objects or four movements—it must consist mentally of four counting acts (Steffe et al., 1982). For example, given a task in which two collections are hidden from view but are said to contain six and four items, respectively, children may put up fingers sequentially while saying, "one, two, three, four, five, six" and then continue on, putting up four more fingers, "seven, eight, nine, ten. Ten!" Others may just start by saying "siiiix . . ." and counting up from there. Such counting-on is a landmark in children's numerical development. It is not a rote step, as is true of all such curtailments of processes. It requires conceptually embedding the six inside the total (Steffe & Cobb, 1988; Steffe et al., 1983). (Recall the discussion of how subitizing supports beginning arithmetic in Chapter 2. At first this embedding is implicit, called the tacitly nested number sequence, Steffe et al., 1982.)

We hypothesize that children accomplish this through a process of *psychological curtailment* (Clements & Burns, 2000; Krutetskii, 1976). Curtailment is an encapsulation process in which one mental activity gradually "stands in for" another mental activity. Children may pass through a phase in which they no longer enumerate each element of the first set on the final count, but name the number of that set with an elongated number word and a sweeping gesture of the hand and pass on to the second addend. For example, after creating sets of five and three, they sweep their hand over the five objects, saying "Fiiiiiiiiiive . . ." and then continue counting as they point to each of the objects in the set of three, ". . . six, seven, eight!" El'konin and Davydov (1975) claim that such abbreviated actions are not eliminated but are transferred to the position of actions which are considered *as if* they were carried out and are thus "implicit." The sweeping movement gives rise to a "mental plan" by which addition is performed, because only in this movement does the child begin to view the group as a unit. The child becomes aware of addition as distinct from counting. This construction of counting on must be based on physically present objects. Then, through introspection (considering the basis of one's own ways of acting), the object set is transformed into a symbol (El'konin & Davydov, 1975).

This research shows that children can follow different developmental paths, some illustrating awareness of the new strategies, others not, and most using a variety of more- and less-advanced strategies at any time. It also shows that failing to solve tasks is not requisite to inventing new strategies; instead, success is often the catalyst (DeLoache, Miller, & Pierroutsakos, 1998; Karmiloff-Smith, 1984, 1986), especially if one is not changing a conception, but only changing to a more efficient or elegant approach to producing the same answer. After concentrated experience, four- to five-year-olds showed a variety of strategies, often the counting-on-from-larger strategy, but their successes, rather than failures, appeared to catalyze the invention of new strategies. Transitional strategies were important, such as the "shortcut-sum" strategy, which appears similar to a counting-all strategy, but involves only one count; for example, to solve 4 + 3, one, two, three, four, five, six, seven and answer seven. This often preceded the counting-on-from-larger strategy, which was preferred by most children once they invented it, especially on problems such as 2 + 23 where it saved the most work (Carpenter & Moser, 1982; Siegler & Jenkins, 1989).

Thus, counting skills—especially sophisticated counting skills—are essential to developing competence with arithmetic. Counting easily and quickly predicts arithmetic competence in kindergarten, and that in turn predicts overall mathematics achievement (Penner-Wilger et al., 2005). In addition, knowing the next number (see the level, "Counter from N (N+1, N−1)," in Chapter 3) predicts arithmetic achievement and addition speed in grades 1 and 2 (and number correct in addition at grade 2).

Large-scale research supports most of these claims (Biddlecomb & Carr, 2008). For example, elementary students who used manipulatives were only at the level of counters of perceptual unit items (e.g., not above the level of Counter and Producer—Counter To (10+), as defined in Chapter 3) and did not use more sophisticated strategies.

In the case where the amount of increase (decrease) is unknown, children often use counting-up-to (counting-backwards-to) to find the unknown amount. However, counting backwards, especially more than three counts, is difficult for most children (Fuson, Smith, & Lo Cicero, 1997) unless they have high-quality instruction in this competence. Instead, many children, especially in countries other than the U.S., learn counting-up-to the total to solve a subtraction situation. This necessitates that children establish the inverse relationship between subtraction and addition. There is little sign that children as young as two years use or understand the principle (Vilette, 2002), but three- and four-year-old children use procedures consistent with the inversion principle (J. S. Klein & Bisanz, 2000; Rasmussen, Ho, & Bisanz, 2003), showing use of arithmetical (quantitative, not just qualitative) principles before formal schooling. This use is inconsistent, however, perhaps reflecting children's creative tendency to try out a variety of procedures (Shrager & Siegler, 1998), limits on their information processing capacities (J. S. Klein & Bisanz, 2000), their nascent understanding of the concept (Vilette, 2002) or some combination. In another study, given a problem with larger numbers, only one four-year-old, one-fourth of the five-year-olds, and three-eighths of the six-year-olds used the addition-subtraction inverse principle (Baroody & Lai, 2007).

Thus, an intuitive, local, and inconsistent use of the inversion principle may emerge about ages three to four years. This may be based on approximate estimations (Gilmore, Katz, & Spelke, 2007). This is a weak scheme, which involves empirical inversion (a computational approach that works only with small numbers). A verbal representation of numbers may facilitate the generalization of this idea. Only in the primary grades do many children understand and use the inversion principle and others (identification and decomposition) in a conscious and interrelated fashion (P. Bryant, Christie, & Rendu, 1999, recall most of these findings show what children learn with traditional instruction, and that is not always ideal). At that time, they often use addition to solve certain subtraction problems. However, many kindergartners do use this mathematically significant principle consistently in a quantitative manner in some situations. Most might be able to do so with good instruction.

As with counting, there is a debate about whether skill or conceptual competence precedes the other. Research shows the two are related; for example, children who succeed on commutativity tasks are more likely than those who did not succeed to use the counting-on-from-larger procedure in solving addition tasks (Rittle-Johnson & Siegler, 1998). Further, children's work seems constrained by understanding of the goals and they judge the counting-on-from-larger as "smart" and incorrect procedures as "not smart." Most kindergartners understood addition concepts of representing each addend once and only once and irrelevance of addend order before they generated the counting-on-from-larger procedure.

However, there is little evidence that creation or use of the counting-on-from-larger strategy is based on an intentional application of commutativity. For example, kindergartners showed little or no relationship between their additional strategies and performance on commutativity tasks (Baroody, 1987b). However, there may be levels of understanding of commutativity that clarify these relationships (Resnick, 1992; 1994, who uses these progressions from protoquantitative schemas to illustrate a synthesis of nativist and social cognitive theories). One recent research review and synthesis (Baroody, Wilkins, & Tiilikainen, 2003) updated this model and proposed four levels of development. At level 0, unary conception + noncommutativity, children possess a unary conception of addition (i.e., having five toys and getting three more is different from having three and getting five) and do not understand the principle of additive commutativity. At level 1, unary conception + non-communativity and binary conception + protocommutativity, children may build a binary conception of addition that is loosely connected to the unary concept and thus view order as a constraint in some situations but as irrelevant in others. These children may use commutativity implicitly to solve problems (e.g., it seems to minimize effort and appears to "work" to address addends in any order), but not "trust" commutativity when asked a question about it explicitly (e.g., they compute 2 + 7 as 7 and 2 more but may not recognize, when asked, that 2 + 7 = 7 + 2). At level 2, unary conception + proto-commutativity and binary conception + part-whole ("true") commutativity, children recognize the commutative relation in part-part-whole situations, but may not in join result unknown situations. At level 3 unary conception + join result unknown commutativity ("pseudocommutativity"—because they recognize that the outcomes are the same but do not necessarily transform the unary to a binary conception) and binary conception + part-whole ("true") commutativity, children recognize that commuted unary situations are equivalent, and they abstract and synthesize their knowledge.

Summary

Early in life, babies are sensitive to some situations that older people view as arithmetic. They may be using an innate subitizing ability that is limited to very small numbers, such as 2 + 1. Or they may be individuating and tracking individual objects. In any case, they possess the beginnings of invariance and transformations and thus have far richer foundations for arithmetic than traditional Piagetian accounts suggested. Further, as with other areas, young children's success in arithmetic does not appear to depend on their ability to conserve number (Frontera, 1994).

The contents of minds can be categorized as data, information, knowledge, understanding, and wisdom (Ackoff, 1989). Infants appear to have data, and perhaps information, but knowledge and understanding develop over considerable time. As for the other areas involving number, calculation first emerges with very small numbers, and then extends to larger numbers. Exact calculation is preceded by a period of approximations that are more accurate than random guessing. Only years later do they extend their abilities to larger collections that, while still small (e.g., 3 + 2), are amenable to solution with other methods. These other methods, usually using concrete objects and based on subitizing and counting, play a critical developmental role, as the sophisticated counting and composition strategies that develop later are all curtailments of these early solution strategies (Carpenter & Moser, 1984; Fuson, 1992a).

Experience and Education

In the U.S., there are many roadblocks to high-quality instruction of arithmetic.

Roadblocks to High-Quality Experience and Education

LIMITING BELIEFS

Most preschool teachers do not believe arithmetic is appropriate, nor do they even think of it as a topic (Sarama, 2002; Sarama & DiBiase, 2004). In multiple countries, professionals in multiple educational roles vastly underestimate beginning students' abilities (Aubrey, 1997; Heuvel-Panhuizen, 1990).

TYPICAL INSTRUCTION

One study, from the Netherlands, paints a depressing picture of the effects of school on children's arithmetic abilities. As mentioned previously, children did improve through the grades from kindergarten to second grade (Frontera, 1994). However, comparing the highest quartile of kindergarteners to the lowest quartile of first and second graders, the kindergarteners do better. The first and second graders used more sophisticated strategies, but that did not imply more correct answers. Qualitative analysis shows that even using more sophisticated numerical strategies, the children did not understand the semantic relationships in the problems, such as in start unknown problems (see Table 5-1). Thus, instruction might be helping students perform arithmetic procedures, but at the expense of conceptual understanding. Instruction was raising their procedural knowledge, but at the expense of their development of conceptual knowledge (and the integration of the two).

TEXTBOOKS

In too many traditional U.S. textbooks, only the simplest meanings are given for addition and subtraction problems join or separate, result unknown (Stigler, Fuson, Ham, & Kim, 1986). However, as we have seen, (a) most kindergarteners can already solve these problem types and (b) other countries first grade curricula include *all* the types in Table 5.1.

Pictures and word problems reflect these and only these interpretations up to the end of first grade. In later years, the sizes of the numbers increase, but the types of word problems do not change substantially. Textbooks from the former Soviet Union, in contrast, posed a great variety of problems, including various problem types and two-step problems (Stigler et al., 1986). A recent comparison of the U.S. and Singapore curricula yielded similar results (A. Ginsburg, Leinwand, Anstrom, & Pollock, 2005).

Given the abilities of even preschool children to directly model different types of problems using concrete objects, fingers, and other strategies (Carpenter et al., 1993), these restricted educational beliefs and strategies are not only unnecessary, but also deleterious. That is, children unfortunately constrain the symbols "+" and "−" to these limited interpretations and lose the flexibility of their intuition-based solution strategies (Carpenter, 1985), and their confidence in themselves as problem solvers decreases. Textbooks also present symbols and number sentences too soon and in the wrong ways (i.e., before meaningful situations); do little with subitizing or counting, automatization of which aids arithmetical reasoning; and de-emphasize counting strategies (Fuson, 1992a). The younger the children, the more problematic these approaches become. The result is that American schooling has a positive effect on children's accuracy on arithmetic, but an inconsistent effect on their use of strategies (Bisanz et al., 2005; Naito & Miura, 2001).

In addition, textbooks offer an inadequate presentation of problems with anything but small numbers. In one kindergarten text, only 17 of the 100 addition combinations were presented, and each of these only a small numbers of times (Hamann & Ashcraft, 1986). Primary students encountered combinations with larger numbers, but less frequently than small-number combinations. Correlational evidence supported that this accounts for difficulty students of all ages have with addition with larger sums (Hamann & Ashcraft, 1986).

Teaching Arithmetic Counting Strategies

There are other reasons to believe that present practice is inadequate with regard to teaching arithmetic counting strategies. For example, longitudinal studies suggest that in spite of the gains many younger children make through adopting efficient mental strategies for computation in the first years of school, a significant proportion of them still rely on inefficient counting strategies to solve arithmetical problems mentally in the upper years of primary school (M. Carr & Alexeev, 2008; B. A. Clarke, Clarke, & Horne, 2006; Gervasoni, 2005; Perry, Young-Loveridge, Dockett, & Doig, 2008). Early strategy use, including fluency and accuracy in second grade, appears to influence later arithmetical competence. Children using manipulatives continued to need to use manipulatives (M. Carr & Alexeev, 2008). Children need to learn to curtail their early creations. When asked to explain a concept they are acquiring, children often convey one procedure in speech and a different procedure in gesture. Such "discordant" children are in a transitional state and are particularly receptive to instruction (Alibali & Goldin-Meadow, 1993; Goldin-Meadow, Alibali, & Church, 1993).

GENERAL APPROACHES

When teaching attends explicitly and directly to the important conceptual issues students are more likely to develop important conceptual understandings, as well as procedural skills (Hiebert & Grouws, 2007).

One study compared two approaches to teaching addition. Children taught using the "atomistic" approach—a traditional sequence—made less progress than those taught the holistic approach where the focus was on counting and the number system (Price, 2001). The atomistic approach emphasized small numbers initially, addition as separate from subtraction, procedural use of physical manipulatives and only cardinal representations. The holistic emphasized numbers of different sizes, patterns in number and arithmetic, inverse relationship between addition and subtraction, and cardinal and ordinal representations. The holistic involved a good deal of counting, including skip counting by 10s to 1000. It also featured different ways to solve problems, including counting strategies. The researchers believe its superior effects were due to its emphasis on the structure of number, number decomposition, and relationships, and thus children's increased opportunities to *mathematize* (Price, 2001).

Other studies confirm the advantages in children inventing, using, sharing, and explaining *different strategies* in developing knowledge and especially adaptive expertise (Baroody & Rosu, 2004). For example, several benefits stem from children's invention and discussion of diverse strategies for more demanding arithmetic problems. *The number of different strategies children show predicts their later learning* (Siegler, 1995). When learning to solve problems involving mathematical equivalence, children were most successful when they had passed through a stage of considering multiple solution strategies (Alibali & Goldin-Meadow, 1993; Siegler, 1995). Also, it is too seldom recognized that the creation and explanation of these strategies are themselves worthwhile mathematical goals (Steffe & Cobb, 1988). Finally, asking children to "check your work" is often not helpful, but *justification* both builds concepts and procedures and serves as a meaningful introduction to checking one's work (Voutsina & Jones, 2001).

COUNTING-ON

Research suggests several teaching approaches that encourage children to invent new strategies. The "Counter from N (N+1, N−1)" level of counting must be well established (Martins-Mourão & Cowan, 1998). If children, especially those with a learning disability, need help with the number-after skill, teacher can provide and then fade a "running start" (Baroody, 1996). If some children do not then invent counting-on for themselves, encouraging understanding and use of the subskills can be helpful (El'konin & Davydov, 1975; Fuson, 1992b).

INVERSION

Kindergartners appear ready for instruction on the inversion principle, once they can verbally subitize small numbers and understand additive and subtractive identity principle (Baroody & Lai, 2007). Given high-quality instruction, children may learn a strong scheme for generalized inversion, earlier than the middle elementary grades (Rasmussen et al., 2003).

INVENTION OR DIRECT INSTRUCTION?

Some researchers have presented evidence that allowing children to invent their own strategies, vs. teaching algorithms directly, has superior outcomes, especially in children's development of mathematical concepts and problem solving (Kamii & Dominick, 1998). Children can be asked to use a specific strategy, and doing so does not affect their accuracy, but it does negatively affect their response time (Torbeyns, Verschaffel, & Ghesquière, 2001).

Another study reported that *children making sense of mathematical relations is key*; the precise pedagogical strategy is sometimes less important. A nine-month training experiment evaluated the effectiveness of a number sense curriculum designed to help at-risk preschoolers develop the prerequisite knowledge and discover the key mathematical relations underlying fluency with $n + 0/0 + n$ and $n + 1/1 + n$ combinations (Baroody, Eiland, Su, & Thompson, 2007). After 12 weeks of core instruction in prerequisite knowledge for mental arithmetic and mental-arithmetic pre-testing, 80 four- and five-year-olds at risk for school failure were randomly assigned to one of four conditions, varying from structured discovery learning and explicit instruction on patterns/relations to haphazard practice. General number sense improved, such as the ability to perform concrete and semi-concrete (items were seen then hidden) addition. However, even the best performers struggled trying to solve non-concrete (mental arithmetic) problems. The type of training did not make a difference; even the explicit instruction, therefore, was not better in developing number sense, which probably develops over time as children construct relationships (but instruction can make a difference, see Baroody, Thompson, & Eiland, 2008, reviewed later in the chapter).

In summary, once children have had the opportunity to invent their own strategies, and discuss different strategies with their peers, encouraging them to adopt more sophisticated, beneficial strategies may be possible with no harmful effects. This is consistent with research with young children up through the intermediate grades that suggests teaching children conceptually—emphasizing conceptual knowledge initially, and in parallel to, procedural knowledge (Rittle-Johnson & Alibali, 1999).

Representations

Here we discuss external representations, from pictures to manipulatives, and internal, or mental representations, development of which should be the goal of work with external representations.

REPRESENTATIONS IN CURRICULA

Primary-grade children (Elia, Gagatsis, & Demetriou, 2007) often ignore external representations such as decorative pictures. Children did attend to informational pictures (containing information required for solution of the problem), but rather encountered a cognitive burden in doing so.

Children often ignore the number line as well (Elia et al., 2007). What could be the problem with such a widely promoted and used mathematical representation? An analysis of early NAEP results suggest that there is a mismatch between children's understanding of arithmetic and the number line model of these operations (Ernest, 1985). The number line is a geometrical model that necessitates connections between a geometric and an arithmetic representation. In the geometric domain, the numbers correspond to vectors, but in the arithmetic domain, the number corresponds to a point. Such dual conceptualizations may limit the effectiveness of the number line (Elia et al., 2007).

In a follow-up study, two groups of children were taught how to use one of the two representations to solve arithmetic problems (Elia & Gagatsis, 2006). The group taught to use informational pictures improved more on tasks involving that representation than the control group, and similarly for those taught to use number lines. Both experimental groups also outperformed the control group on tasks involving other representations, although to a lesser degree; nevertheless, this indicates a general improvement in arithmetic problem-solving ability following explicit instruction on the use of relevant representations.

Supporting these hypotheses, first and second graders perform better on symbolic arithmetic tasks than on corresponding number-line tasks (Shiakalli & Gagatsis, 1990). Further, analyses revealed no relationships between children's symbolic and number line representations. That is, children did not understand the two were expressions of the same idea, although the use of the number line in combination with symbolic representations did not lower children's performance. Along with other researchers' doubts (Dufour-Janvier, Bednarz, & Belanger, 1987), there is much to be cautious about in considering the use of the number line as a representation for beginning arithmetic. However, children in New Zealand do better with the number line (K. Carr & Katterns, 1984), so it is possible that high-quality teaching would make the number line a useful tool. This remains to be seen, but if so, research suggests that students translate in both directions between number line and symbolic representations (Shiakalli & Gagatsis, 1990).

A final study showed one way the number line might be useful. Peer tutoring on using the number line to solve missing addend problems was successful in helping low-performing first graders (Fueyo & Bushell, 1998). The tutors were taught to use a specific teaching procedure.

MANIPULATIVES[1]

Paradoxically, those who are best at solving problems with objects, fingers, or counting are least likely to use those less sophisticated strategies *in the future*, because they are confident in their answers and so move toward accurate, fast retrieval or composition (Siegler, 1993). Manipulatives can be necessary at certain stages of development, such as counters of perceptual unit items (Steffe & Cobb, 1988). Preschoolers can learn nonverbal and counting strategies for addition and subtraction (Ashcraft, 1982; Clements & Sarama, 2007c; Groen & Resnick, 1977), but they may need concrete objects to give meaning to the task, the count words, and the ordinal meanings embedded in the situations. For the youngest children, use of physical objects related to the problem, compared to structured "math manipulatives," may support their informal knowledge to solve the arithmetic problems (Aubrey, 1997). In certain contexts, older students too may need objects to count to create the numbers they need to solve the problem (Steffe & Cobb, 1988).

Teaching children to use their fingers as manipulatives in arithmetic accelerated children's single digit addition and subtraction as much as a year over traditional methods in which children count objects or pictures (Fuson, Perry, & Kwon, 1994).[2] If teachers try to eliminate finger use too soon, children hide their fingers—which are then not as visually helpful—or adopt less useful and more error-prone methods (Fuson et al., 1994; Siegler, 1993). Further, the more advanced methods of counting are sufficiently efficient to allow multidigit and more complex computation and were *not* crutches that held children back (Fuson, 1994, see also Price, 2001).

MOVING BEYOND MANIPULATIVES

Once children have established successful strategies using manipulatives, they can often solve simple arithmetic tasks without them. In one study of kindergarteners, there were no significant differences between those given and not given manipulatives in accuracy or in the discovery of arithmetic strategies (Grupe & Bray, 1999). The similarities go on: children without manipulatives used their fingers on 30 percent of all trials, while children with manipulatives used objects on 9 percent of the trials but used their fingers on 19 percent of trials for a combined total of 28 percent. Finally, children stopped using external aids approximately halfway through the 12-week study.

Similarly, in the level of counting figural items, the goal is to encourage children to reprocess the items of two collections of counted figurative unit items in categorizing the items of the two collections together into a single collection, and then count the items of the single collection, but without perceptual support (Steffe, personal communication).

BUILDING MENTAL (INTERNAL) REPRESENTATIONS IS THE MAIN GOAL

Consistent with the *hierarchic interactionalism* framework's emphasis on mental representation at a more explicit level (i.e., representational redescription, Karmiloff-Smith, 1992), children appear to reorganize their arithmetic activity in the context of successful problem solving. For example, given the task of finding all pairs of whole numbers that sum to a seven, a five-year-old figured out each separate number combination. Asked if he had them all, he replied, "There are more but I don't know them" (Voutsina & Jones, 2001, p. 394). After several sessions of successfully finding all combinations, marked by increasingly systematic listings, he answered the same question: "that's all the different [combinations] that you can make" (p. 396). He starting using number patterns to avoid counting to find the second addend and finally used a strategy of listing $n, 0; n - 1, 1; n - 2, 2. \ldots$ Thus, his initial success was procedural. Using the patterns led him to discover that each new expression was both correct and preserved the pattern's regularity. Based on this, he invented an "ordering" strategy. He "stepped back" and saw the relationships among the various steps in his previously successful but separate procedures and combined them into a more comprehensive strategy. He could justify this on the basis of its accuracy and efficiency, gaining more understanding and control of his problem solving (cf. Karmiloff-Smith, 1992).

Teaching Arithmetic Problem Solving

Although general issues about problem solving are discussed at length in Chapter 13, arithmetic "word problems" play a large and specific role in many curricula, and we discuss several issues here. The limitations of textbook presentations—a critical issue—were described previously.

WORD PROBLEMS AND LANGUAGE DEVELOPMENT

Attention to language is important, especially as there are many terms about which children have limited understanding (Warren, 2003). "Math talk" is essential (Fuson & Murata, 2007 present a complete model). Good teaching of word problems is also good teaching of valuable aspects of language and literacy. Good teaching involves the inclusion of all the problems types (see Table 5.1), as well as two-step problems (Fuson & Abrahamson, in press).

DIFFICULTY LEVELS OF THE PROBLEM TYPES

One of the largest national and international bodies of research (e.g., Carpenter et al., 1993; Carpenter et al., 1999; Fuson, 1992b; Fuson & Abrahamson, in press; Kilpatrick et al., 2001) describes a broad developmental progression of the problem types that children can solve. With the easiest problem types—(a) join, result unknown (change plus); (b) part-part-whole, whole unknown; and (c) separate, result unknown (change minus), children *directly model* the problem's actions, as we have seen. One of the reasons these are easiest is that the problems are usually stated in such a way that the child can duplicate the actions step-by-step. The major difficulty for some children may be learning the mathematical vocabulary (e.g., learning that "altogether" means "in all" or "in total," Fuson & Abrahamson, in press).

Children then move to the various counting strategies, such as counting-on. They can use this to solve join, result unknown (e.g., counting-on and reporting the total), as well as part-part-whole, total unknown problems. Later, they use it to solve join, change unknown (e.g., counting on from the "start" number to the total, keeping track of the number of counts on the fingers, and reporting that number), as well as part-part-whole, part unknown problems.

Solving separate, result unknown problems with counting on or back falls between these two groups in difficulty. There is support for two different pedagogical approaches in the research literature. One approach accepts that counting backwards is difficult, and so teaching children to use counting-on—reconceptualizing a subtraction problem $(11 - 6)$ as a missing-addend addition problem $(6 + \_ = 11)$. Thus, children learn to count on and keep track of the number of counts to solve this problem type (Fuson & Abrahamson, in press). The other pedagogical approach is based on the belief that children need better instruction and practice on counting backwards, but when they do this, they can count back to solve separate, result unknown problems directly (Wright et al., 2002).

Most difficult are the "start unknown" problems. Children might use commutativity so change the join, start unknown problems to those that yield to counting-on (e.g., $\_ + 6 = 11$ becomes $6 + \_ = 11$, and then count on and keep track of the counts). Or, reversal is used to change $\_ - 6 = 5$ to $6 + 5 = \_$.

At this point, all of these types of problems can be solved by new methods that use derived combinations, which are discussed in more detail in chapter 6.

One category, comparison problems, presents children with several unique difficulties, including vocabulary challenges. For example, many children interpret "less" or "fewer," as synonyms for "more" (Fuson & Abrahamson, in press), possibly due to limited exposure to the former terms. Children hear the larger term in many situations (taller, longer) more frequently than the smaller term (shorter), so they need to learn several vocabulary terms. Comparisons can be expressed in several ways, and one way is easier. Following "Jonah has six candies" with "Juanita has three more than Jonah" is easier than following it with "He has three fewer than Juanita." Research shows that for "There are five birds and three worms," the question, "How many birds won't get a worm?" is easier than "How many more birds than worms are there?" (Hudson, 1983).

To use strategies well, children have to understand the mathematics and the language, but also, of course, the situation. The situation may involve characteristics mathematicians often ignore, time (chronology) and dimension (quantities that are not pure numbers but magnitudes of various kinds), which also affect the difficulty of problems for children (Vergnaud, 1978).

A study of the just-mentioned comparison problems provides an illustration (Stern, 1994). Participants were second graders who could solve the easier compare problems. Children were assigned to control (general reasoning tasks) or one of two treatments, situational (learning about the contexts and the language used to describe them) or mathematical (learning part-whole schemes through numerical tasks, including single-digit combinations "fact families"—all pairs and addend with a given sum 20 or less or all subtraction equations that result in a given difference; equivalent equations such as $4 + 2 = 9 - 3$; and missing addend problems such as $? + 3 = 8 - 2$). The training improved children's ability to solve the specific types of exercises. After the first training period, the situational training improved children's ability to solve the easier two types of problems, unknown difference and unknown compare (Mary has three marbles. John has four marbles more than Mary. How many marbles does John have?), but not other types. The mathematical training showed no benefits. The second training period included giving children feedback and another chance to solve the problems, in additional to the specific treatment. Again, the situational training group improved on the easier two types, but now (only) the mathematical training improved on the two more difficult problem types, unknown reference (Mary has nine marbles. *She* has four marbles more than John. How many marbles does John have?) and complex problems (Mary has nine marbles. *She* has four marbles less than John. How many marbles do John and Mary have altogether?).

A similar conclusion might be drawn from a study of 10-year-old children with special needs. Researchers (Van Lieshout & Cornelissen, 1994) postulated that teaching double counting would enable children with mild mental retardation or learning disabilities to solve change unknown problems better (e.g., when manipulatives were not available) than the "visual marker" strategy in which children use, for example, two different colors of cubes. However, results showed the two interventions were equally effective. Given that in the initial testing period children's main error was using irrelevant numbers, it is possible that both training conditions served as situational training, showing children how to interpret the problems with step-by-step modeling.

Thus, children who are novices, poor performers, or who have cognitive impairments or learning difficulties, may benefit particularly from situational training. More experienced and high performing children may profit from mathematical training. Such mathematical training should be combined with help transferring their part-whole knowledge to compare problem settings, by including both in the same instructional settings and discussing the similarities.

One study showed that using a story context for part-whole problems helped first graders develop an abstract additive scheme (Meron & Peled, 2004). For example, the teacher told stories about a grandfather who sent presents to his two grandchildren or, later, about the two children sending presents to him. Another story was about children who live on two islands and travel by boats to school. Children represented these with a part-part-whole board. This combination of context and more abstract mathematical structure helped children learn part-part-whole concepts that transferred to new situations, although some still needed to use the objects and stories to solve new problems (Naito & Miura, 2001).

In summary, professional development and curricula should change substantially based on our present knowledge of research. A full range of activities appropriate to the age (from three years on) should be provided, covering subitizing, counting, counting strategies,[3] and an increasing range of addition and subtraction situations (problem types), which should cover all problem types by the end of first grade. Emphasis should be on meaning and understanding, enhanced through discussions. Slow and inefficient learning occur when principles are not understood, no matter what their source (innate or learned). The tedious and superficial learning of school-age children is too often the product of not understanding goals and causal relations in the particular domain (Siegler & Crowley, 1994). *Meaning for the child must be the consistent focus.*

Learning Trajectories for Adding and Subtracting (Emphasizing Counting Strategies)

As others we have seen, the learning trajectory for adding and subtracting is complex because there are many conceptual and skill advancements. The importance of *goals* for this domain is clear: Arithmetic is a main focus of elementary education. Table 5.2 presents the developmental progression and the mental actions-on-objects for this learning trajectory. A final important note: Most strategies will be used successfully for smaller numbers (totals 10 or less) a year or more before they are used successfully for larger numbers (Frontera, 1994).

Table 5.2 Developmental Progression for Addition and Subtraction (Emphasizing Counting Strategies)

Age (years)	Developmental Progression	Actions on Objects
1	**Pre-Explicit +/−** Sensitivity to adding and subtracting perceptually combined groups. No formal adding. Shows no signs of understanding adding or subtracting.	Use of initial bootstrap abilities (see Chapter 2) to track amounts and approximate the result of joining or separating.
2–3	**Nonverbal +/−** Adds and subtracts very small collections nonverbally. Shown two objects then one object going under a napkin, identifies or makes a set of three objects to "match."	*Figural tracking:* Identifies or makes a set of three objects to "match" using nonverbal (or verbal) representations (see Chapters 2, 3, and 4).
4	**Small Number +/−** Finds sums for joining problems up to 3 + 2 by counting-all with objects. Asked, "You have two balls and get one more. How many in all?" counts out two, then counts out one more, then counts all three: "one, two, three, *three!*"	Real-world experience provides implicit scheme of situations of joining two groups and determining the numerosity of the composite set. Uses the counting competencies of Producer (Small Numbers) (see Chapter 3) to produce each set, then count the total. For very small numbers (e.g., 2 + 1), can count mental representations.

Age (years)	Developmental Progression	Actions on Objects
4–5	**Find Result** +/− Finds sums for joining (you had three apples and get three more, how many do you have in all?) and part-part-whole (there are six girls and five boys on the playground, how many children were there in all?) problems *by direct modeling, counting-all, with objects.* Asked, "You have two red balls and three blue balls. How many in all?" counts out two red, then counts out three blue, then counts all five. Solves take-away problems by separating with objects. Asked, "You have five balls and give two to Tom. How many do you have left?" Counts out five balls, then takes away two, and then counts remaining three.	Competencies from above are extended to larger sets. For example, child forms scheme for combining groups, counts out five, then counts as adds two more to the pile (or makes separate pile and combines piles), then counts all seven. May use fingers, and attenuate the counting process with finger patterns, such as putting up five on one hand and two on the other immediately (subitizing), then counting seven.
	Make It N Adds on objects to "make one number into another," without needing to count from "one." Does not (necessarily) represent how many were added (this is not a requirement of this intermediate-difficulty problem type, Aubrey, 1997). Asked, "This puppet has four balls but she should have six. Make it six," puts up four fingers on one hand, immediately counts up from four while putting up two more fingers, saying, "Five, six.".	A mental representation of the number in the starting set is formed (via a cardinal integration, often directly after counting or subitizing perceptual items) and the skill of counting up from any numbers (Counter from N (N + 1, N − 1, see Chapters 3 and 2) is used to count to the required amount.
	Find Change +/− Finds the missing addend (5 + _ = 7) by adding on objects. *Join-To—Count-All-Groups.* Asked, "You have five balls and then get some more. Now you have seven in all. How many did you get?" counts out five, then counts those five again starting at one, then adds more, counting "Six, seven," then counts the balls added to find the answer, two. (Some children may use their fingers, and attenuate the counting by using finger patterns.)	The scheme for join operations is sufficiently re-represented to allow creation of a mental "placeholder" for the collection of objects that must be added to another group to make the required total. With perceptual support, this allows the separation of the added collection.

Continued Overleaf

Age (years)	Developmental Progression	Actions on Objects
	Separate-To—Count-All-Groups. Asked, "Nita had eight stickers. She gave some to Carmen. Now she has five stickers. How many did she give to Carmen?" Counts eight objects, separates until five remain, counts those taken away. Compares by matching in simple situations. *Match—Count Rest.* Asked, "Here are six dogs and four balls. If we give a ball to each dog, how many dogs won't get a ball?" counts out six dogs, matches four balls to four of them, then counts the two dogs that have no ball.	
5–6	**Counting Strategies** +/− Finds sums for joining (you had eight apples and get three more . . .) and part-part-whole (six girls and five boys . . .) problems with finger patterns and/or by counting on. *Counting-on.* "How much is four and three more?" "Fourrrrr . . . five, six, seven [uses rhythmic or finger pattern to keep track]. Seven!" *Counting-up-to* May solve missing addend ($3 + \_ = 7$) or compare problems by counting up; e.g., counts "Four, five, six, seven" while putting up fingers; and then counts or recognizes the four fingers raised. Asked, "You have six balls. How many more would you need to have eight?" says, "Six, seven [puts up first finger], eight [puts up second finger]. Two!"	The counting scheme (especially the Counter from N ($N + 1, N − 1$) skill) is elaborated so that a number is intuitively conceived simultaneously as a cardinal amount and a part of the total. The starting number therefore represents the number of counting acts it would take to reach that number without perceptual support and the counting continued via a cardinal-to-count transition so as to constitute the second number, with temporal subitizing or perceptual tracking used to keep track of the numerosity of this second number (see Chapter 3). Commutativity, initially a theorem-in-action, is used to reorder addends to save effort (counting-on-from-larger); initially this may be recognized only when adding one.
6	**Part-Whole** +/− Has initial part-whole understanding. Solves all previous problem types using flexible strategies (may use some known combinations, such as $5 + 5$ is 10). Sometimes can do start unknown ($\_ + 6 = 11$), but only by trial and error.	Schemes for join, separate, and part-part-whole situations are sufficiently re-represented and related to form an explicit, although nascent, part-whole scheme. These schemes are also related to various arithmetic strategies, allowing more flexible counting strategies, including some derived combinations.

Age (years)	Developmental Progression	Actions on Objects
	Asked, "You had some balls. Then you get six more. Now you have 11 balls. How many did you start with?" lays out six, then three more, counts and gets nine. Puts one more with the three, . . . says 10, then puts 1 more. Counts up from six to 11, then recounts the group added, and says, "Five!"	
6–7	**Numbers-in-Numbers** +/− Recognizes when a number is part of a whole and can keep the part and whole in mind simultaneously; solves start unknown (_ + 4 = 9) problems with counting strategies.	The part-whole scheme is re-represented at an explicit level, to allow the recognition of additive parts and wholes in multiple situations and the use of inverse operations for calculations.
	Asked, "You have some balls, then you get four more balls, now you have nine. How many did you have to start with?" counts, putting up fingers, "Five, six, seven, eight, nine." Looks at fingers, and says, "Five!"	
	Deriver +/− Uses flexible strategies and derived combinations (e.g., "7 + 7 is 14, so 7 + 8 is 15) to solve all types of problems. Includes Break-Apart-to-Make-Ten (BAMT—explained in Chapter 6). Can simultaneously think of three numbers within a sum, and can move part of a number to another, aware of the increase in one and the decrease in another.	The part-whole scheme, counting strategies, and compositional strategies (see Chapter 6) are related to allow more flexible deployment of strategies.
	Asked, "What's seven plus eight?" thinks: $7 + 8 \rightarrow 7 + [7 + 1] \rightarrow [7 + 7] + 1 = 14 + 1 = 15$.	
	Or, using BAMT, thinks, $8 + 2 = 10$, so separate seven into two and five, add two and eight to make 10, then add five more, 15.	
	Solves simple cases of multidigit addition (sometimes subtraction) by incrementing tens and/or ones.	
	"What's 20 + 34?" Student uses connecting cube to count up 20, 30, 40, 50 plus four is 54.	*Continued Overleaf*

Age (years)	Developmental Progression	Actions on Objects
7	**Problem Solver** +/− Solves all types of problems, with flexible strategies and known combinations.	

Asked, "If I have 13 and you have nine, how could we have the same number?" says, "Nine and one is 10, then three more to make 13. One and three is four. I need four more!"

Multidigit may be solved by incrementing or combining tens and ones (latter not used for join, change unknown).

"What's 28 + 35?" Incrementer thinks: 20 + 30 = 50; +8 = 58; 2 more is 60, 3 more is 63. Combining tens and ones: 20 + 30 = 50. 8 + 5 is like 8 plus 2 and 3 more, so, it's 13. 50 and 13 is 63.

Final Words

Mirroring the two methods of quantification, counting and subitizing, children solving arithmetic tasks with counting-based strategies, as discussed in this chapter, but also composition-based strategies. The latter are discussed in Chapter 6. As we have already seen, especially in the more sophisticated strategies such as those of Deriver +/− and above, children can combine these approaches.

6

Arithmetic

Composition of Number, Place Value, and Multidigit Addition and Subtraction

"Almost all, who have ever fully understood arithmetic, have been obliged to learn it over again in their own way."

(Warren Colburn, 1849)

In the previous chapter, we showed that children who use counting-on—understanding that 5 + 3 can be solving by counting up three times from five—have made a substantial conceptual advance. These children can use increasingly sophisticated arithmetic reasoning. For example, they should be decomposing and recomposing numbers. This chapter reviews research on three topics whose shared core is the increasingly sophisticated composition of number: arithmetic combinations ("facts"), place value, and multidigit addition and subtraction.

Composing Number

Composing and decomposing numbers is another approach to addition and subtraction, one that is often combined with counting strategies, as in the "doubles-plus-one" strategy. Phenomenologically, it can be experienced similarly to subitizing; indeed, conceptual subitizing, previously discussed in Chapter 2, *is* an important case of composition of number. Composing and decomposing are combining and separating operations that help children develop generalized part-whole relations, one of the most important accomplishments in arithmetic (Kilpatrick et al., 2001).

Initial Competencies with Part-Whole Relationships

Toddlers first learn to recognize that sets can be combined in different orders, but may not explicitly recognize that groups are additively composed of smaller groups (Canobi, Reeve, & Pattison, 2002). They do learn to recognize part-whole relations on in nonverbal, intuitive, perceptual situations (Sophian & McCorgray, 1994) and can nonverbally represent parts that make a specific whole. Later, often between four and five years of age, children learn explicitly that (in everyday situations) a whole is bigger than its parts, but may not always accurately quantify that relationship (Sophian & McCorgray, 1994). They do show intuitive knowledge of commutativity, and, measurably later, associativity, with physical groups (Canobi et al., 2002).

Only then do children evince such understandings in abstract arithmetic contexts (Baroody et al., 2005). Such thinking continues to develop. As previously shown, most preschoolers can "see" that two items and one item make three items; even three-year-olds can solve problems such as one and one more, at least nonverbally. However, four-year-olds do not appreciate the part-whole structure of change unknown problems (Sophian & McCorgray, 1994, see Chapter 5 for descriptions of this and other problem structures). They chose a small number as the answer for both addition (join) and subtraction (separate) problems. In contrast, children a year or two older responded with a number that was larger than that given for the final set more often on addition than on subtraction problems, and they responded with a smaller number than that given for the final set more often on subtraction than on addition problems. This is not to say that children always apply such understandings in finding precise answers to arithmetic tasks, but rather that explicit part-whole schemes are developing during the four- to five-year-old range. Such findings are less pessimistic than the view that this level of part-whole thinking is not accessible to children until the primary grades. For example, Piagetian theory might be interpreted as excluding missing-adding tasks until after first or even second grade (Kamii, 1985). However, children appear to understand the part-whole relationships of tasks by kindergarten, although they may not know how or think to apply it to all arithmetic tasks (Sophian & McCorgray, 1994)—and most U.S. children have *not* been provided with high-quality mathematics experiences. In a similar vein, children may not understand explicitly that the sum of two counting numbers must be larger than either addend until the primary grades or later (Prather & Alibali, 2007).

A series of studies (Canobi, Reeve, & Pattison, 1998; Canobi et al., 2002) identified complex relationships between various understandings related to part-whole schemes, including commutativity, additive composition ("larger sets are made up of smaller sets"), associativity, and arithmetic problem solving. For five- to six-year-olds, there was no relationship between knowledge of commutativity and associativity and accuracy of solving arithmetic problems (Canobi et al., 2002). However, it was related to the type of strategy children used. Most children used simple subitizing or counting-all strategies. However, children who used more accurate counting strategies made more accurate order (i.e., commutativity) judgments than other children (this did not apply to their knowledge of the additive composition or associativity principles). Also, children's understanding of commutativity appeared important for their understanding that counters can be used to signify both addends and the total simultaneously (supporting use of the counting-on-from larger strategy, see Chapter 5).

In contrast, for older children, individual differences in knowledge of these principles were systematically related to their skill in solving school addition problems. Thus, children develop an early, primitive understanding of commutativity, then additive composition, commutativity of added groups, and, lastly, associativity, which requires conceptual reasoning concerning how groups can be decomposed and recombined.

Conceptual knowledge is essential even for single-digit additional and subtraction combinations. The more conceptually competent students are, the faster and more accurately they solve such problems and the greater flexibility they show in their use of problem-solving strategies (Canobi et al., 1998). Spontaneous use of concepts predicted procedural skill.

In summary, at least by five years of age, children are ready to engage in tasks that put a substantive demand on their explicit understanding of part-whole relationships, such as join or separate, change unknown problems. However, they may not apply these understandings in all relevant arithmetic tasks (Sophian & McCorgray, 1994). They may not forge any connections between their strong understanding of part-whole concepts in the context of the physical world and school addition problems (Canobi et al., 2002).

How about relationships to counting? In Chapter 5 we described how counting-on strategies relied on the children's use of abstract unit items, and at least the tacitly embedded number sequence (Steffe et al., 1982). Such "nested" number sequences support composition strategies (Biddlecomb & Carr, 2008). (See the description of the construction of part-whole operations in Chapter 3.) They are not required for composition of number, just supportive of its development; however, the "Counter from N (N + 1, N − 1)" level of counting appears to be surprisingly important for both counting on and number composition (Martins-Mourão & Cowan, 1998).

Building on such part-whole understandings, children can learn to separate a group into parts in various ways and then to count to produce (eventually, all of) the number combinations composing a given number; for example, eight as 7 + 1, 6 + 2, 5 + 3, and so on. Eventually, children can generate an image of eight, and mentally operate on the elements of this image, combining them flexibly to produce any of the family of addition situations. They can use such combinations in solving a range of problems (Clements & Conference Working Group, 2004). This is another approach to solving arithmetic problems and knowing the arithmetic combinations, issues to which we now turn.

Learning Basic Combinations ("Facts") and Fluency

GETTING THE FACTS STRAIGHT

Should children memorize the basic facts? Yes . . . but that is misleading as stated. Knowledge of arithmetic *concepts* forms an organizing framework for storing arithmetic combinations (Canobi et al., 1998). Students with greater conceptual knowledge are more likely to use sophisticated strategies *and* retrieve combinations accurately. That is one reason we do not prefer the term "fact"—knowing an arithmetic combination well means far more than knowing a simple, isolated "fact."

MODELS OF RETRIEVAL OF ARITHMETIC COMBINATIONS

Models of "fact retrieval" tend to support this "isolated facts" view. It does appear that skilled people have a "network of associations" in which certain combinations (8 + 7) are connected to a response (15). These models explain this. However, two additional issues should be kept in mind: (a) how strong networks are *best formed* and (b) the existence of other, more complex, components of such networks, including the previously-described properties and relationships.

To begin, research indicates that children increase their use of retrieval (a rapid process of gaining access to a result using automatic mental process) through the years; for example, preschoolers use retrieval on about a fifth of number combinations with operands five or less (Siegler & Jenkins, 1989), compared to adults using retrieval in about 80 percent of the situations (operands less than 10) (LeFevre, Sadeskey, & Bisanz, 1996). Concluding that retrieval is straightforward access of information stored in long-term memory must be done cautiously, however, as what appears, and is reported by young children, to be retrieval often masks covert strategies (Bisanz et al., 2005; Brownell, 1928) and even "memory access" may involve multiple number relations (Dehaene, 1997).

The next questions are, how do children *choose* strategies and how do they learn to "simply retrieve" a combination? An important component of intelligence in a domain is the selection and compilation of strategies (Sternberg, 1985). Siegler and colleagues have created several computational models of the process (Shrager & Siegler, 1998; Siegler & Shipley, 1995; Siegler & Shrager, 1984). For example, if an addition task is recognized, retrieval of the sum is attempted. If it fails, or the result does not pass a confidence criterion level, back up strategies such as counting-on or counting-all are used (see Chapter 5). Retrieval probability is based on hypothesized strengths of associations between combinations and possible results (e.g., 2 + 5 is strongly associated with seven but also weakly associated with six). The model adjusts the associations with experience. With more experience accurately relating 2 + 5 to seven, that association become stronger and the associations to any other potential response such as six become weaker. Later versions also associate combinations with specific solution backup procedures, direct attentional resources to inadequately learned procedures, conduct pattern searching to find and eliminate redundancies to create more efficient procedures, and use "goal sketches" (knowledge structures embodying the hierarchy of subgoals required by correct strategies) to ensure that generated procedures fit the problem guidelines. For example, an addition goal sketch, based on metacognitive knowledge of planning and knowledge of counting, might consist of including each operand once and only once and quantifying the two representations to yield a single number representing the number in both. The latest computational model selected counting-based procedures for combinations that are more difficult, increased efficiency and accuracy, and learned and invented new procedures such as counting-on-from-larger, via a metacognitive system that examines the memory traces of a strategy's operators following execution (Shrager & Siegler, 1998). This system identifies potential improvements and generates new strategies by recombining operations from existing strategies, using heuristics such as eliminating redundant operators, and choosing sequences that are more efficient. A computational model of this system accurately reflects data on children, giving credence to its validity.

Other researchers, however, believe that such models are limited and do not give sufficient attention to fast-but-non-retrieval processes, such as reasoning strategies (Baroody, 1994; Baroody, Wilkins et al., 2003). Further, children do more than these models may appear to imply. For example, they use conceptual knowledge to evaluate strategies they do not yet use but that are more sophisticated than those they presently use. Kindergarteners will judge a shortcut strategy to be smarter than an equally unfamiliar inaccurate strategy, and just as smart as counting from one (Siegler & Crowley, 1994). Further, children use recognition of patterns and relations, to select and design new procedures (Baroody & Tiilikainen, 2003, in a critical review that questions the computational model's assumptions and validity). For example, children notice that the sum of n and 1 is simply the number after n in the counting sequence, resulting in an integration of addition with the well-practiced counting knowledge. From this perspective, conceptual insight, connections, concepts and procedures, and thus development, consist to a substantive degree to the increasing integration of conceptual and procedural knowledge.

NEUROSCIENTIFIC (BRAIN) RESEARCH

We see, then, that cognitive research suggests that when children develop from slow, counting-based strategies, they eventually form long-term representations of combinations (e.g., 5 + 3) and the answer (eight). This is an essential aspect of learning mathematics. Several brain-based studies have confirmed that as children become more fluent with arithmetic their processing shifts from more frontal activation (e.g., the prefrontal cortex, as well as the hippocampus and dorsal basal ganglia) to more activation in regions known to be specialized for arithmetic combinations (parietal regions, Delazer et al., 2004; Rivera, Reiss, Eckert, & Menon, 2005).

Similarly, studying second and third graders who had not yet mastered their addition combinations, researchers recorded how much children used counting or retrieval (via reaction time and observation). Children who retrieved answers were faster, as expected (Anguiano, Wu, Geary, & Menon, 2007). They also showed different brain activation patterns. Those learning to retrieve answers showed increased engagement of brain systems (e.g., medial temporal lobe) involved in storing information before it is consolidated into long-term memory (especially the hippocampus). Also activated was the fusiform gyrus, involved in storing strings of letters or number names (e.g., "5 3 8"). Both these systems would be helping children store the combination in permanent, long-term memory.

Simply said, as students develop, they start storing combinations and relationships into long-term memory. Eventually, they apply less conscious effort and working memory to the task, and they use brain regions more tuned to automatic retrieval. Note though, that other than such shifts in emphasis, brain regions that are activated when doing arithmetic are not very different for children and adults (Kawashima et al., 2004).

One region that seems specialized for arithmetic is the intraparietal sulcus, or IPS. It is also associated with visuospatial processing, so it may include a "mental number line" that people use to estimate or compute answers to addition and subtraction problems (Varma & McDandliss, 2006). Two other regions that are activated help control mental processes (anterior cingulate and bilateral inferior frontal gyrus). So, they may control the "mind's eye" as it scans this mental number line. What is just as interesting is that these regions are not activated for multiplication. It appears that completely different processes are at work (e.g., a specialized "look up table" for multiplication). That does not mean that all addition and subtraction is performed on the mental number line. Indeed, the task of this mental number line may be simply to say whether the answer is positive, zero, or negative—this is not yet known.

However, we suspect that the IPS and its mental number line do more than this. It may *estimate* answers, which helps activate associations that are being formed (see a following section in this chapter on distributions of associations). The IPS may also help "verify" the final result of any "look up."

Several additional studies lend some support to our hypothesis. First, comparing two numbers also activates the IPS. (Some children show a preference for various kinds of visual images in mental calculation, Bills & Gray, 2000.) Also, the study of second and third graders previously discussed also revealed activation in the IPS (Anguiano et al., 2007). This implies that learning to retrieve the answer is a conceptual process too. Development of long-term memories of addition combinations may be dependent in part on the brain and cognitive systems that support a sense of quantity and magnitude, which may have a spatial component. Knowledge of addition combinations may be infused with conceptual knowledge of the magnitudes associated with the problem addends and the answer.

These studies suggest that, at least for addition and subtraction, producing basic combinations is not just a simple "look up" process. Such retrieval is an important part of the process, but many brain systems appear to be involved. One study showed that certain regions of the brain (e.g., cortical networks including the bilateral prefrontal, premotor and parietal regions) are activated in mental calculation and non-mathematical tasks, including that these support general cognitive operations such as working memory, processing symbolic information, and mental images (Gruber, Indefrey, Steinmetz, & Kleinschmidt, 2001). However, only calculation activated other regions (the left dorsal angular gyrus and the medial parietal cortices), suggesting that exact calculation also involves these specialized regions. Similarly, another study showed several general regions activated (e.g., anterior cingulated cortex for attention, executive functions, motor control, spatial working memory, evaluation of performance). Also, certain regions (right inferior parietal lobule, left superior parietal gyrus) engaged relatively specifically for subtraction *and* the entire network supporting addition also activated for subtraction (Kong et al., 2005). Thus, there are also common and specific networks for various arithmetic operations. Consistent with previous studies, other regions are specific for more complex aspects of arithmetic, such as regrouping (left IPS and left inferior frontal gyrus).

Implications are that, with so many brain systems involved, it is no wonder that children need considerable practice, distributed across time. Also, because counting strategies did not activate the same systems, teachers need to guide children to move to more sophisticated composition strategies. Finally, practice should not be "meaningless drill," but should occur in a context of number sense.

CULTURE

Brains operate in cultures, and, once again, the structure of English counting words can interfere with children's learning. Because the numbers 11 to 19 are simple composites of the numbers words for one to nine and ten, Asian-speaking children need only learn the sums to 10 to have usable strategies for all single-digit combinations. For example, $7 + 8$ is thought of as $8 + 2 + 5$ or $10 + 5$, which is directly translatable into the answer 15, for which *their* name is, simple, "ten-and-five" (this is called the "break apart to make tens" strategy and will be described later in this chapter). Similarly, $15 - 8$ is often thought of as $10 - 8 + 5$ (Miura & Okamoto, 2003). Such 10-based decomposition strategies were the primary backup strategies of Chinese, compared to U.S., children (Geary & Liu, 1996). The speed of pronunciation of the Chinese words also adds formation of associations. Some Asian countries, such as Japan, use this strategy of "break apart to make tens" as the main instructional strategy (Murata, 2004). Students show the same broad developmental sequence as students in the U.S. (e.g., from counting all, to counting on, to de/composition strategies), but move to the de/composition strategies reliably, under the influence of this consistent instructional focus.

INVENTION AND USE OF A VARIETY OF STRATEGIES

The research has a strong implication regarding children's invention and use of a variety of arithmetic strategies. Such strategies are developmentally adaptive, both for arithmetic and in general cognition (Alibali & Goldin-Meadow, 1993; Siegler, 1996; Siegler & Jenkins, 1989); useful for all children (Baroody, 1996); and an important aspect of mathematics itself (Steffe & Cobb, 1988). Some might think they are useful only until "facts are memorized." This is only part of the story. While fast and accurate number combinations support mental computation, strong, flexible, computers also know and use number combination *strategies*, and apply those strategies to mental computation of multidigit numbers (A. M. Heirdsfield & Cooper, 2004). If ever educators needed an argument against teaching "one correct procedure," this is it.

Experience and Education

Ultimately, children should be able to reason strategically, adapting strategies for different situations and easily and quickly retrieve the answer to any arithmetic combination when that is appropriate (Baroody & Tiilikainen, 2003; NMP, 2008). Without accurate, fluid knowledge, students are unlikely to make adequate progress in arithmetic (M. Carr & Alexeev, 2008). What do we know about facilitating such adaptive expertise?

HOW NOT TO DEVELOP KNOWLEDGE, FLUENCY, AND ADAPTIVE EXPERTISE

Beginning with a caution, some recent large-scale efforts have been misguided. In 2008, California was one of four states that had standards calling for accelerated addition and subtraction basic-combinations memorization. Textbooks were approved to lead to memorization in first grade, with little guidance for second grade. The result was that barely 26 pecent of the students demonstrated retrieval of 50 percent of addition and subtraction com-binations. Only 7 percent demonstrated adequate progress on California's basic-combinations standard by retrieving at least 80 percent of the combinations (Henry & Brown, 2008).

What instructional practices were related to better basics combinations knowledge? Not many. Teachers' reliance on the state-approved textbooks was *negatively* correlated with basic-combinations retrieval. Students of teachers who relied more heavily on California State-approved textbooks achieved about one-third as well on basic combinations as those who relied less heavily on these textbooks.

Timed tests were *negatively* correlated with knowledge of basic combin-ations. Flash card use was not correlated with better combination knowledge. Similarly, there was little relationship between additional activities the teacher used as supplemental instruction and combination knowledge. Basic-combinations worksheets were positively correlated, but only weakly.

Children were apparently trying to memorize without understanding or strategies, or were still using unsophisticated counting procedures (especially when the teachers over-emphasized correct answers). Neither helps (Henry & Brown, 2008).

HOW TO DEVELOP KNOWLEDGE, FLUENCY, AND ADAPTIVE EXPERTISE

Instead, this study found that using strategies (especially Break-Apart-to-Make-Ten, or BAMT, see the following section) and derived combinations *was* predictive of more difficult basic combinations. The knowledge of "tens complements"—pairs of numbers that add to 10—were more predictive than work on doubles or on smaller sums (Henry & Brown, 2008). Students who learn to use derived-combination strategies in concert with memorization are more likely to develop mathematical proficiency than those who have memorized the combinations without supplementary strategies. Let us turn to other studies that point to more positive pedagogical directions.

COMMUTATIVITY AND ASSOCIATIVITY

Arithmetic properties deserve special attention. Recall that, although understandings of commutativity and associativity is shown in physical contexts as early as four years of age, they often do not develop significantly up to six years of age (Canobi et al., 2002). Commutativity is recognized and explained by students before associativity (Canobi et al., 1998). If commutativity is explicitly used in the study of addition combinations, children can then organize their memories so that both are linked to a single mental representation.

"DOUBLES" AND THE N + 1 RULE

Special patterns such as those involving "doubles" (3 + 3, 7 + 7), also allow access to combinations such as 7 + 8. Research indicates that properly structured computer drill and practice activities can help children master arithmetic combinations. For example, at-risk first graders who practiced using discovery software, which presented $n + 1$ and $1 + n$ problems (e.g., 5 + 1 = 6) improved significantly more than control children on these combinations (Baroody et al., 2008). Surprisingly, children in the control group, who practiced doubles and doubles plus one problems, had little success with *any* group of problems, including the ones they had studied. They may have needed to learn the $n + 1$ rule first. One last finding: The $n + 1$ children outperformed the control children on combinations no group studied, such as 3 + 5 and 5 + 3. Here, the two subgroups of discovery children differed. Those taught with *structured* discovery, pointing out the *patterns* by sequencing the presentation (e.g., what number comes after six, followed immediately by 6 + 1, 1 + 6, 6 + 0, 0 + 6) scored higher than the group that practiced the same combinations, but in random order. So, careful practice that teaches concepts, problem solving, and skills simultaneously, can be particularly effective.

BREAK-APART-TO-MAKE-TEN (BAMT) STRATEGY

Japanese students often proceed through the same general developmental progression as U.S. and other researchers have identified, moving from counting all, to counting on, and to derived combinations and decomposing-composing strategies (Murata, 2004). However, their learning trajectory at that point differs. They begin to coalesce around a single powerful strategy.

Japanese first grade lessons in learning to add using 10 illustrate a powerful learning trajectory, as well as how hierarchic interactionalism synthesizes aspects of constructivism and Vygotsky's Zone of Proximal Development (this description is based on Murata, 2004; Murata & Fuson, 2006). Before these lessons, children work on several related learning trajectories, including numerals, counting, the number structure for teen numbers as 10 + another number, small number arithmetic (i.e., Find Result +/−; in the learning trajectory in Chapter 5; then later, what we call "Composer to 4, then 5" . . . up to Composer to 10 in Table 6–1).

At this point the "break-apart-to-make-ten" (BAMT) strategy is developed. The entire process (to fluency) follows four instructional phases. In Phase 1, teachers elicit, value, and discuss child-invented strategies and encourage children to use these strategies to solve a variety of problems. Supports to connect visual and symbolic representations of quantities are used extensively, and curtailed and phased out as children learn. In Phase 2, teachers focus on mathematical properties and mathematically advantageous methods, especially BAMT. In Phase 3, children gain fluency with the BAMT (or other) methods. In Phase 4, distributed practice is used to increase retention and efficiency and to generalize the use of the method in additional contexts and as a component of more complex methods. Of the means of assistance in Tharp and Gallimore's model (1988), the teacher in the case study (Murata & Fuson, 2006) used questioning and cognitive restructuring extensively and used feeding back, modeling, instructing, and managing to a lesser extent. He also used an additional strategy, engaging and involving.

COMBINED STRATEGIES

In one study, first graders were taught two reasoning strategies, BAMT, and doubles and doubles ± 1, and then asked to solve a series of near ties, such as 8 + 7 (Torbeyns, Verschaffel, & Ghesquière, 2005). Sometimes the students could choose between the strategies, sometimes they were asked to use a specific strategy. Although high-achieving students applied these strategies more efficiently, they were *not* more adaptive than their lower achieving peers. Thus, teachers should support adaptive expertise for all children, because students of a wide range of abilities levels can deploy strategies adaptively and efficiently (Torbeyns et al., 2005). Further, although BAMT is a powerful strategy and more helpful than others for later multidigit computation, it should not be the only strategy children learn.

CHILDREN AT RISK

If children are not making progress in grade 1, and especially grade 2, intensive interventions are warranted (Gervasoni, 2005; Gervasoni, Hadden, & Turkenburg, 2007). See chapters 15 and 16.

ACHIEVING FLUENCY

Research establishes several guidelines for helping children achieve fluency with arithmetic combinations. We define automaticity as correct and accurate knowledge and fluency as automaticity *plus* complex understandings that provide that foundations for that automaticity and for adaptive expertise (Baroody & Tiilikainen, 2003; Fuson, in press; Fuson & Abrahamson, in press).

First, any such intensive work should be reserved for essential, core skill areas—addition and subtraction combinations are such areas.

Second, learning trajectories should be followed so that *children develop the concepts and strategies of the domain first. Understanding should precede practice* (Murata & Fuson, 2006).

Third, research-based strategies for practice should be followed. Practice should be distributed, rather than massed (Cepeda, Pashler, Vul, Wixted, & Rohrer, 2006). For long-term memory, a day or more should eventually separate practice sessions.

Fourth, research-based strategies should be followed in any curricular materials, especially drill and practice software. Such software can be quite effective. Indeed, it is one of the only applications of educational technology where it is better for the software to actually *replace* conventional instruction rather than just supplement it (NMP, 2008). However, few software programs are designed based on explicit strategies. As one example, effect sizes in the National Math Panel's meta-analysis actually might be an *underestimate* of what can be achieved if drill and practice software were more carefully designed. Few curricula or software packages (or teachers) use empirically-validated timetables for practice (e.g., Cepeda et al., 2006) or effective strategies such as increasing ratio review (M. A. Siegel & Misselt, 1984). In increasing ratio review, if a child makes a mistake, that mistake is corrected, but also the same problem is presented as the second, fifth, ninth, and fourteenth problem. This ensures sufficient attention is given to that combination.

Fifth, practice should continue to develop relationships and strategic thinking. For example, research findings support the notion that automatic performance is related to separate associations between (in this case) multiplication problems and division problems (Rickard, 2005). This suggests that at least some practice should occur on all forms of all possible combinations (e.g., including 5 = 8 − 3). This may help children understand properties, including commutativity, additive inverse, and equality, as well as supporting students' retrieval of basic combinations.

Grouping and Place Value

Experiences, rather than age, account for the development of place value understanding (Naito & Miura, 2001). Use of the BAMT strategy, for example, helps children group into tens to solve addition and subtraction problems and to develop place value concepts (Naito & Miura, 2001). Place value has been embedded in the discussions of the learning trajectories of Chapter 2, 3, 4, and 5, but in this section we focus specifically on the concepts of grouping and place value.

Development of Grouping and Place Value Concepts

GROUPING

For the purposes of this discussion, grouping is defined as the operation (process) of combining objects into sets each having the same number of objects. Preschool children show some foundational understandings in this domain. For example, in Brazil, 60% of children attained an understanding of units of different size (four coins of value one vs. four of value 10) before schooling (five to seven years of age). Fewer, but still 39 percent, could produce an exact amount given similar value coins (Nunes & Bryant, 1996). These studies also indicated that competence in counting was not related to understanding of grouping and place value, but experience with additive composition was.

EXTENDING THE PREVIOUS NEUROSCIENTIFIC RESEARCH

There appear to be three regions of the brain that are activated for multidigit numbers. The first is a sort of visual number word form region (ventral visual stream), known for processing the orthographic structure of words (e.g., it activates more for real words than pseudo-words and more for pseudo-words than random letter strings). Apparently, it also processes visual number forms (Varma & McDandliss, 2006). The other regions we met previously, for control, or metacognitive processing, including conflict resolution (Varma & McDandliss, 2006). These might control visual attention as the complex structures of place-value numerals are scanned.

STUDENTS' KNOWLEDGE OF PLACE VALUE

For example, one system states that students asked about the meaning of "1" in 3156 who say only "one" have weak knowledge of place value. At a more sophisticated level, children possess an additive sense of place value; that is, they understand that 546 is equal to 500 plus 40 plus 6. Only later, however, would children understand that 500 is equal to five times 100, 40 is equal to four times 10, and so forth (Wright et al., 2006). Children also learn that the place value in a given place is 10 times the value of the place to its right. In a similar vein, a review of several research studies concluded that children in first grade or younger cannot understand place value (Kamii, 1986, 1989). They develop over the years from not being able to quantify groups at all, to partial understanding (but a need to, or preference for, counting by ones), to understanding the relationships between places.

Researchers have identified five levels of children's conceptual structures about place value (Fuson, in press; Fuson, Smith et al., 1997; Fuson, Wearne et al., 1997).

1. *Unitary multidigit.* Students do not separate numbers into place value groups, nor number words and numerals into their parts. A child who writes "26" for 26 cubes may say that the "2" stands for two single cubes. "Twenty-six" and 26 refer to a group of 26 cubes (26 is simply the number that comes just after 25 and just before 27 and you can only make a group of 26 cubes by counting by ones).

2. *Expanded notion.* Students begin to separate the decade and the ones parts of a number word and relate each part to the quantity to which it refers. A child understand that "twenty-six" means a group of 20 cubes along with a group of six cubes, but for "twenty-six" might write "206."

3. *Count by units within sequence.* Students view each decade as structured into groups of 10. Students can count by tens, and mentally separate out groups of 10 within a quantity so they can count these by tens. Thus, a group of 26 cubes can be created by counting two groups of 10 (10, 20), and then counting up by ones (21, 22, 23, 24, 25, 26).

4. *Regularized named-value English words.* Students think of two-digit numbers as composed of two distinct units—units of ten and units of one. They may count "One ten, two tens . . ." (or even "One, two tens") and then count the ones as before. Students can view each ten as a single 10 or as 10 ones.

5. *Integrated place value understanding.* Students integrate the conceptions from levels 3 and 4 so they can switch back and forth between them effortlessly. The number words (twenty-six), numerals (26), and quantities (26 cubes) are connected. Students can then use a variety of strategies for solving multidigit number problems.

In the latest version of this categorization (from which most of the labeling above came), Fuson emphasizes the understandings that this highest level must eventually include the following (from Fuson, in press).

- *Generalize new places.* Create new places to the left by multiplying the left-most place by ten and to the right by dividing the right-most place by 10 (multiplying by one-tenth).

- *Symmetry around the ones place for English names of places.* The place-value positions the same number of places in both directions from the ones place have the same names except that the decimal name has the fractional suffix "-th".
- *Multiples (powers) of 10.* Each place to the left of the ones place is some number of multiples of 10, and each place to the right is some number of multiples of 0.1 (1/10).
- *Exchanging units.* All adjacent places have the same bidirectional exchange values: exchange one unit to the left for 10 units to the right and vice versa.

In Fuson et al.'s initial model, students' understanding of numbers with three or more digits are direct extensions of these conceptual structures, although, of course, students may operate at different levels for different ranges of numbers, and the developmental progression for one range (e.g., one to 100) is usually not completed before the progression for another (100 to 1000) is begun. Moreover, all numbers from one to 100 may not be operated on at the same level. Also, the hundreds and thousands are understood even more as separate than as sequence structures because of the regularities in the naming structures, such as "three hundred twenty-four thousand."

Finally, students' conceptions and development of them may be strongly affected by the educational environment. The unitary conception may develop first, but after that, students' development may follow different trajectories through the other levels, developing them separately or together and in different sequences (Collet, 2004, as reported in Verschaffel et al., 2007).

Thus, all these categorizations show development, emphasizing different components. Important is the realization that both the "sequence" view and the "composition" view of numbers must be both developed *and* connected. These categorizations discuss sequence, but only in the sense of counting sets of objects. The "mental number line" notion is often left in the background (see Chapter 4), but it needs emphasis as well.

LANGUAGE AND PLACE VALUE

As discussed previously, the patterns in English and French number words are complex and do not help children focus on ten (H. P. Ginsburg, 1977; Kamii, 1985; Miura et al., 1988; Ross, 1986). As discussed in Chapter 3, English has thirteen rather than "threeteen" or, better, "ten-three"; twenty rather than "twoty" or, better, "two tens." Other languages, such as Chinese, in which 13 is read as "ten-and-three," are more helpful to children. Researchers report negative effects of this in the units (coins) tasks: combinations of 20 and 1 (e.g., make 23) were easier than those of 10 and 1 (e.g., make 13) (Nunes & Bryant, 1996).

Research substantiates the effects of language on place value learning (Ross,

1986). For example, Chinese five- (but not four-) year-olds with good verbal counting understood tens-and-ones in a task in which a single-digit number was added to 10, but English-speaking children did not (Ho & Fuson, 1998). These differences are not limited to the surface, but extend to children's cognitive representations of number (Miura & Okamoto, 2003; Miura, Okamoto, Kim, Steere, & Fayol, 1993). For example, Japanese and Korean first graders showed an initial preference for using a canonical base 10 constructions, whereas those using non-Asian languages showed an initial preference for representing numbers with collections of single units. These findings are mirrored by the superiority of first-grade Asian children in performance on place value tasks, including those with written numbers (Miura et al., 1993; Nunes & Bryant, 1996). Their understanding, even in first grade without specific instruction, contradicts claims of children's "inability" to understand place value at young ages (Kamii, 1986), and suggests that helping children overcome language hurdles is an important pedagogical challenge. Thus, the years that it takes English-speaking children to learn concepts of tens and ones and associate them with numerals (Kamii, 1989; Ross, 1986) reflect difficulties English places on their learning. Claims that children are not cognitively "ready" to understand place value need to be rethought. Language is a cultural tool (cf. Vygotsky, 1934/1986) and English is a poor tool compared to other languages such as Chinese, Korean, or Japanese, in certain respects (Miura & Okamoto, 2003). We need to know how much sensitive, consistent instruction, emphasizing the grouping and place value meaning of the words can mitigate that effect. In this vein, changes in tasks, such as demonstrating to children with teen rather than only single-digit numbers, have been found to decrease differences across cultures, led researchers to suggest that differences may be influenced more by sheer exposure to number work (Towse & Saxton, 1998).

GROUPING AND MULTIPLICATION

Of course, grouping also forms a foundation for multiplicative thinking. Here we note that children can make small groups in their early preschool years (K. F. Miller, 1984), although they may not understand the equivalence of the groups. They can also reason about many-to-one correspondences that are not perceptually available. For example, they can associate one doll with the count, "one, two," and the next with the count, "three, four," and so on (Becker, 1993). Although Becker does not discuss this, it is important to note the role of, and preschoolers' competence with, temporal (rhythmic) subitizing in this context. A caveat is that children had difficulty anticipating the number needed for this distribution, apparently not aggregating across repeated iterations, arguably critical to conceptualizing the multiplicative nature of the task. A brief training procedure that highlighted this iterative nature of many-to-one mappings was successful with seven-, but not five- or six-year-olds (Sophian & Madrid, 2003). Still, by kindergarten, children can learn to invent their own solutions to solve simple multiplicative tasks by making groups, modeling the structure of the problem (Carpenter et al., 1999). Counting strategies are usually developed later for multiplicative problems than for addition and subtraction problems, probably because of the large processing demands of aggregating mentally across multiple iterations of many-to-one mappings (cf. Sophian & Madrid, 2003). Thus, many children younger than seven years can solve multiplicative problems at the sensory-concrete, but not higher, level of thinking.

Experience and Education

Solving simple addition problems in the pre-K and kindergarten years helps form a foundation for understanding place value. Following the counting, comparing, and addition learning trajectories in Chapters 3, 4, and 5 is consistent with these findings (Nunes & Bryant, 1996).

There has been debate concerning the relationship between learning place value and learning arithmetic (Baroody, 1990; Fuson & Briars, 1990). One view is that learning place value for numbers of a certain range (the teens, or numbers to 100) first is a prerequisite for learning arithmetic with those numbers. An emerging view is that arithmetic is a good context for the learning of place value (Wright et al., 2006). That is, children can learn place value simultaneously with tackling problems of multidigit arithmetic (Fuson & Briars, 1990).

Effective instruction often uses manipulatives or other objects to demonstrate and record quantities. Further, such manipulatives are used consistently enough that they become tools for thinking (see Chapter 16 in the companion book). They are *discussed* to explicate the place-value ideas. Finally, they are used to solve problems, including arithmetic problems (Hiebert & Wearne, 1992). Such instruction is more effective than conventional textbook instruction in developing concepts of place value *and* addition and subtraction with regrouping (Hiebert & Wearne, 1992). The problem-solving strategies of the first graders who experienced this instruction more often exploited the place value structure of the number system than those taught with textbooks.

MEASUREMENT INSTRUCTION AND PLACE VALUE

Why would instruction in measurement help develop ideas of place value? More will be said of a measure-based approach to early mathematics in Chapter 10, but here we note that such a curriculum can help children be knowledgeable about units (Slovin, 2007). For example, first graders learn to express relationships about physical quantities such as "P > R." They then learn to quantify *how much* two quantities are unequal. This establishes the need to identify the unit *before* number and counting are introduced, because its definition has an impact on both. As two students noted, when asked to comment on the statement 3 < 8, "You don't know; you might have three really, really, really big units and eight small ones, so three is greater than eight. But if you're on a number line, then . . . it's okay. 'Cause you have equal lengths. So you can do that" (Slovin, 2007).

The idea that numbers depend on units is basic to place value understanding. Unsurprisingly, then, this approach introduces place value as a new way of measuring and representing quantities, requiring the construction of new measures. The ratio between consecutive units is the base of the system (10 in our case). This builds directly from experience they already have relating one unit (e.g., a foot) to another (yards . . . or inches), including exchanges between units. Second graders who experienced this approach were skillful in their ability to generate and represent counting numbers in multiple bases; however, they varied in their ability to describe how a place value system works. The researchers then ascertained that sixth- and seventh-graders from a traditional curriculum could not do so either. Therefore, the second graders were apparently making good progress, but more work needs to be done to help them connect the measurement concepts to the place value concepts and skills (Slovin, 2007).

Finally, making equivalent groups for various real-world tasks is appropriate for preschoolers. By kindergarten, children should be modeling simple multiplication problems with sensory-concrete objects.

Multidigit Addition and Subtraction

"To understand is to invent."

(Jean Piaget)

Possessing strong knowledge of arithmetic properties and processes helps students use algorithms adaptively and transfer their knowledge to new situations. Without this knowledge, children often make errors such as subtracting the smaller from the larger digit even if the smaller is in the minuend. Many of these errors stem from children's treatment of multidigit numbers as a series of single-digit numbers, without consideration of their place value and their role in the mathematical situation (Fuson, 1992b). Further, students' knowledge of these concepts and arithmetic procedures is correlated, and conceptual knowledge predicts not only concurrent, but future procedural skill (Hiebert & Wearne, 1996). Finally, instruction designed to emphasize concepts of place value leads to increases in both conceptual and procedural knowledge, more so than instruction that de-emphasizes concepts or that leaves a gap between the two types of knowledge (Verschaffel et al., 2007). This section reviews research on the learning of multidigit arithmetic. Because much learning of this topic is based on formal school experiences, the following section on "Experience and Education" contains the bulk of the research and discussion.

DEVELOPMENT OF MULTIDIGIT ARITHMETIC

Stepping back a bit, we see that explicit knowledge of such mathematics as place value and algorithms are not a prerequisite for the *initial* understandings of *approximate* multidigit arithmetic. Research reviewed in Chapter 2 showed that even infants have an approximate sense of the results of adding or subtracting items from larger visual collections. Also, when five- to six-year-old children were given problems such as "If you had 24 stickers and I gave you 27 more, would you have more or less than 35 stickers?" they answered above chance levels (Gilmore, McCarthy, & Spelke, 2007). This is still less accurate than their ability to estimate the answers when presented similar problems with dot cards, rather than words. However, when simple visual displays were added, including pictures of children and pictures of bags of candies with numerals (only) on them, children's performance was just as good. They appeared to use their existing nonsymbolic number knowledge spontaneously to manipulate quantities that were presented symbolically, without any instruction in arithmetic.

The researchers who reported early competence with nonsymbolic arithmetic suggested that instruction might be enriched by building on these abilities (Gilmore, McCarthy et al., 2007). However, no such instruction has been attempted, to our knowledge. On the other hand, neuroscientific research shows that multidigit mental calculations involve regions of the brain (left inferior frontal regions) that also serve language and working memory, suggesting that general cognitive processes are essential for the use of composition and decomposition strategies (Gruber et al., 2001).

Strategies involving counting by tens and ones can be altered along with children's developing understanding of numeration and place value to lead up to explicit multidigit addition and subtraction knowledge (see Chapter 3). To use such strategies, students need to conceptualize numbers both as wholes (as units in themselves) and composites (of individual units). At this level, a student is capable of viewing number and number patterns as units of units (Steffe & Cobb, 1988).

This is one path for moving along the developmental progression for learning explicit multidigit arithmetic. Recall the development progression for place value described in the previous section (Fuson, Smith et al., 1997; Fuson, Wearne et al., 1997). These concepts are key to enabling students' use of different strategies. As noted previously, like many developmental progressions, the levels of understanding of place value are not absolute or lockstep. Students might use a strategy based on integrated sequence and de/composition strategies when solving horizontally-formatted arithmetic problems, but regress to a type of unary level, called the *concatenated single-digit* conception in vertical format (Verschaffel et al., 2007). The vertical format can lead students to just think of each number as singles, even if they understand place value in different contexts. As we discuss later, this is both the main advantage (efficiency) and disadvantage (loss of a conceptual connections) of standard algorithms. Most of this learning takes place in intentional teaching contexts, to which we turn.

Experience and Education

Second graders in the U.S., Korea, and Taiwan all appeared to understand place value concepts in a subtraction task (Okamoto et al., 1999). However, there were differences among them on representing place value with blocks. For example, children were given 26 unit blocks and six cups and asked to put four blocks into each cup and then to give the total number represented by the blocks. They were then shown the numeral "26" and asked which blocks made the two and which made the six. Children from the U.S. performed the worst on this task, manipulating symbols without signs of meaningful understanding (Okamoto et al., 1999). Thus, U.S. children learn an algorithm, but not conceptual understanding of place value.

HOW SHOULD ALGORITHMS BE TAUGHT?

Earlier we saw that some students remain at an unsophisticated level, for example, remaining counters of perceptual unit items. *Even when they learn a standard algorithm,* their understanding lags behind, even through their intermediate grades (Biddlecomb & Carr, 2008). Carrying out that algorithm should not be considered a success story unless children can use it with understanding, and adaptively.

More forcefully, some have argued, with supporting evidence, that standards algorithms are harmful to children (see Kamii & Dominick, 1998, for their own statement and a review of other researchers with similar conclusions). Algorithms achieve efficiency by separating the place value of, from the addition of (single-digit), numbers. Because teachers often directly teach the standard algorithm regardless of their students' developmental progressions in counting strategies, children treat the standard algorithm as a meaningless but prescribed procedure unconnected to their understandings of counting and other number concepts and processes (Biddlecomb & Carr, 2008; see also Kamii & Dominick, 1997; 1998).

In contrast, studies indicate that curricula and teaching that emphasizes both conceptual understanding simultaneously with procedural skill, and flexible application of multiple strategies, lead to equivalent skill, but more fluent, flexible use of such skills, as well as superior conceptual understanding, compared to approaches that initially emphasize mastery of procedures (Fuson & Kwon, 1992; Hiebert & Wearne, 1996; NMP, 2008).

Thus, explicit teaching of arithmetic does not have to lead to learning problems. Teaching that develops number concepts, counting and compositional strategies, and skills *at students' level in the learning trajectory* benefit students. This teaching must not neglect the connections between, the development of place-value understandings and the procedures for doing multidigit arithmetic. Students' knowledge of these are correlated, and conceptual knowledge predicts not only concurrent, but future procedural skill (Hiebert & Wearne, 1996). Also, better instruction, designed to emphasize concepts of place value, leads to increases in both conceptual and procedural knowledge, better than instruction that de-emphasizes concepts or that leaves a gap between the two types of knowledge (Verschaffel et al., 2007).

Research supports the notion that inventing one's own procedures is often a good first phase in ensuring these advantages (Carpenter et al., 1993; Carpenter & Moser, 1984; Fennema, Carpenter, & Franke, 1997; Kamii & Dominick, 1997, 1998). As a specific example, a three-year longitudinal study of students' multidigit number concepts and operations in grades 1–3 showed that about 90 percent of all children used invented procedures to solve multidigit addition and subtraction problems (Carpenter et al., 1998). Those students who used invented strategies *before* they learned standard algorithms demonstrated better knowledge of base-ten number concepts and were more successful in extending their knowledge to new situations than were students who initially learned standard algorithms. These results support students' use of invented procedures *first*, as reflected in the Curriculum Focal Points.

These results also support the position of some researcher/developers that place value itself may be best taught in the context of solving multidigit addition and subtraction problems (Fuson & Briars, 1990). As another specific example, low SES urban Latino first graders experienced a year-long curriculum that supported their thinking of two-digit quantities as tens and ones. They worked through a learning trajectory (the UDSSI model) and most could accurately add and subtract two-digit numbers by using drawings or base ten blocks. Their performance was on a par with East Asian children (Fuson, Smith et al., 1997). In contrast to these positive pictures, U.S. students taught standard algorithms focusing only on mastery of procedures often do *not* show flexible or intelligent use of those algorithms or other strategies (Anghileri, 2004).

Some contend that students' invention at this level is not the critical feature, but rather the *sense*-making in which students engage whether or not they invent, adapt, or copy a method (Fuson, in press; Fuson & Abrahamson, in press). Sense making is probably the essence; however, the bulk of research indicates that initial student invention develops multiple interconnecting concepts, skills, and problem solving. This does not mean that children must invent every procedure, but that conceptual development, adaptive reasoning, and skills are developed simultaneously and that initial student invention may be a particularly effective way of achieving these goals.

MENTAL PROCEDURES BEFORE ALGORITHMS

Many researchers believe that use of written algorithms is introduced too soon and that a more beneficial approach is the initial use of mental computation. A recent research review concludes that standard written algorithms intentionally relieve the user of thinking about where to start, what place value to assign to digits, and so forth (Verschaffel et al., 2007). This is efficient for those who already understand, but often has negative effects on initial learning. In comparison, mental strategies are derived from and support underlying concepts. Conventionally taught students usually take a long time to master algorithms and often never master them. They often find it difficult to relate the algorithm to problems in which it is relevant and perform badly on assessments that ask for understanding or insight into the algorithm (Verschaffel et al., 2007).

Through several small case studies, Heirdsfield and her colleagues (A. Heirdsfield, 2005; A. Heirdsfield, Dole, & Beswick, 2006; A. Heirdsfield & Lamb, 2006a, 2006b, 2006c) have shown that mental computational procedures and professional development regarding such practices, can help students become more accurate, sophisticated, and flexible in their methods for solving arithmetic problems. The researchers' model for mental computation includes a range of metacognitive, cognitive, and affective components, which differ for flexible and accurate students and those who are inflexible. Flexible students used more and more efficient mental strategies, had broader numeration understanding, were more metacognitive (strategies and beliefs, including at the final, "checking" stage), understood the effects of arithmetic operations on number understanding, and held strong positive beliefs in their own strategies. For all students, fluency with arithmetic combinations, including retrieval but also strategies for combinations (such as derived combinations), was important. Computational estimation was not important to these mental calculations (along with the age of the children considered in this book, this is why we do not review research on that skill, for information, see Verschaffel et al., 2007). The inflexible students mostly used mental images of standard paper-and-pencil algorithms. Flexible students instead might compute as follows: 199 is close to 200; 246 + 200 = 446, take away one; 445. The flexible students used strategies such as the following to compute 28 + 35: compensation (30 + 35 = 65, 65 − 2 = 63), leveling (30 + 33 = 63), aggregation, right to left (28 + 5 = 33, 33 + 30 = 63), and separation, right to left (8 + 5 = 13, 20 + 30 = 50, 63).

A separate analysis classified mental calculation strategies into two primary categories, decomposition (similar to "separation") and begin-with-one-number ("jumping" the place values of the other number, similar to "aggregation"), and a third category of mixed strategies (Fuson, Wearne et al., 1997, see also T. J. Cooper, Heirdsfield, & Irons, 1997).

As we saw, Heirdsfield and others have identified a compensating category, wherein the given numbers are altered in a flexible way, such as 48 + 26 = 50 + 25 − 2 + 1 = 75 − 1 = 74, whereas others (Fuson, Wearne et al., 1997) consider these as subcategories of the main two categories. Decomposition and jump are the main two strategies, which align with two ways of interpreting two-digit numbers, the "collection-based" and "sequence-based" interpretations, respectively. In turn, the composition strategy is aligned with base ten blocks and other such manipulatives, whereas the jump strategy is aligned with 100s charts or number lines (especially the empty number line, discussed later in this chapter). Further, U.S. and U.K. emphases on base ten blocks and column addition supports these countries' emphasis on only decomposition strategies. In contrast, jump strategies are dominant among continental European students, probably due to the greater emphasis on mental calculation and focus on these strategies in instructional materials. However, in all countries, students use both, even if both strategies have not been explicitly taught. Importantly, the jump strategies are more effective and accurate.

The Dutch curriculum, based on the belief that the use of mental arithmetic helps develop concepts and skills, uses mental arithmetic up through second grade and only introduces written algorithms in higher grades (Beishuizen, 1993). Some studies compared specific strategies, for example the decomposition (they call it "10–10") strategy, in which the tens are split from both numbers and added (for 46 + 23, 40 + 20 = 60 and 6 + 3 = 9, so, 69), and the jump (they call it N10) strategy, in which one jumps by tens from the first (non-decomposed) number (46 + 20 = 66, 66 + 3 = 69). Both strategies do not process numbers from the right, commonly taught to U.S. children (although they prefer to process from the left, if encouraged to make sense of the arithmetic, Kamii & Dominick, 1998). Dutch children appear to prefer the decomposition strategy initially, possibly because moving along a mental number line by tens and ones is difficult for them (recall that their counting words are even less helpful than English, see Chapter 3). However, the decomposition strategy puts a larger strain on working memory when renaming is involved, especially for subtraction. For 42 − 15, children may think, 40 − 10 = 30, 2 − 5 = ?, 30 + 2 = 32, 32 − 2 − 3 = 27. Using the jump strategy, they would think, 42 − 10 = 32, 32 − 2 − 3 = 27. Use of a hundreds chart helped Dutch children use the jump strategy. In contrast, use of blocks (here, connecting cubes in 10-blocks and singles) increased lower-achieving students into use of the decomposition strategy. It also encouraged a passive "reading off the answer" from the blocks. Blocks still might serve a purpose at some levels, but their limitations must also be considered (Beishuizen, 1993).

The Dutch more recently promote the use of the "empty number line" as a support for the jump strategy (Beishuizen, 1993). Use of this model has been reported as supporting more intelligent arithmetical strategies. For example, they would use a compensation strategy when adding numbers with "nine" in the ones place (A. S. Klein, Beishuizen, & Treffers, 1998). Further, children taught with the empty number line learned procedural knowledge as well as or better than those taught more procedures. The number line is "empty" in that it is not a measurement/ruler model, but simply keeps the order of numbers and the size of "jumps" recorded, such as shown in Figure 6.1.

$$85 - 68$$

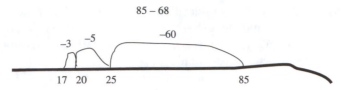

Figure 6.1 The empty number line supporting arithmetic.

Additional research indicates that we should not just teach but also *connect* these strategies. For example, the jump strategy may de-emphasize decade structures, but maintain number sense. Decomposition strategies emphasize place value, but often lead to errors (Blöte, Van der Burg, & Klein, 2001).

<small>WHICH ALGORITHMS?</small>

There are many arguments about whether to teach the standard algorithms. Too often, such arguments have generated more heat than light, for several reasons. First, there is no single standard algorithm. Many different ones have been used in the U.S. and around the world. All are valid (Kilpatrick et al., 2001). Second, what are taken as different "standard" algorithms by teachers and lay people are often *not* viewed as different by mathematicians, who believe they are all just simple *modifications* (often in the way numbers are recorded) of general place-value based algorithms. That is, different algorithms all subtract in same-place-value columns and compose/decompose as necessary; they just do these processes and notate them in slightly different ways.

A classic, and still useful, study by Brownell and Moser (1949) compared the benefits of teaching decomposition and equal addends subtraction algorithms (see the companion book) either meaningfully or mechanically. The meaningful or conceptual approach used manipulatives for grouping, expanded notation, connections between representations, and delaying the written algorithm until the meanings were established. The mechanical approach taught the algorithm step-by-step and used the saved time for practice. On the immediate posttest, the mechanical group scored higher on speed and accuracy. But on retention and transfer, the meaningful approach scored better. The meaningful approach was better for the decomposition method or for students who had already learned an algorithm. The main message is that for retention, transfer, and understanding, meaningful teaching was superior (Brownell & Moser, 1949).

Given instruction that focuses on flexible application of a variety of strategies, students are more likely to adaptively fit their strategies to the characteristics of the problems (A. S. Klein et al., 1998; Verschaffel et al., 2007). However, many second graders, although they do adapt to item characteristics, do not frequently take into consideration the characteristics of the strategies (e.g., accuracy, speed) and themselves (competence with strategies) (Torbeyns, Verschaffel, & Ghesquière, 2006). This may be due to instructional emphasis on routines in the instructional environment (Verschaffel et al., 2007). *In contrast, research suggests a consistent emphasis on adaptive expertise.*

If teachers are helped to understand students' thinking, studies show that they help students invent and use adaptive calculation strategies (e.g., Carpenter et al., 1998). Further, if students invent their own strategies first, they have fewer errors than students who were taught algorithms from the start.

Finally, a consistent result is that *conceptually based instruction supports mathematical proficiency* (Carpenter et al., 1998; Fuson & Briars, 1990; Fuson, Wearne et al., 1997; Resnick, 1992; Verschaffel et al., 2007). This point is so critical, that we provide additional research supporting it as "final words" for this section.

In one study, most of the students who developed conceptual knowledge either first or simultaneously with procedural knowledge could invent new solution procedures, or use their knowledge adaptively, whereas those who learned procedures first could not. They relied on conventional procedures and, more frequently, on buggy procedures than those receiving non-traditional instruction. This non-traditional instruction encouraged students to develop their own procedures and to make sense of others' procedures. Thus, conceptual knowledge facilitates procedure selection, procedure monitoring, and transfer. Also, once again, students' invented strategies are a good starting point (Hiebert & Wearne, 1996). Finally, important for us as early childhood educators, it is important to promote such creativity and understanding *early*. Students with strong concepts from the first year were able to participate more fully in learning mathematics for the three years of this study.

In contrast, students taught in conventional classrooms, focusing on the mastery of (only) the standard paper-and-pencil algorithms for solving multi-digit additions and subtractions, more frequently use erroneous, or "buggy" procedures and make more systematic errors than students instructed in non-conventional classrooms (Hiebert & Wearne, 1996).

In another study, second-grade classes were randomly assigned to one of two instructional programs (Blöte et al., 2001). The first was a reform-based program based on the Dutch Realistic Mathematics Education, in which students invent and discuss their solution procedure. From the beginning of instruction, this program emphasizes developing conceptual understanding simultaneously with procedural skill, as well as flexible application of multiple strategies. These students outperformed those in a traditional textbook program that focused on mastery of procedures initially, and varied application of strategies only toward the end of instruction. The reform group children more often selected strategies related to the number properties of the problems and used strategies more adaptively, such as solving problems with "8" or "9" in the one's place with compensation strategies. That is, these were flexible problem solvers who adapted their strategies to the number characteristics of the problem at hand. For example, they solved $62 - 49$ as $62 - 50 = 12$, $12 + 1 = 13$, but solved $62 - 44$ as $44 + 6 = 50$, $50 + 10 = 60$, $60 + 2 = 62$, and $6 + 10 + 2 = 18$. Such flexible strategy use indicates both conceptual understanding and procedural skill. The traditional group did not use the procedures flexibly, even after months of instruction in that program emphasized such flexible use. The reform group scored higher on three measures, showing superior conceptual understanding. Children in both groups developed conceptual understanding before achieving procedural skill, but the two domains were more interconnected for the reform group (Blöte et al., 2001).

Although involving intermediate-grade students, a third study indicated that conceptual instruction led to increased conceptual understanding and to generation and transfer of a correct procedure. Procedural instruction led to increased conceptual understanding and to adoption, but only limited transfer, of the instructed procedure (Rittle-Johnson & Alibali, 1999).

Learning Trajectory for Composing Number and Multidigit Addition and Subtraction

Table 6.1 provides the developmental progression and the mental actions-on-objects for this learning trajectory. We first make three brief notes.

- Unlike any other developmental progression, Table 6-1 is split into two parts: first composing, and then multidigit addition and subtraction. This was done to emphasize that the second part is a *copy* of the developmental progression already included in the learning trajectory in Chapter 5, enhanced with the information from this chapter.
- Place value is fundamental to all number, so it is embedded in the learning trajectories in Chapters 2, 3, 4, and 5, as well as this one. This chapter is merely the most specific focus on place value.
- Recall again that the ages in all the learning trajectory tables are only approximate, especially because the age of acquisition usually depends heavily on experience.

Table 6.1 Developmental Progression for Composing Number and Multidigit Addition and Subtraction

Age (years)	Developmental Progression	Actions on Objects
Composing Numbers		
0–2	**Pre-Part-Whole Recognizer** Only nonverbally recognizes parts and wholes. Recognizes that sets can be combined in different orders, but may not explicitly recognize that groups are additively composed of smaller groups. When shown four red blocks and two blue blocks, intuitively appreciates that "all the blocks" include the red and blue blocks, but when asked how many there are in all, may name a small number, such as one.	(See Chapter 2's learning trajectory for underlying cognitive mechanisms.)
3–4	**Inexact Part-Whole Recognizer** Knows that a whole is bigger than parts, but may not accurately quantify. (Intuitive knowledge of commutativity, and, later, associativity, with physical groups, later in more abstract contexts, including numbers.) When shown four red blocks and two blue blocks and asked how many there are in all, names a "large number," such as five or 10.	(See Chapters 2–5 learning trajectories for underlying cognitive mechanisms.)
4–5	**Composer to Four, then Five** Knows number combinations. Quickly names parts of any whole, or the whole given the parts. Shown four, then one is secretly hidden, and then is shown the three remaining, quickly says "one" is hidden.	Chapter 2's level of "Conceptual Subitizer to Five" describes initial underlying cognitive mechanisms for this level. These are internalized as networks of mental images—including partitioned mental objects (e.g., abstract mental images of [•••|••] connected to number line representations of jumps of three and two to five—and of abstract representations of part-part-whole triads (two, three . . . five). As the competence develops within this level, and through later levels, the symbolic representations attain prominence and the others recede into supportive roles in cognition.

Age (years)	Developmental Progression	Actions on Objects
	Composer to Seven Knows number combinations to totals of seven. Quickly names parts of any whole, or the whole given parts. Doubles to 10.	As above, extended with other combinations and increasingly abstract representations.
	Shown six, then four are secretly hidden, and shown the two remaining, quickly says "four" are hidden.	
	Composer to 10 Knows number combinations to totals of 10. Quickly names parts of any whole, or the whole given parts. Doubles to 20.	As above, extended with other combinations and increasingly abstract representations.
	"Nine and nine is 18."	
7	**Composer with Tens and Ones** Understands two-digit numbers as tens and ones; count with dimes and pennies; two-digit addition with regrouping.	As above, extended with other combinations, especially with fives and tens and explicit place value knowledge.
	"17 and 36 is like 17 and 3, which is 20, and 33, which is 53."	

Addition and Subtraction (extending the Chapter 5 Learning Trajectory)

Age (years)	Developmental Progression	Actions on Objects
6–7	**Deriver +/−** Uses flexible strategies and derived combinations (e.g., "7 + 7 is 14, so 7 + 8 is 15) to solve all types of problems. Includes Break-Apart-to-Make-Ten (BAMT). Can simultaneously think of three numbers within a sum, and can move part of a number to another, aware of the increase in one and the decrease in another.	The part-whole scheme, counting strategies, and compositional strategies are related to allow more flexible deployment of strategies.
	Asked, "What's seven plus eight?" thinks: $7 + 8 \rightarrow 7 + [7 + 1] \rightarrow [7 + 7] + 1 = 14 + 1 = 15$.	
	Or, using BAMT, thinks, $8 + 2 = 10$, so separate 7 into 2 and 5, add 2 and 8 to make 10, then add 5 more, 15.	
	Solves simple cases of multidigit addition (and often subtraction) by incrementing tens and/or ones.	
	"What's 20 + 34?" Student uses connecting cube to count up 20, 30, 40, 50 plus 4 is 54.	

Continued Overleaf

Age (years)	Developmental Progression	Actions on Objects
7	**Problem Solver +/−** Solves all types of problems, with flexible strategies and known combinations.	
	Asked, "If I have 13 and you have nine, how could we have the same number?" says, "Nine and one is 10, then three more to make 13. One and three is four. I need four more!"	
	Multidigit may be solved by incrementing or combining tens and ones (latter not used for join, change unknown).	
	"What's 28 + 35?" Incrementer thinks: 20 + 30 = 50; + 8 = 58; two more is 60, three more is 63. Combining tens and ones: 20 + 30 = 50. 8 + 5 is like 8 plus 2 and 3 more, so, it's 13. 50 and 13 is 63.	
7–8	**Multidigit +/−** Uses composition of tens and all previous strategies to solve multidigit +/− problems.	*Flexibly Uses All Strategies*, from compensating to written algorithms.
	Asked, "What's 37 − 18?" says, "I take one ten off the three tens; that's two tens. I take seven off the seven. That's two tens and zero . . . 20. I have one more to take off. That's 19."	
	Asked, "What's 28 + 35?" thinks, 30 + 35 would be 65. But it's 28, so it's two less—63.	

Final Words

Research on number and quantitative supports the tenets of the *hierarchic interactionalism* framework. For example, cognitive progressions through levels in the specific domains of number, such as counting, comparing, and arithmetic, are evident, building on initial bootstraps, yet undergoing significant development through the early years. There are different courses for such development. Two examples, emphasizing experiences in the social environment, briefly illustrate these possibilities. First, children from low-income homes may engage in informal premathematical activity and possible premathematical knowledge (H. P. Ginsburg et al., 1999), but, due to different experiences, may still lack components of the conceptual structures possessed by children from more affluent homes (Griffin et al., 1994). Second, educational emphases on skills, for example, can lead to instrumental knowledge of, and beliefs about, mathematics (Kamii & Housman, 1999; Skemp, 1976). More specifically, experiences with sophisticated counting strategies, composition/decomposition, and other imagistic approaches lead children to develop different strategies and understandings of number than, for example, experiences limited to simple counting strategies and memorization. Relevant here is the notion, perhaps expressed best by Wittgenstein (1953/1967), but expressed by several others (e.g., Douglass, 1925; Glasersfeld, 1982), of weaving together various threads to form number concepts, in which various different weavings create different number concepts of various strength and applicability. The tenet of progressive hierarchization is illustrated by the connections children come to make between various mathematically-relevant concepts and procedures (e.g., connecting experiences with nonverbal subitizing, hearing number words applied to particular situations, and counting to learn cardinality, Klahr & Wallace, 1976; Sophian & Adams, 1987), creating more robust understandings (e.g., of number, or, at higher levels, of mathematics) that are hierarchical in that they employ generalizations (e.g., of additive composition) while maintaining differentiations (e.g., discrete vs. continuous compositions).

The domains of number and geometry share commonalities that emerge from the loosely-differentiated competencies of the young child. For example, Mix, Huttenlocher, and Levine suggested that "the quantification of infants and young children could be accurately termed 'spatial quantification' " (Mix et al., 2002, p. 139). In this view, spatial thinking is essential in its role in the development of number and quantification. It is important for many other reasons. This essential area is introduced next in Part III.

Part III
Geometry and Spatial Thinking

Geometry and spatial reasoning are inherently important because they involve "grasping . . . that space in which the child lives, breathes and moves . . . that space that the child must learn to know, explore, conquer, in order to live, breathe and move better in it."

(Freudenthal, in NCTM, 1989, p. 48)

For early childhood, the area of geometry is the second most important area of mathematics learning. One could argue that this area—including spatial thinking—is as important as number. Viewed broadly, for example, geometric and spatial thinking are not only important in and of themselves, but—as we have seen through Part II—they *also* support number and arithmetic concepts and skills (Arcavi, 2003). Indeed, some research suggests that the very ability to represent *magnitude* is dependent on visuospatial systems in regions of the parietal cortex of the brain (Dehaene, Spelke, Pinel, Stanescu, & Tsivkin, 1999; Geary, 2007; Pinel, Piazza, Le Bihan, & Dehaene, 2004; Zorzi, Priftis, & Umiltà, 2002).

In Part III, we begin with just that space in which the child lives and we examine how the child learns to know it better (Chapter 7). We then turn to issues of geometric *shape*, including identifying and analyzing shapes (Chapter 8) and the composition and decomposition of shapes (Chapter 9). The separation of these two basic geometric domains is based on distinct systems in the primate brain for object perception, or recognizing *what* an object is (inferior temporal cortex, ventral pathway) and for spatial perception, or *where* an object is (posterior parietal cortex, ventral stream) (Stiles, 2001; Ungerleider & Mishkin, 1982).

Spatial Thinking

Spatial thinking is an essential human ability that contributes to mathematical ability. It is a process that is distinct from verbal reasoning (Shepard & Cooper, 1982) and that functions in distinct areas of the brain (Newcombe & Huttenlocher, 2000; O'Keefe & Nadel, 1978). Further, mathematics achievement is related to spatial abilities (Ansari et al., 2003; Fennema & Sherman, 1977; Fennema & Sherman, 1978; Guay & McDaniel, 1977; Lean & M. A. Clements, 1981; Stewart, Leeson, & Wright, 1997; Wheatley, 1990). As an example, empirical evidence indicates that spatial imagery reflects not just general intelligence but also a specific ability that is highly related to the ability to solve mathematical problems, especially nonroutine problems (e.g., Wheatley, Brown, & Solano, 1994). Finally, we know that girls, certain other groups who are underrepresented in mathematics, and some individuals are harmed in their progression in mathematics due to lack of attention to spatial skills, and benefit from more geometry and spatial skills education (e.g., Casey & Erkut, 2005; Casey, Nuttall, & Pezaris, 2001).

However, the relationship between spatial thinking and mathematics is not straightforward. For example, some research indicates that students who process mathematical information by verbal-logical means outperform students who process information visually (for a review, see Clements & Battista, 1992). Clearly, the type of spatial competencies matters. Two major type of competencies are spatial orientation and spatial visualization (Bishop, 1980; Harris, 1981; McGee, 1979). We first discuss spatial orientation, which involves an extensive body of research, then spatial visualization and imagery.

Spatial Orientation

Spatial orientation involves understanding and operating on relationships between different positions in space, at first with respect to one's own position and your movement through it, and eventually from a more abstract perspective that includes maps and coordinates at various scales. This essential competence is even linked to memory systems (Nadel & Moscovitch, 1998). Like number, spatial orientation has been postulated as a core domain, for which competencies, including the ability to actively and selectively seek out pertinent information and certain interpretations of ambiguous information, are present from birth (Gelman & Williams, 1997). Infants focus their eyes on objects and then begin to follow moving objects (Leushina, 1974/1991). Toddlers ignore other cues and instead use geometric information about the overall shape of their environment to solve location tasks (Hermer & Spelke, 1996). Again, however, evidence supports the interaction of inborn endowments, (possibly) maturation, experience, and sociocultural influences.

Piaget maintained that children are born without knowledge of space, or even permanent objects (Piaget & Inhelder, 1967). His topological primacy thesis posited that they move through stages of egocentric spatial constructions (e.g., objects within reach, or those in front of the child, including topological relations of connectedness, enclosure, and continuity) to allocentric constructions (e.g., objects farther away, including having relationships to one another). Studies can be interpreted in that light. For example, if six- to 11-month old children are placed in a maze and repeatedly find a toy by crawling straight and then turning left at an intersection, then are moved to the other end, most will incorrectly turn in the same direction that originally led to the toy (Acredolo, 1978). At 16 months of age, children correctly compensate for the change in their position. Piaget claimed that children's first notions are of topological space (e.g., understanding closure and connectedness) and later build notions of projective (relations between the child and objects, establishing a "point of view") and "Euclidean," or coordinate, space.

Research supports Piaget's prediction about development of near space before far space (see Haith & Benson, 1998, for a review). However, Piaget's topological primacy thesis appears of limited usefulness. In addition, we shall see again that research also suggests that young children are more, and adults less, competent than the Piagetian position indicated, although substantial development does occur. Young children can reason about spatial perspectives and spatial distances, although their abilities develop considerably throughout the school years. In the first year of life, infants can perceive the shape and size of objects and can represent the location of objects in a three-dimensional space (Haith & Benson, 1998; Kellman & Banks, 1998). As another example, "egocentrism" is not displayed if landmarks provide cues (Rieser, 1979). Between five and nine months, infants develop a geometric mechanism that allows them to identify an object to which another person is pointing (Butterworth, 1991). At the other end, older students and adults still display biases and errors in spatial reasoning (Fischbein, 1987; Uttal & Wellman, 1989) and do not always perform successfully on tasks designed by Piaget to assess an underlying Euclidean conceptual system (Liben, 1978; Mackay, Brazendale, & Wilson, 1972; H. Thomas & Jamison, 1975). Thus, both the topological primacy thesis and the traditional egocentric-to-allocentric theory should be replaced. However, Piaget's constructivist and interactionist positions remain viable, especially that the representation of space is not a perceptual "reading off" of the spatial environment, but is built up from active manipulation of that environment (Piaget & Inhelder, 1967). We review research on spatial orientation in four categories: spatial location and intuitive navigation, spatial thought, models and maps, and coordinates and spatial structuring.

Spatial Location and Intuitive Navigation

Although both children and adults develop "mental maps," these are not like a mental picture of a paper map. Instead, they consist of private knowledge and idiosyncrasies. Children learn about space by developing two types of self-based reference systems and two types of external-based reference systems (Newcombe & Huttenlocher, 2000). The younger the child, the more loosely linked these systems are.

SELF- AND EXTERNAL-BASED SYSTEMS

Self-based spatial systems are related to the Piagetian construct of egocentric space and encode the position of the moving self. The most primitive, both in its early emergence and its limited power, is response learning, or sensorimotor coding. The child records a location or route to a location by a pattern of movements that have been associated with a goal (e.g., looking to the left from a high chair to see a parent cooking). The second is path integration, in which locations are coded based on the distance and direction of one's own movement. One's location is continually updated based on input regarding movement (as well as from landmarks encountered-integrated with external-based systems). Such automatic processes could serve as the foundation for explicit mathematics (Newcombe & Huttenlocher, 2000).[1]

External-based reference systems are based on environmental structures and landmarks. The landmarks are usually salient, familiar, and/or important objects. Cue learning associates an object with a coincident landmark, such as a toy on a couch. As with response learning, cue learning is the more limited and less powerful of two systems. The more powerful, place learning, comes closest to people's intuition of "mental maps" (albeit, as we shall see, this is a limited metaphor), as it builds locations from distances and directions among environmental landmarks. One example of place learning, taking the edges of a region or walls of a room as a frame of reference, illustrates a possible early, implicit foundation for later learning of coordinate systems.

Finally, when information from these four systems is combined, it is combined hierarchically (e.g., chair in a room, school, city . . .), with different precisions at each level. This provides a best estimate of locations, but can also introduce systematic biases (Newcombe & Huttenlocher, 2000). For example, knowing an object was dropped and lost in the left half of the backyard might be combined with a memory of a specific location via path integration, but it may bias the estimate toward the center of the region.

When do these systems emerge? Once they do, how do they develop? Development consists of two interrelated aspects. First, children learn through experience which coding systems are more effective and accurate in which situations. (Following Newcombe & Huttenlocher, 2000, we use the term "coding" to mean a memory trace of some type in the information-processing system that supports action in the environment without any commitment to a cognitively accessible "representation" that will, eventually, support explicit thinking about space.) Second, each of these coding systems becomes more effective, although the simple systems of response and cue learning only extend the situations to which they apply. We begin by describing this latter aspect of development.

RESPONSE LEARNING AND CUE LEARNING

In the first year of life, stationary infants rely on response learning to locate objects in their environment. An example is children who incorrectly turn in the same direction that originally led to a toy even after being physically reoriented (Acredolo, 1978; see also Acredolo & Evans, 1980).

In addition to response learning, two other systems, cue learning and path integration emerge by at least six months of age (Newcombe & Huttenlocher, 2000). As an example of cue learning, seven-month-olds can remember which of two containers contains an object, even after a minute's delay filled with distractions (McDonough, 1999). Landmarks can help children depress an incorrect response after they are rotated, although six-month-olds were uncertain of the correct choice; nine- and 11-months olds used the cues successfully (Acredolo & Evans, 1980). As another example, infants associate objects as being adjacent to a parent (Presson, 1982; Presson & Somerville, 1985), but cannot associate objects to distance landmarks. By the age of one year, they can use a different colored cushion among an array of cushions to locate a toy (Bushnell, McKenzie, Lawrence, & Com, 1995). Toddlers and three-year-olds can place objects in pre-specified locations near distant landmarks, but "lose" locations that are not specified ahead of time once they move. Wang and Spelke (2002) describe a "view-dependent place recognition" system that operates similarly in animals such as ants and bees, and argue that in humans as well, determining location and navigating are based on view-specific representations.

Such cue learning may seem early, considering the Piagetian notion of object permanence. In that framework, children still make the A-not-B error at nine months; that is, after successfully searching for an object at one location, A (several times), they continue to search for it at that location, even after observing that the object is hidden at a new location, B. The Piagetian interpretation confounds object permanence with object location, an issue to which we will return. Experiments varying factors such as measures (infants have better location knowledge as assessed by looking rather than reaching) have shown earlier competence under specific conditions and also suggest new analyses. For example, children must choose between the most frequently executed look (A) and the most recently executed look (B), whereas in reaching, both the most recently and frequently executed action is to location A. Thus, the correct choice of B requires overcoming considerable conflict from other sources of input (Newcombe & Huttenlocher, 2000).

Other related models have been proposed. One is a Parallel Distributed Processing (PDP, aka connectionist) model (see Clements & Battista, 1992; McClelland, Rumelhart, & the PDP Research Group, 1986). The researchers propose conflict between traces that are latent (change in weights or strength of individual connections, stored in long term memory) and active (sustained activation of connections in short term, or working, memory). Development in this theory is mainly the increasing ability to maintain and use active traces (Munakata, 1998). A similar, dynamic systems account provides evidence that the A-not-B phenomenon does not indicate a unique early level of development, but one phase in the development of general and life-long processes that guide actions to remembered locations (Spencer, Smith, & Thelen, 2001). In the account, inputs to the system change over the few seconds of the task's duration. The repeated activation of location A builds a strong memory trace that then begins to fade. Later input activating B is stronger at that moment, but fades more quickly over time, as it was but a single experience. So, the more delay, the more likely activation will be stronger at A than B. Empirical results supported this account over other theoretical positions. The center of the search space was also source of bias, but was not the dominant factor and was not a consistent effect (as implied in Huttenlocher, Newcombe, & Sandberg, 1994).

This account also explains other tasks and performance at other ages. For example, two-year-olds' responses were also biased toward location A. However, they develop stronger external-based location memory and maintain information over longer periods and thus perform more accurately than infants. In addition, children may learn that recency is more important than frequency in such search tasks and that codings of external frameworks are more important than response systems when they are in conflict (Newcombe & Huttenlocher, 2000), as well as developing the efficiency of those external-based systems. Although the use of the A-not-B tasks (at least solely) to inform us about the object concept is debated (Haith & Benson, 1998), it does appear to inform the processes of location coding and searching (Spencer et al., 2001).

PATH INTEGRATION ("DEAD RECKONING")

Infants use response and cue learning when they are stationary. They ignore movement when they are carried (Acredolo, Adams, & Goodwyn, 1984), but use path integration (aka "dead reckoning"—see note 1) as early as six months of age when they have actively moved themselves (Newcombe, Huttenlocher, Drummey, & Wiley, 1998). By one year of age, they can encode both distance and direction with some degree of accuracy during self movement (Bushnell et al., 1995). Thus, self-movement appears important, although infants as young as six, but not four months, of age can demonstrate above-chance performance after training (to localize a fixed location from two orientations) (see also Haith & Benson, 1998, for a review and statement of methodological challenges; D. Tyler & McKenzie, 1990). They can internally represent the amount of rotational movement about their own axis by at least eight months, and code amount of movement along a straight line by at least nine months. By 16 months, children are likely to perform path integration following movements involving both translation and rotation. They sometimes use this system, even more than other systems for certain tasks (Bremner, Knowles, & Andreasen, 1994). A general point is that spatial systems that produce motor activity and spatial representations are intimately connected (Rieser, Garing, & Young, 1994). Path integration has been identified in insects, birds and mammals, and findings support that aspects of it are funda-mental inborn endowments in humans as well (Wang & Spelke, 2002). The fine calibration of the system, and the ability to ignore distracting visual information, improves from four years of age to adulthood, probably based on fine-tuning from the senses, including proprioception and kinesthesia (Newcombe & Huttenlocher, 2000).

PLACE LEARNING

During their second year, children develop the ability to code locations using objects in their external environment. They also become capable of spatial reasoning, in that they can solve problems with that information. They con-tinue to grow in their abilities in spatial coding, reasoning, and symbolizing through their elementary school years, as they develop spatial visualization abilities such as maintaining and operating on mental images (e.g., mental rotation) and learn to use such tools as language and maps.

The first of these abilities is place learning, which involves creating a frame of reference by coding objects' positions with respect to perceptually available landmarks, using information of their distances and directions. In contrast to Piaget's topological primacy thesis, in which children build a "Euclidean system" only by age nine or 10, research indicates that toddlers are able to code distance information and use that to locate objects. For example, infants as young as five months use spatiotemporal information to track and even individuate objects and from 12 months of age, can code distance to support the search for hidden objects (Bushnell et al., 1995; Newcombe & Huttenlocher, 2000); however, in one of these studies they could not use separate indirect landmarks at one year of age (Bushnell et al., 1995). They can also use simple geometric properties of a room to guide a search; for example, looking more often in two corners of a rectangular room with the long wall on the right and the short wall on the left (Hermer & Spelke, 1996).

Although some findings support those (Fodor, 1972; Hermer & Spelke, 1996; Wang & Spelke, 2002) who believe that there are innate, encapsulated, cognitive "modules," in this case, a "geometric module" (Hermer & Spelke, 1996), results are sufficiently variable to place the existence of such a geometric module in doubt. For example, Gouteux and Spelke (2001) replicated others' findings but with variations. They found that early-developing navigational abilities depend on a mechanism that is sensitive to the shape of the permanent, extended surface layout, but that is not sensitive to geometric or non-geometric properties of objects in the layout. In addition, when landmarks appeared to be permanent, toddlers did use this information, even after disorientation (Learmonth, Newcombe, & Huttenlocher, 2001). Children also used a colored wall, at least in rooms that were larger (12 by 8 feet) than rooms used in previous research (Hermer & Spelke, 1996). Such findings leave the relative precedence of the two spatial systems, and the possible domain specificity of the geometric coding, as open questions. It may be there are task-specific mechanisms that search, for cues like size, stability, and geometric configuration of environmental features, just those cues that have ecological validity for navigating animals (Shusterman & Spelke, 2004). In any case, even place learning starts early, in the use of a surrounding surface layout as a framework (and continues to exert influence on searches). However, cues are also used early in some situations, and use of other geometric information and more complex place learning follow.

Place learning using multiple objects may appear after 21 months of age (Newcombe et al., 1998). For example, after shown an object hidden in a sandbox, children were taken around the other side of it. Children 21 months or younger were not helped by the availability of landmarks around the sandbox (that is, they did no worse when these landmarks were hidden by a curtain), but older children were significantly more accurate with the visible landmarks. By five years of age, children can represent an object's position relative to multiple landmarks, such as an object midway between two other objects (Newcombe, 1989). From five to seven years, children increase their ability to keep track of their locations in mazes or open areas.

Functional use of such spatial knowledge for searching, which requires coding spatial information and forming and utilizing spatial relationships, develops over the toddler and preschool years (Newcombe & Sluzenski, 2004). There is a significant growth in the ability to search for multiple objects between 18 and 24 months of life and an increase in the ability to use relations among objects between 24 and 42 months (Newcombe & Sluzenski, 2004). In addition, toddlers can systematically check an array by exhaustively searching within groupings at three sites. (Note that even in place-based learning, children need to establish a relationship to themselves: Lourenco, Huttenlocher, & Vasilyeva, 2005.) Preschoolers can plan comprehensive searches in a small area, including memory of sites that have been checked, often using a circular search path (Cornell, Heth, Broda, & Butterfield, 1987). Lastly, only five-year-olds can use higher-order spatial configurations or patterns to aid searches, probably because that is the age at which they develop the ability to perceive spatial figures in more than one way (Uttal, Gregg, Tan, & Sines, 2001).

SELECTION OF SYSTEMS

As mentioned, the second aspect of development involves learning to select the coding systems that are more effective and accurate in different situations. Evidence of early appearance of all systems and gradual growth favor the view that children change the relative importance they assign to different types of spatial information when these types provide conflicting information (Newcombe & Huttenlocher, 2000), possibly through the formation of metacognitive strategies (Minsky, 1986). Infants' choices among conflicting spatial systems depend on a combination of cue salience, complexity of movement, whether or not response learning has been recently reinforced, and whether the infant is emotionally secure or under stress (N. S. Newcombe & Huttenlocher, 2000). Further development depends on experience. For example, when children attain self-mobility by crawling between six and nine months of age, they can experience failures in response learning. Infants who crawl, and even those with extensive experience with a walker, succeed more often in locating objects' spatial positions (Bertenthal, Campos, & Kermoian, 1994). The longer they have been moving themselves, the greater the advantage, probably because they learn to attend to relevant environmental information and update their spatial codings as they move. This is supported by research showing that when 12-month-old children walk to the other side of a layout and have the opportunity to look at all times (as opposed to being guided by their mother or having their vision blocked), they both look more than children who are guided and also subsequently do better in turning toward the object from the new position (Acredolo et al., 1984). There is great variability on the onset of crawling (Bertenthal et al., 1994), which, along with failures in the codes from response learning, probably leads to developmental advances via the variation-and-selection process.

This perspective does not deny the possibility of an apparently qualitative, or general, shift in default propensities (Newcombe & Huttenlocher, 2000), which may be the result of newly available experiences (e.g., crawling) or of the gradual growth in the effectiveness of a new system that has achieved ascendance in the overlapping stages of development theory (Minsky, 1986, see also a later but more developed version in Siegler, 1996). Such shifts may also result from biological maturation, although some argue that experience may be the cause of the development of the nervous system (Thelen & Smith, 1994).

HIERARCHICAL COMBINATION OF SYSTEMS

Before their second birthday, at about 16 months, children show the beginnings of a hierarchical combination of spatial reference frames, including categorical coding of regions and fine-grained information, although the categories and combinations of categories develop considerably after that age (Newcombe & Huttenlocher, 2000). For example, children form categories that are not physically demarcated (e.g., the left half of a field), beginning in a limited way at four to six years of age (in small rectangles) and expand to larger regions at about 10 years. Second, they develop the ability to code hierarchically along two dimensions simultaneously. For example, to recall the location of a point in a circular region, people 10 years of age and older code locations for both the distance from the center of a circle and angle, as well as categorical information about the quadrant. Children younger than seven years do not code the categorical information about quadrants in such tasks, whereas seven-year-olds do code those categories if angle information is requested. In general, as they age, children divide regions into smaller and more abstract categorically-coded regions. Such changes, rather than a qualitative shift to Euclidean space, appear to explain changes in performance. In summary, hierarchical coding begins at 16 months, but not until 10 years of age do children reach sophisticated levels (Newcombe & Huttenlocher, 2000).

SUMMARY

Children are born with potential abilities in response learning, cue learning, path integration, and place learning. at least in limited circumstances that include a simple frame. During the first year of life, these systems are further integrated, based on feedback from experiences with their physical environment. During the second year, starting at about 21 months, children develop place learning proper, that is, they begin to use distance information from multiple environmental landmarks to define location. Development of symbolic skills may play an important role. From that point forward, the path integration and place learning systems develop in effectiveness and accuracy. Path integration improves from four years of age on. By five years of age, children can represent a location in terms of multiple landmarks, and from five to seven years, develop in their ability to maintain locations in challenging circumstances such as open areas. All four systems are further reconfigured in their application and integration. Finally, there are changes in the size and nature of categories used in hierarchical spatial coding, but these remain limited in the preschool years.

Further, the systems are used with increasing efficiency. At six months of age, children are more likely to rely on response learning, but older children, with more visual and especially self-produced movement experiences, rely more on cue learning and path integration (Newcombe & Huttenlocher,

2000). This variation-and-selection approach is similar to Siegler's (1996) approach, as previously discussed regarding the learning of number. Again, we see the phenomenon of increased variability leading eventually to greater stability and generalizability.

We now turn to what Piaget and Inhelder's (1967) research focused upon, representation that would support reflection. They separated representation that would support action in the world (what we called spatial coding) and that would support reflection about the world (spatial thought).

Spatial Thought

As children gain the capacity for symbolic thought in their second year, they begin to gain access to their spatial knowledge and thus build upon spatial codings to create accessible representations, supporting the emergence of spatial thought. We first address the question of whether spatial reasoning is an innate or developed ability, and then consider spatial perspective taking, navigation through large-scale environments, and the language of space.

DEVELOPMENT OF SPATIAL THOUGHT

Some have argued that abilities such as spatial inference are innate, based on, for example, the finding that children who are blind can infer paths that they have not been taught (Landau, Gleitman, & Spelke, 1981). Kelli, for example, a two and a half-year-old blind child, could infer paths to be taken between novel pairs of locations after moving between other pairs. However, evidence supports the interpretation that children construct spatial relations. Kelli may have built her abilities upon other available senses, including those supporting path integration. Further, in other research, blind children performed less accurately in the key aspect of the task (accuracy at final position) than age-matched sighted, but blindfolded, children performed in similar tasks. This is noteworthy given that the blindfolding created an artificial task for sighted children (Morrongiello, Timney, Humphrey, Anderson, & Skory, 1995). In addition, congenitally blind people have difficulties with spatial tasks, with inaccuracy in encoding distance and angle increasing with distance between objects (Arditi, Holtzman, & Kosslyn, 1988). They also tend to represent routes as a sequence of landmarks, rather than having an overall path or two-dimensional representation, the formation of which may require simultaneously experiencing multiple locations (Iverson & Goldin-Meadow, 1997). Thus, at least some visual experience appears important for full development of spatial knowledge (Morrongiello et al., 1995; Newcombe & Huttenlocher, 2000).

Given that most studies show that blind children and blindfolded sighted children can point to an inferred location at better than chance levels, and that they do not differ in accuracy, there are three additional implications (Newcombe & Huttenlocher, 2000). First, spatial codings and representations are spatial rather than visual. Even congenitally blind children are aware of spatial relationships. By three years, they begin to learn about spatial properties of certain visual concepts represented in language (Landau, 1988). They can learn from spatial-kinesthetic practice (Millar & Ittyerah, 1992). They perform many aspects of spatial tasks similar to blindfolded sighted children (Morrongiello et al., 1995). Second, visual input is important, but spatial relations can be constructed without it (Morrongiello et al., 1995). Third, we see again that Piaget's notion that early spatial knowledge is not metric ("Euclidean") has not been supported. In summary, then, the research indicates that abilities have inborn beginnings, but are realized slowly over years of development.

SPATIAL PERSPECTIVE TAKING

A component of Piaget's topological primacy thesis was that "projective relations" did not develop until elementary school age. When they developed, children considered figures and locations in terms of a "point of view." As an example, the concept of the straight line results from the child's act of "taking aim" or "sighting." Children perceive a straight line from their earliest years, but they initially cannot independently place objects along a straight path. They realize, based on perception, that the line is not straight, but cannot construct an adequate conceptual representation to make it so. At about seven years of age, children spontaneously "aim" or sight along a trajectory to construct straight paths.

The Piagetians confirmed these theoretical claims with other experiments, such as the "three mountains" task in which children had to construct a scene from the perspective of a doll. For each new position of the doll, young children methodically went about their task of re-creating the appropriate viewpoint, but it always turned out to be from the same perspective—their own! Thus, Piaget and Inhelder infer that children must construct systems of reference, not from familiarity born of experience, but from operational linking and coordination of all possible viewpoints, each of which they are conscious. They conclude that such global coordination of viewpoints is the basic prerequisite in constructing simple projective relations. For although such relations are dependent upon a given viewpoint, nevertheless a single "point of view" cannot exist in an isolated fashion, but necessarily entails the construction of a complete system linking together all points of view.

However, other studies have shown conflicting results. For example, young children do recognize that other observers see something different, and develop in their ability to construct those viewpoints (Pillow & Flavell, 1986). They may use a "line-of-sight" idea, in which they reason that people can see any object for which one can imagine an unobstructed line between their eyes and the object. Some ability to coordinate perspectives mentally is present in children as young as 18 months. For example, children perform better than chance in retrieving a reward after it was hidden randomly in one of two identical left-right locations on a turntable, then its location reversed via either a 180-degree rotation of the turntable by the experimenter or a move by the child to the opposite side of the table (Benson & Bogartz, 1990).

Several factors affect children's responses, including attributes of the subject (intellectual realism, cognitive style), task (naturalism, experience with difference viewpoints, actual vs. imagined movement, availability of outside landmarks, attributes of the display), and response mode (Newcombe, 1989). Several of these factors have implications for children's coding of location. For example, perspective-taking tasks are easier if the children move around the objects or are provided a model of the room, suggesting that the locations of the objects are coded individually with respect to an external framework of landmarks. Thus, coding the location of small objects may develop from association (coincidence) with a single external landmark, to proximity to a single landmark, to distance from several landmarks. By the age of five, and possibly as early as three for some situations, children encode the location of small objects with respect to a framework of landmarks. Starting at age seven, and more fully by ages nine or ten, children can focus on a single item, imagine that from a different perspective, and then use this information to choose a corresponding picture in a three mountains task. Such encoding continues into adulthood (Newcombe, 1989).

In summary, the development of projective space may involve not just the coordination of viewpoints but also the establishment of an external framework. That is, a key to solving the three mountains task may be, again, the conflict between frames of reference, experienced and imagined. Full competence in dealing with such conflicts is achieved at approximately the ages Piaget originally claimed. Simultaneously, children are developing additional knowledge of projective relations. At four years of age, but not three, children begin to understand that moving objects nearer or farther increases and decreases its apparent size; they can also indicate how a circular object should be rotated to make it appear circular or elliptical (Pillow & Flavell, 1986).

NAVIGATION THROUGH LARGE SCALE ENVIRONMENTS

Navigation in large environments requires integrated representations, because one can see only some landmarks at any given point. Some researchers believe that people learn to navigate using landmarks; then routes, or connected series of landmarks; then scaled routes; and finally survey knowledge, a kind of "mental map" that combines many routes and locations (Siegel & White, 1975). Only older preschoolers learn scaled routes for familiar paths; that is, they know about the relative distances between landmarks (Anooshian, Pascal, & McCreath, 1984). Even young children, however, can put different locations along a route into some relationship, at least in certain situations. For example, they can point to one location from another even though they never walked a path that connected the two (Uttal & Wellman, 1989).

Children as young as three and a half years were able, like adults, to accurately walk along a path that replicated the route between their seat and the teacher's desk in their classroom (Rieser et al., 1994). Self-produced movement is again important. Kindergartners could not imagine similar movements and point accurately, but they could imagine and recreate the movements and point accurately when they actually walked and turned. Thus, children can build imagery of locations and use it, but they must physically move to show their competence. However, with no landmarks, even four-year-olds make mistakes (Huttenlocher & Newcombe, 1984). Kindergartners build local frameworks that are less dependent on their own position and that constrain paths. They still rely, however, on relational cues such as being close to a boundary. By third grade, children can use larger, encompassing frameworks that include the observer of the situation.

Comparing routes, as in finding the shortest of several routes, is a difficult task. Children as young as one or two years can plan shortest routes only in simple situations. For example, one and a half year-olds will choose the shortest route around a wall separating them from their mothers (Lockman & Pick, 1984). Such early planning may depend on direct sighting of the goal and on an obvious choice of a shorter or more direct route to the goal (Wellman, Fabricius, & Sophian, 1985). Children three and a half to four and a half years of age show a mixture of sighting and planning, that is, considering extended courses of action taking into account the overall distances of competing routes, probably based on qualitative distance-relevant aspects of routes, such as the necessity of backtracking (Wellman et al., 1985). There is some evidence that young children can compute shortest routes even when the goal is not visible (Newcombe & Huttenlocher, 2000). A significant proportion (40 percent) of four-year-olds can not only identify that a direct and indirect route to a given location are not the same distance, but can explain why the direct route was shorter (Fabricius & Wellman, 1993). However, ability to plan routes in situations in which the optimal route involves locations that are not close or in sight (when others are) appears at five to six years of age.

Considering these results in the context of the broad research on spatial orientation, it is not surprising that children grow over a number of years in their ability to form integrated spatial representations. However, evidence does not support a simple, qualitative shift from "landmark" to "route" to integrated, two-dimensional representations (Newcombe & Huttenlocher, 2000). Instead, development results from substantive refinements in the effectiveness and connectedness of already-existing representational systems, including hierarchical categorization (e.g., children create more precise embedded categories as they age). Young children undoubtedly rely on cues (landmarks) and partially-connected landmark-and-route representations when they have limited experience in an environment and when information-processing demands, such as those on memory, use of strategies (e.g., turning around to visualize how a route will look on the return trip), and inferences required to combine spatial knowledge from different systems, overwhelm their cognitive abilities. They develop abilities such as recognition-in-context memory that facilitates acquisition of landmark knowledge (Allen & Ondracek, 1995).

Also important is the realization that, again, adults do not achieve perfect accuracy in their ideas about space. Intuitive representations of space are non-homogeneous and anisotropic (exhibiting properties with different values when measured along axes in different directions). For example, people tend to attribute absolutely privileged directions to space, such as "up" and "down." They view space as centered (e.g., at one's home), and as having increasing density as one approaches the centration zones, with the effect that distances are increasingly amplified upon approach. Thus, people's intuitive representation of space is a mixture of often-contradictory properties, all related to their terrestrial life and behavioral adaptive constraints (Fischbein, 1987).

THE LANGUAGE OF SPACE

The development of both geometric domains, the "what" and "where" systems (Ungerleider & Mishkin, 1982), begins early in life as children represent objects at a detailed level of shape, and simply as a set of axes (i.e., a representation of an object allowing a region in front and a region in back, Landau, 1996). However, spatial relations are not perceived "automatically"; they require attention (Logan, 1994; Regier & Carlson, 2002). Children learning English show strong biases to ignore fine-grained shape when learning novel spatial terms such as "on" or "in front of" or when interpreting known spatial terms, and equally strong biases to attend to fine-grained shape when learning novel object names. For example, three-year-olds will ignore shape and generalize primarily on the basis of an object's demonstrated location when shown an unusual object and told, "This is acorp my box" (Landau, 1996). That is, they interpret that the unknown word "acorp" refers to a spatial relationship between the object and the box, and thus infer it refers to its location, not the shape of it. Conversely, if told "This is a prock", they would attend to the unusual object's shape.

Children represent objects in terms of axes by the second year of life; contrary to Piagetian theory, the development of regions appears to begin with the axis and broaden afterward. However, spatial terms are acquired in a consistent order, even across different languages (Bowerman, 1996), and this is one of the few sequences that is consistent with the Piagetian topological primacy thesis. The first terms acquired are "in," "on," and "under," along with such vertical directionality terms as "up" and "down." These initially refer to transformations of one spatial relationship into another ("on" not as a smaller object on top of another, but only as making an object become physically attached to another, Gopnik & Meltzoff, 1986). Second, children learn words of proximity, such as "beside" and "between." Third, children learn words referring to frames of reference such as "in front of," "behind." The words "left" and "right" are learned much later, and are the source of confusion for many years.

The consistency of acquisition order, along with early learning of space and the reliance on spatial understanding in learning new words (e.g., predicting what new words mean and extending their use to new situations) argue that spatial language builds upon already-constructed spatial concepts (Bowerman, 1996; Regier & Carlson, 2002; Spelke, 2002). However, that does not mean that children merely map spatial words directly onto extant spatial concepts. The concepts may be just forming, and change from attempts to change spatial relationships of objects ("down" as "get me down") to references to all such changes, and finally to static spatial relationships. The words children use encode concepts that are problematic for the child—that the child is developing—and are used as a cognitive tool to support that development. In addition, adult language helps children consolidate their emerging understandings (Gopnik & Meltzoff, 1986). Further, semantic organization of language appears to influence children's development of spatial concepts (Bowerman, 1996). For example, while English uses "on" for contact with and support by a surface (on a table and handle on a door) and "in" for containment, Finnish categorizes the handle on a door and apple in a bowl together; the horizontal support of "on a table" requires a different construction. In Dutch, the hanging attachment of "handle on a door" is a separate construct (Bowerman, 1996). Consistent with the notion that these differences affect children's special learning, cross-cultural studies show that, for example, children learning English acquire concepts referring to verticality faster than children learning a language such as Korean, for which those terms are less central, whereas Korean children learn different meanings for terms that mean "in" as in "fit tightly" and as in "inside a larger container", whereas English-speaking children are slower to learn that differentiation, with these differences occurring both in production (Choi & Bowerman, 1991) and in comprehension (Choi, McDonough, Bowerman, & Mandler, 1999) as early at 18 to 23 months. Thus, even if it does not change perception at a low level in a Whorfian manner—with language determining what is perceived and thought—it appears likely that language appears to affect conceptual growth by affecting what kind of spatial relationships and categories children attend to and build. As we stated previously, however, language and culture are intricately interwoven and vocabulary focuses thought but also reflect cultural *practices* that may be at the root of these differences.

By two years of age, children have considerable spatial competence on which language might be based. Further, in contrast to many who emphasize children's naming of objects, children use spatial relational words more frequently, and often earlier, than names (Gopnik & Meltzoff, 1986). Moreover, the use of even a single-word utterance by a 19-month-old, such as "in" may reflect more spatial competence than it first appears when the contexts differ widely, such as saying, "in" when about to climb into the child seat of a shopping cart and saying "in" when looking under couch cushions for coins she just put in the crack between cushions (Bowerman, 1996). However, notions such as "left" and "right," whose relative understanding may require mental rotation (Roberts & Aman, 1993), may not be fully understood until about six to eight years of age. Between these ages, children also learn to analyze what others need to hear to follow a route through a space. To a large degree, however, development past pre-K depends on sociocultural influences on children's understanding of conventions, such as negotiating which frame of reference is used (Newcombe & Huttenlocher, 2000). Such influences have strong effects. For example, achieving flexible spatial performance is correlated, and may be caused by, acquisition appropriate spatial vocabulary (Wang & Spelke, 2002). Indeed, it may be the unique way that people combine concepts from different inborn spatial systems into mature and flexible spatial understandings. Training preschoolers on the spatial terms "left" and "right" helped them reorient more successfully (Shusterman & Spelke, 2004). Finally, while language supports simple representations such as cue learning, place learning is difficult to capture verbally because of the multiple simultaneous relationships, This leads us to more apropos external representations, such as models and maps.

Models and Maps

Young children can represent and, to an extent, mathematize, their experiences with navigation. They begin to build mental representations of their spatial environments and can use and create simple maps. Children as young as two years of age can connect oblique and eye-level views of the same space, finding their mother behind a barrier after observing the situation from above (Rieser, Doxsey, McCarrell, & Brooks, 1982). In another study, two and a half-, but not two-year-olds, could locate a toy, shown a picture of the space, even when two-year-olds are given help (DeLoache, 1987; DeLoache & Burns, 1994).

To make sense of maps, children have to create relational, geometric correspondences between elements, as these vary in scale and perspective (Newcombe & Huttenlocher, 2000). It is noteworthy that essential mathematical notions of *representation* and *symbolization* (one thing "stands for" something else) and specific *correspondences* appear in a *limited* form in children as young as three years (Liben & Myers, 2007). Thus, even three-year-olds may be able to build simple, but meaningful, models with landscape toys such as houses, cars, and trees (Blaut & Stea, 1974), although this ability is limited through the age of six years (Blades, Spencer, Plester, & Desmond, 2004). However, we know less about what specific abilities and strategies they use to do so. For example, kindergartners making models of their classroom cluster furniture correctly (e.g., they put the furniture for a dramatic play center together), but may not relate the clusters to each other (Siegel & Schadler, 1977).

Thus, preschoolers have some impressive initial competencies, but these are just starting to develop. We begin a more in depth look at this development by considering children's use, rather than production, of models and maps. One study confirms that children can use both models and maps by two and a half to three years of age, but with a twist. Children were shown a location on a scale model of a room then asked to find same object in the actual room (DeLoache, 1987). For example, a miniature dog was hidden behind a small couch in the model, and the child was asked to find a larger stuffed dog hidden behind a full-sized couch. Interestingly, raising a point to which we shall return, three-, but not two and a half-, year-olds could find the corresponding object (the authors do not state, but we assume, the two were in alignment). However, both ages were successful with line drawings or photographs of the room. It may be that the younger children saw the model as an interesting object, but not as a symbol for another space, leading to the counterintuitive result that the more "concrete" model was less useful to them. In support of this notion, having these children play with the model decreased their success using it as a symbol in the search task, and eliminating any interaction increased their success. The threes were successful with either, revealing cognitive flexibility in their use of the model, as an object per se and a symbol for another space.

In a similar vein, beginning about three, and more so at four, years of age, children can interpret certain symbols on maps, such as a blue rectangle standing for blue couch, or "x marks the spot" (Dalke, 1998). Their abilities lack sophistication; for example, preschoolers recognized roads on a map, but suggested that the tennis courts were doors (Liben & Downs, 1989). Some believe that the colors on a map represent colors of the real-world objects (Liben & Myers, 2007). In another study, four- and five-year-olds criticized symbols that lacked features (e.g., tables without legs), but could recognize a plane view of their classroom, so findings such as these may be the result of children merely voicing preferences. All could distinguish between representational (in room) and nonrepresentational (outside of room) paper space (Liben & Yekel, 1996). In any case, by age five or six, children can consistently interpret the arbitrary symbolic relationships used in maps (Newcombe & Huttenlocher, 2000). Yet children may understand that symbols on maps represent objects but have limited understanding of the geometric correspondence between maps and the referent space. As we shall see, both understandings are developing, but have far to go, by the end of the preschool years (Liben & Yekel, 1996).

Shortly after three years of age, children are able to scale distance across simple spatial representations, a fundamental competence (Huttenlocher,

Newcombe, & Vasilyeva, 1999). However, they perform better with symmetric than asymmetric configurations (Uttal, 1996). Children also understand that a map represents space (Liben & Yekel, 1996). By four years of age, they can build upon these abilities and begin interpreting maps, planning navigation, reasoning about, and learning from maps, at least in simple situations (Newcombe & Huttenlocher, 2000). For example, four-year-olds benefit from maps and can use them to guide navigation (i.e., follow a route) in simple situations (Scholnick, Fein, & Campbell, 1990). In a similar study, four- to seven-year-olds had to learn a route through a six-room playhouse with a clear starting point. Children who examined a map beforehand learned a route more quickly than those who did not (Uttal & Wellman, 1989). Children younger than six, however, have trouble knowing where they are in the space; therefore, they have difficulty using information available from a map relevant to their own present position (Uttal & Wellman, 1989). Preschoolers also have difficulty aligning maps to the referent space, a skill that improves by age five (Liben & Yekel, 1996). Competencies in geometric distances and scaling are underway by age six or seven, and primary grade children can recognize features on aerial photographs and large-scale plans of the same area (Blades et al., 2004; Boardman, 1990), but these abilities continue to improve into adulthood. However, even adults do not attain perfect competence.

The ability to use a map to plan routes is more challenging than following specified routes. This ability is forming at about age five, although the spaces researchers use are usually simple and rectangular. By six years, children can plan routes in more complex environments with multiple alternatives, using distance information. For example, by five to six years of age, children can use maps to navigate their way around a school, but are less successful navigating complex streets or a cave (Jovignot, 1995). More research is needed on naturalistic spaces, as well as on children's ability to plan efficient routes (Newcombe & Huttenlocher, 2000).

As we saw, young preschoolers show some ability to create models of spaces such as their classrooms (Blaut & Stea, 1974; Siegel & Schadler, 1977). Preschoolers, like older people, could preserve the configuration of objects when reconstructing a room depicted on a map. However, preschoolers placed objects far from correct locations and performed worse with asymmetric than symmetric configurations (Uttal, 1996). Most four-year-olds can locate clusters of model furniture items in a scale model of their classroom, but get confused when they must position the items, getting only about half the items correct (Golbeck, Rand, & Soundy, 1986; Liben, Moore, & Golbeck, 1982). Much of the difficulty may be not be in coding and producing locations, but rather in scaling distances, especially as that difficulty is compounded with multiple elements (Newcombe & Huttenlocher, 2000).

There are individual differences in such abilities. In one study, most preschoolers rebuilt a room better using real furniture than toy models. For some children, however, the difference was slight. Others placed real furniture correctly, but grouped the toy models only around the perimeter. Some children placed the models and real furniture randomly, showing few capabilities (Liben, 1988). Even children with similar mental representations may produce quite different maps due to differences in drawing and map-building skills (Uttal & Wellman, 1989). Nevertheless, by the primary grades, most children are able to draw simple sketch-maps of the area around their home from memory (Boardman, 1990).

What accounts for differences and age-related changes? Maturation and development may be significant. Children need mental processing capacity to update directions and location. The older they get, the more spatial memories they can store and transformations they can perform. Such increase in processing capacity, along with general experience, determines how a space is represented more than the amount of experience with the particular space (Anooshian et al., 1984). Students continue to learn about the role of symbols, including understanding the intent of the creator of the symbols, throughout elementary school (Myers & Liben, 2008). Other learning is also important, as will be discussed in a following section. For now, we emphasize that although the modal number correct on a map assessment was zero for kindergarteners, several were correct on every item (Liben & Myers, 2007). Similarly, some sixth-graders and adults show little competence with maps. Thus, experience probably plays a major role in understanding spatial representations such as maps.

Fundamental is the connection of primary to secondary uses of maps (Presson, 1987). Even young children can form primary relations to spaces on maps, once they see them as representing a space at about two and a half to three years of age (DeLoache, 1987). This ability is probably an *initial bootstrap* in that it appears in children and adults in cultures that have no maps or other explicit representational tools (Dehaene, Izard, Pica, & Spelke, 2006). They must learn to treat the spatial relations as separate from their immediate environment. These secondary meanings require people to take the perspective of an abstract frame of reference ("as if you were there") that conflicts with the primary meaning. You no longer imagine yourself "inside," but rather must see yourself at a distance, or "outside," the information. Showing children several models, and explicitly comparing them using language, and possibly visual highlights, can help (Loewenstein & Gentner, 2001), probably because it helps children notice common relationships on subsequent tasks. Such meanings of maps challenge people from preschool into adulthood, especially when the map is not aligned with the part of the world it represents (Uttal & Wellman, 1989). For example, successful map use and mental rotation abilities are correlated in four- to six-year olds (Scholnick et al., 1990). Ability to use misaligned maps, especially those 180° misaligned, shows considerable improvement up to about eight years of age. In addition, children may learn other strategies to deal with the basic problem of conflicting frames of reference (Newcombe & Huttenlocher, 2000). These findings re-emphasize that we must be careful how we interpret the phrase "mental (or cognitive) map." Spatial information may be different when it is garnered from primary and secondary sources such as maps.

Coordinates and Spatial Structuring

Young children can learn to relate various reference frames, and they appear to use, implicitly, two coordinates in remembering direction, either polar or Cartesian. This appears inconsistent with the Piagetian account of the development of two-dimensional space, in which only in later years do children come to "see" objects as located in a two-dimensional frame of reference. That is, Piaget and Inhelder (1967) challenged the claim that there is an innate tendency or ability to organize objects in a two- or three-dimensional reference frame. Spatial awareness does not begin with such an organization; rather, the frame itself is a culminating point of the development of Euclidean space.

To test their theory in the case of horizontality, Piaget and Inhelder showed children jars half-filled with colored water and asked them to predict the spatial orientation of the water level when the jar was tilted. For verticality, a plumb line was suspended inside an empty jar, which was similarly tilted, or children were asked to draw trees on a hillside. Children initially were incapable of representing planes; a scribble, for example, represented water in a tilted jar. At the next state, the level of the water was always drawn perpendicular to the sides of the jar, regardless of tilt. Satisfaction with such drawings was in no way undermined even when an actual water-filled tilted jar was placed next to the drawing. It is, then, quite striking "how poorly commonly perceived events are recorded in the absence of a schema within which they may be organized" (p. 388). Sometimes, sensing that the water moves towards the mouth of the jar, children raised the level of the water, still keeping the surface perpendicular to the sides. Only at the final stage—at about nine years of age—did children ostensibly draw upon the larger spatial frame of reference (e.g., tabletop) for ascertaining the horizontal.

Ultimately, the frame of reference constituting Euclidean space is analogical to a container, made up of a network of sites or positions. Objects within this container may be mobile, but the positions are stationary. From the simultaneous organization of all possible positions in three dimensions emerges the Euclidean coordinate system. This organization is rooted in the preceding construction of the concept of straight line (as the maintenance of a constant direction of travel), parallels, and angles, followed by the coordination of their orientations and inclinations. This leads to a gradual replacement of relations of order and distance between objects by similar relations between the positions themselves. It is as if a space were emptied of objects so as to organize the space itself. Thus, intuition of space is not a "reading" or innate apprehension of the properties of objects, but a system of relationships borne in actions performed on these objects.

Once again, however, subsequent research indicates that young children are more competent, and adolescents and adults less competent, than the theory might suggest. Regarding the latter, not all high school seniors or college students perform successfully on tasks designed by Piaget to assess an underlying Euclidean conceptual system (Liben, 1978; Mackay et al., 1972; H. Thomas & Jamison, 1975). On the other hand, it appears that young children's grasp of Euclidean spatial relationships is more adequate than the theory posits. Very young children can orient a horizontal or vertical line in space (Rosser, Horan, Mattson, & Mazzeo, 1984). Similarly, in very simple situations, four- to six-year-old children (a) can extrapolate lines from positions on both axes and determine where they intersect, (b) are equally successful going from point to coordinate as going from coordinate to point, and (c) extrapolate as well with or without grid lines (Somerville & Bryant, 1985). Piagetian theory seems correct in postulating that the coordination of relations develops after such early abilities. Young children fail on double-axis orientation tasks even when misleading perceptual cues are eliminated (Rosser, Horan et al., 1984). Similarly, the greatest difficulty is in coordinating two extrapolations, which has its developmental origins at the three- to four-year-old level, with the ability to extrapolate those lines developing as much as a year earlier (Somerville, Bryant, Mazzocco, & Johnson, 1987).

These results suggest an initial inability to utilize a conceptual coordinate system as an organizing spatial framework (Liben & Yekel, 1996). Only some four-year-olds can use a coordinate reference system, whereas most six-year-olds can (Blades & Spencer, 1989) at least in scaffolded situations. However, most four-year-olds can coordinate dimensions if the task is set in a meaningful, guided context in which the orthogonal dimensions are cued by the line of sights of imaginary people (Bremner, Andreasen, Kendall, & Adams, 1993). Conceptual integration of coordinates is not limited to two orthogonal dimensions. Children as young as five years can metrically represent spatial information in a polar coordinate task, using the same two dimensions as adults, radius and angle, although children do not use categorizations of those dimensions until age nine (Sandberg & Huttenlocher, 1996).

However, performance on coordinate tasks is influenced by a variety of factors at all ages. Performance on horizontality and verticality tasks may reflect bias toward the perpendicular in copying angles, possibly because this reference is learned early (Ibbotson & Bryant, 1976). Representations of figures also are distorted either locally by angle bisection, or by increasing symmetry of the figure as a whole (Bremner & Taylor, 1982). Finally, performance on these Piagetian spatial tasks correlates with disembedding as well as with general spatial abilities (Liben, 1978). Such results indicate a general tendency to produce symmetry or simplicity in constructions that confound the traditional Piagetian interpretation (Bremner & Taylor, 1982; Mackay et al., 1972).

Thus, young children have nascent abilities to structure two-dimensional space (which they often have to be prompted to use), but older students often have not developed firm conceptual grounding in grid and coordinate reference systems. To consciously structure space with such systems requires considerable conceptual work. Spatial structuring is the mental operation of constructing an organization or form for an object or set of objects in space (Battista, Clements, Arnoff, Battista, & Borrow, 1998). Structuring is a form of abstraction, the process of selecting, coordinating, unifying, and registering in memory a set of mental objects and actions. Structuring takes previously abstracted items as content and integrates them to form new structures. Spatial structuring precedes meaningful use of grids and coordinate systems. On the one hand, grids that are provided to children may aid their structuring of space; but children still face hurdles in understanding these grid and coordinate systems. The grid itself may be viewed as a collection of square regions, rather than as sets of perpendicular lines. In addition, order and distance relationships within the grid must be constructed and coordinated across the two dimensions. Labels must be related to grid lines and, in the form of ordered pairs of coordinates, to points on the grid, and eventually integrated with the grid's order and distance relationships so that they constitute numerical objects and ultimately can be operated upon.

Even as late as fourth-grade, many children still need to learn to spatially structure two-dimensional grids in this fashion (Sarama, Clements, Swaminathan, McMillen, & González Gómez, 2003). They need to overcome conceptual hurdles of (a) interpreting the grid structure's components as line segments or lines rather than regions; (b) appreciating the precision of location the lines required, rather than treating them as fuzzy boundaries or indicators of intervals and (c) learning to trace vertical or horizontal lines that were not axes. When using coordinates, children may have needed to reconstruct the levels of counting and quantification that they had already constructed in the domain of counting discrete objects.

In summary, even young children can use coordinates that adults provide for them. However, when facing traditional tasks, they and their older peers may not yet be able or predisposed to spontaneously make and use coordinates for themselves. Performance on coordinate tasks progresses uniformly and continuously from preschool to grade 6 (G. R. Carlson, 1976).

As a final note, we argue that that the term "spatial structuring" be reserved for this specific construct of organizing such two- or three-dimensional concepts, the context in which the term was created (Battista & Clements, 1996; Battista et al., 1998; Sarama et al., 2003). Although one could think of all geometric and spatial activity discussed in this section as "structuring space," this would enervate the construct. Furthermore, better, specific local theories exist for other areas of geometry and spatial thinking. Building stronger and more detailed local theories is a superior approach for psychology and education (Newcombe & Huttenlocher, 2000).

Imagery and Spatial Visualization

Visual representations are central to our lives, including most domains of mathematics (Arcavi, 2003). In this broad sense, visualization is "the ability, the process, and the product of creation, interpretation, use of and reflection upon pictures, images, diagrams, in our minds, on paper, or with technology tools, with the purpose of depicting and communicating information, thinking about and developing previously unknown ideas and advancing understandings" (p. 56). Data representations are one example (see Chapter 12).

Spatial images are internally experienced, holistic representations of objects that appear (to the individual) to be similar to their referents. Kosslyn (1983) defines four classes of image processes: generating an image, inspecting an image to answer questions about it, maintaining an image in the service of some other mental operation, and transforming and operating on an image. Thus, spatial visualization involves understanding and performing imagined transformations of two- and three-dimensional objects, including motions, matching, and combining.

To do this, people need to be able to create a mental image and manipulate it. An image is not a "picture in the head," although some have argued that the mental processes are similar to those that underlie the perception of objects (Shepard, 1978). For example, they are integrated and can be scanned or rotated as one would do to perceptually available objects, with transitional images and times in proportion to those of perceptual activity (Eliot, 1987; S. M. Kosslyn, Reiser, & Ball, 1978). Images are more abstract, more malleable, and less crisp than pictures. They are often segmented into parts and represent relationships among those parts (Shepard, 1978). Some images can cause difficulties, especially if they are too inflexible, vague, or filled with irrelevant details.

Not everyone agrees with the close comparison between real-world objects and images. Pylyshyn argues that the cognitive foundation of these images may be the same kind of conceptual structures that underlie other knowledge (Pylyshyn, 1973, 2003). For example, when recollections of spatial objects are vague, certain perceptual qualities are absent, not geometrically definable components. As another example, children's difficulty discriminating a figure and its mirror image may indicate that their mental representations do not include relations such as "to the left of," but do include general relations such as adjacent to.

Pylyshyn also argues that the personal experience of mental images has fooled researchers into erroneous interpretations of experiments. Some experiments have found, for example, that it takes longer to mentally scan a path on a map from cities that are a greater distance apart. However, it may be that the tasks themselves suggest or tell subjects to scan, and that they therefore reproduce the very time lags that they implicitly believe would be characteristic of such scanning (Pylyshyn, 1981). Subjects under different conditions perform many tasks that do not form linear relationship with time. Thus, the precise cognitive nature of mental images is still under debate.

Such debates indicate that imagery and visualization are difficult areas to study. Even more so than other areas, they are high-inference research fields, in which we often assume that what people discuss or draw is an indication of what they visualize and provides insight into how it affects their thinking; however, we have little reliable evidence on the validity of this assumption.

Whatever their precise cognitive basis, spatial visualization abilities are processes involved in generating and manipulating mental images, as well as guiding the drawing of figures or diagrams on paper or computer screens (Presmeg, 1997). For example, children might create a mental image of a shape, maintain that image, and then search for that same shape, perhaps hidden within a more complex figure. To do so, they may need to mentally rotate the shapes, one of the most important transformations for children to learn. These spatial skills directly support children's learning of specific topics, such as geometry and measurement, but they also can be applied to mathematical problem solving across topics (Battista, 1990; Kersh, Casey, & Young, in press). This may account for the consistent finding that spatial skills and mathematics achievement are connected in older students (Casey, Nuttall, & Pezaris, 1997; Casey et al., 2001; Delgado & Prieto, 2004; Friedman, 1995; Hegarty & Kozhevnikov, 1999). Few studies have investigated this relationship with young children, but high correlations have been found in mathematically precocious preschool and kindergarten children (Robinson, Abbot, Berninger, & Busse, 1996).

In Piagetian theory (Piaget & Inhelder, 1967, 1971) children up to four years of age cannot construct an entire image of a two-dimensional shape after only tactile-kinesthetic experience (visual experiences were thought to rely overly on perceptual thinking) because preschoolers are too passive, touching one part of a shape only. Children aged four to seven would touch another part and regulate their actions by establishing relations among them, building a more accurate representation of the shape. Such processes allow them to accurately distinguish between rectilinear (e.g., a triangle) and curvilinear (e.g., circle) shapes and build images of simple shapes. Children older than seven years systematically return to each movement's starting point, allowing the parts of the figure to be synthesized into a complete whole. Mental actions are then reversible, and distinct yet coordinated with other actions, allowing complete and accurate image building. At this point, children can use anticipatory schemes that include possible features such as straight or curved lines, angles, parallels, order, and equal or unequal lengths. In this way, images are said to be internal imitations of actions, even perceptual actions such as eye movements.

Although Piaget argued that most children cannot perform full dynamic motions of images until the primary grades (Piaget & Inhelder, 1967, 1971), pre-K children show initial transformational abilities. Some researchers have reported that second graders learned only manual procedures for producing transformation images, but could not mentally perform such transformations (Williford, 1972). In contrast, other studies indicate that even young children can learn something about these motions and appear to internalize them, as indicated by increases on spatial ability tests (Clements, Battista, Sarama, & Swaminathan, 1997; Del Grande, 1986). Slides appear to be the easiest motions for children, then flips and turns (Perham, 1978); however, the direction of transformation may affect the relative difficulty of turn and flip (Schultz & Austin, 1983). Results depend on specific tasks, of course; even four- to five-year olds can do turns if they have simple tasks and orientation cues (e.g., one or more markers of orientation are on the edge of a shape and the "flipped" shape is not a distractor, Rosser, Ensing et al., 1984). Further, some studies indicate that second-grade students are capable of mental rotation involving imagery (Perham, 1978; Rosser, Lane, & Mazzeo, 1988). In one study of children of ages four to eight, there were no significant effects of showing the motion to reproduce the effects of the transformation for slides and flips (with the trend being a negative effect for younger children) but a dramatic beneficial effect for turns. A slide task was at least as easy as a flip, and turns were most difficult (J. C. Moyer, 1978).

From geometric motions to using maps, children have to be able to perceive that two shapes or sets of objects in space are the "same" and to make correspondences between them (see the discussion in Chapter 8 on comparing shapes and congruence). Transformations and perspective taking appear to follow the development of perceptual and imagistic reproduction. There is a hierarchical developmental sequence of reproduction of geometric figures requiring only encoding (i.e., building a matching configuration of shapes, with the original constantly in sight), reproduction requiring memory (building a matching configuration from recall), and transformation involving rotation and visual perspective-taking (building a matching configuration either from recall after a rotation or from another's perspective), with pre-K children able to perform at only the first two levels (Rosser et al., 1988). In a similar vein, a framework of imagery for early spatial mathematics learning that is generally consistent with the research reviewed here has been proposed by Owens (1999). In each of three categories, orientation and motion, part-whole relationships, and classification and language, children develop strategies in five categories: emergent (beginning to attend, manipulate, and explore), perceptual (attend to features and make comparisons, relying on what they can see or do), pictorial (mental images and standard language), pattern and dynamic imagery (conceptual relationships), and efficient strategies. Preliminary evidence suggests the validity and usefulness of the framework for researchers and teachers. Using a similar framework, it was found that 11 percent of Australian kindergarteners were unable to visualize simple shapes at the beginning of the year (2 percent at the end of the year in the experimental group), 70 percent were at the level of forming static, pictorial images in conjunction with models or manipulatives (37 percent of the experimental children at the end), with only 19 percent at the level of visualizing effects of motions (52 percent by the end for experimentals) and 1 percent using dynamic imagery (10 percent by the end for experimentals) (D. M. Clarke et al., 2002). Thus, there is much room for growth in the earliest year, but helping teachers understand developmental progressions and learning trajectories can promote that growth.

One additional issue regarding transformations deserves attention. First graders discriminate between mirror-image reversals (b vs. d) better than kindergarteners (Cronin, 1967). After experience with reading, children regard orientation as a critical criterion for differences between geometric shapes. This can work *against* geometric development (if not discussed).

From experiments on people who are congenitally blind, we know that their imagery is in some ways similar, and some ways different from normally sighted people. For example, only sighted people image objects of different size at different distances, so the image will not overflow a fixed image space. They image objects at distances so that the objects subtend the same visual angle. Thus, some aspects of visual imagery are visual, and not present in blind people's images, but some aspects of imagery may be evoked by multiple modalities (Arditi et al., 1988).

TYPES OF CHILDREN AND MATHEMATICAL PROBLEM SOLVING

Krutetskii classified gifted children into categories depending on the way they used mathematical abilities, especially verbal-logical components and visual-pictorial components (Krutetskii, 1976).

1. *Analytic* children used strong verbal-logical abilities, which dominated their weak visual abilities.
2. *Geometric* children used strong visual abilities, which dominated their above-average verbal-logical abilities.
3. *Harmonic* children had both strong verbal-logical and strong visual abilities. Some could use visual supports but preferred not to, and others preferred to do so.

This classification system is also relevant for children of all abilities levels (Presmeg, 1997). This classification returns us to the question of when visual thinking is helpful and when it is not. The strong visual thinkers synthesized their visual/concrete and abstract knowledge (Clements, 1999a; we also discuss this at length in Chapter 16 in the companion book). They had visual "schemes" (Krutetskii, 1976), leading to our next point.

TYPES OF IMAGES AND MATHEMATICAL PROBLEM SOLVING

High-achieving children build images that have a spectrum of quality and a more conceptual and relational core. They are able to link different experiences and abstract similarities. Low-achieving children's images tended to be dominated by surface features. Instruction might help them develop more sophisticated images (Gray & Pitta, 1999).

The *schematic images* of high-achieving children are thus more general and abstract. They contain the spatial relationships relevant to a problem and thus support problem solving (Hegarty & Kozhevnikov, 1999).

The *pictorial images* of low-achieving children do not aid problem solving and actually can impede success. They represent mainly the visual appearance of the objects or persons described in a problem. Thus, just using pictures or diagrams or encouraging children to "visualize" may not be at all useful. Instead, educators should help students develop and use specific types of schematic images. The diagrams for arithmetic (e.g., Figure 6.1 in this book or Figures 5.2 and 6.3 in the companion book) illustrate that such images are useful in many mathematics contexts.

Other categories of images are consistent, but more elaborate. For example, according to one categorization, images can be automatic or intentional, and intentional images can be analogical (graphs, geometrical) or not (statements or formulas) (Duval, 1999).

Experience and Education

Spatial thinking can be learned and should be taught at all educational levels, according to a report by the National Research Council (NRC, 2006). However, we are only beginning to learn about specific cultural and educational experiences and their impact on these capabilities, especially for young children. Experience-expectant processes (Greenough et al., 1987) appear to account for much of children's development. Universal experiences, such as our physical world provides, lead to an interaction of inborn capabilities and environmental inputs that guide development in similar ways across cultures and individuals. However, other competencies, such as spatial reasoning and the use and creation of external spatial representations, such as language, models and maps, probably develop via experience-dependent processes (Greenough et al., 1987), and thus capability differs across cultures and individuals. For example, preschool teachers spend more time with boys than girls, and usually interact with boys in the block, construction, sand play, and climbing areas, and with girls in the dramatic play area (Ebbeck, 1984). Boys engage in spatial activities more than girls at home, both alone and with caretakers (Newcombe & Sanderson, 1993). Such differences may interact with biology to account for early spatial skill advantages for boys (note that some studies find no gender differences, e.g., Brosnan, 1998; see Chapter 15 for a discussion; Ehrlich, Levine, & Goldin-Meadow, 2005; Jordan, Kaplan, Oláh, & Locuniak, 2006; Levine, Huttenlocher, Taylor, & Langrock, 1999; Rosser, Horan et al., 1984).

As a more general note, we are not advocating teaching "spatial thinking" as a part of math instruction divorced from teaching other mathematical content and processes. Teaching isolated spatial skills, especially to children with special needs, has a long history, most of which has been unsuccessful (Hofmeister, 1993). Thus, there are important questions not only for cognitive psychology, but also for mathematics education research.

Spatial Orientation, Navigation, and Maps

Psychological research once again indicates that active experiences, here emphasizing both physical and mental activity, are appropriate, and, in some cases, critical, for children, especially as they are just developing a skill, such as spatial orientation. For example, one-year-olds who walk themselves around a display are more active observers and better locators than those who are carried (Acredolo et al., 1984). Similarly, self-directed movement at five years of age led to superior recall of distances in a spatial layout of a room (Poag, Cohen, & Weatherford, 1983). As they develop, they become able to perform well under a greater variety of conditions (e.g., outcomes did not differ among self- or other-directed movement and viewing conditions for seven-year-olds). These and other studies (Benson & Bogartz, 1990; Newcombe & Huttenlocher, 2000; Rieser et al., 1994) emphasize the importance of self-produced movement for success in spatial tasks and suggest the benefit of maximizing such experience for all young children.

Given the early competence in foundational spatial representational systems, there is every reason to assume that rich environments will contribute to spatial competence at the intuitive and explicit levels. For example, young children learn practical navigation early, as adults responsible for their care will agree. Channeling that experience is valuable. For example, when nursery-school children tutor others in guided environments, they build geometrical concepts (Filippaki & Papamichael, 1997). Parents vary widely in the quantity and quality of the experiences they provide their children about space and spatial relations, and this is related to children's competence with maps and other spatial skills (Liben & Myers, 2007). Such environments might include interesting layouts, experiences with landmarks and routes, and frequent discussion about spatial relations on all scales, including distinguishing parts of their bodies (Leushina, 1974/1991) and spatial movements, finding a missing object, and finding the way back home from an excursion. Verbal interaction is important. For example, parental scaffolding of spatial communication helped both three- and four-year-olds perform direction-giving tasks, in which they had to disambiguate by using a second landmark ("it's in the bag *on the table*"), which children are more likely to do the older they are. Both age groups benefited from directive prompts, but four-year olds benefited more quickly than younger children from nondirective prompts (Plumert & Nichols-Whitehead, 1996). Control children never disambiguated, showing that inter-action and feedback from others is critical to certain spatial communication tasks.

Representing spatial environments with models and maps, as well as implicitly or verbally, is less likely to be spontaneously developed. Specific teaching strategies may therefore yield as yet largely unexplored benefits. Models and maps are sociocultural tools (Gauvain, 1991), but ones whose development is not well supported in the U.S. culture. For example, school experiences are limited and fail to connect map skills with other curriculum areas, including mathematics (Muir & Cheek, 1986).

Such deficits may have negative ramifications past map use. Using and thinking about maps may contribute to spatial development by helping children acquire abstract concepts of space, the ability to think systematically about spatial relationships that they have not experienced directly, and the ability to consider multiple spatial relations among multiple locations (Uttal, 2000). Some evidence supports this possibility. As we have seen, children benefit from exposure to overhead views (Rieser et al., 1982), at least when children *use* the information (cf. Liben & Yekel, 1996), and to maps (Uttal & Wellman, 1989). Indeed, using maps to teach children locations before they entered the space helped children to identify rooms out of the learned sequence, thus it improved their mental representation of that space (Uttal & Wellman, 1989).

Research provides suggestions. Instruction on spatial ability, symbolization, and metacognitive skills (consciously self-regulated map reading behavior through strategic map referral) can increase four- to six-year-olds' competence with reading route maps, although it does not overcome age-related differences (Frank, 1987). Using oblique maps aids preschoolers' subsequent performance on plan ("bird's-eye view") maps, perhaps because symbolic understanding was developed (Liben & Yekel, 1996). Telling very young children that a model was the result of putting a room in a "shrinking machine" helped the children see the model as a symbolic representation of that space (DeLoache, Miller, Rosengren, & Bryant, 1997). Using structured maps that help pre-schoolers match the elements on the map with the corresponding elements in the space facilitated their use of maps (DeLoache, Miller, & Pierroutsakos, 1998).

Similarly, many of young children's difficulties do not reflect misunder-standing about space, but the conflict between such sensory-concrete and abstract frames of reference. Thus, adults might guide children to (a) develop abilities to build relationships among objects in space, (b) extend the size of that space, (c) link primary and secondary meanings and uses of spatial infor-mation, (d) develop mental rotation abilities, (e) go beyond "map skills" to engage in actual use of maps in local environments (Bishop, 1983), and (f) develop an understanding of the mathematics of maps.

There is some research indicating that navigation activities that combine physical movement, paper-and-pencil, and computer work can facilitate learning of mathematics and map skills. For example, young children can abstract and generalize directions and other map concepts working with the Logo turtle (Borer, 1993; Clements, Battista, Sarama, Swaminathan, & McMillen, 1997; Clements & Meredith, 1994; Goodrow, Clements, Battista, Sarama, & Akers, 1997; Kull, 1986; Try, 1989; J. A. Watson, Lange, & Brinkley, 1992; Weaver, 1991) although results are not guaranteed (Howell, Scott, & Diamond, 1987). The interface must be appropriate and activities must be well planned (J. A. Watson & Brinkley, 1990/91). Logo can also control a floor turtle robot, which may have special benefits for certain populations. For example, blind and partially sighted children using a computer-guided floor turtle developed spatial concepts such as right and left and accurate facing movements (Gay, 1989). Other simple (non-Logo) navigational programs may have similar benefits. For example, using such software (with on-screen navigation) has shown to increase kindergartners' understanding of the concepts of left and right (S. L. Carlson & White, 1998).

Such work integrates naturally with Logo experiences in which students examine shapes from the perspective of movement, as in walking a rectangular path. This perspective, corresponding roughly with differential geometry, considers the local, or intrinsic, properties of figures. Instructing the computer's Logo turtle to define figures using commands such as "forward 100" and "right 90" to help children learn geometric properties is explored in Chapter 8.

Most children probably encounter maps incidentally. Therefore, although the research reviewed here is suggestive, we know little about the potential of planned educational opportunities with maps, and the efficiency of introducing such opportunities to children of different ages. We do know children develop abilities with navigation, models, and maps early in their life. We need more research on systematic, research-based education, especially before recommendations for wide-scale changes can be made. Although children begin to develop skill with maps by the time they reach elementary school, they continue to build concepts and skills for many years to come. Most adults do not really understand maps, and often naively believe that maps are simply miniaturizations of the world. We do not yet know if early experiences are effective and efficient (e.g., first grade may be more efficient than earlier, Frank, 1987), and need to learn more about the nature of efficacious educational experiences.

Similarly, young children can use coordinates on maps or graphs that are provided for them, but we have too little evidence of the short- and long-range effects of structured experiences. Across the early childhood and primary grades, children should learn to (a) quantify what the grid labels represent,

(b) connect their counting acts to those quantities and to the labels, (c) subsume these ideas to a part-whole scheme connected to both the grid and to counting/arithmetic, and eventually (d) construct proportional relationships in this scheme. Children who do so can mentally structure grids as two-dimensional spaces, demarcated and measured with "conceptual rulers" ("mental number lines"—see Chapter 10). To achieve this, they need to learn to mentally internalize the structure of grids as two-dimensional spaces, demarcated and measured with conceptual rulers. They must integrate their numerical and spatial schemes to form a conceptual ruler (Clements, Battista, Sarama, Swaminathan et al., 1997; Steffe, 1991). They must then integrate conceptual rulers into two orthogonal number lines that define locations in that space. This integration is a distributive coordination; that is, one conceptual ruler must be taken as a mental object for input to another, orthogonal, conceptual ruler (Sarama et al., 2003).

Real-world contexts can be helpful in teaching coordinates initially, but mathematical goals and perspectives should be clearly articulated throughout instruction and the contexts should be faded from use as soon as students no longer need them (Sarama et al., 2003). Computer environments can additionally aid in developing children's ability and appreciation for the need for clear conceptions and precise work. The ethereal quality of a toggled screen grid can help scaffold children's creation of a mental construct that they project on the plane. Coordinate-based games on computers can help older children learning location ideas (Sarama et al., 2003). When children enter a coordinate to move an object but it goes to a different location, the feedback is natural, meaningful, and nonevaluative.

Research also suggests cautions regarding some popular teaching strategies. For example, phrases such as "over and up" and "the x-axis is the bottom," which we recorded on numerous occasions, do not generalize well to a four-quadrant grid. The "over and up" strategy also hinders the integration of coordinates into a coordinate pair (Sarama et al., 2003). Overall, coordinates can serve as a useful vehicle to develop geometric concepts and divergent thinking (Arnold & Hale, 1971).

Previously we considered the Logo turtle's command intrinsic commands of "FD" and "RT." This perspective can be contrasted with an extrinsic perspective, in which one "looks down" on the plane, as in coordinate systems. Logo also includes coordinate commands, suggesting that a curriculum might use both to help children learn more about, and distinguish between, intrinsic and extrinsic conceptualizations. The importance of this can be argued from a mathematical standpoint—laying the foundation for both differential and analytic geometry—and from a psychological standpoint—there is evidence that intrinsic geometry has its developmental roots in a coordination of the somatic and locomotive sensorimotor subsystems, whereas extrinsic geometry has it roots in visual subsystems (Lawler, 1985). Research indicates that use of

Logo's coordinate commands aid learning, especially mathematical generalization and abstraction, in both grid and coordinate systems (Sarama et al., 2003). Illustrations of these approaches can also be found in the companion book.

Building Imagery and Spatial Visualization

As early as the preschool years, through to first grade, U.S. children perform lower than children in countries such as Japan and China on spatial visualization and imagery tasks (Starkey et al., 1999; Stigler et al., 1990). There is more cultural support for activities in these countries (e.g., using visual representations, expecting competency in drawing), and, similarly, within cultural groups within the U.S., and within higher SES families in all countries (Starkey et al., 1999; Thirumurthy, 2003). Research shows that even pre-K and kindergarten children show initial transformational abilities in certain settings. Although incomplete, research suggests that all children benefit from developing their ability to create, maintain, and represent mental images of mathematical objects.

There is limited research on the precise nature of tasks that effectively develop other spatial visualization and imagery competencies. Research indicates that several approaches may be beneficial for primary-grade children, and similar activities may help younger children. For example, primary grade children whose schools use manipulatives performed better on tests of spatial ability than in those schools lacking use of such materials (Bishop, 1980). There is correlational evidence that puzzle play at home, and talk with parents, improves children's mental transformation scores, especially for girls (Cannon, Levine, & Huttenlocher, 2007). Further, play with "boys' toys" may lead to higher visual-spatial skills—at least the two are correlated (Serbin & Connor, 1979). Girls more than boys used verbally-mediated strategies to solve spatial problems, which may have accounted for the facilitation of parent talk.

Educational experiences can help children of almost any age. Spatial training in identifying a fixed location from two orientations was effective with infants as young as six (but not four) months of age (D. Tyler & McKenzie, 1990).

In a similar vein, primary-school children who engaged in spatial problem-solving activities requiring diverse imagery improved in spatial thinking (Owens, 1999). A unit emphasizing transformational geometry improved spatial perception of grade 2 students (Del Grande, 1986). Specific training on simple mental transformations of shapes was not more effective than simple practice in one study (Ehrlich, Levine, & Goldin-Meadow, 2006). But both increased competence, suggesting that intentional activities can be valuable, and may be especially important for girls.

Finally, suggestions can be garnered from tasks included in curricula that have significant effects on spatial competencies (even though the nature of the studies do not allow delineating the specific effects of individual tasks). These include tactile kinesthetic tasks, geometric "snapshots" activities (Clements & Sarama, 2003a; Razel & Eylon, 1986, 1990; Wheatley, 1996; Yackel & Wheatley, 1990), constructing shapes from parts with multiple media (C. Edwards, Gandini, & Forman, 1993), composing and decomposing shapes (Clements & Sarama, 2003a; Klein, Starkey, & Ramirez, 2002; Razel & Eylon, 1986, 1990) and geometric motions on the computer (Clements et al., 2001).

How do children learn *mental* transformations from such activities? There is some evidence that they *curtail* physical movement as they slowly develop mental visualization competence (Clements & Burns, 2000; Krutetskii, 1976). For example, primary-grade students learn turns by progressively constructing imagery and concepts related to turns (Clements, Battista, Sarama, & Swaminathan, 1996). They gain experience with physical rotations, especially rotations of their own bodies. In parallel, they gain limited knowledge of assigning numbers to certain turns, initially by establishing benchmarks. Through a synthesis of these two schemes, they build dynamic, quantitative mental transformations that they can project onto static figures. They do this through *psychological curtailment* (recall Chapter 5's discussion of curtailment in the developing of the ability to use counting-on). Curtailment is the gradual construction of mental images and manipulations of those images to "stand in for" what was a physical strategy (global, whole body, L-hands, etc.). We posit that this is an image schema, (M. Johnson, 1987) or a mental model. That is, it is an internalized dynamic mental image acquired through bodily experience that allows the individual to "re-present" relevant features of that experience. So, we see progressive development from movements of large portions of the body to smaller portions (hand, head); we see movement from pronounced full movement of these portions to abbreviated movement of them, to no movement but staring at the screen, which we theorize is the enactment of the mental image-based version of those movements. In a later phase, compilation process may make these mental processes quicker and more effortless (Anderson, 1983). Teachers aware of this process can observe the behavioral signs and support the curtailment with modeling and discussions. They can also use environments, like Logo's turtle math, that support these learning processes.

Building spatial abilities early is effective and efficient. For example, grade 2 children benefitted more than grade 4 children from lessons taught to develop spatial thinking (Owens, 1992). In 11 lessons, children described the similarities and differences of shapes, made shapes from other shapes, made outlines using sticks, compared angles, made pentomino shapes and found their symmetries. Those children outperformed a control group in a randomized field trial on a spatial thinking test, with differences attributable to the grade 2 children. No difference was found between groups that worked cooperatively or individually, with whole-class discussions. Nearly all interactions that led to heuristics about what to do or to conceptualizations were between the teacher and the student, not between students (Owens, 1992).

Learning Trajectories for Spatial Thinking

Table 7.1 provides the developmental progression and the mental actions-on-objects for *two* learning trajectories for spatial thinking: spatial orientation (maps and coordinates) and spatial visualization and imagery. *However, these two learning trajectories represent only a small bit of the role of spatial thinking in mathematics.* We saw that spatial and structural thinking is critical in (visual) subitizing, counting strategies, and arithmetic. Such spatial knowledge

Table 7.1 Learning Trajectories for Spatial Thinking

Age (years)	Developmental Progression	Actions on Objects
a. Spatial Orientation (including maps and coordinates)		
0–2	**Landmark and Path User** Uses a distance landmark to find an object or location near it, if they have not personally moved relative to the landmark. Understands initial vocabulary of spatial relations and location.	To simple response learning (associating an object with a given perceptual-motor response), the system develops and uses cue learning, in which landmarks are associated with objects in proximity to that landmark. The particular, single, visual perspective of the system (i.e., when the system is not moved) supports the association in the first year of life. When the system is moved, bootstrapped path integration systems allow encoding of approximate distance and direction, especially when the movement is self-directed.
2–3	**Local-Self Framework User** Uses distant landmarks to find objects or location near them, even after they have moved themselves relative to the landmarks, *if* the target object is specified ahead of time. Orients a horizontal or vertical line in space (Rosser, Horan et al., 1984).	Increasing ability to code spatial information for multiple objects and form and use spatial relations between those objects—as long as those objects include the system's own position (that is, the objects are coded in relation to the self)—allows better use of objects' locations. This depends on the self's own location, which may not be maintained after movement. Over the years 3 to 6, the system develops better coding for the spatial relationships between the objects independent of the self, including frameworks using its own (remembered) position. Making correspondences between familiar spaces and aligned, direct representations (photographs or simple models) is a bootstrapped ability.

Age (years)	Developmental Progression	Actions on Objects
4	**Small Local Framework User** Locates objects after movement, even if target is not specified ahead of time. Searches a small area comprehensively, often using a circular search pattern. Extrapolates lines from positions on both axes and determines where they intersect in meaningful contexts.	Codes the locations of several objects in a small area, along with their relationships, and stores and mentally marks that locations that have been searched. Path integration improves in accuracy. In perceptually supported tasks, creates an imagistically-guided direction from given lines and traces these to where they meet. (May not be able to hold this in memory or explicitly understand the process.)
5	**Local Framework User** Locates objects after movement (relates several locations separately from own position), maintaining the overall shape of the arrangement of objects. Represents objects' positions relative to landmarks (e.g., about half way in between two landmarks) and keeps track of own location in open areas or mazes. Some use coordinate labels in simple situations.	System can retain memory of multiple objects and relationships without self-reference and place them into hierarchically-embedded relationships, allowing the construction and retrieval of the general shape of the arrangement of the objects and locations in the arrangement. The resulting *local* framework is used to encode the location of each object separately (e.g., an object is not tied only to nearby landmarks). Metric accuracy of place and path integration systems improves with age (for years).
6	**Map User** Locates objects using maps with pictorial cues. Can extrapolate two coordinates, understanding the integration of them to one position, as well as use coordinate labels in simple situations.	Increasing ability to integrate various systems of spatial orientation, to view spatial figures from multiple perspectives, and to hierarchically relate regions, allows use of higher-order spatial configurations and patterns to locate objects or plan searches.
7	**Coordinate Plotter** Reads and plots coordinates on maps.	Previous abilities are integrated to allow spatial structuring, mentally constructing an organization into two-dimensional space, the basis of coordinates.
8+	**Route Map Follower** Follows a simple route map, with more accurate direction and distances.	

Continued Overleaf

Age (years)	Developmental Progression	Actions on Objects
	Framework User Uses general frameworks that include the observer and landmarks. May not use precise measurement even when that would be helpful, unless guided to do so.	
	Can follow and create maps, even if spatial relations are transformed.	

b. Spatial Visualization and Imagery

Age (years)	Developmental Progression	Actions on Objects
0–3	**Simple Slider** Can move shapes to a location.	Bootstrap abilities.
4	**Simple Turner** Mentally turns object in easy tasks.	With immediate perceptual support, can build image of object and maintain it sufficiently to reproduce basic geometric motions on the image and enact that on the physical object represented.
	Given a shape with the top marked with color, correctly identifies which of three shapes it would look like if it were turned "like this" (90° turn demonstrated) before physically moving the shape.	Explicit concepts only about limited aspects of images (e.g., that moving objects nearer or farther from self increases or decreases its apparent size).
5	**Beginning Slider, Flipper, Turner** Uses the correct motions, but not always accurate in direction and amount.	With perceptual support, builds and maintains a mental image and (intuitively) applies slides, flips, or turns in simple situations (e.g., flip over vertical axes; 90° turns), but that intuition can be misdirected by misleading perceptual cues (e.g., specifying a left, rather than the correct right, turn to get a point at the bottom of a figure to orient to the left). Also, stimulus elements (especially those on edges) rather than wholes may be moved. Bootstrap sensitivity to symmetry is represented to allow the explicit recognition of simple symmetric figures.
	Knows a shape has to be flipped to match another shape, but flips it in the wrong direction.	
6	**Slider, Flipper, Turner** Performs slides and flips, often only horizontal and vertical, using manipulatives. Performs turns of 45, 90, and 180 degrees.	Previous competence extended to resist misleading perceptual cues and to increasingly coordinate movement of multiple elements of the object, leading to more accurate performance in similarly simple situations. Anticipates motions on objects (but not representational levels).
	Knows a shape must be turned 90° to the right to fit into a puzzle.	

Age (years)	Developmental Progression	Actions on Objects
7	**Diagonal Mover** Performs diagonal slides and flips. Knows a shape must be turned and flipped over a oblique line (45° orientation) to fit into a puzzle.	Extends abilities to perform diagonal slides and flips. System can mentally represent simple slides and turns without perceptual support, storing initial state, motion, and ending state.
8+	**Mental Mover** Predicts results of moving shapes using mental images. "If you turned this 120°, it would be just like this one."	Mental representation of initial state, motion, and final state support the prediction of various shape transformations using mental imagery.

is central to geometry, measurement, patterning, data presentation, and the other topics discussed in chapters to come.

Final Words

Research does not support a qualitative shift in spatial thinking, such as from egocentric to allocentric representations, nor does development proceed from topological to "Euclidean." Instead, children develop several spatial systems, they develop the effectiveness of each of these systems, and they develop more powerful ways of selecting or combining the information from each of the systems. They extend these abilities, especially as they represent space, starting in the second year of life. By connecting spatial representations to each other and to language, they gain the ability to *reason* and *communicate* about space. They use all these competencies to construct and select increasingly coordinated reference systems as frameworks for spatial organization.

Further, although infants are endowed with potential spatial competencies, experience-expectant processes (Greenough et al., 1987) engender their development. That is, experiences with space are sufficiently similar across cultures and individuals that developmental processes are almost guaranteed to have certain environmental inputs. Thus, inborn potentialities are no more or less fundamental than these expected environmental inputs; rather, the key is in their interaction. In summary, the infant possesses biologically-provided tools, which "bootstrap" and guide, but do not determine, development; instead, they interact with maturation and physical and social experience, with the role of these differing depending on the subdomain.

Although maps and models appear more apt representations of space than non-graphic language, it is interesting that children appear to use language to express and understand spatial concepts earlier and more easily than they use models and maps. Whether this is the result of language forms being more fundamental to human development (Newcombe & Huttenlocher, 2000) or merely the result of the relative amount of experience children receive with each form is an open research question.

The view expressed in this chapter clears up some confusion regarding the role of spatial sense in mathematics thinking. "Visual thinking" and "visual strategies" are not the same as spatial sense. Spatial sense as we describe it—all the abilities we use in "making our way" in the spatial sphere—is related to mathematical competencies (D. L. Brown & Wheatley, 1989; Clements & Battista, 1992; Fennema & Carpenter, 1981; Wheatley et al., 1994).

Visual thinking, as in the initial levels of geometric thinking, is thinking that is limited to surface-level, visual ideas. Given high-quality education, children move beyond that kind of visual thinking as they learn to manipulate dynamic images, as they enrich their store of images for shapes, and as they connect their spatial knowledge to verbal, analytic knowledge.

Perhaps most important for mathematics education is that children develop increasingly integrated representations that synthesize flexible imagery and geometric conceptualizations. We continue to discuss these issues in the following two chapters on shape and shape composition.

8
Shape

Shape is a fundamental construct in cognitive development in and beyond geometry. For example, young children form artifact categories characterized by similarity among instances in shape (Jones & Smith, 2002). Even very young children show strong biases to attend to fine-grained shape when learning novel object names, at least when directed to a rigid object. We begin by extending the arguments that opened Chapter 7 concerning the importance of geometric and spatial thinking. Then we introduce several theoretical perspectives on children's development of shape concepts, followed by our own hierarchic interactionist position that we believe is most consistent with existing evidence.

Background—Why Geometry and Spatial Thinking?

Performance in the U.S. and Other Countries

International comparisons show that (a) the poor performance of U.S. students in mathematics is as bad or worse in geometry than in most other topics and that (b) U.S. students do not learn much geometry from grade to grade (Mullis et al., 1997). In the TIMMS work, U.S. students scored at or near bottom in every geometry task (Beaton et al., 1996; A. Ginsburg, Cooke, Leinwand, Noell, & Pollock, 2005; Lappan, 1999). Indeed, geometry and measurement are the *weakest* areas in the most recent TIMSS and PISA international comparisons.

One intensive comparison of the math achievement of eighth-grade students in 30 countries covered 23 specific content knowledge and processing subskills. Findings revealed clear differences. U.S. students were particularly weak in geometry. More important, success in geometry was highly associated with logical reasoning and other important mathematical skills across the sampled countries (Tasuoka & Corter, 2004).

These differences emerge in the earliest years of life. In a study of preschoolers' mathematical knowledge, Chinese children outperformed U.S. children (matched on SES) on a test of numerical knowledge by 15 percent, but they outperformed U.S. children in spatial/geometric knowledge twice as much: 30 percent (Starkey et al., 1999).

A considerable research corpus from psychology and mathematics education shows that developmental levels of geometric and spatial thinking exist (have been empirically supported in many studies) and yet are oft-neglected in the U.S. (Clements, 2003; Clements & Battista, 1992; van Hiele, 1986). There is every reason, then, to suspect that students in the U.S. are not prepared for higher levels of thinking and therefore do not benefit from the (admittedly deficient) geometry education that is offered to them. Further, there is some research that shows that certain geometric and spatial experiences are achievable by young children and contribute to their mathematical development.

Professional Judgment

Some mathematicians go even farther than Freudenthal, positing that, except for simple calculation, geometric concepts underlie all of mathematical thought (e.g., Bronowski, 1947). Smith (1964) argues that mathematics is a special kind of language through which we communicate ideas that are essentially spatial; mathematics is a visual language. For Smith, this is increasing as one reaches college mathematics. From number lines to arrays, even quantitative, numerical, and arithmetical ideas rest on a geometric base. Cross-cultural research substantiates that core geometrical knowledge, like implicit basic number or quantitative knowledge, appears to be a universal capability of the human mind (Dehaene et al., 2006). For example, people from an isolated Amazonian community spontaneously made use of foundational geometric concepts, including points, lines, parallelism, and right angles when trying to identify intruders in pictures, and used distance and angular relationships in geometrical maps to locate hidden objects. Further, their profiles of difficulty were similar to those of American adults. They performed remarkably well in core concepts in topology (connectedness, closed shapes), Euclidean geometry (points, lines, parallelism, right angles), and geometric figures (square, circle, triangle). They had more difficulty, but performed above chance, in detecting symmetries and metric properties (e.g., equidistance between points). They had the most difficulty with geometric motions and mirror images, both of which require a mental transformation of one shape into another, followed by a second-order evaluation of this transformation (Dehaene et al., 2006).

We should not forget geometry's relation to science and mathematics. Two of the most prominent physicists of the last 100 years attributed their advancements to geometry. As a boy, Einstein was fascinated by a compass, leading him to think about geometry and mathematics. He taught himself extensively about geometry by age 12. Later in life, Einstein said that his elements of thought were always initially geometric and spatial, including "certain . . . more or less clear images which can be voluntarily reproduced or combined." "Conventional words or other signs have to be sought for laboriously only in a secondary stage, when the associative play is sufficiently established." Hawking put it this way: "Equations are just the boring part of mathematics. I attempt to see things in terms of geometry." They are not exceptions. Visual thinking played a dominant role in the thinking of Michael Faraday, Sir Francis Galton, Nikola Tesla, James D. Watson, René Thom and Buckminster Fuller, among others (Shepard, 1978a).

There are mathematicians who study geometry who agree. "Geometry should be a focus at every age, in every grade, every year. Math curricula are often criticized for their insularity—'what does this have to do with the real world?' No mathematical subject is more relevant than geometry. It lies at the heart of physics, chemistry, biology, geology and geography, art and architecture. It also lies at the heart of mathematics, though through much of the 20th century the centrality of geometry was obscured by fashionable abstraction. This is changing now, thanks to computation and computer graphics which make it possible to reclaim this core without loss of rigor. The elementary school curriculum should give the children the tools they will need tomorrow" (Marjorie Senechal, personal communication).

Further, a report by a committee including eminent mathematicians H. S. M. Coxeter and W. W. Sawyer proclaimed that geometry was essential for all grades, especially because "geometric literacy is lower than numerical literacy" (K-13 Geometry Committee, 1967). They also stated that geometry plays a basic role in physical science, engineering, and some role in nearly every other subject, and that it has strong aesthetic connections.

A major researcher and developer in mathematics, Zal Usiskin, has repeatedly made strong cases that geometry is the domain that (a) connects mathematics with the real, physical world (critical for numerous fields), (b) studies visual structures and patterns, (c) represents phenomena whose original is not physical or visual (e.g., graphs, networks), and (d) brings coherence to all of these, because they all use the same mathematical language for describing space (Usiskin, 1997). Usiskin argued geometry must start in the earliest year of schooling.

Research on Geometric Thinking

As seen in Chapter 7 regarding spatial thinking, developing geometric knowledge contributes to a growth in mathematical competence and in other cognitive abilities, including IQ (Clements & Battista, 1992; Clements & Sarama, 2007b). Geometric knowledge, in particular, is highly related to mathematical reasoning and a host of other mathematics concepts and skills (Tasuoka et al., 2004). This included proportional reasoning, judgmental application of knowledge, concepts and properties, and managing data and processing skills, leading the authors to conjecture that geometry may be a gateway skill to the teaching of higher-order mathematics thinking skills. Further, we know that spatial ability contributes to cognition in broad and multiple ways (Newcombe & Huttenlocher, 2000).

Considering these bodies of research and professional judgments, it is probable that U.S. students' learning not only of all topics geometric, but also of measurement, coordinates, graphs and other visual displays, the large number of geometric models for arithmetic and algebraic concepts and operations, and yes, even proof, suffers as a result of inattention to geometric and spatial thinking from the earliest years. Even less salient, but perhaps just as important, is the harm such spatial ignorance does to students' learning of related topics in other subject-matter domains such as computer graphics, navigation, geography, the visual arts, and architecture. The U.S. Employment Service estimates that most technical-scientific occupations such as draftsman, airplane designer, architect, chemist, engineer, physicist, and mathematician require persons having spatial ability at or above the 90th percentile.

Theories of Young Children's Perception and Knowledge of Shape

Piaget

Piaget and Inhelder (1967) claimed that young children initially discriminate objects on the basis of "topological" features, such as being closed or otherwise topologically equivalent, especially when given only tactile, rather than visual, perceptions of the shapes. Only older children could discriminate rectilinear from curvilinear forms and, finally, among rectilinear closed shapes, such as squares and diamonds, via systematic and coordinated explorations. However, as previously discussed with regard to spatial thinking, there has been decreasing support for this view. One criticism has been that Piaget and Inhelder's use of the terms such as topological, separation, proximity, and Euclidean, as well as the application of these and related concepts to the design of their studies, are not mathematically accurate (Darke, 1982; Kapadia, 1974; Martin, 1976b). For example, proximity, in Piaget and Inhelder's interpretation of "nearbyness," is not topological, for it involves distance. Piaget and Inhelder also claim that only by the stage of formal operations (11 or 12 years) do children synthesize notions of proximity, separation, order, and enclosure to form the notion of continuity. However, continuity is not the synthesis of these concepts; it is a defining concept of topology. If it does not develop until a late stage, the argument for the primacy of topological concepts is weakened (Darke, 1982; Kapadia, 1974). In a similar vein, classifying figures as topological or Euclidean is problematic, as all figures possess both these characteristics and many of the figures Piaget and Inhelder used were topologically equivalent (see Figure 8.1). Decades ago, researchers reported that even at the earliest ages (two to three years), children can distinguish between curvilinear and rectilinear shapes, contrary to the theory (Lovell, 1959; Page, 1959).

Other studies showed children a test shape and then, after its removal, asked children to identify a shape "most like" it. One (Esty, 1970, cited in Darke, 1982) found that four-year-olds classified the topologically-equivalent shapes

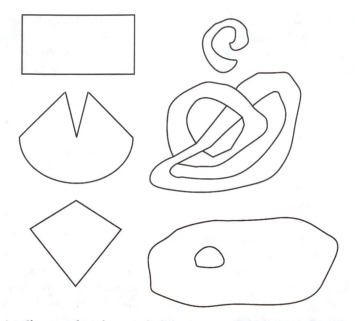

Figure 8.1 Shapes such as those on the left were considered "Euclidean" by Piaget and Inhelder in their haptic perception experiments; those on the right were considered to be "topological forms."

to be most like the original. However, older groups of children chose them as least like the original. Martin (1976a) used a set of shapes and three variants: A was topologically equivalent to the model. B and C, though not strictly equivalent to the model in a Euclidean sense, preserved as many Euclidean properties of the model as consistent with the fact that they had been altered to eliminate a particular topological property. Thus, B and C preserved properties such as straightness, curvature, line segment length, and angle size that A failed to preserve. But B failed to preserve connectedness and C varied closedness. Four-year-olds tended to choose the copy that was topologically equivalent as the "worst" copy of the model less often than older children. But, the "worst" scores were at or above chance levels and thus did not lend support to Piaget and Inhelder's theory. In addition, four-year-olds sacrificed topological properties in their selections as freely as did eight-year-olds.

A difficulty in designing such experiments is in quantifying the degree of equivalence of the shapes. Geeslin and Shar (1979) modeled figures via a finite set of points on a grid. Degree of distortion was defined as the sum of displacements of these points. The authors postulate that children compare two figures in terms of the amount of "distortion" necessary to transform one figure into another, after an attempt at superimposition using rigid motions and dilations. This model received strong support; however it is more pre-dictive than explanatory. In agreement with other research, preschool to grade 4 children were cognizant of both topological and Euclidean properties and how these properties distinguished variants. A small number of students at each level favored either topological or Euclidean properties. Note that, as the authors admit, these studies dealt with perception, whereas Piaget and Inhelder specifically addressed representation.

In sum, results of many of the Piagetian studies may be an artifact of the particular shapes chosen and the abilities of young children to identify and name these shapes (G. H. Fisher, 1965). This does not support a strong version of the topological primacy thesis. It may not be topological properties as a class that enable young children to identify certain shapes. Visually salient properties such as holes, curves, and corners; simplicity; and familiarity may underlie children's discrimination.

However, this discrimination *is*, at least in some sense, mathematical—a first rendering of considerable capability, the *initial bootstraps* of hierarchic interactionalism. That is, children probably have innate knowledge of (Euclidean/topological) geometric properties. A study of children and adults from the U.S. and an isolated Amazonian community with no presence of geometric representations or vocabulary revealed that all groups performed quite well on geometric oddity task (which one is not like the others). For example, when shown six shapes, five rectangles and one non-square rhombus, as in Figure 8.2, 86 percent of the Amazonians chose the rhombus.

Across tasks, they performed remarkably well in core concepts in topology (connectedness, closed shapes), Euclidean geometry (parallelism, right angles), and geometric figures (square, circle, triangle). They had more difficulty, but performed above chance, in detecting symmetries and metric properties (e.g., equidistance between points). They had the most difficulty with geometric motions (e.g., two triangles in a line- or mirror-symmetry relation) and mirror

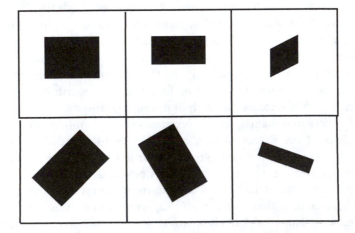

Figure 8.2 Which of these shapes does not belong with the others?

images. These both require a mental transformation of one shape into another, followed by a second-order evaluation of this transformation. This property, or the difficulty of depicting such transformations in static pictures, may have caused the low performance. Amazonian children and adults, and U.S. children, scored about the same on all tasks. U.S. adults performed better. So, culture and learning make a substantial difference, but core geometrical knowledge, like implicit basic number or quantitative knowledge, appears to be a universal capability of the human mind.

Although the topological primacy thesis is not supported, Piaget and Inhelder's theory included a second theme. They claim that children's representation of space is not a perceptual apprehension of their spatial environment, but is constructed from prior active manipulation of that environment. From this perspective, abstraction of shape is the result of a coordination of children's actions. Children "can only 'abstract' the idea of such a relation as equality on the basis of an action of equalization, the idea of a straight line from the action of following by hand or eye without changing direction, and the idea of an angle from two intersecting movements" (p. 43). The Piagetian's tactile-kinesthetic experiments appeared to support this view.

Gibson

In contrast, Gibson (1969) stated that motor activity plays at most an indirect role in perception. She also disagreed with the empiricists who believed perception was a matter of association. Instead, she claimed that perception involves both learning and development, increasing the person's ability to (selectively) extract information from the stimulation in the environment. Her theory is similar to Gestalt theory, which emphasized (a) wholes, irreducible to parts, that drive toward "best structures," and (b) developmental processes including articulation and differentiation, rather than accretion by association. However, Gibson emphasizes learning in sensory reorganization through processes of filtering and abstraction. Perception begins as only crudely differentiated and grossly selected. With growth and exposure, perception becomes better differentiated and more precise, as the person learns detection of properties, patterns, and distinctive features. Gibson suggested that learning is facilitated by instructors emphasizing distinctive features and by beginning with broad differences in those features and moving toward finer distinctions.

From this perspective, perception is active, adaptive, internally directed, and self-regulated. In contrast to a radical constructivist orientation, Gibson assumes an external reality, including structure and information already existing in the stimulus, without the need for cognitive mediation. Consistent with the constructivist interpretation, other research indicates that, although components such as edge-lines may already be discrete, and basic perceptual competencies such as size constancy (correcting for variations in distance) inborn (Granrud, 1987; Slater, Mattock, & Brown, 1990), one cannot claim ontological reality is divided into invariants (E. Wright, 1983). That is, there is no "information" in the environment separate from the individual.

Van Hieles

Also in the constructivist tradition, but addressing later development, the theory of Pierre and Dina van Hiele posits that students progress through qualitatively distinct levels of thought in geometry (van Hiele, 1986; van Hiele-Geldof, 1984). At Level 1, the "visual" level, students can only recognize shapes as wholes and cannot form mental images of them. A given figure is a rectangle, for example, because "it looks like a door." They do not think about the defining attributes, or properties,[1] of shapes. At level 2, descriptive/analytic, students recognize and characterize shapes by their properties. For instance, a child might think of a square as a figure that has four equal sides and four right angles. Students find that some combinations of properties signal a class of figures and some do not; thus the seeds of geometric implication are planted. Students at this level do not, however, see relationships between classes of figures (e.g., a child might believe that a figure is not a rectangle because it is a square). Many students do not reach this level until middle or even high school.

Hierarchic Interactionalism

The hierarchic interactionalism perspective builds most directly on elaborations and revisions of the most educationally relevant theory, that of the van Hieles, introducing other theoretical and empirical contributions. To begin, although both theories posit domain specific developmental progressions, hierarchic interactionalism hypothesizes several revisions of the van Hiele levels (Clements & Battista, 1992). These revisions have been subsequently supported (Clements, Battista et al., 2001b; Clements et al., 1999; Yin, 2003).

THE FIRST LEVEL OF GEOMETRIC THOUGHT

A level antecedent to the visual level is required to describe the empirical corpus. At level 0, pre-recognition, children cannot reliably distinguish circles, triangles, and squares from nonexampless of those classes. Children at this level are just starting to form visual schemes for the shapes. These early, unconscious schemes are formed through several initial bootstrap competencies. For example, pattern matching through a type of feature analysis (Anderson, 2000; E. J. Gibson, Gibson, Pick, & Osser, 1962) is conducted after the visual image of the shape is transformed by heuristics built into the visual system that imposes an intrinsic frame of reference on the shape, possibly using symmetry (Palmer, 1989).

BUILDING WHOLES AND PARTS OF SHAPES

Research indicates that even infants can perceive wholes as well as parts of geometric patterns (Bornstein & Krinsky, 1985) and that children as young as three years engage in active spatial analysis in both construction (Tada & Stiles, 1996) and in perception (Feeney & Stiles, 1996), a process that changes with development. That is, children will draw a "+" sign using four separate line segments, treating intersections as junctions of separate parts, and will even choose four small segments as being most like the goal object. Older children produce one long vertical and two short horizontal segments, and adults two long segments. As another example, when copying a square divided into fourths (all lines parallel or perpendicular), some young children use all short segments, and others use multiple closed forms (e.g., four squares drawn inside the larger square). As early as four and a half years, most children's constructions are similar to those of adults. Thus, the youngest children parse out simple, well-formed, spatially independent parts and use simple combination rules such as seriation and adjacency, then organization around a central point, to connect these parts. Older children relate parts across intersections and parse out continuous unsegmented parts, coordinating relations across boundaries (Tada & Stiles, 1996). These first units may be inborn, well-defined, rigid, unarticulated primary structures that may not follow Gestalt principles. Indeed, Gestalt processes themselves, and what adults perceive, may be a result of a developmental process. Development includes both components of "spatial analysis"—identification of the parts of a geometric form and, most importantly, *integration of those parts into a coherent whole*. Whereas four-year-olds use fragmented strategies, such as drawing segmented forms radiating around a central point, children as young as six years of age possess multiple spatial analytic strategies and can, in simple situations, use strategies like those of adults. The strategy they use is a function of both their capabilities and the complexity of the pattern they are copying (Akshoomoff & Stiles, 1995). Throughout development, children process more parts and more difficult sets of relations, such as intersections and oblique segments, in increasingly higher-order *hierarchical* units (Akshoomoff & Stiles, 1995).

Simple, closed shapes may initially tend to form undifferentiated, cohesive units in children's phenomenological perceptual experiences (cf. L. B. Smith, 1989). (Research suggests that shapes are perceived holistically with a separate subsystem: Ganel & Goodale, 2003.) For example, contour is a salient characteristic for young children (e.g., Tada & Stiles, 1996) that, when suggestive of a spatially continuous object, may direct the perception of the shape as a whole unit. Nascent schemes may ascertain the presence of the features of closed and "rounded" to match circles, "pointy" features along a figural scan-path to match triangles (without necessarily attaching numerical significance to this path, cf. Glasersfeld, 1982; Piaget & Szeminska, 1952), four near-equal sides with approximately right angles to match squares, and approximate parallelism of opposite "long" sides to match rectangles.

Experiencing multiple examples of a shape begins the formation of a class of shapes. This often begins with exemplars[2] of a shape category, which engenders the formation of a mental prototype, one form of semanticized episodic memory in which multiple cases are very similar. The memory of these cases loses any trace to specific time and place, because the neocortex region of the brain records similar events/objects in overlapping ensembles of neurons (Nadel & Moscovitch, 1998).

Research has substantiated that children possess several different prototypes for figures (e.g., a vertically and a horizontally-oriented rectangle) without accepting the "middle" case (e.g., an obliquely-oriented rectangle). In one study, subjects studied a preponderance of rectangles with extreme values and few intermediate values of variables such as size (Neumann, 1977). Subjects were presented with test items and asked to rate their confidence that they had already studied that particular item. Interestingly, the subjects rated the extremes (e.g., large or small rectangles) much higher than items created by using the mean of these values (e.g., middle-sized rectangles), showing that they extracted multiple foci of centrality, thereby creating several visual prototypes. Thus, they did not cognitively "average" what they had studied. This finding is consistent with studies on the van Hiele theory (Burger & Shaughnessy, 1986; Clements & Battista, 1992; Clements, Battista et al., 2001b; Fuys, Geddes, & Tischler, 1988).

As they refine these prototypes into increasingly elaborated triangle schemas (cognitive networks of relationships connecting geometric concepts and processes in specific patterns), children develop, tacitly at first, the ability to "see" both the parts *and* the whole so that they do not consider an angle (e.g., an upside-down "V") to be a triangle. Similarly, they learn not to focus only on the enclosing, simple contour of the shape that initially led them to consider shapes such as chevrons (deltoids) to be triangles (K. Owens, 1999).

Typical "geometry deprived" (Fuys et al., 1988) young children have a limited number of imagistic schemes for triangle, such as isosceles triangles. That is, their schemes remain chained to a prototype. One five-year-old, for example, separated the triangles as in Figure 8.3, arguing that the ones on the right were "half triangles" and placing them so that, together, they approximated an isosceles triangle that apparently corresponded to his prototype (B. A. Clarke, 2004).

Other children may have two imagistic schemes, such as an equilateral triangle and a right triangle, both with a horizontal base (Hershkowitz et al., 1990; Vinner & Hershkowitz, 1980). These prototype schemes are not absolutely rigid, but they have constraints. For example, the more the lengths of the legs of a right triangle differ in length, the less likely it will be assimilated to that prototype. Such schemes can be thought of as having multivariate distributions

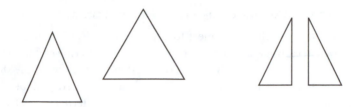

Figure 8.3 Two isosceles triangles and two right triangles.

of possible values (e.g., for the relationships between the side lengths and for degree of the base's rotation from the horizontal) in which the nearer to the mode of the distribution the perceived figure is (equal for the side lengths and 0° rotation of the base for this example), the more likely it will be assimilated to that prototype (parallel distributed processing, or PDP, networks and other structural theories model this type of system, see Clements & Battista, 1992; McClelland et al., 1986).

THE ROLE OF LANGUAGE

As the initial schemas are developing, so do mappings similar to those of number, color, and other properties (Sandhofer & Smith, 1999). That is, children first learn that the question "what shape?" is answered by words such as "circle" and "square." They then map these shape words to a few sensory-concrete examples. Next, they combine these abilities to produce correct shape names for prototypical examples of common shapes. Only after these experiences do they build shape categories (probably because the PDP-type networks of each of these examples contains much more information than geometric shape and thus property-to-property matching and shape category creation is a slower developmental process, cf. Sandhofer & Smith, 1999). Thus, shape words and names help organize and direct attention to the relevant features of objects.

This analysis reveals that the nature of the van Hielian levels also requires clarification. The "visual" level includes visual/imagistic and verbal declarative knowledge ("knowing what") about shapes. That is, it is not viable to conceptualize a purely visual level (1), followed and replaced by a basically verbal descriptive level (2) of geometric thinking—a common interpretation. Instead, different types of reasoning—those characterizing different levels—coexist in an individual and can be developing simultaneously but at different rates. Consistent with the tenet of *progressive hierarchization*, levels do not consist of unadulterated knowledge of only one type. This view is consistent with literature from Piagetian and cognitive traditions (e.g., Minsky, 1986; Siegler, 1996; Snyder & Feldman, 1984), as well as reinterpretations of van Hielian theory (Clements & Battista, 1992; Gutiérrez, Jaime, & Fortuny, 1991; Lehrer, Jenkins, & Osana, 1998; Pegg & Davey, 1998).

LEARNING ABOUT FEATURES, COMPONENTS, AND PROPERTIES

Certain conditions, such as a request to explain one's decision, may prompt children, even at early levels, to abstract, attend to, and describe certain features ("this is pointy"). They might also consciously attend to a subset of the shape's visual characteristics and use such a subset to identify geometric shapes. Thus, their descriptions of shapes may include a variety of terms and attributes (Clements, Battista et al., 2001b; Lehrer, Jenkins et al., 1998). However, these are "centrations" in the Piagetian sense, not integrated with other components of the shape. This supports the recognition of both comparison-to-prototype and attention-to-attributes in young children's geometric categorization (Clements et al., 1999; see also Lehrer, Jenkins et al., 1998). Conditions also affect how such features and prototype matching are processed. For example, young children's overall acceptance rate of both examples and nonexamples increases with the inclusion of palpable distractors (Hannibal & Clements, 2008).

Thus, even at a very early age children attend to some attribute of their imagistic scheme, even if it is only its "prickliness" for triangles (cf. Lehrer, Jenkins et al., 1998). Then, as the scheme becomes better formed, and, importantly, as the child gains the ability and predisposition to give increased selective attention to single dimensions when comparing objects (L. B. Smith, 1989), the child is able to discern more attributes (both defining and non-defining) that s/he uses to construct her or his definition of a triangle. They can match and identify many shapes (most reliably, exemplars determined by both biology and culture). However, they often attend only to a proper subset of a shape's visual characteristics and are unable to identify many common shapes. In tactile contexts, they can distinguish between figures that are curvilinear and those that are rectilinear but not among figures within those classes. Even in visual contexts, they may not be able to construct an image of shapes, or a representation of the image. They are unable to rotate shapes and place them into part-whole relationships (Wheatley & Cobb, 1990). Thus, before level 1, children lack the ability to construct and manipulate visual images of geometric figures. This example of *cyclic concretization* is consistent with the Piagetian tradition of the construction of geometric objects on the "perceptual plane" before a reconstruction on the "representational" or "imaginal plane" (Piaget & Inhelder, 1967).

Later in development, additional visual-spatial elements, such as the right angles of squares, are incorporated into these schemes and thus traditional prototypes may be produced. Further, older children can attend to these features separately, whereas younger children are not able or predisposed to focus on single features analytically (L. B. Smith, 1989; Vurpillot, 1976). Therefore, younger children can produce a prototype in identifying rectangles without necessarily attending to the components or specific features that constitute these prototypes. For children of all ages, the prototypes may be overgeneralized or undergeneralized compared to mathematical categorization, of course, depending on the examples and nonexamples and teaching acts children experience. Also, progress to strong level 1 and eventually to level 2 understanding is protracted. For example, primary grades continue to apply many different types of cognitive actions to shapes, from detection of features like fat or thin, to comparison to prototypical forms, to the action-based embodiment of pushing or pulling on one form to transform it into another (Clements, Battista et al., 2001b; Lehrer, Jenkins et al., 1998).

Thus, young children operating at levels 0 and 1 show evidence of recognition of components and attributes of shapes, although these features may not be clearly defined (e.g., sides and corners). Some children operating at level 1 appear to use both matching to a visual prototype (via implicit feature analysis) and reasoning about components and properties to solve these selection tasks. Thus, level 1 geometric thinking as proposed by the van Hieles is more syncretic (a fusion of differing systems) than visual, as Clements (1992) suggested. That is, this level is a synthesis of verbal declarative and imagistic knowledge, each interacting with and enhancing the other. We therefore suggest the term *syncretic level* (indicating a fusion of different perspectives), rather than *visual level*, because we wish to signify a global combination of verbal and imagistic knowledge without an analysis of the specific components and properties of figures. At the syncretic level, children more easily use declarative knowledge to explain why a particular figure is not a member of a class, because the contrast between the figure and the visual prototype provokes descriptions of differences (S. Gibson, 1985).

Children making the transition to the next level sometimes experience conflict between the two parts of the combination (prototype matching vs. component and property analysis), leading to mathematically incorrect and inconsistent task performance. For example, one girl started pre-K with a stable concept, a scheme of the triangle as a visual whole. However, when introduced instructionally to the attributes of triangles, she formed a separate scheme for a "three-sided shape." For some time thereafter, she held complex and unstable ideas about triangles, especially when the two schemes conflicted (Spitler, Sarama, & Clements, 2003). As another example, many young children call a figure a square because it "just looked like one," a typical holistic, visual response. However, some attend to relevant attributes; for them, a square had "four sides the same and four points". Because they had not yet abstracted perpendicularity as another relevant and critical attribute, some accept certain rhombi as squares (Clements, Battista et al., 2001b). That is, even if their prototype has features of perpendicularity (or aspect ratio—the ratio of height to base—near 1), young children base judgments on similarity (in this case, near perpendicularity) rather than on identity (perpendicularity), and therefore they accept shapes that are "close enough" (L. B. Smith, 1989). The young child's neglect of such relevant (identity) attributes or reliance on irrelevant attributes leads to categorization errors. This is consistent with early findings that preschoolers show a slow development of skills, sudden insight, and regression (Fuson & Murray, 1978).

Mervis and Rosch (1981) theorized that generalizations based on similarity to highly representative exemplars will be the most accurate. This theory would account for the higher number of correct categorizations by those children who appeared to be making categorization decisions on the basis of comparison to a visual prototype without attention to irrelevant attributes. Finally, strong feature-based schemes and integrated declarative knowledge, along with other visual skills, may be necessary for high performance, especially in complex, embedded configurations. To form useful declarative knowledge, especially robust knowledge supporting transition to level 2, children must construct and consciously attend to the components and properties of geometric shapes as cognitive objects (a learning process that requires mediation and is probably aided by physical construction tasks as well as reflection often prompted by discussion, points to which we return).

Thus, the hierarchic interactionalism theory predicts that children are developing stronger imagistic prototypes and gradually gaining verbal declarative knowledge. Those culturally popular classes of figures that are more symmetric and have fewer possible imagistic prototypes (circles and squares) are more amenable to the development of imagistic prototypes and thus show a straightforward improvement of identification accuracy. Rectangles and triangles have more possible prototypes. Rectangle identification may improve only over substantial periods of time. Similarly, shapes such as triangles, the least definable by imagistic prototypes discussed here, may show complex patterns of development as the scheme widens to accept more forms, overwidens, and then must be further constrained.

For example, many children might possess verbal declarative knowledge that may include the name "triangle" and a few statements of components, such as "three sides" and possibly "three corners." However, these statements are not constrained further; for example, there are few limitations placed on the nature of these sides (e.g., they might be curved) and corners. Such prototypes match many forms, so there is a wide acceptance. With repeated exposure to exemplars in the culture, these prototypes grow stronger; to the extent these exemplars are limited (e.g., mostly equilateral for many shape categories), acceptance decreases radically, leading to the child's rejection of both distractors and variants that do not closely match the visual prototype, which may have rigid constraints regarding aspect ratio, skewness, and orientation. This rejection may be particularly noticeable in situations in which shapes are drawn (or otherwise cannot be manipulated) and are presented in a canonical rectangular frame. Nascent declarative knowledge, while developing, does not gain transcendence in the scheme (consistent with the *hierarchic development* tenet of the theory). (Note this provides an elaboration and mechanism for the construct of concept images—a combination of all the mental pictures and properties that have been associated with the concept, Vinner & Hershkowitz, 1980.) Even people who know a correct verbal description of a concept and possess a specific visual image (or concept image) associated strongly with the concept may have difficulty applying the verbal description correctly. Eventually, exposure to a wider variety of examples and a strengthening of declarative knowledge ("three straight sides") leads to a wider acceptance of varieties of geometric figures while rejecting nonmembers of the class. Each type of knowledge increasingly constrains the other (*co-mutual development of concepts and skills*).

Children's variegated responses (some visual, some verbal declarative) may be another manifestation of this syncretic level. Further, they substantiate Clements' (1992) claim that geometric levels of thinking coexist, as previously discussed. Progress through such levels is determined by social influences, specifically instruction, as much or more than by age-linked development, especially beyond the preschool years. Although each higher level builds on the knowledge that constitutes lower levels, the nature of the levels does not preclude the instantiation and application of earlier levels in certain contexts (not necessarily limited to especially demanding or stressful contexts). For each level, there exists a probability for evocation for each of numerous different sets of circumstances, but this process is codetermined by conscious metacognitive control, control that increases as one moves up through the levels, so people have increasing choice to override the default probabilities (*progressive hierarchization*). The use of different levels is environmentally adaptive; thus, the adjective *higher* indicates a higher level of abstraction and generality, without implying either inherent superiority or the abandonment of lower levels as a consequence of the development of higher levels of thinking. Nevertheless, the levels would represent veridical qualitative changes in behavior, especially the construction of mathematical representations (i.e., construction of geometric objects) from action.

In summary, geometric knowledge at every level maintains nonverbal, imagistic components; that is, every mental geometric object includes one or more image schemes—recurrent, dynamic patterns of kinesthetic and visual actions (M. Johnson, 1987). Imagistic knowledge is not left untransformed and merely "pushed into the background" by higher levels of thinking. Imagery has a number of psychological layers, from more primitive to more sophisticated (each connected to a different level of geometric thinking), which play different (but always critical) roles in thinking depending on which layer is activated. Even at the highest levels, geometric relationships are intertwined with images, though these may be abstract images. Thus, images change over development. The essence of level 2 thinking, for example, lies in the integration and synthesis of properties of shapes, not merely in their recognition. Through the process of *progressive hierarchization*, children at this level have transcended the perceptual and have constructed the properties as singular mental geometric objects that can be acted upon, not merely as descriptions of visual perceptions or images (cf. Steffe & Cobb, 1988). Ideally, however, these objects are "neither words nor pictures" (Robert B. Davis, 1984, p. 189), but a synthesis of verbal declarative and rich imagistic knowledge, each interacting with and supporting the other. The question, therefore, should not be whether geometric thinking is visual or not visual, but rather, whether imagery is limited to unanalyzed, global visual patterns or includes flexible, dynamic, abstract, manipulable imagistic knowledge (Clements et al., 1999), knowledge has been representationally redescribed and is available for explicit conceptualization and verbalization. Figures 8.4 and 8.5 illustrate two contrasting conceptualizations of geometric levels of thinking.

It is important to note that this is educational/experiential, not merely maturational, growth. We describe the implications to these results in the following section.

Thinking and Learning about Specific Shapes

With these processes in mind, it is useful to consider children's learning about specific shapes. Infants may be born with a tendency to form certain mental prototypes. When people in a Stone Age culture with no explicit geometric

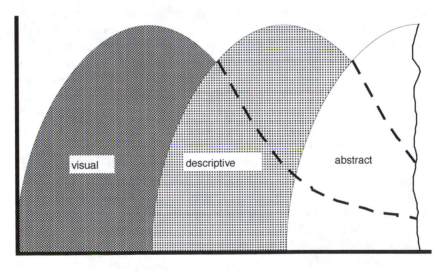

Time

Figure 8.4 Hypothesized linear view of the levels of geometric thinking.

Note: In the traditional view illustrated above, each level ripens to fruition, engenders the beginning of the next level—which incorporates and subordinates the earlier level—and finally fades away.

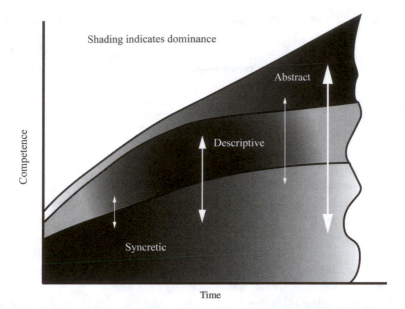

Figure 8.5 Hypothesized hierarchic interactionalism view of the levels of geometric thinking.

Note: In the hierarchic interactionalism view illustrated above, types of knowledge develop simultaneously. Although syncretic knowledge is dominant in the early years (darker shading indicates dominance of a particular level of thinking), descriptive knowledge is present and interacts with it, though weakly (symbolized by the small double arrow at the left). Syncretic knowledge, descriptive verbal knowledge, and, to a lesser extent initially, abstract symbolic knowledge grow simultaneously, as do their connections. When abstract knowledge begins ascendance, connections among all types are established and strengthened (symbolized by thicker arrows). Indicated only by the shading are the unconscious probabilities of instantiation associated with each level; in a related vein, but not illustrated, are the executive processes that also develop over time, serving to integrate these types of reasoning and, importantly, to determine which level of reasoning will be applied to a particular situation or task.

concepts were asked to choose a "best example" of a group of shapes, such as a group of quadrilaterals and near-quadrilaterals, they chose a square and circle more often, even when close variants were in the group (Rosch, 1975). For example, the group with squares included square-like shapes that were not closed, had curved sides, and had non-right angles. So, people might have innate preferences for closed, symmetric shapes (cf. Bornstein, Ferdinandsen, & Gross, 1981). Further, symmetry affects shape perception in two ways, on the global level (e.g., preference for symmetry about the vertical, and to lesser extent, horizontal axis) and local level (symmetries within a shape even if the axes are not vertical or horizontal). For example, global symmetries support the recognition of a prototypical "diamond" (with the long diagonal vertical) but the local symmetry still affects the recognition of any rhombus, even if oriented with a horizontal side (Palmer, 1985). Recall that implicit sensitivity to these geometric properties appears to be an initial bootstrap (Dehaene et al., 2006).

Culture influences these preferences. Educational materials introduce U.S. children to triangles, rectangles, and squares overwhelmingly in limited, rigid ways (see the companion book). These results are strikingly consistent with a similar study conducted in Turkey (Aslan & Aktas-Arnas, 2007a). Such limited conceptualizations are directly reflected in children's behaviors (Clements et al., 1999; Lehrer, Jenkins et al., 1998). In one study, four- to five-year olds considered rotated squares no longer the same shape or even size, six- to seven-year-olds retained its characteristics, but lost its category and name—it was no longer a square, and only by eight to nine years did students achieve invariance (Vurpillot, 1976). This may reflect systematic bias for horizontal and vertical lines and a need for perceptual learning and flexibility, but restricted experiences exacerbate such limitations. Research indicates that such rigid visual prototypes can rule children's thinking throughout their lives (Burger & Shaughnessy, 1986; N. D. Fisher, 1978; Fuys et al., 1988; Kabanova-Meller, 1970; Vinner & Hershkowitz, 1980; Zykova, 1969).

Research also identifies specific prototypes. Decades ago, Fuson and Murray (1978) reported that by three years of age over 60 percent of children could name a circle, square, and triangle. More recently, Klein, Starkey, and Wakeley (1999) reported shape-naming accuracy of middle-income five-year-olds as: circle, 85 percent, triangle, 80 percent (note all were close to isosceles), square, 78 percent, rectangle, 44 percent (note squares were not scored as correct choices). About a quarter of five-year-olds in Australia were able to name these common shapes, including a range of triangles, before any school experience (B. A. Clarke, 2004).

A study of young children used the same line drawings previously used with elementary students for comparison purposes (Clements et al., 1999); replication studies have been conducted in Singapore (Yin, 2003) and Turkey (Aslan, 2004). Children identified the circles accurately: 92 percent, 96 percent, and 99 percent for four-, five-, and six-year-olds, respectively in the U.S. (see the companion book for the figures). Only a few of the youngest children chose an ellipse and another curved shape. Most children described circles as "round," but few could offer any description. Evidence suggests that they matched the shapes to a visual prototype. Turkish children showed the same pattern (Aktas-Arnas & Aslan, 2004; Aslan, 2004; Aslan & Aktas-Arnas, 2007b).

Children also identified squares fairly well: 82 percent, 86 percent, and 91 percent for four-, five-, and six-year-olds, respectively. Younger children tended to mistakenly choose nonsquare rhombi; 25 percent of six-year-olds and 5 percent of seven-year-olds did so in Singapore. However, they were no less accurate in classifying squares without horizontal sides. In Singapore, seven-year-olds were less likely to correctly identify these as squares than were six-year-olds (Yin, 2003). Children in all three countries were more likely to be accurate in their square identification when their justifications for selection were based on the shape's defining attributes. In one study, children from Turkey did not give any property-based justifications until age four; 41 percent did so by the age of six years (Aktas-Arnas & Aslan, 2004). Further, when children did use properties they were correct most of the time (compare 70.2 percent correctness for visual responses to 91.3 percent for property responses).

Children were less accurate at recognizing triangles and rectangles (except in Turkey, where children identified these shapes only slightly less accurately, 68 percent and 71 percent, than squares, 73 percent, Aslan, 2004). However, their scores were not low; about 60 percent correct for triangles. Although ages differed, both the U.S. and Singapore data revealed a phase in which children chose more triangle examples and distractors, then "tightened" their criteria to omit some distractors but also some examples. The children's visual prototype seems to be of an isosceles triangle. Turkish children found triangles the most difficult to classify (Aslan & Aktas-Arnas, 2007b).

Young children tended to accept "long" parallelograms or right trapezoids as rectangles. Thus, children's visual prototype of a rectangle seems to be a four-sided figure with two long parallel sides and "close to" square corners.

Additionally interesting are cross-cultural and longitudinal comparisons. Similarly-aged children in the U.S. were slightly better than Singapore children on circles and squares, but the reverse was true for triangles, rectangles, and embedded figures (Yin, 2003)—the more complex tasks. However, these differences lacked statistical significance, so no conclusions can be drawn as yet.

Although young children in this study were less accurate recognizing triangles and rectangles, their performance shows considerable knowledge, especially given the abstract nature of the test and the variety of exemplars and nonexemplars employed. Striking was the lack of significant change from the preschool years to six grade (Clements, Battista et al., 2001b; Clements et al., 1999) as shown in Figures 8.6 and 8.7 (in addition, many of the elementary students were from high SES, high-achieving populations). Indeed, for all shapes assessed two trends were evident. First, as discussed previously, very young children possess knowledge of geometric figures. Second, children show a steady, but hardly remarkable, improvement from pre-K through the elementary grades.

In the follow-up study, children aged three to six were asked to sort a variety of manipulative forms (Hannibal & Clements, 2008). Certain mathematically irrelevant characteristics affected children's categorizations: skewness, aspect ratio, and, for certain situations, orientation. With these manipulatives, orientation had the least effect. Most children accepted triangles even if their base was not horizontal, although a few protested. Skewness, or lack of

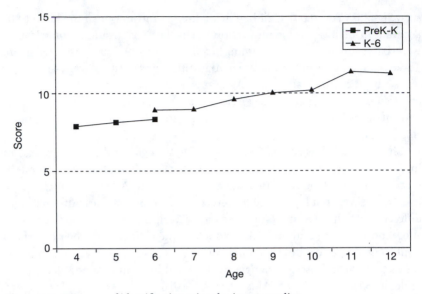

Figure 8.6 Accuracy of identification triangles in two studies.

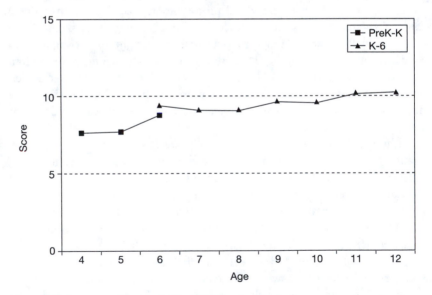

Figure 8.7 Accuracy of rectangle identification in two studies.

symmetry, was more important. Many rejected triangles because "the point on top is not in the middle." Turkish children showed the same pattern (Aslan & Aktas-Arnas, 2007b). For rectangles, on the other hand, many children accepted non-right parallelograms and right trapezoids. Also important was aspect ratio. Children preferred an aspect ratio near one for triangles; that is, about the same height as width. Other forms were "too pointy" or "too flat." Children rejected both triangles and rectangles that were "too skinny" or "not wide enough." These same factors (with an additional one of size in some cases) similarly affected children's judgments in Turkey (Aslan, 2004; Aslan & Aktas-Arnas, 2007b).

Another study addressed recognition of squares at various orientations. The percentage of primary children recognizing squares was 96.1 for squares with a horizontal base, and 93.2, 84.5, and 73.8 for rotated squares, the last 45° from the horizontal (Kerslake, 1979). It was not until the age of eight that children begin to generalize the concept of square. Again, the explanation for such phenomena may be that shapes are perceived relative to a reference-frame structure in which the orientation of the axes is taken as the descriptive standard. The visual system has heuristics for assigning the frame, which usually, but not always, allows the detection of shape equivalence. However, the reference orientation results from an interaction of intrinsic structure (e.g., symmetry) and orientation relative to the environment (verticality or gravity) and the observer (Palmer, 1989).

A study not designed to test the van Hiele theory also provides evidence on classification schemes. Children of three, four, five, seven, and nine years of age, and adults, were asked to sort shapes including exemplars, variants, and distractors (Satlow & Newcombe, 1998). A substantial change occurred between four and especially five years of age to seven years, consistent with Keil's description of characteristic-to-defining shifts, in which older children relied more on rule-based definitions and less on perceptual similarity than younger children. Younger children were more likely to accept distractors with characteristic features and reject variants. Development regarding recognition of variants was incremental, but identification of distractors showed sudden improvement. Consistent with research discussed, shapes with multiple variants, such as triangles, were more difficult. The authors state that this evidence refutes theories of general development, including Piaget's or the van Hieles'. However, the shift itself is consistent with our hierarchic interactionalism reinterpretations of van Hielian theory (Clements, Battista et al., 2001b).

In their play, children's behaviors were coded as "pattern and shape" more frequently than six other categories (Seo & Ginsburg, 2004). About 47 percent of these behaviors involved recognizing, sorting, or naming shapes. However, children's capabilities, in play and other situations, exceed just naming and sorting shapes. This continues into the primary grades, as we have seen (Lehrer, Jenkins et al., 1998). As a final example from the U.K., seven-year-olds were given a set of shapes in random order and asked to match and name each. More than 90 percent easily matched the shapes, but the percentage naming each was circle, 97.4, square, 96.4, equilateral triangle, 92.8, rectangle, 78.1, regular hexagon, 55.3, and regular pentagon, 31.1. They were also less confident about drawing those they had more difficulty naming. The percentage able to name properties of the shapes varied from 92 for the square to 80 for the pentagon. These data substantiate the conclusion, consistent across the studies reviewed here, that children can easily distinguish the shapes, but are exposed to a limited number of shape concepts and names. Although their performance is lower for unfamiliar shapes, these children can still name properties, further evidence that they are in "geometrically deprived" environments. We turn to additional aspects of children's knowledge of shape and spatial structure.

Representing (Drawing)

According to the Piagetian position, a drawing is an act of representation, not perception, so it also illustrates children's understanding of ideas. Young children's inability to draw or copy even simple shapes again argues that this understanding stems from coordinating their own actions, rather than passive perception. But could this be due simply to motor difficulties? Such difficulties do limit children's drawings. However, Piaget and Inhelder provide many examples that "motor ability" does not explain, such as the child who could draw a pine tree with branches at right angles but could not draw a square with right angles. Also, most children take two years to progress from drawing a (horizontal) square to drawing a (non square) rhombus. So, children need far more than a visual "picture." Again, we see the importance of action and exploration. Children benefit from trying to represent shapes in many ways, from drawing to building specific shapes with sticks or with their bodies.

Piagetian (Piaget & Inhelder, 1967) stages in drawing have been generally confirmed by mathematics education researchers. For example, an early study confirmed a sequence of drawings using scalogram analysis (Noelting, 1979). By one to two years of age, children may produce different kinds of scribbles and, after coordinating initially movement-centrated scribbles (Figure 8.8a), many represent a circle and a line by the end of this time period, coordinating movement with external cues, as in Figure 8.8b (Brittain, 1976; Noelting, 1979).

By three to four years of age, they can draw more well-formed circles, disjoint circles, and a "plus" (Figure 8.8c). Thus, they can separate figures in space and draw segments in reciprocal directions.

At age four, children can draw squares, oblique crossing lines, and intersecting circles (Figure 8.8d). This requires recognition of closure, coordination of distance and direction, intuitive representation of vertices, and coordination of separation and union. An "X" as drawn becomes a plus. More complex figures are often represented as a square-with-additions. As figures become more complex, the age at which children can reproduce them varies considerably.

By five to six years of age, children produce two new elements, oblique lines

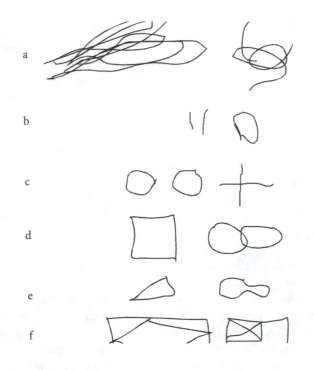

a

b

c

d

e

f

Figure 8.8 Geometric drawings.

and curves that include changes in the directions of curvature (e.g., convex to concave, such as a drawing a "key"; see Figure 8.8e). Thus, they can draw triangles. Later, often at about seven years of age, they can draw a rhombus, which involves oblique lines and a similar reversal in the directionality. They also move toward geometric patterning in their paintings, including systematic repetition of an element or division of the plane resulting in translation, reflection, or even rotational patterns (e.g., painting one side of the paper as a "mirror image" of the other) (D. Booth, 1984).

By eight to nine years of age, children create hierarchical figures, made up of parts of a whole and symmetrical orientation (e.g., a rhombus drawn inside of a rectangle by connecting the midpoints of the rectangle's sides; see Figure 8.8f). Thus, the child has to see line segments as consisting of both a part and a whole. The hierarchical inclusion of both inclusion and direction relates to a "good gestalt" in drawings.

These drawings are *usually done on rectangular paper*. That makes a difference. In one study, drawing a triangle on triangular-shaped paper was as easy for children as copying a square on square piece of paper (Brittain, 1976). Thus, we must be careful about saying the developmental sequence is "circle, square, triangle" unless we consider the shape of the background (paper). Nevertheless, the order is fairly consistent, especially the complexity of lines, the use of oblique lines and intersecting figures. They gradually master perspective through coordination of part-whole relations and direction.

There is a paucity of research on very young children's knowledge of three-dimensional figures. Babies only one or two days old can maintain object size despite changes in distance (and thus change in size of the retinal image, Slater et al., 1990). That is, they habituate in looking at a sphere of constant size that changes in distance from the newborn, but not when both this distance and the size of the sphere is changed so that the sphere subtends the same angle on the retina (Granrud, 1987). In addition, infants can perceive three-dimensional shapes, however, this is limited to continuously moving objects, rather than single or even multiple static views of the same object (Humphrey & Humphrey, 1995).

As with two-dimensional figures, children do not perform well in school-based tasks involving three-dimensional shapes, even into the intermediate grades (Carpenter, Coburn, Reys, & Wilson, 1976). South African first graders used different names for solids (such as "square" for cube), but were capable of understanding and remembering features they discussed (Nieuwoudt & van Niekerk, 1997). U.S. students' reasoning about solids was much like that about plane figures; they referred to a variety of characteristics, such as "pointyness" and comparative size or slenderness (Lehrer, Jenkins et al., 1998). Students also treated the solid wooden figures as malleable, suggesting that the rectangular prism could be transformed into a cube by "sitting on it." Use of plane figure names for solids may indicate a lack of discrimination between two and three dimensions (Carpenter et al., 1976).

Two related studies asked children to match solids with their nets. Kindergarteners had reasonable success when the solids and nets both were made from the same interlocking materials (Leeson, 1995). An advanced kindergartener had more difficulty with drawings of the nets (Leeson, Stewart, & Wright, 1997), possibly because he was unable to visualize the relationship with the more abstract materials.

Congruence, Symmetry, and Transformations

Young children develop beginning ideas not just about shapes, but also about symmetry, congruence, and transformations. The ability to detect symmetry develops early (Vurpillot, 1976). Infants as young as four months dishabituate more quickly to symmetric figures than asymmetric figures, at least for vertical symmetry (Bornstein et al., 1981; Bornstein & Krinsky, 1985; Ferguson, Aminoff, & Gentner, 1998; C. B. Fisher, Ferdinandsen, & Bornstein, 1981; Humphrey & Humphrey, 1995). A preference for vertical symmetry seems to develop between four and 12 months of age and vertical bilateral symmetry remains easier for children than horizontal symmetry, which in turn is easier than diagonal symmetries (Genkins, 1975; Palmer, 1985; Palmer & Hemenway, 1978). Extreme spatial separation of components of the pattern caused infants to lose the advantage for vertical symmetry (Bornstein & Krinsky, 1985). Further, they do not dishabituate to horizontal symmetry or different vertical patterns (C. B. Fisher et al., 1981), so initial competence is limited to "goodness of organization."

There appear to be two phases in recognition of symmetry (Palmer & Hemenway, 1978). The system first selects potential axes of symmetry defined by symmetric components via a crude, but rapid, analysis of symmetry in all orientations simultaneously. It maps alignment relations, using detection of closed loops, (non-)perpendicularity, intersections and protrusions, to produce structured representations (i.e., structurally consistent matches between identical attributes and relations of the objects in each). Vertical, and to a lesser extent, horizontal axes are preferred, because orientation relationships, such as above and beside, develop early; vertical is preferred because beside is bidirectional (Ferguson et al., 1998). The system then evaluates specific axes sequentially in a detailed comparison (Palmer & Hemenway, 1978), which has a significant influence on shape recognition (Palmer, 1989).

Children often use and refer to rotational symmetry as much as they do line symmetry in working with pattern blocks (Sarama, Clements, & Vukelic, 1996). For people of all ages, symmetric shapes are detected faster, discriminated more accurately, and often remembered better than asymmetrical ones (Bornstein et al., 1981). However, many explicit concepts of symmetry are not firmly established before 12 years of age (Genkins, 1975).

Many young children judge *congruence* (Are these two shapes "the same"?) based on whether they are, overall, more similar than different (Vurpillot, 1976). As with symmetry, the comparison of two figures may evoke a pair of structured representations, and the comparison is represented as a mapping between sets of relations between components of the representations (Ferguson et al., 1998). Children younger than five and a half years may not do an exhaustive comparison, and until about seven years of age, may not attend to the spatial relationships of all the parts of complex figures (Vurpillot, 1976). Shown pairs of figures, some congruent, but all rotated, kindergartners tend to judge all pairs as "different," considering orientation a significant feature (Rosser, 1994a). Even third graders may have difficulty rotating an entire complex stimulus and may rotate only parts of it, or may ignore parts of a complex stimulus. Not until later, at age 11, did most children perform as adults.

With guidance, however, even four-year-olds and some younger children can generate strategies for verifying congruence for some tasks. Preschoolers often try to judge congruence using an edge matching strategy, although only about 50 percent can do it successfully (Beilin, 1984; Beilin et al., 1982). They gradually develop a greater awareness of the type of differences between figures that are considered relevant and move from considering various parts of shapes to considering the spatial relationships of these parts (Vurpillot, 1976). In about first grade, they consider both multiple attributes and their spatial relationships and begin to use superposition. Thus, strategies supersede one another in development (e.g., motion-based superposition) becoming more powerful, sophisticated, geometrical, and accurate (recall that rigid motions were discussed in the section on spatial thinking).

The origins of the symmetry and equivalence concepts, however, may lie in early actions. Evidence indicates that children as young as 18 months will pick up two blocks and bang them together and are more likely to choose equivalent blocks than other available blocks. Children may progress through levels, from experiencing similar input between two hands (symmetry in action), to bilateral banging, to relating the block forms (at about two years of age), stacking equivalent blocks (an early explicit attempt to create a static expression of equivalence), placing blocks side by side, and eventually spacing equivalent blocks (Forman, 1982). Thus, human sensitivity to symmetry and equivalences may be prefigured in the bilateral symmetry of our anatomy, prefigured in the sense that particular types of object manipulatives are more likely to occur as a result of our having hands bilaterally opposed, and the feedback that is thus pleasing, as having identical objects in two hands (Forman, 1982), perhaps reflecting perception of the equivalence of our own bodies and even neurological symmetries.

Under the right conditions, children of all ages can apply similarity transformations to shapes. Even four- and five-year-olds can identify similar shapes in some circumstances (Sophian & Crosby, 1998). The coordination of height and width information to perceive the proportional shape of a rectangle (fat vs. skinny, wide or tall) might be a basic way of accessing proportionality information. This may serve as a foundation for other types of proportionality, especially fractions. Similarly, other research shows first graders can engage in and benefit from similarity tasks (Confrey, 1992).

In early childhood, children also progress in drawing transformations of two-dimensional shapes (Gagatsis, 2003; Gagatsis, Sriraman, Elia, & Modestou, 2006). Children asked to draw a "stairway" of specific shapes, such as rectangles, used one of three strategies: (approximate) similarity transformations (increasing both dimensions, Figure 8.9a), increasing one dimension only (Figure 8.9b), and producing defective series.

From four to eight years of age, children moved from defective series to either of the other two strategies (note that similarity may be a visually or analytically based transformation). Similarly, higher-IQ children used more sophisticated strategies. However, older children more often increased only one dimension. The strategy of increasing one dimension only may appear to indicate a pre-recognition level of geometric thinking in which children attended to only a subset of a shape's characteristics, whereas increasing

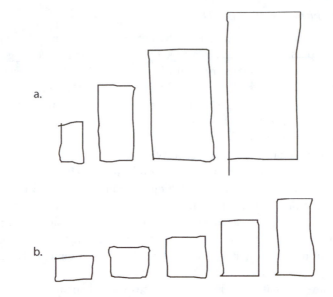

Figure 8.9 Children's "stairways" of rectangles.

both dimensions indicated a syncretic level of thinking (Gagatsis, 2003). Thus, another interpretation is that increasing one dimension signifies a global visual view with partial analysis, placing it in transition between the syncretic and descriptive levels (Gagatsis et al., 2006). (Similarly, increasing both dimensions may reflect a visual/syncretic or descriptive/analytic cognitive basis; the studies could not distinguish between these possibilities.) Lack of recognition of shapes was associated with defective strategies (which reflected a pre-recognition level of thinking), but did not differentiate among more sophisticated strategies.

Thus, teaching both shape recognition and transformations may be important to children's mathematical development. Traditional teaching of separate categories of "squares" and "rectangles" was assumed to underlie children's difficulties in relating these shape classes and their characteristics. The use of the strategy of increasing one dimension of a rectangle may allow children to develop dynamic intuition that a square may thus be produced.

Experience and Education

Around 300 BC, a king named Ptolemy I ruled in Alexandria, Egypt, a center of science, culture and learning of those times. A learned man himself, Ptolemy asked Euclid, the father of geometry, to teach him. Euclid began this "13 steps" but Ptolemy became impatient. He proposed to Euclid that a shortcut would be desirable. Euclid responded, "Sire, there is no royal road to geometry."

Hierarchical Interactionalism and Different Educational Paths

Consistent with the tenet of *different developmental courses* and the evidence that children possess multiples types of geometric knowledge, we suggest that children's knowledge of geometry might be enhanced in different ways. First, their imagistic prototypes might be vastly elaborated by the presentation of a variety of variants, via the systematic variation of irrelevant and relevant attributes (e.g., through dynamic media such as the computer). Children must actively attend to the examples and connect them as through verbal labeling. Such enhancement is accomplished mainly through a usually unconscious visual induction process. Second, through the presentation of particular tasks and engagement in dialogue about them, children's verbal declarative knowledge might be refined to extend, elaborate, and constrain their visual knowledge. Preschoolers exposed to such discussions consciously used and were excited about their ability to tell if any figure was a triangle just by counting to see if it had three straight sides (Clements & Sarama, 2007).

We hypothesize that each of these two paths toward enhancing knowledge of geometry can be followed separately or together. If separately, knowledge of one type can "substitute" for knowledge of another type on certain tasks, within certain limits (including a performance decrement, in accuracy or speed of execution). For example, a rich and varied exposure to various examples could allow near-perfect performance on triangle discrimination tasks such as those discussed previously. Performance would suffer only if a figure were presented that fell outside the range of any of the multiple imagistic prototypes developed by the children, or if the task demanded reasoning based on properties not supported by such imagistic-oriented schemes (e.g., calculations regarding angle relationships), in which case the schemes would be inadequate to the task.

Similarly, well-developed verbal declarative knowledge, even in the absence of exposure to various examples could allow perfect performance on such simple discrimination tasks. However, performance would suffer (at least in speed of execution) because a chain of reasoning would be required for every figure that could not be immediately assimilated into the (hypothesized-limited) range of imagistic prototypes. In each of these cases, the characteristics of the figures would have to be "read off" the figure and compared to those that are held in verbal declarative knowledge as characteristics of the class. This type of verbal knowledge would support more sophisticated analysis of geometric figures. Without the imagistic knowledge, however, the range and flexibility of the application of this knowledge would be limited. Research on the learning of geometry shows that students limit their conceptualizations to studied exemplars and often consider common but nondefining features (e.g., an altitude of a triangle is always located inside the triangle) as essential features of the concept (Burger & Shaughnessy, 1986; Fisher, 1978; Fuys, Geddes, & Tischler, 1988; Kabanova-Meller, 1970; Zykova, 1969). Further, students who know a correct verbal definition of a concept but also have a limited visual prototype associated with it, may have difficulty applying the verbal description correctly (Clements & Battista, 1989; Hershkowitz et al., 1990; Vinner & Hershkowitz, 1980). This is consistent with the theory of simultaneous and sequential processing. In this view, pictorially-presented materials may be more likely to evoke the visual/holistic/simultaneous processing, whereas aurally-presented materials would be more likely to evoke verbal/sequential/linear processing. The type of presentation may interact with individual differences in abilities in these two domains.

This view is consistent with the work of Karmiloff-Smith (1984; 1986; 1990), who postulates a repeating three-phase cycle of representational re-description. Phases, in contrast to structurally-constituted stages or levels, are recurrent, general (across-domain) processes that people work through during development or learning. At phase 1, the building of mental representations is predominantly driven by interactions of the children's goal-directed schemes with the environment. The children's goal is behavioral success, or the reaching of that goal, which sometimes is evaluated by consistency with adult responses and feedback.[3] Such success leads to the recording of isolated correspondences between environmental situations that do or do not allow or aid the attainment of the goal in a form inaccessible to the system (i.e., input-output correspondences along with their contexts in compiled form). In this form, any relationship between bits of knowledge is, at best, implicit.

When behavioral success is achieved, a phase 2 metaprocess (a procedure that operates on internal knowledge structures) evaluates the knowledge base. Now, the goal is not to behave successfully, but to gain control over the representational forms (Vygotsky, 1934/1986, similarly stated that the development of thought cannot be derived from the failure of thought and postulated a genetic predisposition to gain control of mental representations). The first operation of phase 2 is to re-record phase 1 representations in a form which can be accessed, though not yet consciously. The implicit representations are analyzed into semanticized components, linking them into a simplified but growing network structure that is predicated on the usefulness of the initial correspondences to goal attainment. The second operation is to form relationships between bits of knowledge. These two new operations place demands on cognitive processing, which, together with the (over)simplified structure and the need to test the mental representation in new situations, often leads to new "errors"— ostensibly a step backward to phase 1 (or earlier) from an adult's perspective—that mask the progress in explicating representations of the domain. Finally, these two operations constitute an internalization of relationships and processes that were previously only implicit (cf. Steffe & Cobb, 1988).

Once successful re-representation is achieved, children develop phase-3 control mechanisms that integrate and balance consideration of the external environment and the new internal representational connections forged in phase 2. At the end of phase 3, these connections are re-recorded again in abstract symbolic form, the first form accessible to conscious thought. Now, performance improves beyond that which was achieved at either of the two earlier phases.

At the syncretic level of geometric thinking, children are implicitly recognizing the properties of shapes. For example, their schemes for squares and for rectangles both contain patterns for right angles. However, these are patterns in spatial subsystems that emerge when instantiated, they are not conceptual objects (mental entities that can be manipulated or scrutinized, Davis, 1984). Right angles are not represented explicitly and, therefore, no relationship is formed between them. In general, this type of representation explains how operation at one level can presuppose knowledge from the succeeding level, without allowing access to knowledge at the higher level because the form of such knowledge is proceduralized or schematized behaviorally and is, therefore, inaccessible to the rest of the cognitive system.

When shapes are dealt with successfully on the level of behavior, meta-processes re-record the mental representations, creating a mental geometric object for the visual image of the right angles and a link between these mental objects for different cases of right angles, including links between those in rectangles and those in squares. Because children in phase 2 are seeking control over their representations of these geometric forms, some increases in "errors" (from an adult's point of view) may occur (e.g., maintaining the notion that a nonrectangular parallelogram is a rectangle "because you're only looking at it from the side").

Eventually, the properties become conceptual objects that are available as data to conscious processes. That is, visual features become sentient in isolation and are linked to a verbal label; and the child becomes capable of reflecting on the visual features and thus can explicitly recognize the shape's properties. At first, however, the flexibility of application is limited. Indeed, children can be expected not only to think at different levels for different topics (Clements & Battista, 1992), but also to think at different phases for different topics. Problem solving and discussion involving the geometric objects help build connections between the constructed knowledge (e.g., of right angles) and other similarly-accessible knowledge (e.g., of parallelism and side lengths of rectangles and squares). Eventually, connections are built between properties of figures such as rectangles and squares and of properties of other geometric objects. In this manner, children's geometric knowledge can become increasingly abstract, coherent, and integrated, because it is freed from the constraints of compiled, and thus inflexible, mental representations. At each level, the degree of integration increases as the connections span greater numbers of geometric, and eventually, nongeometric topics (cf. Gutiérrez & Jaime, 1988). As another example, recall children's creations of "stairways" of specific shapes (Gagatsis, 2003). Defective series would be signs of developing (but not yet achieving) behavioral success. Early use of similarity transformations would indicate achieving that success (cf. Gagatsis, Sriraman, Elia, & Modestou, 2006). A shift to increasing only one dimension might indicate phase 2 redescriptions, but at first only on one dimension, with two-dimensional, similarity transformations eventually signaling the development of phase-3 control mechanisms.

Here again, instruction has a strong influence. Ideally, it encourages unification; however, the instruction of isolated bits of knowledge at low levels retards such development. Unfortunately, the latter is pervasive in both curriculum materials (Fuys et al., 1988) and teaching (Clements & Battista, 1992; Porter, 1989; B. Thomas, 1982).

To place instructional implications in a different light, it is only after the third phase that children become explicitly aware of their geometric conceptualizations; therefore, it is after phase 3 that the last three instructional steps in the van Hiele model (explicitation, free orientation, and integration) can begin.[4] An implication is that short-circuiting this developmental sequence (e.g., by beginning with explicitation) is a pedagogical mistake. Deprived of the initial construction of their own mental geometric objects and relationships (images), children construct phase 1 (behaviorally "correct") verbal responses based on "rules without reason" (Skemp, 1976). A more viable goal is the construction of mathematical meaning from actions on geometric objects and subsequent reflections on those actions.

In summary, development of geometric properties as conceptual objects leads to pervasive level 2 thinking. This development represents a reconstruction on the abstract/conscious/verbal plane of those geometric conceptualizations that Piaget and Inhelder (1967) hypothesized were first constructed on the perceptual plane and then reconstructed on the representational/imaginal plane. Thus, level 2 thinking requires what Piaget called the construction of articulated mental imagery, which develops most fully via the combined enhancement of both imagistic and verbal declarative knowledge, as previously discussed. We posit that the same recurrent phases explain the reconstruction on each new plane (level), but that the role of social interaction and instruction increases in importance with higher levels.

The theory of reiterated phases of re-representation applies equally to children and adults, regardless of their overall stage of cognitive development (Karmiloff-Smith, 1990). This is consonant with reports of low van Hiele levels among high school students and preservice teachers (Burger & Shaughnessy, 1986; Denis, 1987; Gutiérrez & Jaime, 1988; Mayberry, 1983; Senk, 1989). We now turn to the effects of experiences on particular shape concepts.

SHAPES: 2-D

Research indicates the importance of educational experiences. If the examples and nonexamples children experience are rigid, not representing the range of the shape category, so will be their concepts. This is not a developmental limitation; one of the youngest three-year-olds scored higher than every six-year-old on shape recognition tasks (Clements et al., 1999). Concepts of two-dimensional shapes begin forming in the pre-K years and stabilize as early as age six (Gagatsis & Patronis, 1990; Hannibal & Clements, 2008), so early experiences are important. This learning will be more effective if it includes a full range of examples and distractors to build valid and strong concept images, including dynamic and flexible imagery (Owens, 1999).

Language should also be developed. Many children describe triangles as having "three points and three sides," but up to half were not sure what a "point" or "side" was (Clements et al., 1999). As with the number word sequence, the English language presents more challenges than others, such as East Asian languages. For example, in those languages, every "quadrilateral" is called simply, "four-side-shape." For most terms, judges evaluated the East Asian versions to have more mathematical clarity; for example, "sharp angle" vs. English's "acute angle"; or, "parallel-four-sided-shape" vs. English's "paral-lelogram" (Han & Ginsburg, 2001).

Typical U.S. instruction in geometry is not of high quality. One early study found that kindergarten children had a great deal of knowledge about shapes and matching shapes before instruction began. Their teacher tended to elicit and verify this prior knowledge but did not add content or develop new know-ledge. That is, about two-thirds of the interactions had children repeat what they already knew in a repetitious format as in the following exchange:

Teacher: Could you tell us what type of shape that is?
Children: A square.
Teacher: Okay. It's a square (B. Thomas, 1982).

When teachers did elaborate, their statements were often filled with math-ematical inaccuracies.

A more recent study confirmed that current practices in the primary grades also promote little conceptual change: First grade students in one study were more likely than older children to differentiate one polygon from another by counting sides or vertices (Lehrer, Jenkins, & Osana, 1998). Over time, children were less likely to notice these attributes, given conventional instruction of geometry in the elementary grades. Such neglect evinces itself in student achievement. Students are not prepared for learning more sophisticated geometry, especially when compared to students of other nations (Carpenter, Corbitt, Kepner, Lindquist, & Reys, 1980; Fey et al., 1984; Kouba et al., 1988; Stevenson, Lee, & Stigler, 1986; Stigler et al., 1990). In one TIMMS study, U.S.

students scored at or near bottom in every geometry task (Beaton et al., 1996; Lappan, 1999).

Such comparisons may be present even among preschoolers in various countries (Starkey et al., 1999). On a geometry assessment, four-year-olds from America scored 55 percent compared to those from China at 84 percent. Thus, cultural supports are lacking from the earliest years in the U.S.

The work of the ENRP project similarly shows that children learn geometry considerably earlier and better in educational environments based explicitly on children's development of geometric thinking (B. A. Clarke, 2004). Clarke's "growth points" are consistent with the developmental levels discussed here and are based on the same notion that the van Hiele levels need to be further delineated to serve educational needs, especially in early childhood. The instructional approach is that there is little value in extensive formal naming of shapes until children are beginning to classify by properties, which helps children organize their knowledge of shapes in a categorization structure. Second graders using this approach were at levels of thinking beyond those in a comparison second grade group; indeed, children as young as kindergarten, provided these high-quality learning experiences, were achieving what the comparison second graders achieved.

In a similar vein, early childhood curricula traditionally introduce shapes in four basic level categories: circle, square, triangle, and rectangle. The idea that a square is not a rectangle is rooted by age five (Clements et al., 1999; Hannibal & Clements, 2008). It is time to re-think our presentation of squares as an isolated set. If we try to teach young children that "squares are rectangles," especially through direct telling, confusion is likely. If, on the other hand, we continue to teach "squares" and "rectangles" as two separate groups, we will block children's transition to more flexible categorical thinking (cf. Gagatsis, 2003).

In our study (Clements et al., 1999), four-year-olds were more likely to accept the squares as rectangles, possibly because they were less predisposed (because their prototype of rectangles was less distinguished from that of squares) or able to judge equality of all sides. Although the squares were included in the rectangle-recognition task (by the original task designers) to assess hierarchical inclusion, we did not expect or find such thinking in these young children. Their responses do show, however, that the path to such hierarchical thinking is a complex and twisting one with changes at several levels. This again raises the question of whether the strictly visual prototype approach to teaching geometric shapes is a necessary prerequisite to more flexible categorical thinking or a detriment to the early development of such thinking. Kay (1987) provided first graders with instruction that (a) began with the more general case, quadrilaterals, proceeded to rectangles, and then to squares; (b) addressed the relevant characteristics of each class and the hierarchical relationships among classes; and (c) used terms embodying these relationships ("square rectangle"). At the end of instruction, most children identified characteristics of quadrilaterals, rectangles, and squares, and about half identified hierarchical relationships among these classes, although none had done so previously. Although the depth of these first-graders' understanding (especially of hierarchical relations) and the generalizations made on the basis of the empirical results must be questioned (Clements & Battista, 1992), so too should we question the wisdom of the traditional, prototype-only approach, which may lay groundwork that must be overturned to develop hierarchical thinking.

Probably the best approach is to present many examples of squares and rectangles, varying orientation, size, and so forth, including squares as examples of rectangles (with double naming—"it's a square rectangle"). Older children can discuss "general" categories, such as quadrilaterals and triangles, counting the sides of various figures to choose their category. Also, teachers might encourage them to describe why a figure belongs or does not belong to a shape category.

Logo microworlds can be evocative in generating thinking about squares and rectangles for young children. In one large study (Clements et al., 2001), some kindergarteners formed their own concept (e.g., "it's a square rectangle") in response to their work with the microworlds. This concept was applied only in certain situations: squares were still squares, and rectangles, rectangles, unless you formed a square while working with procedures—on the computer or in drawing—that were designed to produce rectangles. The concept was strongly visual in nature, and no logical classification per se, such as class inclusion processes, should be inferred. The creation, application, and discussion of the concept, however, were arguably a valuable intellectual exercise.

Many researchers have studied the effects of Logo on students' understanding of two-dimensional geometric shapes in general (for reviews, see Clements et al., 2001; Clements & Sarama, 1997a). More recent studies are relatively positive; for example, McCoy (1996) stated that: "Logo programming, particularly turtle graphics at the elementary level, is clearly an effective medium for providing mathematics experiences. . .when students are able to experiment with mathematics in varied representations, active involvement becomes the basis for their understanding. This is particularly true in geometry . . . and the concept of variable" (p. 443). In the area of geometry, research has focused on concepts of plane figures, especially students' levels of geometric thinking about those figures; angle and angle measurement; and motion geometry.

Guided Logo experience can significantly enhance students' concepts of two-dimensional figures (Butler & Close, 1989; Clements, 1987). When asked to describe geometric shapes, students with Logo experience give more statements overall and more statements that explicitly mention geometric properties of shapes than students with no Logo experience (Clements & Battista, 1989, 1990; Lehrer & Smith, 1986). In one study, students were able to apply their knowledge of geometry better than a comparison group, but there was no difference in their knowledge of basic geometric facts. The researchers concluded that the use of Logo influenced the way in which students mentally represented their knowledge of geometric concepts (Lehrer, Randle, & Sancilio, 1989).

Similarly, Logo experience appears to affect students' ideas about angle significantly. Responses of control students in one study reflected common usage, such as describing an angle as "a line tilted," or no knowledge of angle. In comparison, the Logo students indicated more mathematically oriented conceptualizations, such as "Like where a point is. Where two lines come together at a point" (Clements & Battista, 1989). Several researchers have reported that Logo experience has a positive effect on students' angle concepts (Clements & Battista, 1989; du Boulay, 1986; Frazier, 1987; Kieran, 1986a; Kieran & Hillel, 1990; Noss, 1987; Olive, Lankenau, & Scally, 1986). However, in some situations, benefits do not emerge until students have more than a year of Logo experience (Kelly, Kelly, & Miller, 1986–87).

On the other hand, Logo experiences may also foster some unintended conceptions of angle measure. For example, students may confuse angle measure with the amount of rotation along the path (e.g., the exterior angle in a polygon) or the degree of rotation from the vertical (Clements & Battista, 1989). In addition, concepts generated while working with Logo do not replace previously-learned concepts of angle measure. For example, students' conceptions about angle measure and difficulties they have coordinating the relationships between the turtle's rotation and the constructed angle have persisted for years, especially if not properly guided by their teachers (Clements, 1987; Cope & Simmons, 1991; Hoyles & Sutherland, 1986; Kieran, 1986a; Kieran, Hillel, & Erlwanger, 1986). In general, however, appropriately designed Logo experience appears to facilitate understanding of angle measure. After working with Logo, students' concepts of angle size are more likely to be mathematically correct, coherent, and abstract (Clements & Battista, 1989; Kieran, 1986b; Noss, 1987), while showing a progression from van Hiele Level 0 to Level 2 in the span of the Logo instruction (Clements & Battista, 1989). If Logo experiences emphasize the difference between the angle of rotation and the angle formed as the turtle traces a path, confusions regarding the measure of rotation and the measure of the angle may be avoided (Clements & Battista, 1989; Kieran, 1986b).

Generally, then, studies support the use of Logo as a medium for learning and for teaching mathematics.[5] Results especially support Logo as a medium for learning and teaching geometry (Barker, Merryman, & Bracken, 1988; Butler & Close, 1989; Clements & Meredith, 1993; Hoyles & Noss, 1987; Kynigos, 1991; Miller, Kelly, & Kelly, 1988; Salem, 1989). However, not all research has been positive. First, few studies report that students "master" the mathematical concepts that are the teachers' goals for instruction. Second, some studies show no significant differences between Logo and control groups

(Johnson, 1986). Without teacher guidance, mere "exposure" to Logo often yields little learning (Clements & Meredith, 1993). Third, some studies have shown limited transfer. For example, the scores of students from two ninth-grade Logo classes did not differ significantly from those of control students on subsequent high school geometry grades and tests (Olive, 1991; Olive et al., 1986). One reason is that students do not always think mathematically, even if the Logo environment invites such thinking (Noss & Hoyles, 1992). For example, some students rely excessively on visual/spatial cues and avoid analytical work (Hillel & Kieran, 1988). This visual approach is not related to an ability to create visual images but to the role of the visual "data" (i.e., the students' perceptions) of a geometric figure in determining students' Logo constructions. Although helpful initially, this approach inhibits students from arriving at mathematical generalizations if overused. Further, there is little reason for students to abandon visual approaches unless teachers present tasks that can only be resolved using an analytical, generalized, mathematical approach. Finally, dialogue between teacher and students is essential for encouraging predicting, reflecting, and higher-level reasoning.

In sum, studies showing the most positive effects involve carefully planned sequences of Logo activities. Appropriate teacher mediation of students' work with those activities is necessary for students to construct geometric concepts successfully. This mediation must help students forge links between Logo and other experiences and between Logo-based procedural knowledge and more traditional conceptual knowledge (Clements & Battista, 1989; Lehrer & Smith, 1986). Care must be taken that such links are not learned by rote (Hoyles & Noss, 1992).

A large project addressed these concerns with a carefully sequenced curriculum in Logo (Clements et al., 2001). The findings were clear that Logo programming can help students construct elaborate knowledge networks (rather than mechanical chains of rules and terms) for geometric topics. One main effect was increasing students' ability to describe, define, justify, and generalize geometric ideas. Students' greater explication and elaboration of geometric ideas within the Logo environments appear to facilitate their progression to higher levels of geometric thinking. For example, in programming the Logo turtle, there is a need to analyze and reflect on the components and properties of geometric shapes and to make relationships explicit. In addition, the necessity of building Logo procedures encourages students to build understandable, implicit definitions of these shapes. Students construct more viable knowledge because they are constantly using graphical manifestations of their thinking to test the viability of their ideas. There is also support for the linkage of symbolic and visual external representations.

In a similar vein, there was a positive effect on students' flexible consideration of multiple geometric properties. As we previously hypothesized (Clements & Battista, 1994), computer environments can allow the manipulation of specific screen objects in ways that assist students to view them as geometric (rather than visual/spatial) and to recognize them as representatives of a class of geometric objects. The power of the computer is that students simultaneously confront the specific and are concrete with the abstract and generalized (as represented by the Logo code). Students treat a figure both as having characteristics of a single shape and as one instance of many such figures.

Logo environments appear to demand and thus facilitate precision in geometric thinking. In contrast, there is imprecision when students work with paper and pencil, and they can be distracted by the actual effort of drawing. The need in Logo environments for more complete, exact, and abstract explication may account for students' creation of richer concepts. That is, by using Logo students have to specify steps with thorough specification and detail to a noninterpretive agent. The results of these commands can be observed, reflected on, and corrected; the computer serves as an explicative agent. In noncomputer manipulative environments, a student can make intuitive movements and corrections without explicit awareness of mathematical objects and actions. For example, even young children can move puzzle pieces into place without conscious awareness of the geometric motions that can describe these physical movements. In noncomputer environments, attempts are sometimes made to promote such awareness. Still, descriptions of motions tend to be generated from, and interpreted by, physical action of students (Johnson-Gentile, Clements, & Battista, 1994). This interpretation of the results is consonant with previous research indicating prolonged retention and continuous construction of early Logo-based schemes for geometric concepts (Clements, 1987).

Finally, computer and classroom environments that promote a problem-solving approach to education appear to have benefits for the development of both mathematical concepts and processes (e.g., reasoning, connecting, problem-solving, communicating, and representing). They seem especially beneficial for developing student competence in solving complex problems. Further, because students test ideas for themselves, computers can aid them to move from naive to empirical to logical thinking and encourage them to make and test conjectures. Thus, it can be argued that *high-quality implementations of Logo experiences places as much emphasis on the spirit of mathematics— exploration, investigation, critical thinking, and problem solving—as it does on geometric ideas.* We believe that it has the potential to develop valid mathematical thinking in students (Clements et al., 2001).

SHAPES: 3-D

Less is known about teaching concepts of three-dimensional shapes. Certainly, consistent experience with building materials such as building blocks appears warranted (Leeb-Lundberg, 1996), especially as children engage in considerable pre-mathematical play with these materials (Seo & Ginsburg, 2004) and can build general reasoning skills in this geometric context (Kamii et al., 2004). However, it is critical that teachers mathematize such activity. Using specific terminology for solids, faces, and edges makes such discussion particularly beneficial (Nieuwoudt & van Niekerk, 1997). Much more is known about building with blocks and other three-dimensional shapes—see Chapter 9.

GEOMETRIC MOTIONS, CONGRUENCE, AND SYMMETRY

There is mixed evidence regarding young children's ability with geometric motions. Pre-K to kindergarten children may be limited in their ability to mentally transform shapes, although there is evidence that even these sophisticated processes are achievable (Ehrlich et al., 2005; Levine et al., 1999). Further, these children can learn to perform rotations on objects (physical or virtual), and a rich curriculum, enhanced by manipulatives and computer tools, may reveal that knowledge and mental processes are valid educational goals for most young children. For example, interventions improve the spatial skills of low-income kindergartners, especially when embedded in a story context (Casey, 2005). Computers are especially helpful, as the screen tools make motions more accessible to reflection, and thus bring them to an explicit level of awareness for children (Clements & Sarama, 2003b; Sarama, Clements, & Vukelic, 1996).

Children's painting and constructions, discussed previously, might be used as models in introducing symmetry, including two-dimensional creations of painting, drawing, and collage, and three-dimensional creations of clay and blocks (Booth, 1984)

Computer environments also can be helpful in learning congruence and symmetry (Clements et al., 2001). Indeed, the effects of Logo microworlds on symmetry were particularly strong for kindergarten children. Writing Logo commands for the creation of symmetric figures, testing symmetry by flipping figures via commands, and discussing these actions apparently encouraged children to build richer and more general images of symmetric relations (with possibly some overgeneralization). Children had to abstract and externally represent their actions in a more explicit and precise fashion in Logo activities than, say, in free-hand drawing of symmetric figures.

Research supports the use of manipulatives in developing geometric and spatial thinking in young children (Clements & McMillen, 1996). Using a variety of manipulatives is more beneficial than the typically abstract-verbal textbook-only presentation. For example, an experiment with random assignment of both students (seven to nine years of age) and teachers compared a textbook-only lessons on geometry to the same lessons with additional concrete and pictorial materials systematically incorporated (across visual, auditory, and tactile modes). Even with lessons and total time held constant, the group participating in the lessons with a wider variety of stimuli performed significantly better on the geometry posttest (Greabell, 1978).

Such tactile-kinesthetic experiences as body movement and manipulating geometric solids help young children learn geometric concepts (Gerhardt, 1973; Prigge, 1978). Children also fare better with solid cutouts than printed forms, the former encouraging the use of more senses (Stevenson & McBee, 1958). If manipulatives are accepted as important, what of pictures? Pictures also can be important; even children as young as five or six years (but not younger) can use information in pictures to build a pyramid, for example (Murphy & Wood, 1981). Thus, pictures can give children an immediate, intuitive grasp of certain geometric ideas. However, pictures need to be sufficiently varied so that children do not form limited ideas. Further, research indicates that it is rare for pictures to be superior to manipulatives. In fact, in some cases, pictures may not differ in effectiveness from instruction with symbols (Sowell, 1989). But the reason may not lie in the "nonconcrete" nature of the pictures as much as it lies in their "nonmanipulability"—that is, that children cannot act on them as flexibly and extensively. Research shows that manipulatives on computers can have real benefit.

Instructional aids help because they are manipulable and meaningful. In providing these features, computers can provide representations that are just as real and helpful to young children as physical manipulatives. In fact, they may have specific advantages (Clements & McMillen, 1996). For example, children and teachers can save and later retrieve any arrangement of computer manipulatives. Similarly, computers allow us to store more than static configurations. They can record and replay *sequences* of our actions on manipulatives. This helps young children form dynamic images. Computers can help children become aware of, and mathematize, their actions. For example, very young children can move puzzle pieces into place, but they do not think about their actions. Using the computer, however, helps children become aware of, and describe, these motions (Clements & Battista, 1991; Johnson-Gentile et al., 1994).

Further, computer manipulatives can facilitate students' thinking about the properties of geometric shapes (P. S. Moyer, Niezgoda, & Stanley, 2005; Sarama, Clements, & Vukelic, 1996).

In general, research indicates that Logo experiences can also aid the learning of motion geometry and related ideas such as symmetry. Working with a Logo unit on motion geometry, students' movement away from van Hiele Level 0 was slow. There was, however, definite evidence of a beginning awareness of the properties of transformations (A. T. Olson, Kieren, & Ludwig, 1987). In another study, middle school students achieved a working understanding of transformations and used visual feedback to correct overgeneralizations when working in a Logo microworld (L. D. Edwards, 1991). Logo experiences may also help develop notions of symmetry. Students as young as first grade have been observed using such mathematical notions as symmetry (Kull, 1986). In addition, symmetry concepts are learned by students involved in Logo through middle school (Edwards, 1991; Gallou-Dumiel, 1989; (J. K. Olson, 1985). One student used a specially designed Logo symmetry microworld to learn such concepts and effectively transferred her mathematical understandings to a paper and pencil problem (Hoyles & Healy, 1997).

ANGLE, PARALLELISM, AND PERPENDICULARITY

Angles are critical but often are not learned or taught well. Many children young and old believe that an angle must have one horizontal ray, a right angle is an angle that points to the right, two right angles in different orientations are not equal in measure, or even that angles have wings (Clements & Battista, 1992). Children may describe an angle as "a shape," a side of a figure, a tilted line, an orientation or heading, a corner, a turn, and a union of two lines (Clements & Battista, 1990). Children do not find angles to be salient properties of figures (Clements et al., 1996; Mitchelmore, 1989). When copying figures, children do not always attend to the angles. As described in the following section, children ignore angles during early levels of development of shape composition abilities.

To understand angles, children must discriminate angles as critical parts of geometric figures, compare and match angles, and construct and mentally represent the idea of turns, integrating this with angle measure. Children possess intuitive knowledge of turns and angles and five-year-olds can match angles in correspondence tasks (Beilin et al., 1982).

Research has not adequately compared different approaches to teaching angle, but some teaching strategies have been suggested based on studies. Mitchelmore and colleagues have proposed a sequence of tasks, described in the companion book (Mitchelmore, 1989, 1992, 1993, 1998), and summarized as follows.

Begin by providing practical experiences with angle in various contexts, including corners, bends, turns, openings, and slopes. The first examples for each should have two "arms of the angle" physically present, such as in scissors, roach junctions, a corner of a table. Corners are the most salient for children and should be emphasized first. The other physical models can follow. Experience with bending (e.g., a pipe cleaner) and turning (e.g., doorknobs, dials, doors) would be introduced last in this early phase.

Then help children understand the angular relationships in each context by discussing the common features of similar contexts, such as bends in lines or in paths on maps.

Next, help students bridge the different contexts by representing the common features of angles in each context. For example, that they can be represented by two line segments (or rays) with a common endpoint. Once turns are understood, use the dynamic notion of turning to begin measuring the size of the angles.

Learning Trajectory for Shapes

As others we have seen, the learning trajectory for shapes is complex. First, there are several conceptual and skill advancements that makes levels more complicated. Second, there are four *subtrajectories* that are related, but can develop somewhat independently. (a) The *Comparing* subtrajectory involves matching by different criteria in the early levels and determining congruence. (b) The *Classifying* subtrajectory includes recognizing, identifying ("naming"), analyzing, and classifying shapes. (c) The *Parts* subtrajectory involves distinguishing, naming, describing, and quantifying the components of shapes, such as sides and angles. (d) The closely related *Representing* subtrajectory involves building or drawing shapes.

Table 8.1 provides the developmental progression and the mental actions-on-objects for this learning trajectory. Given the poor educational experiences provided most children in the studies on which this is based, the age of acquisitions are particularly variable.

Table 8.1 Learning Trajectory for Shapes

Age (years)	Developmental Progression	Actions on Objects
0–2	**"Same Thing" Comparer** *Comparing* Compares real-world objects (Vurpillot, 1976). Says two pictures of houses are the same or different. **Shape Matcher—Identical** *Comparing* Matches familiar shapes (circle, square, typical triangle) with *same size and orientation*. Matches  . —**Sizes** Matches familiar shapes with *different sizes*. Matches  . —**Orientations** Matches familiar shapes with *different orientations*. Matches  .	"Bootstrap" competences encourage active engagement (physically and perceptually) with shape, including parsing objects and figures into implicitly-recognized components such as edges, maintenance of size constancies, pattern matching through feature analysis (guided by heuristics that use symmetry or other features to impose an intrinsic framework on the perceptual input), bias toward symmetry, and regularity detection. Match based on meaning of objects; e.g., two houses. Congruence: 3s·* responses, to comparison task with verbal instructions show little relation to the characteristics of the stimulus; first "same" judgments express a communality of representational meaning between two objects; there does not appear to be any extraction of a common part or attribute (all houses are the same). *It must be acknowledged that there are no present studies which might tell us what it is in the perceived object that makes it possible for the two to three-year-old child to identify the house or duck. (Vurpillot, 1976).

Continued Overleaf

Age (years)	Developmental Progression	Actions on Objects
3	**Shape Recognizer—Typical** *Classifying* Recognizes and names typical circle, square, and, less often, a typical triangle. May physically rotate shapes in atypical orientations to mentally match them to a prototype.	The above competencies, along with repeated social experience with the culturally-determined shape classes generates networks sensitive to the exemplars for those classes. Salient perceptual characteristics (e.g., contour or a angle with the vertex at the top) may activate these nascent schemes.

Names this a square .

Some children correctly name different sizes, shapes and orientations of rectangles, but also call some shapes rectangles that look rectangular but are not rectangles.

Names these shapes "rectangles" (including the non-rectangular

parallelogram) .

"Similar" Comparer *Comparing* Judges two shapes the same if they are more visually similar than different.

"These are the same. They are pointy at the top."

Implicit quantification of the similarity of objects being compared via salient characteristics results in judgments of two objects as "the same shape" when they are computed to be more similar than they are different.

| 3–4 | **Shape Matcher—More Shapes** *Comparing* Matches a wider variety of shapes with *same size and orientation*. | |

—Sizes and Orientations Matches a wider variety of shapes with *different sizes and orientations*.

Matches these shapes

—Combinations Matches *combinations* of shapes to each other.

Matches these shapes .

Age (years)	Developmental Progression	Actions on Objects
4	**Shape Recognizer—Circles, Squares, and Triangles+** *Classifying* Recognizes some less typical squares and triangles and may recognize some rectangles, but usually not rhombuses (diamonds). Often doesn't differentiate sides/corners. Names these as triangles .	Schemes for shapes are expanded to includes multiple prototypes that are more flexible, but nevertheless operate within constraints. Each shape name serve as nexus for attention to the relevant characteristics which (especially under favorable social interactions) are increasingly representationally redescribed.
	Part Comparer *Comparing* Says two shapes are the same after matching one side on each (Beilin, 1984; Beilin et al., 1982). "These are the same" (matching the two sides).	Scanning of images results in identification of sides of approximately the same length. This guides the matching of those edges of the physical shapes, and if they approximately coincide, a "match" is determined (mathematically inaccurately generalized to indicate congruent shapes). If the physical match is rejected, the process is repeated.
	Constructor of Shapes from Parts—Looks Like *Parts* Uses manipulatives representing parts of shapes, such as sides, to make a shape that "looks like" a goal shape. May think of angles as a corner (which is "pointy"). Asked to make a triangle with sticks, creates the following 	Perceptually available model (or, for familiar forms, global and static mental image), implicitly analyzed, guides the physical placement of manipulatives to create an approximate configuration for a given shape. Initially, the implicit analysis considers each component (even lines transversed by others) separately (integration is limited to approximate relative location and orientation). These gradually become more integrated into a coherent whole.
	Some Attributes Comparer *Comparing* Looks for differences in attributes, but may examine only part of shape. "These are the same" (indicating the top halves of the shapes are similar by laying them on top of each other).	Items scanned to compare attributes. A result of "the same" is produced if there is an *absence* of relevant differences and "not the same" by presence of at least one relevant difference. However, scanning is not necessarily comprehensive of all the items' attributes and not all scanned attributes are necessarily compared; comprehensiveness of both processes increases with age. *Continued Overleaf*

Age (years)	Developmental Progression	Actions on Objects
4–5	**Shape Recognizer—All Rectangles** *Classifying* Recognizes more rectangle sizes, shapes, and orientations of rectangles. Correctly names these shapes "rectangles" .	The right angle is more firmly embedded in schemes for rectangles (especially in favorable environments in which children are encouraged to focus on this and other single characteristics).
	Side Recognizer *Parts* Identifies sides as distinct geometric objects. Asked what this shape is , says it is a quadrilateral (or has four sides) after counting each, running finger along the length of each side.	System explicitly can "pull out" each side as a separate conceptual object while simultaneously considering it part of the whole shape.
	Most Attributes Comparer *Comparing* Looks for differences in attributes, examining full shapes, but may ignore some spatial relationships. "These are the same."	Scans shapes comprehensively and compares most attributes (more accurately than in previous levels). After the scan of the shapes, most likely component is selected and physical match is attempted. The other components are then visually estimated (for some, all components are physically matched). If all components match, the result is "the same shape." However, physical and especially visual matching may not be exact and the spatial relationships among components (i.e., what we call "properties" of shapes) may be ignored (e.g., only a small percentage begin to conceptualize such properties as right angles).
	Corner (Angle) Recognizer—*Parts* Recognizes angles as separate geometric objects, at least in the limited context of "corners." Asked, why is this a triangle, says, "It has three angles" and counts them, pointing clearly to each vertex.	System explicitly can "pull out" each angle as a separate conceptual object while simultaneously considering it part of the whole shape.
5	**Shape Recognizer—More Shapes** *Classifying* Recognizes most familiar shapes and typical examples of other shapes, such as hexagon, rhombus (diamond), and trapezoid. Correctly identifies and names all the following shapes, .	Schemes for shapes, even those with few prototypes (circle, square) are developed based on the synergistic combination of rich visual/constructive experiences and verbal declarative knowledge that constrains the visual components of the scheme.

Age (years)	Developmental Progression	Actions on Objects

6 | **Shape Identifier** *Classifying* Names most common shapes, including rhombuses, avoiding mistakes such as calling ovals circles. Recognizes (at least) right angles, so distinguishes between a rectangle and a parallelogram without right angles. | Verbal declarative knowledge is evoked in more contexts to constrain visual/spatial aspects of shape schemes and to analyze geometric shapes. Visual/spatial knowledge is more differentiated and specific. Thus, children are more accurate in classifications.

Correctly names all the following shapes .

7 | **Angle Recognizer—More Contexts** *Parts* Can recognize and describe contexts in which angle knowledge is relevant, including corners (can discuss "sharper" angles), crossings (e.g., a scissors), and, later, bent objects and bends (sometimes bends in paths and slopes). Only later can explicitly understand how angle concepts relate to these contexts (e.g., initially may not think of bends in roads as angles; may not be able to add horizontal or vertical to complete the angle in slope contexts; may even see corners as more or less "sharp" without representing the lines that constitute them). Often does not relate these contexts and may represent only some features of angles in each (e.g., oblique line for a ramp in a slope context).

Parts of Shapes Identifier
Classifying Identifies shapes in terms of their components.

"No matter how skinny it looks, that's a triangle *because* it has three sides and three angles." ⎯⎯⎯ | Verbal declarative knowledge is evoked deliberately to analyze geometric shapes. Visual/spatial knowledge is increasingly specific and under metacognitive control. Cognitively, components are explicitly separated out from a figure while remaining integrated with other components.

Congruence Determiner
Comparing Determines congruence by comparing all attributes and all spatial relationships. | Scans shapes and compares attributes comprehensively. Increasing visual inspection of sides and angles

Continued Overleaf

Age (years)	Developmental Progression	Actions on Objects
	Says that two shapes are the same shape and the same size after comparing every one of their sides and angles.	integrated into a totality producing a superposition strategy; i.e., system directs the use of physical motions to produce superposition; if all components (do not) match, the result is a determination of (non) congruence (note that "same" and "not the same" may regain two different structures, Vurpillot, 1976).
	Congruence Superposer *Comparing* Moves and places objects on top of each other to determine congruence.	
	Says that two shapes are the same shape and the same size because they can be laid on top of each other.	
	Constructor of Shapes from Parts—Exact *Representing* Uses manipulatives representing parts of shapes, such as sides and angle "connectors," to make a shape that is completely correct, based on knowledge of components and relationships.	Perceptually available model or mental image now supplemented with explicit knowledge of geometric properties guides the physical placement of manipulatives to create an accurate (within perceptual-motor limits) configuration for a goal shape. With age and experience, components and relations, such as intersections and oblique orientations, are increasingly organized hierarchically.
	Asked to make a triangle with sticks, creates the following. △	
8+	**Angle Representer** *Parts* Represents various angle contexts as two lines, explicitly including the reference line (horizontal or vertical for slope; a "line of sight" for turn contexts) and, at least implicitly, the size of the angle as the rotation between these lines (may still maintain misconceptions about angle measure, such as relating angle size to the length of sides distance between endpoints and may not apply these understandings to multiple contexts).	As above with explicit concepts for angles and their measure.
	Congruence Representer *Comparing* Refers to geometric properties and explains with transformations.	As previously, but with explicit knowledge of geometric properties and criteria for mathematical explanations (e.g., congruence of all properties, superimposition), produces accurate determination of congruence and explanation.
	"These must be congruent, because they have equal sides, all square corners, and I can move them on top of each other exactly."	

Age (years)	Developmental Progression	Actions on Objects
	Shape Class Identifier *Classifying* Uses class membership (e.g., to sort), not explicitly based on properties.	Schemes for shapes are organized hierarchically, based on a combination of visual imagery and "double-naming" and other linguistic aids (e.g., "a square is a special type of rectangle").
	"I put the triangles over here, and the quadrilaterals, including squares, rectangles, rhombuses, and trapezoids over there."	
	Shape Property Identifier *Classifying* Uses properties explicitly. Can see the invariants in the changes of state or shape, but maintaining the shapes' properties.	Schemes for shapes are organized hierarchically, based on a combination of flexible visual imagery and especially analysis of shared and non-shared components and properties.
	"I put the shapes with opposite sides parallel over here, and those with four sides but not both pairs of sides parallel over there."	
	Property Class Identifier *Classifying* Uses class membership for shapes (e.g., to sort or consider shapes "similar") explicitly based on properties, including angle measure. Is aware of restrictions of transformations and also of the definitions and can integrate the two. Sorts hierarchically, based on properties.	Classes are connected to, and can be operated in terms of, their properties.
	"I put the equilateral triangles over here, and scalene triangles over here. The isosceles triangles are all these . . . they included the equilaterals."	
	Angle Synthesizer *Parts* Combines various meanings of angle (turn, corner, slant), including angle measure.	A network for various meanings of angles is established, interrelating these meanings.
	"This ramp is at a 45° angle to the ground."	

Final Words

Geometric thinking are essential human abilities that contribute to mathematical ability. Their importance is highlighted by findings that infants assign greater weight to spatiotemporal information than color or form in their definition of what an object is (Newcombe & Huttenlocher, 2000).

Thereafter, toddlers use the shape of objects as the essential cue used in learning the identity and names of objects. For example, training 17-month-olds to attend to shape led them to generalize that objects with similar shape have the same name, and engendered a dramatic increase of 350 percent in learning new words outside of the laboratory (L. B. Smith, Jones, Landau, Gershkoff-Stowe, & Samuelson, 2002).

Although far less developed than our knowledge of number, research provides guidelines for developing young children's learning of geometric and spatial abilities. However, we do not know the potential of children's learning if a conscientious, sequenced development of spatial thinking and geometry were provided to children throughout their earliest years. This can also be seen as a caveat. Research on the learning of shapes and certain aspects of visual literacy suggest the inclusion of these topics in the early years. We have insufficient evidence on the effects (efficacy and efficiency) of including topics such as congruence, similarity, transformations, and angles in curricula and teaching at specific age levels. Such research, and longitudinal research on many such topics, is needed.

Finally, competencies in these first two major realms, spatial/geometric and quantitative/number, are connected, probably at deep levels, throughout development. The earliest competencies may share common perceptual and representational origins (Mix et al., 2002). Infants are sensitive to both amount of liquid in a container (Gao, Levine, & Huttenlocher, 2000) and distance a toy is hidden in a long sandbox (Newcombe, Huttenlocher, & Learmonth, 1999). Visual-spatial deficits in early childhood are detrimental to children's development of numerical competencies (Semrud-Clikeman & Hynd, 1990; Spiers, 1987). Other evidence shows specific spatially-related learning disabilities in arithmetic, possibly more so for boys than girls (Share, Moffitt, & Silva, 1988). Children with Williams Syndrome, who show impairment on visuo-spatial construction tasks, can learn reading and spelling, but have difficulty learning mathematics (Bellugi, Lichtenberger, Jones, Lai, & St. George, 2000; Howlin, Davies, & Udwin, 1998). Primary school children's thinking about "units" and "units of units" was found to be consistent in both spatial and numerical problems (Clements, Battista, Sarama, & Swaminathan, 1997). In this and other ways, specific spatial abilities appear to be related to mathematical competencies (D. L. Brown & Wheatley, 1989; Clements & Battista, 1992; Fennema & Carpenter, 1981; Wheatley et al., 1994). Geometric measurement connects the spatial and numeric realms explicitly and is the topic of Chapters 10 and 11. First, we complete the discussion of shapes with Chapter 9's focus on shape composition.

9

Composition and Decomposition of Shapes

The ability to describe, use, and visualize the effects of composing and decomposing geometric regions is significant in that the concepts and actions of creating and then iterating units and higher-order units in the context of constructing patterns, measuring, and computing are established bases for mathematical understanding and analysis (Clements, Battista, Sarama, & Swaminathan, 1997; Reynolds & Wheatley, 1996; Steffe & Cobb, 1988). Additionally, there is suggestive evidence that this type of composition corresponds with, and may support, children's ability to compose and decompose numbers (Clements, Sarama, Battista, & Swaminathan, 1996).

In this chapter we examine three related topics. First, we discuss composition of three-dimensional shapes in the restricted but important early childhood setting of building with blocks. Second, we discuss composition and decomposition of two-dimensional shapes. Third, we discuss disembedding of two-dimensional shapes, such as in embedded (hidden) figure problems.

Composition of 3-D Shapes

Block building provides a view of children's initial abilities to compose three-dimensional objects (as well as their formation of a system of logic, cf. Forman, 1982). Children initially build structures from simple components and later explicitly synthesize three-dimensional shapes into higher-order three-dimensional shapes. In their first year, children either engage in little systematic organization of objects or show little interest in stacking (Forman, 1982; Kamii et al., 2004; Stiles & Stern, 2001). Instead, they pound, clap together, or slide the blocks (Goodson, 1982) or use single blocks to represent an object, such as a house or vehicle (Reifel, 1984). The first composite constructions are simple combinations of pairs.

Even when combining more than two blocks, children remain in one dimension. Stacking begins at one year, thus showing use of the spatial relationship of "on" (Kamii et al., 2004). Occasionally, children balance blocks intuitively as a stack of rectangular prisms, for example, but often they place a block off center or on an edge of a triangular prism. In the latter case, they recognize lack of success when the block falls, but do not attempt to understand

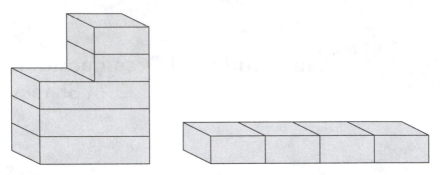

Figure 9.1 At two years, children place blocks, often congruent blocks, on or next to other blocks.

it. The next-to relation, creating structures such as a road or "train," develops at about one and a half years (Goodson, 1982; Stiles-Davis, 1988).

At about two years, children place each successive block congruently on or next to the one previously placed (Stiles-Davis, 1988), respectively, shown in Figure 9.1. They appear to recognize that blocks stacked vertically do not fall when so placed. At this point, children begin to reflect (think back) and anticipate (Kamii et al., 2004). Around two to three years of age, children begin to extend their building to two dimensions, covering to an extent a plane in creating a floor or wall (Guanella, 1934).

At three to four years of age, children regularly build vertical and horizontal components within a building (Stiles & Stern, 2001). They can use the relations only in sequence at age two and a half or three years, creating multicomponent structures, but within a limited range, such as the simple arch. This involves the simplest hierarchical integration, in that blocks are combined to create increasingly complex structures using blocks to integrate other blocks, as in the case of a horizontal block in an arch spanning and thus uniting, two vertical blocks (Goodson, 1982; Guanella, 1934; Reifel, 1984; Sluss, 2002).

When asked to build "a tall tower," they use long blocks vertically, because they have added to the goal of making a stable tower, making a stable tall tower, first using only one block in this fashion, then several (Kamii et al., 2004). At four years, they can use multiple spatial relations, extending in multiple directions and with multiple points of contact among components, showing flexibility in how they generate and integrate parts of the structure. A small number of children will build a tower with all blocks; for example, by composing the triangular blocks, making subparts to coordinate with the whole (Kamii et al., 2004). For example, a four-year-old built the tower in Figure 9.2, intuitively classifying the blocks by stability, and ordering them by that categorization, using the more stable blocks at the bottom, combining triangular prisms in the layer near the top and another triangular prism in unstable position at the top.

Figure 9.2 A children's building shows evidence of using blocks that will build a stable tower.

Figure 9.3 Slightly higher levels of block composition show working in two directions.

This developmental progression was used to study children's processes in relation to task complexity (Stiles & Stern, 2001). Three-year-olds could not produce the more complex constructions, including an enclosure, "+," and horizontal corner (illustrated respectively in Figure 9.3). Their strategy was simple and unsystematic accretion of parts. Children of four or five years could use a more sophisticated strategy organized around main construction components, but they regressed to simpler strategies for the most difficult tasks. Children of six years did not differ from adults on these tasks. The authors concluded that spatial processing in young children is not qualitatively different from that of older children or adults. However, with age, children produce progressively more elaborate constructions. The way they analyze spatial arrays also changes; they segment out different elements and relational structures. For example, to make a "+," adults often complete one long segment and add two short segments, but children build four components around a point. Finally, as children develop, they choose more advanced strategies, but this is influenced by the task.

Consistent with our theoretical standpoint, this development reflects *progressive hierarchization*. There is some evidence that at about four to five years of age, children develop an internalized representation of a spatial arrangement before and during a block construction, without needing to refer to a perceptually available model (e.g., Goodson, 1982). Before that level of thinking, their reproductions mirror a global aspect of a model or capture isolated parts, but only later do they reproduce individual parts (without organization) and then, finally, integrate the parts and the whole. For example, children learn to build an arch, such as Figure 9.4, by two and a half to three years, and most three-year-olds can build a row of arches. By four years of age, they could relate arches in two dimensions (Fig. 9.5), and between four and five years, can build a simple hierarchical structure of arches: an "arch of arches" as shown in Figure 9.6. Only children more than five years of age could build more complex hierarchical figures, in which, for example, eight arches on three levels related in two dimensions, as in Figure 9.7 (an arch of arch-of-arches). This implies a mental plane that organizes substructures. For example, building an arch of arches is related to building a "arch" as a mental unit and then organizing multiple copies of those units (Goodson, 1982). For the construction of Figure 9.7, children might build the arches in each layer, then follow the same strategy on the next higher layer, or build by layers.

In summary, to develop, children have to understand and relate both parts and whole, by analyzing the structure into component parts and organizing those parts to reconstruct the whole. Such understanding of the whole integrates the hierarchical relationships between the parts, units composed of parts, and the whole. For example, children understand how individual blocks combine (both in spatial position and functional relationship) to make an arch, similarly understand how individual arches can combine to make an arch-of-arches, and can simultaneously recognize the individual parts and their role in the structure of the whole. Their ability to build and manipulate individual

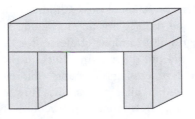

Figure 9.4 A building blocks arch.

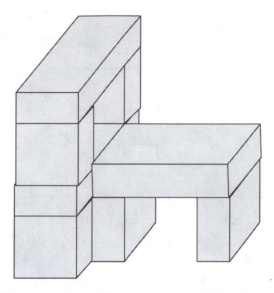

Figure 9.5 Relating arches in two dimensions.

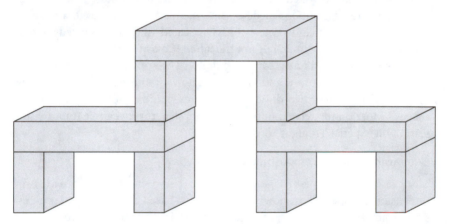

Figure 9.6 An arch of arches.

(blocks) and composite (arches) units *mentally* allows them to build and follow a mental plan for construction.

Kamii (2004) argues for focusing on children's general reasoning with a Piagetian perspective. From a different perspective, children's performance on a block design task was consistent with Vygotskian theory, predicted both by preschoolers' initial abilities and a dynamic assessment of their learning potential (Day, Engelhardt, Maxwell, & Bolig, 1997). Both these areas were domain-specific, supporting the position that cognition is multidimensional.

Figure 9.7 An arch of arches of arches.

A related study asked children to make cube buildings from two-dimensional representations or determine the number of cubes in a pictured cube building. An included case study indicated that an advanced kindergartner could do the former, but not the latter. It may be that he was unable to visualize the shapes and needed manipulatives (Leeson et al., 1997). Thus, less advanced children in pre-K and kindergarten may require hands-on materials to help them interpret two-dimensional representations of three-dimensional shapes. (More on the related notion of spatial structuring can be found in the section on "Spatial Thought" on pp. 296–299.)

Composition and Decomposition of 2-D Shapes

More research on actual shape composition has been conducted with two-dimensional shapes. The following is a research-based developmental progression, which approximately spans ages three to eight years (Clements, Sarama, & Wilson, 2001; Sarama, Clements, & Vukelic, 1996). This learning trajectory, first noted in Sarama, Clements, & Vukelic, 1996, has been explicated by these researchers in and for the *Buildings Blocks* project (Clements, Sarama et al., 2001). From lack of competence in composing geometric shapes, children gain abilities to combine shapes—initially through trial and error and gradually by attributes—into pictures, and finally synthesize combinations of shapes into new shapes (composite shapes). The basic competence is combining shapes to produce composite shapes. We hypothesized the following levels of thinking.

PRE-COMPOSER

Children manipulate shapes as individuals, but are unable to combine them to compose a larger shape. Children cannot accurately match shapes to even simple frames (closed figures that can be filled with a single shape).

PIECE ASSEMBLER

Children at this level are similar to Pre-composers, but they place shapes contiguously to form pictures, often touching only at vertices. In free form "make a picture" tasks, for example, each shape used represents a unique role, or function in the picture (e.g., one shape for one leg). Children can fill simple frames using trial and error (Mansfield & Scott, 1990; Sales, 1994), but have limited ability to use turns or flips to do so; they cannot use motions to see shapes from different perspectives (Sarama, Clements, & Vukelic, 1996). Thus, children at the first two levels view shapes only as wholes and see few geometric relationships between shapes or between parts of shapes (i.e., a property of the shape).

PICTURE MAKER

Children can concatenate shapes contiguously to form pictures in which several shapes play a single role (e.g., a leg might be created from three contiguous rhombuses, as in Figure 9.8), but use trial and error and do not anticipate creation of new geometric shapes. Shapes are chosen using gestalt configuration or one component such as side length (Sarama, Clements, & Vukelic, 1996). If several sides of the existing arrangement form a partial boundary of a shape (instantiating a schema for it), the child can find and place that shape. If such cues are not present, the child matches by a side length. The child may attempt to match corners, but does not possess angle as a quantitative

Figure 9.8 Children at the *Picture Maker* level can concatenate several blocks to make one part of a construction, such as an arm or leg.

entity, so they try to match shapes into corners of existing arrangements in which their angles do not fit (a "picking and discarding" strategy). Rotating and flipping are used, usually by trial-and-error, to try different arrangements (Sarama, Clements, & Vukelic, 1996; Wheatley & Cobb, 1990). Thus, children can complete a frame that suggests that placement of the individual shapes but in which several shapes together may play a single semantic role in the picture.

SHAPE COMPOSER

Children combine shapes to make new shapes or fill puzzles, with growing intentionality and anticipation. Shapes are chosen using angles as well as side lengths. Eventually, the child considers several alternative shapes with angles equal to the existing arrangement. Rotation and flipping are used intentionally and mentally (i.e., with anticipation) to select and place shapes (Sarama, Clements, & Vukelic, 1996; Wheatley & Cobb, 1990). They can fill complex frames (figures whose filling requires multiple shapes) (Sales, 1994) or cover regions (Mansfield & Scott, 1990). Imagery and systematicity grow within this and the following levels. In summary, there is intentionality and anticipation, based on the shapes' attributes, and thus, the child has imagery of the component shapes, although imagery of the composite shape develops within this level (and throughout the following levels).

SUBSTITUTION COMPOSER

Children deliberately form composite units of shapes (Clements, Battista, Sarama, & Swaminathan, 1997) and recognize and use substitution relationships among these shapes.

SHAPE COMPOSITE ITERATER

Children construct and operate on composite units (units of units) intentionally. They can continue a pattern of shapes that leads to a "good covering," but without coordinating units of units (Clements, Battista, Sarama, & Swaminathan, 1997).

SHAPE COMPOSER WITH SUPERORDINATE UNITS

Children build and apply (iterate and otherwise operate on) units of units of units.

Three sources of evidence supported the validity of this theory (Clements, Sarama et al., 2001; Clements, Wilson et al., 2004). First, the original hypothetical learning trajectory and the developmental progression underlying it emerged from naturalistic observations of young children composing shapes (Clements, Battista, Sarama, & Swaminathan, 1997; Mansfield & Scott, 1990; Sales, 1994; Sarama, Clements, & Vukelic, 1996, Sarama & Clements, in preparation). Second, the levels of the developmental progression were tested iteratively in formative research that involved researchers and teachers. Their case studies indicated that about four-fifths of the children studied evinced behaviors consistent with the developmental progression (using an early version of the instrument). By the end of this phase, all participants believed the developmental progression and the items retained to measure levels in the progression to be valid and that they could reliably classify children as exhibiting thinking on the progression. Third, a summative study employed the final instrument with 72 randomly selected children from pre-K to grade 2. Analyses revealed that the level scores fit the hypothesized structure in which scores from one level would be more highly correlated with scores immediately adjacent to that level than to scores on levels nonadjacent to the given level. Further, the developmental progression showed development across ages, with children at each grade scoring significantly higher than those at the preceding grade. In addition, support for this theory lies in its consistency with previously discussed research on children's perceptions of shape. In both, parts are related to wholes, with each part initially playing a single functional role in the pattern structure (cf. Tada & Stiles, 1996). Indeed, children spatially isolate parts at first, then arrange them contiguously, and later combine them in an integrative manner, eventually creating more complex units within different structural layers. In both cases, mature cognition is an end result of a developmental process in which parts and wholes are interrelated across hierarchical levels.

Disembedding 2-D Shapes

Children develop over years in learning how to separate structures within embedded figures. Visual discrimination, including figure-ground discrimination, appears to be innate, and visual stimuli are perceptually organized in the first year of life (Vurpillot, 1976). Vurpillot's work is grounded in Gestalt theorists, who, as we briefly described previously (e.g., p. 205), argue that the mind organizes input into a limited number of perceptual structures, called primary structures, essentially determined by the laws of "good" continuity and "good" form (closure, symmetry, internal equilibrium). For Vurpillot, the primary perceptual structures operate as rigid, indivisible, unanalyzable and unarticulated up to about four years of age, but between six and eight years they become flexible, decomposable and composable. Eventually these concepts and operations operate hierarchically (i.e., units can be combined, each one serving as a whole to the smaller units of which it is composed and, at the same time, as a component part of the comprehensive structure). Thus, in this age range, children develop the ability to break down line figures and reassemble them in new forms (as in embedded-figures problems), link up isolated perceptual units by means of imaginary lines to identify the more complex structures of incomplete figures, and pass from one structure to another when these are reversible figures (like Necker's cube in Figure 9.9).

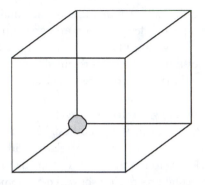

Figure 9.9 Necker's cube, a reversible figure in which the dot can be seen on the front or the back face of the cube.

Logically, a line segment has an infinite number of points, and the number of elements into which a line drawing can be broken is infinite. Even assuming every segment is perceived as a whole, there are a large number of possible combinations among those elements. Therefore, there is a large number of ways in which a perceiver might organize any line drawing of at least moderate complexity.

Gestalt theory leads to the following principles. (Figure 9.10 provides illustrations of the terms used, including primary and secondary structures for contours and areas.)

1. All the line segments of a figure are involved in construction of the primary contour structures (PCS; see Figure 9.10, rows 1 and 2).
2. No segment or part can belong to more than one primary structure.
3. A segment belongs in its entirety to a single primary contour structure.
4. The PCS are preferably symmetrical or at least as regular as possible.
5. The number of PCS must be the fewest possible.
6. Each area entirely surrounded by the line segments of a figure and not crossed by another line segment constitutes a primary area structure (PAS; see Figure 9.10, row 3).

Solving embedded-figures problems requires going beyond the primary structure to create secondary structures, which include segments borrowed from one or more PCS.

The preschooler can thus find a figure identical to a given PCS, but in other cases will incorrectly designate a PCS as the solution, as empirical findings suggest. The following problems present increasing degrees of difficulty, the first three primary levels of organization, the second three secondary levels of organization (in which parts can belong simultaneously to several structures, allowing the construction of new units).

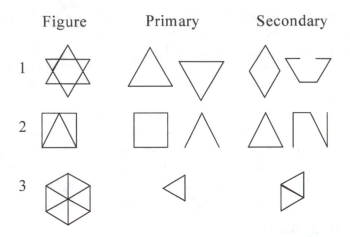

Figure 9.10 Rows 1 and 2 show contour structures (row one overlapping, row 2 juxtaposed) and Row 3 shows area structures.

1. The PCS that is the frame, or external contour (e.g., largest square, or outside contour, in the 3 by 3 arrangement of squares shown in Figure 9.11).
2. A PCS of a complex figure (triangle of Star of David, such as the PCS of Figure 9.10, row 1).
3. A PCS other than the frame (e.g., the tic-tac-toe layout of the arrangement of squares in Figure 9.11, that is, all *but* the largest square).
4. A figure that is not a PCS, but encloses a PAS (e.g., one of the smallest squares of the arrangement of squares in Figure 9.11.
5. Similar, but a sum of several PASs (e.g., a block "L" of squares, or a 2 by 2 square, from Figure 9.11.
6. A nonclosed figure that is not a PCS.

In finding a secondary structure, children less than six years of age often identify a PCS instead. Circles appear to be the easiest shapes to disembed, with rectangles, and then squares, more difficult (Ayers, Cannella, & Search, 1979).

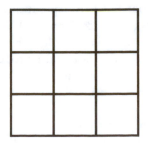

Figure 9.11 A 3-by-3 grid.

No gender differences were found. Even seven- to ten-year-olds may have difficulty finding embedded triangles (Bright, 1975).

There is limited recent research on this topic, but one study confirmed that few four-year-olds could find embedded circles or squares embedded in square structures (Clements et al., 1999). However, five-year-olds were more likely to do so.

In sum, before six years of age, what children perceive is organized in a rigid manner into structures whose form is determined by Gestalt principles. Children grow in the flexibility of the perceptual organizations they can create. They eventually integrate parts and use imaginary components, with anticipation. Beyond a certain level of complexity, people of any age cannot perceive secondary structures, but must construct them piece-by-piece.

Experience and Education

Composition of 3-D Shapes

Research indicates that block building is important for development of shape and shape composition ability, to say nothing of the general reasoning that it may also facilitate (Forman, 1982; Kamii et al., 2004; Stiles & Stern, 2001). A longitudinal study indicated that block building may help lay a foundation for mathematics achievement in later years (Wolfgang, Stannard, & Jones, 2001). Ratings of the sophistication of block building in preschool had no signification relationship to achievement in grades 3 and 5, but did correlate to standardized math scores in grade 7 and, at high school, positive and significantly correlated with all assessments, including number of mathematics courses taken, number of honors courses, advanced math courses taken and grades (Wolfgang et al., 2001). This evidence is only correlational, and the ratings were not solely based on mathematical aspects of block building, but they are suggestive.

Block building also has been linked to spatial skills. Most studies again have been only correlational; for example, nine-year-olds who build a specific model out of Lego blocks scored higher in spatial ability (e.g., mental rotation) than those who did not complete the model (Brosnan, 1998). The amount of time children spent in spatial-manipulative play has been correlated with performance on a spatial visualization test, here, reproducing patterns using the tops of small red and white cubes (Serbin & Connor, 1979). Similarly, in a preschool population, two types of block building skills—the complexity of block structures built during an open-ended task and reproducing a model of a block structure—were associated with two measures of spatial visualization, block design and analyzing and reproducing abstract patterns (Caldera et al., 1999).

Peers may have a positive influence on children's block building ability. For example, three-year-olds in a classroom with four- and five-year-olds showed more rapid development in block building than those in classrooms without more experienced peers (Gura, 1992).

These studies could not test for causal relationships. An experimental study provided one group with spatial-manipulative instruction. Only this group improved in spatial visualization skills (Sprafkin, Serbin, Denier, & Connor, 1983), providing evidence that the relationship is one of cause and effect.

Research suggests that teachers should not only provide materials, facilitate peer relationships, and time to build, but also incorporate planned, systematic block building into their curriculum, which they rarely do (Kersh et al., in press). Children should have open exploratory play and solve semi-structured and well-structured problems, with intentional teaching provided for each. Preschoolers who are provided such scaffolding display significant increases in the complexity of their block building (Gregory, Kim, & Whiren, 2003). Important to our learning trajectories approach, the teachers' scaffolding was based on professional development in recognizing developmental progressions in the levels of complexity of block building. They provide verbal scaffolding for the children based on those levels, but do not directly assist children, or engage in any block building themselves. Other studies intervened with full learning trajectories—that is, a goal, a developmental progression, and matched activities. Groups of kindergarteners who experienced such a learning trajectory improved in block-building skill more than control groups who received an equivalent amount of block-building experience during unstructured free play sessions (Kersh et al., in press). Thus, research provides guidelines, but we have only a few studies that compare approaches. We need additional research comparing strategies as well as more research on complementary approaches.

As we saw previously, spatial training may be more important for girls than boys (Connor, Serbin, & Schackman, 1977). Block building is another case in point. Girls and boys often differ in the ways they engage in block building (Farrell, 1957; Farwell, 1930; Kersh et al., in press; Margolin & Leton, 1961; Saracho, 1995). A smaller proportion of girls play with blocks. Boys tend to approach block building as an *engineering* task, often balancing a complex edifice upon a small, and thus risky, base (Kersh et al., in press). Thus, boys challenge themselves to create more *spatially* complex structures (Erikson, 1963; Kersh et al., in press). These differences are observed from the earliest years into adolescence (B. Casey, Pezaris, Anderson, & Bassi, 2004). The greater experience often leads to advantages for boys in measures of block-building ability, in middle-income children (Goodfader, 1982; Kersh et al., in press; Sluss, 2002). (Some authors argue that both experience and innate, psycho-analytic, factors play roles in gender differences, e.g., Goodfader, 1982.) However, in a three-year longitudinal study that exposed children to equal amounts of block building, no similar gender differences were found (Hanline, Milton, & Phelps, 2001). No differences were found in a university early childhood program either (Caldera et al., 1999). It may be that tasks were different, an issue to which we turn next, but it may also be that such programs attempt to involve girls in block play (Kersh et al., in press). Thus, children from higher-income, compared to lower-income, subcultures and boys, compared to girls, may often be provided more experience in block building.

Whatever the reason for the differences in girls' and boys' engagement in activities such as block play, it is reasonable to assume that planned, systematic activities will be relatively more beneficial for girls in today's U.S. culture. Girls tend not to engage in as much, or as spatially complex, block play during free choice activities as boys (Kersh et al., in press). Further, girls score lower on tasks in such settings. That is, gender differences favoring males appear in open-ended, unstructured block building tasks (Goodfader, 1982; Sluss, 2002), whereas there are little or no gender differences in semi-structured tasks that pose more specific problem-solving challenges (Reifel, 1984) or in highly structured tasks, for instance, in copying a building (Caldera et al., 1999). However, they can solve problems in structured activities and seem to gain from them as much as do boys. Thus, girls may develop valuable spatial and geometric knowledge and abilities if teachers are intentional about providing them with opportunities and encouragement for block play, intervening during block play based on developmental progressions, and especially engaging them in a sequence of semi- and well-structured construction tasks, based on a learning trajectory for block building.

These findings lead to an important implication: more structured and sequenced block-building interventions will help provide boys and girls with equitable, beneficial opportunities to learn about the structural properties of blocks and thus spatial skills. Research confirms that block-building skills improve more if kindergartners experience systematic interventions (Kersh et al., in press).

Learning Trajectory for Composition of 3-D Shapes

Table 9.1 provides the developmental progression and the mental actions-on-objects for this learning trajectory. This is *only* for the set of unit blocks; composition of more complex and less familiar three-dimentional shapes would follow the same developmental progression but at later ages and with more dependence on experiences.

Composition and Decomposition of 2-D Shapes

The content and effects of one program illustrate the importance of shape and shape composition. An artist and collaborating educational researchers developed the Agam program to develop the "visual language" of children ages three to seven years (Eylon & Rosenfeld, 1990). (A description of the activities is provided in the companion book.) The results of using the program, especially for several consecutive years, are positive. Children gain in geometric and spatial skills and show pronounced benefits in the areas of arithmetic and writing readiness (Razel & Eylon, 1990). These results support systematic

Table 9.1 A Developmental Progression for the Composition of 3-D Shape

Age (years)	Developmental Progression	Actions on Objects
0–1	**Pre-Composer (3-D)** Manipulates shapes as individuals, but does not combine them to compose a larger shape. May pound, clap together, or slide blocks or use single blocks to represent an object, such as a house or truck.	
1	**Stacker** Shows use of the spatial relationship of "on" to stack blocks, but choice of blocks is unsystematic.	See the learning trajectory for motions and spatial sense.
1½	**Line Maker** Shows use of relationship of "next to" to make a line of blocks.	See the learning trajectory for motions and spatial sense.
2	**Congruency Stacker** Shows use of relationship of "on" to stack congruent blocks, or those that show a similarly helpful relationship to make stacks or lines.	See the learning trajectories for matching shapes and for motions and spatial sense. With immediate perceptual support of and feedback from action upon physical 3-D shapes, selects a shape that appears to correspond to another shape and moves it into correspondence.
2	**Piece Assembler (3-D)** Builds vertical and horizontal components within a building, but within a limited range, such as building a "floor" or simple "wall."	With the perceptual support of concrete objects, uses trial and error strategy to apply slide and turn motions to shapes so the shapes correspond with a model (or perceptually supported mental image). Recognition of the composite is based on a provided visual gestalt and is post hoc.
3–4	**Picture Maker (3-D)** Uses multiple spatial relations, extending in multiple directions and with multiple points of contact among components, showing flexibility in integrating parts of the structure. Produces arches, enclosures, corners, and crosses, but may use unsystematic trial and error and simple addition of pieces.	In addition to previous actions-on-objects, with perceptual support of concrete objects, mentally fills in one or two missing components of a simple building, at least maintaining a length and global shape, then finds an approximately corresponding shape from a provided set of concrete shapes. Visualizes extent in two and three dimensions.

Continued Overleaf

Age (years)	Developmental Progression	Actions on Objects
4–5	**Shape Composer (3-D)** Composes shapes with anticipation, understanding what 3-D shape will be produced with a composition of two or more other (simple, familiar) 3-D shapes. Can produce arches, enclosures, corners, and crosses systematically. Builds enclosures and arches several blocks high (Kersh et al., in press).	A turning point in shape composition, builds, maintains, and manipulates *mental* images of 3-D shapes and builds images of how these combine to create other shapes. For simple combinations, relates the image's parts to wholes. Uses the three rigid motions with anticipation.
5–6	**Substitution Composer and Shape Composite Repeater (3-D)** Substitutes a composite for a congruent whole. Builds complex bridges with multiple arches, with ramps and stairs at the ends.	Uses, and synthesizes, composition and decomposition strategies mentally and intentionally, allowing the composition or decomposition of shapes and substitution of a composition of shapes for other shapes (and vice versa).
6–8+	**Shape Composer—Units of Units (3-D)** Makes complex towers or other structures, involving multiple levels with ceilings (fitting the ceilings), adult-like structures with blocks, including arches and other substructures.	Builds, maintains, and manipulates units of units of units.

long-term instruction in the domain of geometry and spatial thinking in early childhood (Razel & Eylon, 1990). Children are better prepared for all school tasks when they gain the thinking tools and representational competence of geometric and spatial sense.

Two studies using puzzles found some success in raising children's ability to compose with two-dimensional shapes (M. B. Casey, Erkut, Ceder, & Young, 2008). In the first, kindergarteners were given a story-based geometry intervention. Compared to a control group, girls, but not boys, increased their scores on a near- but not a far-transfer test. In the second study, low-income kindergarteners increased both near-and far-transfer test scores more in a storytelling-context than in a de-contextualized format. Girls again benefited more than boys from the geometry-content interventions (both with and without a story context). Caveats include that this was a quasi-experimental study, whose analyses treated the student as the unit of analyses, even though children were clustered in classrooms.

Supporting these results, emphasis on the learning trajectory for composition of shape in the *Building Blocks* program led to strong effects in this area. The first study revealed that preschoolers in the *Building Blocks* curriculum, compared to those in a control group, developed competencies in two-dimensional composition, with effect sizes greater than two dimensions—equivalent to effects usually found for individual tutoring (Clements & Sarama, 2007c). In a follow-up, large-scale randomized field trial with 36 classrooms, the *Building Blocks* curriculum (Clements & Sarama, 2007a) made the most substantial gains compared to both a non-treatment and another preschool math curriculum, the *Pre-K Mathematics Curriculum* (A. Klein et al., 2002) and other groups in shape composition (and several other topics). Especially because the *Pre-K Mathematics Curriculum* also included shape composition activities, we believe that the greater gains caused by the *Building Blocks* curriculum can be attributed to its explicit use of the sequenced activities developed from, and the teachers' knowledge of, the learning trajectory, to which we turn.

Learning Trajectories for Composition and Decomposition of Geometric Shapes (2-D)

Because the developmental progressions for the composition and decomposition of two-dimensional geometric shapes are closely connected, we present them together, in Table 9.2 along with the mental actions on objects.

Table 9.2 A Developmental Progression for the Composition of 2-D Shapes

Age (years)	Developmental Progression	Actions on Objects
0–3	**Pre-Composer** Manipulates shapes as individuals, but is unable to combine them to compose a larger shape. Make a picture **Pre-DeComposer** Decomposes only by trial and error. Given *only* a hexagon, can break it apart to make this simple picture, by random placement.	See the learning trajectories for shapes and matching shapes. (Assumes perceptual support.)
4	**Piece Assembler** Makes pictures in which each shape represents a unique role (e.g., one shape for each body part) and shapes touch. Fills simple "Pattern Block Puzzles" using trial and error.	Sees the learning trajectories for matching shapes and for motions and spatial sense. Intuitively recognizes a manipulative shape that corresponds to a distinct outlined shape, with continuous perceptual support.

Continued Overleaf

Age (years)	Developmental Progression	Actions on Objects

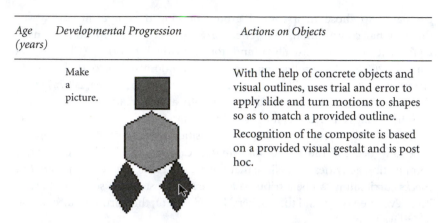

Make a picture.

With the help of concrete objects and visual outlines, uses trial and error to apply slide and turn motions to shapes so as to match a provided outline.

Recognition of the composite is based on a provided visual gestalt and is post hoc.

5	**Picture Maker** Puts several shapes together to make one part of a picture (e.g., two shapes for one arm). Uses trial and error and does not anticipate creation of new geometric shape. Chooses shapes using "general shape" or side length. Fills "easy" "Pattern Block Puzzles" that suggest the placement of each shape (but note below that the child is trying to put a square in the puzzle where its right angles will not fit).	In addition to previous actions-on-objects, completes a (gestalt) shape by mentally filling in one or two missing components (e.g., to build an image of a hexagon from the figure below), then finds a corresponding shape from a provided set of concrete shapes.

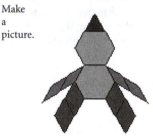

Make a picture.

Similarly, especially when such a gestalt is unavailable, but with consistent perceptual supports, maintains an approximate visual image of a side length, using this to choose a shape that matches the side of another shape or one line segment of an outline (as in selecting the square to fit in the non-square rhombus-shaped region in the "main" on the right).

Simple DeComposer. Decomposes ("takes apart" into smaller shapes) simple shapes that have obvious clues as to their decomposition.

Given the support of a concrete shape with perceptual cues as to a canonical decomposition, acts on the immediate visual field to direct the physical decomposition.

Given hexagons, can break it apart to make this picture.

Age (years)	Developmental Progression	Actions on Objects
	Shape Composer Composes shapes with anticipation ("I know what will fit!"). Chooses shapes using angles as well as side lengths. Rotation and flipping are used intentionally to select and place shapes. In the "Pattern Block Puzzles" below, all angles are correct, and patterning is evident.	A turning point in shape composition actions-on-objects, builds, maintains, and manipulates *mental* images of shapes and begins to build similar images of how they combine to create other shapes. Use the three rigid motions with anticipation.

Make a picture.

6	**Substitution Composer** Makes new shapes out of smaller shapes and uses trial and error to substitute groups of shapes for other shapes to create new shapes in different ways.	Use, and synthesizes, composition and decomposition strategies, allowing the composition or decomposition of a shape and the substitution of a composition of shapes for other shapes (and vice versa).

Make a picture with intentional sub- stitutions.

Shape DeComposer (with Help) Decomposes shapes using imagery that is suggested and supported by the task or environment.

Given the support of a concrete shape with cues as to a decomposition, acts on the immediate visual field to direct the physical decomposition.

Given hexagons, can break one or more apart to make this shape.

7	**Shape Composite Repeater** Constructs and duplicates units of units (shapes made from other shapes) intentionally; understands each as being both multiple small shapes *and* one larger shape. May continue a pattern of shapes that leads to tiling.	Builds, maintains, and manipulates *mental* images of composite shapes, structuring them as composites of individual units and as a single entity (a unit of units).

Children use a shape composition repeatedly in constructing a design or picture.

Continued Overleaf

Age (years)	Developmental Progression	Actions on Objects
	Shape DeComposer with Imagery Decomposes shapes flexibly using independently generated imagery.	Builds, maintains, and manipulates *mental* images of shapes and their constituent components, using a synthesis of decomposition and composition actions to direct those interacting processes.

Given hexagons, can break one or more apart to make shapes such as these.

| 8 | **Shape Composer—Units of Units** Builds and *applies* units of units (shapes make from other shapes). For example, in constructing spatial patterns, extend patterning activity to create a tiling with a new unit shape—a unit of unit shapes that they recognize and consciously construct. | Builds, maintains, and manipulates units of units of units. |

Builds a large structure by making a combination of pattern blocks over and over and then fitting them together.

| | **Shape DeComposer with Units of Units** Decomposes shapes flexibly using independently generated imagery and planned decompositions of shapes that themselves are decompositions. | As above. |

Given only squares, can break them apart—*and then break the resulting shapes apparent again*—to make shapes such as these.

Disembedding 2-D Shapes

There is a limited amount of research on the *educational* importance of the topic of disembedding two-dimensional shapes. Clearly, students need to do so to solve complex geometric problems. For example, success in geometry proofs often depends on the ability to see geometric figures in new ways (including extending and adding line segments). It may be that there are other advantages, in supporting composition and decomposition processes in general and in examining geometric structures. At least some researchers report that success on such tasks is directly related to children's overall success in school (Ayers et al., 1979), but they also report that (very simple) instructions did not raise competence. Thus, more research is needed before a confident recommendation could be made to spend a substantial amount of instructional time on this topic in the early years. As mentioned, however, the ability and predisposition to see embedded figures in different ways, and to construct—physically or mentally—extensions and additions to geometric diagrams, is necessary for the successful solution of many geometric problems, especially proofs. Thus, this is an important, under-appreciated skill (Schoenfeld, personal communication, June 6, 2008), and we need research to see when and how it can be best developed.

The primary task we use is a direct application of the skill: find figures in increasingly complex geometric figures, including embedded figures. Some research suggests that, pedagogically, it would be wise to have children embed figures themselves before finding already-embedded figures (Bright, 1975).

Learning Trajectories for Embedded Geometric Figures (2-D)

There is also little research from which to build a learning trajectory for disembedding. Relying heavily on older research, we present our development progression and mental actions-on-objects in Table 9.3.

Table 9.3 A Developmental Progression for Embedded Geometry Figures (2-D)

Age (years)	Developmental Progression	Actions on Objects
3	**Pre-Disembedder** Can remember and reproduce only one or small collection of nonoverlapping (isolated) shapes.	
4	**Simple Disembedder** Identifies frame of complex figure. Finds some shapes in arrangements in which figures	Maintains a visual trace or path along sides or curves of familiar shapes (with perceptual support), even if they are interrupted by the sides of another figure.

Continued Overleaf

Age (years)	Developmental Progression	Actions on Objects
	overlap, but not in which figures are embedded in others. 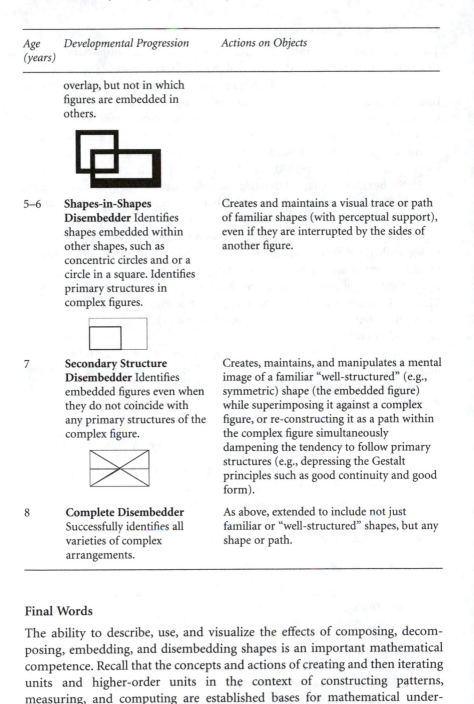	
5–6	**Shapes-in-Shapes Disembedder** Identifies shapes embedded within other shapes, such as concentric circles and or a circle in a square. Identifies primary structures in complex figures.	Creates and maintains a visual trace or path of familiar shapes (with perceptual support), even if they are interrupted by the sides of another figure.
7	**Secondary Structure Disembedder** Identifies embedded figures even when they do not coincide with any primary structures of the complex figure.	Creates, maintains, and manipulates a mental image of a familiar "well-structured" (e.g., symmetric) shape (the embedded figure) while superimposing it against a complex figure, or re-constructing it as a path within the complex figure simultaneously dampening the tendency to follow primary structures (e.g., depressing the Gestalt principles such as good continuity and good form).
8	**Complete Disembedder** Successfully identifies all varieties of complex arrangements.	As above, extended to include not just familiar or "well-structured" shapes, but any shape or path.

Final Words

The ability to describe, use, and visualize the effects of composing, decomposing, embedding, and disembedding shapes is an important mathematical competence. Recall that the concepts and actions of creating and then iterating units and higher-order units in the context of constructing patterns, measuring, and computing are established bases for mathematical understanding and analysis (Clements, Battista, Sarama, & Swaminathan, 1997; Reynolds & Wheatley, 1996; Steffe & Cobb, 1988). Additionally, this type of composition corresponds with, and supports, children's ability to compose and decompose numbers (Clements, Sarama et al., 1996). More directly, the abilities serve people well in solving a wide variety of problem, from geometric proofs to the design of a floor space. Of course, such designs also require geometric measurement, the topic of Part IV.

Part IV
Geometric Measurement

"Really to interpret the child's present crude impulses in counting, measuring, and arranging things in rhythmic series, involves mathematical scholarship—a knowledge of the mathematical formulae and relations which have, in the history of the race, grown out of such crude beginnings."

(Dewey, 1902/1976, p. 282)

"Geometry" means "earth measure." Geometric measurement is an essential part of people's lives. This alone justifies an emphasis on this topic.

Also, geometric measurement can serve as a bridge between the two critical domains of geometry and number, with each providing conceptual support to the other. Indications are, however, that this potential is usually not realized, as measurement is not taught well. Many children use measurement instruments or count units in a rote fashion and apply formulas to attain answers without meaning (Clements & Battista, 1992). For some attributes, children have difficulty establishing a proper unit for measurement, such as area (some erroneously count lengths), volume (some count faces) and, especially, angle (some use distance between rays, length of rays, etc., Clements & Battista, 1990; Clements, Battista, & Sarama, 2001a). In international comparisons, U.S. students' performance in measurement was low (NCES, 1996).

There are also equity concerns. Boys outperform girls, and higher SES children outperform lower SES children by a large amount, 20–30 percent (Vasilyeva & Casey, 2007, in a fourth grade sample). Boys had no such advantage on number tests, so their spatial abilities, or experience with measurement outside of school, may account for their better performance in measurement.

10
Geometric Measurement, Part 1
Length

We begin with a brief consideration of children's development of geometric measurement competencies from the earliest years. We then turn to measurement of length.

Children's Development in Geometric Measurement

Children's understanding of measurement has its roots in infancy and the preschool years, but grows over many years, as the work of Piaget and his collaborators has shown (Piaget & Inhelder, 1967; Piaget et al., 1960). As with number, however, Piagetians underestimated the abilities of the youngest children. For example, shown an object that was then occluded by a drawbridge, infants looked longer when the drawbridge rotated past the point where the object should have stopped it (Baillargeon, 1991). Thus, even infants are sensitive to continuous quantity (Gao et al., 2000), and even comparisons (Spelke, 2002) and accumulations (Mix et al., 2002) of continuous quantity at least in some conditions (cf. Huntley-Fenner et al., 2002). These studies show that early cognitive foundations of mathematics are not limited or unique to number. As with number, however, these abilities have limits. Infants and toddlers can discriminate between lengths of dowels, but only when a salient standard (a same-length dowel or container) was present; four-year-olds could discriminate with or without such a standard (Huttenlocher, Duffy, & Levine, 2002). Infants and toddlers may lack the ability to create and maintain a mental image of a length in all but special situations.

As we discussed, some believe that humans may be sensitive to amounts of continuous quantity and not discrete number (Clearfield & Mix, 1999). However, they do make distinctions. For example, when a small number of objects or portions of a substance is hidden and then revealed, 12- to 13-month-old infants expect that the former cannot be combined to make a larger object but that the latter can be coalesced into larger portions (Huntley-Fenner, 1999a). Recall that 11-, but not nine-month-old infants could discriminate sequences of number (Brannon, 2002). Noteworthy here is that the nine-month-olds could discriminate sequences of size; therefore, non-numerical ordinal judgments may develop before the capacity for numerical ordinal judgments.

Preschool children know that continuous attributes such as mass, length, and weight[1] exist, although they cannot quantify or measure them accurately.

Children two to four years of age can use the same three types of standards when judging "big" and "little" that adults use: perceptual (object is compared to another physically present object), normative (object is compared to a class standard stored in memory, such as a chihuahua is small for a dog), and functional (is this hat the right size for this doll?) (Ebeling & Gelman, 1988). Children also can coordinate these, preferring the perceptual to the normative if there is a conflict (asked if an object is larger than an egg, but then given an even larger egg, children will compare to the larger egg) and preferring either of these to the functional (which must be brought to the attention of three-, but not four-year-olds) (S. A. Gelman & Ebeling, 1989). Finally, children can switch within contexts and from a normative context to the others, but have difficulty switching to a normative context. The normative context may differ from the perceptual and functional contexts in that there are not physically present stimuli and thus may be accessible only when no other context has been recently experienced (Ebeling & Gelman, 1994).

As young as three years of age, children know explicitly that if they have some clay and then are given more clay, they have more than they did before. However, preschoolers cannot reliably make judgments about which of two amounts of clay is more; they use perceptual cues such as which is longer. Children do not reliably differentiate between continuous and discrete quantity, for example, basing equal sharing on the number of cookie pieces rather than the amount of substance (K. F. Miller, 1984; Piaget et al., 1960).

Further, they have not yet integrated their counting (e.g., of discrete entities) with measurement (counting units of continuous quantity). For example, four- and five-year olds were more likely to count when asked which group had "more glasses" than if asked which had "more sand," even though in each comparison the same sand was in the same glasses (Huntley-Fenner, 1999b). Younger children responded inaccurately when asked to compare sand that was not in glasses. When children observed cupfuls of sand poured into boxes they again did not use counting, and used the rate, not duration, of pouring as the basis of judgment (if the pouring acts were hidden, younger children performed the worst). Thus, children must learn to apply their counting skills to unitized measures of continuous quantities. They appear to do so first for small numerosities. For example, six-year-olds were more accurate in addition tasks when red blocks were placed in cylinders, instead of liquid, but only for small numerosities (five or less). To measure, children have to overcome a natural inclination to quantify continuous substances with mental processes that are analogously continuous (i.e., that do *not* involve discrete units and counting). In a striking example, three- to five-year-old children were no less successful comparing amounts of sand in piles than when the same amount was shown in three vs. two discrete glasses (Huntley-Fenner, 2001b).

Despite such challenges, young children can be guided to have appropriate measurement experiences. They naturally encounter and discuss quantities

(Seo & Ginsburg, 2004). They initially learn to use words that represent quantity or magnitude of a certain attribute. Then they compare two objects directly and recognize equality or inequality (Boulton-Lewis, Wilss, & Mutch, 1996). At age four to five years, most children can learn to overcome perceptual cues and make progress in reasoning about and measuring quantities. They are ready to learn to measure, connecting number to the quantity (even though the average U.S. child, with limited measurement experience, exhibits limited understanding of measurement until the end of the primary grades). We next examine this development in more detail for the attribute of length.

Length Measurement

Length is a characteristic of an object found by quantifying how far it is between the endpoints of the object. "Distance" is often used similarly to quantify how far it is between any two points in space. The discussion of the number line is critical here, because this defines the number line used to measure length (see Chapter 4—both in this and in the companion book). Measuring length or distance consists of two aspects, identifying a unit of measure and *subdividing* (mentally and physically) the object by that unit, placing that unit end to end (*iterating*) alongside the object. Subdividing and unit iteration are complex mental accomplishments that are too often ignored in traditional measurement curriculum materials and instruction. Therefore, many researchers go beyond the physical act of measuring to investigate children's understandings of measuring as covering space and quantifying that covering.

We discuss length in the following three sections. First, we identify several key concepts that underlie measuring (from Clements & Stephan, 2004; Stephan & Clements, 2003). Second, we discuss early development of some of these concepts. Third, we describe research-based instructional approaches that were designed to help children develop concepts and skills of length measurement.

Concepts in Linear Measurement

At least eight concepts form the foundation of children's understanding of length measurement. These concepts include understanding of the attribute, conservation, transitivity, equal partitioning, iteration of a standard unit, accumulation of distance, origin, and relation to number.

UNDERSTANDING OF THE ATTRIBUTE

Understanding of the attribute of length includes understanding that lengths span fixed distances ("Euclidean" rather than "topological" conceptions in the Piagetian formulation).

CONSERVATION

Conservation of length includes the understanding that as an object is moved, its length does not change. For example, if children are shown two equal length rods aligned, they usually agree that they are the same length. If one is moved to project beyond the other, children 4.5 to 6 years often state that the projecting rod is longer. At 5 to 7 years, many children hesitate or vacillate; beyond that, they quickly answer correctly. Conservation of length develops as the child learns to measure (Inhelder, Sinclair, & Bovet, 1974).

TRANSITIVITY

Transitivity is the understanding that if the length of object X is equal to (or greater/less than) the length of object Y and object Y is the same length as (or greater/less than) object Z, then object X is the same length as (or greater/less than) object Z.

EQUAL PARTITIONING

Equal partitioning is the mental activity of slicing up an object into the same-sized units. Asking children what the hash marks on a ruler mean can reveal how they understand partitioning of length (Clements & Barrett, 1996; Lehrer, 2003). Some children understand "five" as a single hash mark, not as a space that is partitioned into five equal-sized units. As children come to understand that units can also be partitioned, they come to grips with the idea that length is continuous (e.g., any unit can itself be further partitioned).

UNITS AND UNIT ITERATION

Unit iteration requires the ability to conceptualize the length of a small unit such as a block as part of the length of the object being measured and to place the smaller block repeatedly along the length of the larger object (Kamii & Clark, 1997; Steffe, 1991), tiling the length without gaps or overlaps, and counting these iterations. Such tiling, or space-filling, is implied by partitioning, but that is not well established for young children, who also must see the need for equal partitioning and thus the use of identical units.

ACCUMULATION OF DISTANCE AND ADDITIVITY

Accumulation of distance is the understanding that as you iterate a unit along the length of an object and count the iteration, the number words signify the space covered by all units counted up to that point (Petitto, 1990). Piaget et al. (1960) characterized children's measuring activity as an accumulation of distance when the result of iterating forms in nesting relationships to each other. That is, the space covered by three units is nested in or contained in the space covered by four units. Additivity is the related notion that length can be decomposed and composed, so that the total distance between two points is equivalent to the sum of the distances of any arbitrary set of segments that subdivide the line segment connecting those points.

ORIGIN

Origin is the notion that any point on a ratio scale can be used as the origin. Measures of Euclidean space conform to ratios (the distance between 45 and 50 is the same as that between 100 and 105), implying that any point can serve as the origin.

RELATION BETWEEN NUMBER AND MEASUREMENT

Children must reorganize their understanding of the items they are counting to measure continuous units. They make measurement judgments based upon counting ideas, often based on experiences counting discrete objects. For example, Inhelder et al. (1974) showed children two rows of matches. The matches in each row were of different lengths, but there was a different number of matches in each so that the rows were the same length. Although, from the adult perspective, the lengths of the rows were the same, many children argued that the row with shorter matches was longer because it had more matches. One needs to understand the relationship between the units and the number of units to understand measurement situations, unlike counting discrete items. In addition, measurement contexts may differ from the discrete cardinal situations in other ways. For example, when measuring with a ruler, every element should not necessarily be counted and in those cases, the order-irrelevance principle does not apply in the same way (i.e., you can count units out of order if and only if they are units on the ruler corresponding to the length of the object you are measuring, Fuson & Hall, 1982).

Another relation children must learn is the proportionality of measurements, including the inverse relationship between the size of a unit and the number of units in a given measure.

Researchers debate the order of the development of these concepts and the ages at which they are developed; it may be that education and experience has a large effect on both. Researchers generally agree that these ideas form the foundation for various aspects of measurement. Traditional measurement instruction is insufficient for helping children build these conceptions.

Early Development of Length Measurement Concepts

The same landmarks that aid children in cue or place learning also can affect their representations of the distances separating objects. Piaget, Inhelder, and Szeminska (1960) reported that after placing a third object between two objects, young children claim that the distance is smaller or larger than before. In another study, children judged that two routes, one direct and one indirect, cover the same distance. Subsequent studies have confirmed that most four-year-olds, and about half of five- and six-year-olds, show such patterns

(Fabricius & Wellman, 1993; K. F. Miller & Baillargeon, 1990). Thus, the Piagetian position was that young children did not possess understanding of distance and length.

However, mistakes on tasks may not be due to the misconceptions of space that Piagetian theory assumed. First, children can encode and apply distance information. For example, preschoolers do well at simple distance judgment tasks, with this competence appearing as early as 12 to 16 months of age (Huttenlocher et al., 1999).

Second, there are inconsistencies in the literature on Piagetian tasks. About 40 percent of four-year-olds could avoid errors on direct and indirect routes, including giving correct explanations (Fabricius & Wellman, 1993). Further, children three and a half to five years of age appear to understand both the direct-indirect principles and the same-plus principle (if two routes are the same up to a point, but only one continues, it is longer), in a task modification in which the items were screened, so responses would not be the result of perceptual scanning (Bartsch & Wellman, 1988).

In a variation of the conservation-of-length task, children were asked which of five boxes a stick would fit into (Schiff, 1983). Children's judgments remained consistent after sliding. Thus, they correctly judged that a stick would go into the same box after it was moved (e.g., apparently believing that sliding the stick across the table did not change the physical dimensions of the stick). In another study, children were asked to choose a stick to bridge a gap. They appeared to understand that occlusion of the stick did not affect the length (K. F. Miller & Baillargeon, 1990). Children first understand affordances, such as "will this stick fit here," and later integrate knowledge between length and distance (K. F. Miller, 1984).

Across several experiments, then, there is little empirical support for the notion, such as in the Piagetian topological primary thesis, that conceptualizations underlying children's reasoning about distance and length differ from those of adults. Preschoolers understand that lengths span fixed distances. Still, some researchers hold that complete conservation is essential for, but not equivalent to, a full conception of measurement. Piaget, Inhelder, and Szeminska (1960) argued that transitivity is impossible for children who do not conserve lengths because once they move a unit, it is possible, in the child's view, for the length of the unit to change. Many researchers agree that children develop the notion of conservation before transitivity (Boulton-Lewis, 1987). Further, although researchers agree that conservation is essential for a complete understanding of measurement, children do not necessarily need to develop conservation before they can learn some measurement ideas (Boulton-Lewis, 1987; Clements, 1999c; Hiebert, 1981; Petitto, 1990). Two measurement ideas that seem to depend on conservation and transitivity are the inverse relation between the size of the unit and the number of those units and the need to use equal length units when measuring. However, there are several anecdotal reports of preschoolers understanding the inverse relation in reform curricula contexts, and one study (Sophian, 2002) showed an increase in the understanding of effect of object size on measurement of volume in three- and four-year-olds, when children are given the opportunity to compare the result of measurements made with different units.

Most researchers argue that children must reason transitively before they can understand measurement adequately (Boulton-Lewis, 1987). Some researchers conclude that the ruler is useless as a measuring tool if a child cannot yet reason transitively (Kamii & Clark, 1997). As with conservation, this may only be true for some tasks. Further, as we have seen before, understanding is not a dichotomous phenomenon. Children as young as pre-K and kindergarten age use transitivity in simple measurement tasks. For example, given two holes and a marked stick, they can compare the depth of the holes by inserting the stick and comparing the marks (Nunes & Bryant, 1996). Such abilities appear in even younger children on some tasks (K. F. Miller, 1989).

On many tasks that *appear* to require general logical reasoning, children find their own strategy to measure, and they do so correctly. These solution strategies do not necessarily match the structural logic of the task. For example, children use intermediate measurements to compare two lengths without explicitly asking the transitivity question. They move a unit to measure the length of an object and do not worry about whether the length is being conserved. Finally, children of all developmental levels solve simple measurement tasks that do not appear to rely heavily on general reasoning.

In summary, children have an intuitive understanding of length on which to base reasoning about distance and length, but that reasoning develops considerably. They may have difficultly mapping words such as "long" onto the adult concept, instead assuming it means end point comparison (Schiff, 1983). They need to learn to coordinate and resolve perceptual and conceptual information when it conflicts. Finally, they need to learn to use measurement, understanding that units of lengths can be iterated along successive distances and these iterations counted to determine length. Thus, young children know that properties such as length (as well as area, volume, and mass, and weight) exist early, but they do not initially know how to reason about these attributes or to measure them accurately. Using an example outside of length, if three-year-olds have some amount of quantity (e.g., clay) and then are given an additional amount of quantity (more clay), they know that they have more than they did before. Three- and four-year-olds encounter difficulty, however, when asked to judge which of two amounts that they currently have (e.g., which of two mounds of clay) is more. They tend to use perceptual cues to make this judgment. For example, when one of two identical balls of clay is rolled into a long sausage-like shape, children do not "conserve" the initial equivalence of the clay balls, and instead judge that the sausage has more clay than the ball because it is longer. Nevertheless, when there are no perceptually conflicting cues, preschoolers are accurate comparing objects directly.

Before kindergarten, many children lack measurement rules such as lining up an end when comparing the lengths of two objects (Piaget & Inhelder, 1967; Piaget et al., 1960), although they can learn about such ideas. Even five- to six-year-olds, given a demarcated ruler, wrote in numerals haphazardly with little regard to the size of the spaces. Few used zero as a starting point showing a lack of understanding of the origin concept. At age four to five years, however, many children can, with opportunities to learn, become less dependent on perceptual cues and thus make progress in reasoning about or measuring quantities. From kindergarten to grade 2, children significantly improve in measurement knowledge (Ellis, Siegler, & Van Voorhis, 2000). They learn to represent length with a third object, using transitivity to compare the length of two objects that are not compared directly in a wider variety of contexts (Hiebert, 1981). They can also use given units to find the length of objects and associate higher counts with longer objects (Hiebert, 1981, 1984). Some five-year-olds, and most seven-year-olds, can use the concept of unit to make inferences about the relative size of objects; for example, if the numbers of units are the same, but the units are different, the total size is different (Nunes & Bryant, 1996). However, even the seven-year-olds found tasks demanding and conversion of units challenging.

Kindergarteners can become fairly proficient with a conventional ruler and understand quantification in measurement contexts, but their skill decreases when features of the ruler deviate from the convention. Thus, measurement is supported by characteristics of measurement tools, but children still need to develop understanding of key measurement concepts. In one study, all K-2 understood several measurement concepts. But there were significant age differences on understanding concepts such as iterating a standard unit and the cardinality principle (Ellis et al., 2000). Children initially may iterate a unit leaving gaps between subsequent units or overlapping adjacent units (Horvath & Lehrer, 2000; Lehrer, 2003), therefore, it is a physical activity of placing units along a path in some manner, not an activity of covering the space/length of the object with no gaps or overlaps. Furthermore, students often begin counting at the numeral "1" on a ruler (Lehrer, 2003) or, when counting paces heel-to-toe, start their count with the movement of the first foot, missing the first foot and counting the second foot as one (Lehrer, 2003; Stephan, Bowers, Cobb, & Gravemeijer, 2003). Students probably are not thinking about measuring as covering space. Rather, the numerals on a ruler (or the placement of a foot) signify when to start counting, not an amount of space that has already been covered (i.e., "one" is the space from the beginning of the ruler to the hash mark, not the hash mark itself). Many children initially find it necessary to iterate the unit until it "fills up" the length of the object and will not extend the unit past the endpoint of the object they are measuring (Stephan et al., 2003). Finally, many children do not understand that units must be of equal size. They will even measure with tools subdivided into different size units and conclude that quantities with more units are larger (Ellis et al., 2000). This may be a deleterious side effect of counting, in which children learn that the size of objects does not affect the result of counting (Mix et al., 2002, although we disagree with the authors' claim that units are always "given" in counting contexts—along with most teachers, Mix et al. do not consider counting contexts, such as counting whole toy people constructed in two parts, top and bottom, when some are fastened and some are separated, cf. Sophian & Kailihiwa, 1998).

A study of second graders' understanding of rules supports these points. Before formal instruction, most children had a subjective impression of rulers (Nührenbörger, 2001). They drew pictures that indicated they had a mental picture of rules and key aspects of measuring. For example, a third drew rulers with equal-interval unit markings, a starting point, subdivisions, and numerals. Drawings of another third suggested equal intervals, markings, and numerals, but subdivisions and other aspects were not represented as well. The bottom third either used marks and numerals but with the marks appearing as "decorations" or numerals only. After instruction, most students in the lowest two-thirds increased their levels of thinking. However, students often remained unaware of the concepts underlying the construction, iteration, and subdivision of units. Their actions often reflect dominance of their experience with counting discrete items and reading of numerals.

Children are also learning accumulation of distance. Some, for example, measured the lengths of objects by pacing heel to toe and counting their steps (Stephan et al., 2003). As one child paced the length of a rug, the teacher stopped the child mid-measure and asked her what she meant by "eight". Some children claimed that eight signified the space covered by the eighth foot, while others argued that it was the space covered from the beginning of the first foot to the end of the eighth. These latter children were measuring by accumulating distances. This type of interpretation may not appear until students are nine or 10 year old (Clements, 1999c; Kamii & Clark, 1997). However, with meaningful instruction, children as young as six years old can learn to measure by accumulating distance (Stephan et al., 2003).

Finally, young children are developing the foundational ideas of origin and relation between number and measurement. As Piagetian research indicated, they draw on their counting experiences to interpret their measuring activity, to which the "starting at one" error may be related. If children understand measuring only as "reading the ruler," they may not understand this idea (Lehrer, 2003; Nührenbörger, 2001). Children also have to understand and apply counting concepts, including one-to-one correspondence and the cardinality principle.

Thus, significant development occurs in the early childhood years. By first or second grade, most children understand the inverse relationship between unit size and number of units, although they may have difficulty applying these concepts (Carpenter & Lewis, 1976; Lehrer, Jenkins et al., 1998). Many children develop these concepts before instruction. However, the foundational length ideas are usually not integrated. For example, children may still not understand the importance of, or be able to create, equal size units, even into the primary grades (Clements, Battista, Sarama, Swaminathan et al., 1997; Lehrer, Jenkins et al., 1998; K. F. Miller, 1984). This indicates that children have not necessarily differentiated fully between counting discrete objects and measuring. Even if they show competence with rulers and are given identical units, children may not spontaneously iterate those they have if they do not have a sufficient number to measure an object (Lehrer, Jenkins et al., 1998)—even when the units are rulers themselves (Clements, 1999c). Even up to the primary grades, some children cannot or do not mentally partition the object to be measured.

Another important aspect of measurement that we shall only briefly mention is that of precision. In one study, explicit attention to the ways of ordering and structuring trial-to-trial variability in measuring helped second graders make sense of that variation by suggesting representative values of sets of trials of measures (Lehrer, Schauble, Carpenter, & Penner, 2000).

Estimation

Real-world applications of length often involve estimation. There is little research on measurement estimation, and most of it is with older students and adults (see Sowder, 1992a). Briefly, research suggests that skilled estimators move fluently back and forth between written or verbal linear measurements and representations of their corresponding magnitudes on a mental number line (Joram et al., 1998). Although having real-world "benchmarks" is useful, instruction should also help children build understandings of scales and concepts of measurement into their estimation competencies.

Measurement estimation depends on concepts and skills with physical measurement, so that foundations should be laid first. One group of researchers applied the accumulator model to build a theory of measurement. They hypothesize that people can obtain a verbal or written numerical representation of a magnitude in three ways. In the direct verbal way, people mentally divide the magnitude under consideration into discrete intervals and verbally count the intervals (the authors do not say much about the process of mentally dividing the magnitude, a weakness of the model). In an indirect way, people divide the magnitude into discrete intervals, counting the interval nonverbally to obtain a mental magnitude that represents numerosity, and then access a verbal representation of the corresponding numerosity. Another indirect way is used when the magnitude (e.g., a length) directly generates a nonverbal magnitude (a perceived magnitude) for which a measurement has been already learned (this rug is about the length of an eight-foot plank). This relates the magnitude to the magnitudes that represent a given numerosity. This third way is only available to someone with repeated estimating experiences of the first two ways, because it is only those kinds of experiences that can establish the scaling factor that relates perceived magnitudes to numerical magnitudes.

Most people probably use the iteration strategy. Research indicates that the number of "iterations" of this mental unit predicts the time it takes people to make an estimate, rather than the total length of the object. The unit can be large (e.g., a six-foot person), decreasing the number of iterations necessary. The so called "mental number line" actually *becomes* a mental number line, with all that implies (actual length units, and possibly multiply interrelated units), when students develop this skill.

Students may not have the ability to generate and manipulate such constrained mental units and number lines well until third grade (Joram et al., 1998). How should estimation abilities be developed? One popular approach is guess and check (practice with feedback). This can be effective, but the skills taught are often fragile and limited to the contexts in which people were taught (i.e., it does not transfer). Guess and test does not improve what strategies they use. More promising might be training strategies and "measurement sense" by prompting students to learn reference or benchmark (e.g., an inch-long piece of gum and also a six-inch dollar bill) lengths; order points along a continuum; and build up mental number lines ("mental rulers") (Joram, Gabriele, Bertheau, Gelman, & Subrahmanyam, 2005).

Experience and Education

Young children naturally encounter and discuss quantities in their play (H. P. Ginsburg et al., 1999). They first learn to use words that represent quantity or magnitude of a certain attribute. Facilitating this language is important not only to develop communication abilities, but for the development of mathematical concepts. Simply using labels such as "Daddy/Mommy/Baby" and "big/little/tiny" helped children as young as three years to represent and apply higher-order seriation abilities, even in the face of distracting visual factors, an improvement equivalent to a two-year gain. Language provides an invitation to form comparisons and a method to remember the newly represented relational structure (Rattermann & Gentner, 1998). Thus, language can modify thought (cf. Vygotsky, 1934/1986). Along with progressive alignment, in which children are presented with easy literal similarity matches prior to difficult matches, language provides powerful scaffolding potential (Kotovsky & Gentner, 1996).

Next, children compare two objects directly and recognize equality or inequality, for example, of the length of two objects (Boulton-Lewis et al.,

1996). Following this, children can to learn to measure, connecting number to length. Again, language, such as the differences between counting-based terms and continuous-quantity terms can help children form relationships between counting and continuous measurement (Huntley-Fenner, 2001b). Before turning to measurement proper, we should recall a related competence, ordering or seriating multiple objects by length. Piagetian theory (1952) held that this was one of the two foundational concepts that lead to number, as discussed previously. While it may not function in that central role, it remains important to measurement, to learning number, and to general thinking (Ciancio, Rojas, McMahon, & Pasnak, 2001; Lebron-Rodriguez & Pasnak, 1977; Pasnak, Madden, Malabonga, & Holt, 1996).

Kamii and Clark (1997) argue that comparing lengths is at the heart of developing the notions of conservation, transitivity, and unit iteration, but most textbooks do not have these types of tasks. Textbooks tend to ask questions such as "How many paper clips does the pencil measure?" rather than "How much longer is the blue pencil than the red pencil?" Although Kamii and Clark advocate beginning instruction by comparing lengths with nonstandard or standard units (not a ruler), they caution that such an activity is often done by rote. Teachers must focus children on the mental activity of transitive reasoning and accumulating distances. One type of task that involves indirect comparisons is to ask children if the doorway is wide enough for a table to go through. This involves an indirect comparison and transitive reasoning.

Many recent curricula advise a sequence of instruction in which children compare lengths, measure with nonstandard units, incorporate the use of manipulative standard units, and measure with a ruler (Clements, 1999c; Kamii & Clark, 1997). The basis for this sequence is, explicitly or implicitly, Piaget et al.'s (1960) theory of measurement. The argument is that this approach motivates children to see the need for a standard measuring unit. Researchers who advocate this approach argue that, when classroom discussions focus on children's meaning during measuring, they are able to construct sophisticated understanding (Lehrer, 2003; McClain, Cobb, Gravemeijer, & Estes, 1999; Stephan et al., 2003).

Although such an approach has shown to be effective, it may not be necessary to follow a nonstandard-to-standard units approach. For example, Boulton-Lewis et al. (1996) found that children used nonstandard units unsuccessfully, but were successful at an earlier age with standard units and measuring instruments. The researchers concluded that nonstandard units are not a good way to initially help children understand the need for standardized conventional units in the length measuring process. Just as interesting were children's strategy preferences. Children of every age, especially in Years 1 and 3, preferred to use standard rulers, even though their teachers were encouraging them to use nonstandard units. One teacher did not allow use of rulers in her classroom, saying they had become a distraction because children wanted to use them. Further, children measured correctly with a ruler before they could devise a measurement strategy using nonstandard units.

As another example, a substantial number of first and second graders do not recognize that using a smaller unit increases number of units in measurement of a fixed quantity (Carpenter & Lewis, 1976). These children acquire the knowledge that the number of units measured is inversely related to the size of the unit, at least in some form, but they still did not recognize the importance of maintaining a standard unit of measure (Carpenter & Lewis, 1976).

Taken as a whole, these studies suggest that early experience measuring with different units may be the *wrong* thing to do. To realize that arbitrary units are not reliable, a child must reconcile the varying lengths and numbers of arbitrary units. Emphasizing nonstandard units too early may defeat the purpose it is intended to achieve. That is, early emphasis on various nonstandard units may interfere with children's development of basic measurement concepts required to understand the need for standard units. In contrast, using manipulative standard units, or even standard rulers, is less demanding and appears to be a more interesting and meaningful real-world activity for young children (Boulton-Lewis et al., 1996). These findings have been supported by additional research (Boulton-Lewis, 1987; Clements & Battista, 2001; Clements, Battista, Sarama, Swaminathan et al., 1997; Héraud, 1989).

Another study (Nunes, Light, & Mason, 1993) suggests that children can meaningfully use rulers before they "reinvent" such ideas as units and iteration. Children six to eight years of age communicated about lengths using string, centimeter rulers, or one ruler and one broken ruler starting at 4 cm. The traditional ruler supported the children's reasoning more effectively than the string; children's performance almost doubled. Their strategies and language (it is as long as the "little line [half] just after three") indicated that children gave "correct responses based on rigorous procedures, clearly profiting from the numerical representation available through the ruler" (p. 46). They even did better with the *broken* ruler than the string, showing that they were not just "reading numbers off" the ruler. The unusual context confused children only 20 percent of the time. The researchers concluded that conventional units already chosen and built into the ruler do not make measurement more difficult. Indeed, children benefitted from the numerical representation provided even by the broken ruler.

Further, their research has led several authors to argue that early rule use should be encouraged, not avoided or delayed (Clements, 1999c; Nühren-börger, 2001; Nunes et al., 1993). Rulers allow children to connect instruction to their previous measurement experiences with conventional tools. In contrast, dealing with informal, three-dimensional units de-emphasizes the one-dimensional nature of length and unfortunately focuses on counting of discrete objects. Thus, both the zero point and the iteration of line segment lengths as units is de-emphasized (Bragg & Outhred, 2001).

With typical instruction, no first graders and only 21 percent of second graders could construct a ruler that used the length of a paper clip as a measure (Bragg & Outhred, 2001). Slightly more could measure a length by iterating a paper clip and accurately indicate that the result involved a fraction of the unit. However, even those students who could perform these tasks could not identify units *as linear* in various contexts, such as indicating what a "5" meant on a ruler, or that part of a 1 cm cube used when measuring a length. Thus, children's understanding of unit is weak under typical instruction.

The Piagetian-based argument, that children must conserve length before they can make sense of ready-made systems such as rulers (or computer tools, such as those discussed in the following section), may be an overstatement. Findings of these studies support a Vygotskian perspective (Ellis et al., 2000; K. F. Miller, 1989), in which rulers are viewed as cultural instruments children can appropriate. That is, children can use rulers, appropriate them, and so build new mental tools. Not only do children prefer using rulers, but they can use them meaningfully and in combination with manipulable units to develop understanding of length measurement. In general, measurement procedures can serve as cognitive tools (K. F. Miller, 1989) that develop to solve certain practical problems and organize the way children think about amount. Measurement concepts may originally be organized in terms of the contexts and procedures used to judge, compare, or measure specific attributes (K. F. Miller, 1989). If so, transformations that do not change length but do change number, such as cutting, may be particularly difficult for children, more so than traditional conservation questions. Children need to conceptually distinguish the different attributes and learn which transformations affect which attributes. Children should be helped to introduce measurement problems, introduce such tools, and use children's solutions as a way to extend their thinking about the attributes and their measure.

Another Piaget-based idea, from the field of social cognition, is that conflict is the genesis of cognitive growth. One series of studies, however, indicated this is not always so. If two strategies, measurement and direct comparison, were in conflict, children learned little. They benefited little from verbal instruction. However, children who saw that the results of measurement and direct comparison agreed were more likely to use measurement later than were children who observed both procedures but did not have the opportunity to compare their results (P. E. Bryant, 1982). Here, then, is another case that engaging children in conflict (between strategies, or between results of measuring with different units) too soon is unhelpful or deleterious.

Based on this research corpus, Clements (1999c) suggests a sequence of instruction we have enhanced here and in the companion volume. Children should be given a variety of experiences comparing the size of objects. Next, children should engage in experiences that allow them to connect number to length, using both conventional rulers and manipulative units using standard units of length, such as centimeter cubes (specifically labeled "length-units" with the children, from Dougherty & Slovin, 2004). As they explore with these tools the ideas of length-unit iteration, correct alignment, (with a ruler) and the zero-point concept are developed. In second or third grade, teachers might introduce the need for standard length-units and the relation between the size and number of length-units. The early use of *multiple* nonstandard length-units would not be used until this point (cf. Carpenter & Lewis, 1976). Instruction focusing on children's interpretations of their measuring activity can enable children to use flexible starting points on a ruler to indicate measures successfully (Lubinski & Thiessen, 1996). Without such attention, children just read off whatever ruler number aligns with the end of the object into the intermediate grades (Lehrer, Jacobson et al., 1998).

Based on the work of Russian researchers, the Measure Up curriculum emphasizes abstract, algebraic thinking early (Dougherty & Slovin, 2004, see also Chapters 6 and 13). For example, first graders might solve problems in which they have to physically compare two lengths A and B and then represent how to equalize them. They might draw a diagram and explain how C could be added to A or taken away from B, as in Figure 10.1.

Students also solve numerical problems using similar diagrams. For example, one problem tells second or third graders that a girl had 43 volume-units of water in one container and eight volume-units less in another and asks how many volume-units she would have if she combined the containers. Students might solve this at three levels of sophistication, illustrated in Figure 10.2.

Second graders who experience this approach showed skillfulness in counting and representing the numbers, but analysis of their responses showed different levels of generalization of method and explanation of underlying principles (Slovin, 2007).

Children must eventually learn to subdivide length-units. Making one's own ruler and marking halves and other partitions of the unit may be helpful in this regard. Children could fold a unit in halves, mark the fold as a half, and then continue to do so, to build fourths and eighths.

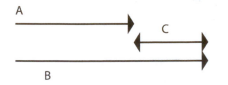

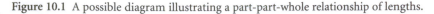

Figure 10.1 A possible diagram illustrating a part-part-whole relationship of lengths.

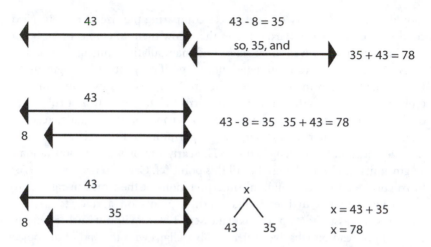

Figure 10.2 Possible solution strategies at different levels of sophistication.

Computer experiences also can help children link number and geometry in measurement activities and build measurement sense. Even young children can abstract and generalize measurement ideas working with computers (Clements, Battista, Sarama, Swaminathan et al., 1997; Clements & Meredith, 1994; Kull, 1986; Try, 1989) if the interface is appropriate and activities well planned (J. A. Watson & Brinkley, 1990/91). In a combination of these approaches, eight- and nine-year-old students learned about units, subdividing units and fractions, as they made maps of their playground (Lehrer & Pritchard, 2002). They used their previous experience with Logo to build these and other concepts and skills, including polar coordinates and scaling.

Cross-cultural research has shown that influences of other experiences can affect measurement practices. For example, Filipino children's rounding of monetary transactions to include only whole numbers probably is the cause of their rounding measurement of a length to the whole numbers. Other differences in the student's performance on the measurement tasks may be related to differences in curricula. In addition, children from two cultures were equally competent at measuring, but Filipino children were not as successful as the New Zealand children on tasks requiring visualization, probably reflecting curricular differences, such as the New Zealand Curriculum's emphasis on informal measurement and visualization (Irwin, Vistro-Yu, & Ell, 2004).

Learning Trajectory for Length Measurement

Table 10.1 provides the developmental progression and the mental actions-on-objects for this learning trajectory.

Table 10.1 A Developmental Progression for Length Measurement

Age (years)	Developmental Progression	Actions on Objects
2	**Pre-Length Quantity Recognizer** Does not identify length as attribute. "This is long. Everything straight is long. If it's not straight, it can't be long."	Action schemes, both physical/kinesthetic and visual, implicitly trace linear extents. In certain situations, from infancy children are sensitive to linear extent, including comparisons and accumulations. These are initially not, and later only partially, connected to explicit vocabulary.
3	**Length Quantity Recognizer** Identifies length/distance as attribute. May understand length as an absolute descriptor (e.g., all adults are tall), but not as a comparative (e.g., one person is taller than another). "I'm tall, see?" May compare non-corresponding parts of shape in determining side length.	Action schemes are connected to length vocabulary. In some situations, such vocabulary is connected to categories of linear extent, such as "tall/long" or "short." In others, action schemes are used to compare lengths—one object is longer if a scan lasts perceptibly longer than the scan of another object. Thus, intuitive comparisons are made on direct perceptual, normative (one object can be a class standard stored in memory, such as a doll's length), or functional (if guided/prompted; e.g., is this block long enough?) bases. However, in some situations salient differences at one end of the objects are substituted for a scan (potentially leading to inaccuracies if the other endpoints are not aligned) Also, irrelevant details such as the shape of objects can affect these categorizations and comparisons.
4	**Length Direct Comparer** Physically aligns two objects to determine which is longer or if they are the same length. Stands two sticks up next to each other on a table and says, "This one's bigger."	The scheme addresses length as a linear extent from endpoint to endpoint of a path. Shape of the objects and path can affect the application of the scheme. With perceptual support, objects can be mentally and then physically slid and rotated into alignment and their endpoints compared.
	Indirect Length Comparer Compares the length of two objects by representing them with a third object. Compares length of two objects with a piece of string.	A mental image of a particular length can be built, maintained, and (to a simple degree) manipulated. With the immediate perceptual support of some of the objects, such images can be compared. For some, explicit transitive

Continued Overleaf

Age (years)	Developmental Progression	Actions on Objects
	When asked to measure, may assign a length by guessing or moving along a length while counting (without equal length units). Moves finger along a line segment, saying 10, 20, 30, 31, 32. May be able to measure with a ruler, but often lacks understanding or skill (e.g., ignores starting point). Measures two objects with a ruler to check if they are the same length, but does not accurately set the "zero point" for one of the items.	reasoning may be applied to the images or their symbolic representations (i.e., object names). If asked to measure, a counting scheme operates on an intuitive unit of spatial extent or amount of movement, directing physical movements (or, less frequently, eye movements) along a length while counting (resulting in a "trace-and-count" or "point-and-count" strategy). The sensory-concrete mental actions require the perceptual support of the object to be measured.
5–6	**Serial Orderer to 6+** Orders lengths, marked in one to six units. (This develops in parallel with "End-to-End Length Measurer.") Given towers of cubes, puts in order, one to six.	A scheme organized in a hierarchy, with the higher-order concept a (possibly implicit) image of an ordered series. Ability to estimate relative lengths (driving a trial and error approach) is eventually complemented by a scheme that considers each object in such a series to be longer than the one before it and shorter than the one after it (resulting in a more efficient strategy).
	End-to-End Length Measurer Lays units end-to-end. May not recognize the need for equal-length units. The ability to apply resulting measures to comparison situations develops later in this level. (This develops in parallel with "Serial Orderer to 6+"). Lays nine inch cubes in a line beside a book to measure how long it is.	An implicit concept that lengths can be composed as repetitions of shorter lengths underlies a scheme of laying lengths end to end. (This scheme must overcome previous schemes, which use continuous mental processes to evaluate continuous extents, and thus are more easily instantiated.) This is initially only applied to small numerosities (e.g., five or fewer units). Starting with few restrictions (i.e., only weak intuitive constraints to use equal-size units or to avoid gaps between "units") the scheme is enhanced by the growing conception of length measuring as covering distance (or composing a length with parts) with further application of these constraints.

Age (years)	Developmental Progression	Actions on Objects
7	**Length Unit Relater and Repeater** Measures by repeated use of a unit (but initially may not be precise in such iterations). Relates size and number of units explicitly (but may not appreciate the need for identical units in every situations). Relates size and number of units explicitly. "If you measure with centimeters instead of inches, you'll need more of them, because each one is smaller." Can add up two lengths to obtain the length of a whole. "This is five long and this one is three long, so they are eight long together." Iterates a single unit to measure. Recognizes that different units will result in different measures and that identical units should be used, at least intuitively and/or in some situations. Uses rulers with minimal guidance. Measures a book's length accurately with a ruler.	Actions schemes include the ability to iterate a mental unit along a perceptually-available object. The image of each placement can be maintained while the physical unit is moved to the next iterative position (initially with weaker constraints on this placement). With the support of a perceptual context, scheme can predict that fewer larger units will be required to measure an object's length. These action schemes allow the application of counting-all addition schemes to be applied to measures.
8	**Length Measurer** Considers the length of a bent path as the sum of its parts (not the distance between the endpoints). Measures, knowing need for identical units, relationship between different units, partitions of unit, zero point on rulers, and accumulation of distance. Begins to estimate. "I used a meter stick three times, then there was a little left over. So, I lined it up from 0 and found 14 centimeters. So, it's 3 meters, 14 centimeters in all."	The length scheme has additional hierarchical components, including the ability simultaneously to image and conceive of an object's length as a total extent and a composition of units. This scheme adds constraints on the use of equal-length units and, with rulers, on use of a zero point. Units themselves can be partitioning, allowing the accurate use of units and subordinate units.

Continued Overleaf

Age (years)	Developmental Progression	Actions on Objects
	Conceptual Ruler Measurer Possesses an "internal" measurement tool. Mentally moves along an object, segmenting it, and counting the segments. Operates arithmetically on measures ("connected lengths"). Estimates with accuracy. "I imagine one meter stick after another along the edge of the room. That's how I estimated the room's length is nine meters."	Interiorization of the length scheme allows mental partitioning of a length into a given number of equal-length parts or the mental estimation of length by projecting an image onto present or imagined objects.

Final Words

This chapter described children's development of geometric measurement competencies from the earliest years and their learning of length measurement. Chapter 11 addresses other domains of geometric measurement: area, volume, and angle.

11
Geometric Measurement, Part 2
Area, Volume, and Angle

As with length, measurement of area, volume, and angle connects to other areas of mathematics and to children's experience with the physical world. Developing concepts and skills therefore builds a foundation for understanding topics from multiplication to fractions and for solving real world problems from deforestation to navigation.

Area Measurement

Area is an amount of two-dimensional surface that is contained within a boundary. Area measurement assumes that a suitable two-dimensional region is chosen as a unit, congruent regions have equal areas, regions do not overlap, and the area of the union of two regions (disjoint union; i.e., regions that do not overlap) is the sum of their areas (Reynolds & Wheatley, 1996). Thus, finding the area of a region can be thought of as tiling (or equal partitioning) a region with a two-dimensional unit of measure.

As with number, sensitivity to area is present in the first year of life. However, infants' approximate number sense may be more accurate than their corresponding sense of area (Xu & Spelke, 2000).

These area understandings do not develop well in traditional U.S. instruction and have not for a long time (Carpenter, Coburn, Reys, & Wilson, 1975), not only for young children, but also preservice teachers (Enochs & Gabel, 1984). A study of children from grades 1, 2, and 3 revealed little understanding of area measurement (Lehrer, Jenkins et al., 1998). Asked how much space a square (and a triangle) cover, 41 percent of children used a ruler to measure length. When asked what "nine" would mean in that context, they said it would be "inches." The second most frequent response, 22 percent, was "I don't know." Only 11 percent said they would find an area unit to cover the region. About a third of the children did not suggest any way of measuring the areas. When these children were provided with manipulatives, including small squares, 78 percent used some combination of the manipulatives to cover the square region and 22 percent persisted with the idea of area as length. Some treated area as "iterated length," measuring a length of a side of a square, then moving the ruler to a parallel position slightly toward the opposite side, and repeating this process, adding the values of the lengths. Those who used manipulatives as units of covering were split between those who used only squares (45 percent) and those who used both squares and another shape, such as triangles (55 percent). When measuring triangles, 70 percent preferred triangular shapes as the covering shape; for rectangles, 68 percent used only rectangles and only 16 percent also used squares. Thus, children used resemblance to choose a unit of measure.

Concepts of Area Measurement

Understanding of area measurement involves learning and coordinating many ideas (Clements & Stephan, 2004). Many of these ideas, such as transitivity and relation between number and measurement, operate in area measurement in a manner similar to length measurement, as discussed in the previous chapter. Other foundational concepts for the domain of area measurement include understanding the attribute of area (including comparison of areas), equal partitioning, units of area and unit iteration, structuring an array, conservation, and linear measurement.

UNDERSTANDING THE ATTRIBUTE OF AREA

Understanding the attribute of area involves giving a quantitative meaning to the amount of bounded two-dimensional surface. Initially, preschoolers may use only one dimension or one salient aspect of the stimulus to compare the area of two surfaces (Bausano & Jeffrey, 1975; Maratsos, 1973; Mullet & Paques, 1991; Piaget et al., 1960; Raven & Gelman, 1984; J. Russell, 1975; Sena & Smith, 1990). For example, four- and five-year-olds may match only one side of figures when attempting to compare their areas (Silverman, York, & Zuidema, 1984). Others claim that children can integrate more than one feature of a region, but judge areas with *additive* combinations, for example, making implicit area judgments based on the longest single dimension (Mullet & Paques, 1991) or height + width rules (Cuneo, 1980; Rulence-Paques & Mullet, 1998). Children from six to eight years use a linear extent rule, such as the diagonal of a rectangle. Only after this age do most children move to explicit use of spatial structuring of multiplicative rules to solve those studies' tasks. (Spatial structuring, the mental operation of constructing an organization into rows and columns, is discussed in more detail in a following section.) Note this does not imply formal use of multiplication, but only that their estimates are best modeled (approximated) by the normative multiplicative rule.

In most of these studies, children did not interact with the materials. Doing so often changes their strategies and improves their estimates. Children as young as three years are more likely to make estimates consistent with multiplicative rules when in a problem-solving setting using manipulatives than when just asked to make a perceptual estimation. For example, they are more accurate when asked to count out the right number of square tiles to cover a floor and put them in a cup (K. F. Miller, 1984). Similarly, children of five to six years of age were more likely to use strategies consistent with multiplicative rules after playing with the stimulus materials (Wolf, 1995). Children were to estimate the size of rectangular pieces of baking chocolate on a graphic rating scale. Control group children estimate using a height + width rule; however, children who played with the materials first used a multiplicative rule.

Wolf (1995) argues that more complex rules are often used when people are more familiar with the materials involved in a task. This may be so, however, children did better when their manipulation followed their estimation of sizes. Thus, it may be that small numbers of objects and familiarity with materials is beneficial, but that also familiarity with the task (the conceptual goal) and the physical and cognitive actions applied to the materials encourage more accurate strategies, such as scanning one length through another.

Although some researchers imply multiplicative thinking on the part of the child, we take the conservative position that there is little evidence of true two-dimensional spatial structuring in these studies. Children may be using linear or additive strategies that are more consistent with the result of accurate multiplicative rules or other implicit estimation strategies. We return to this issue in the discussion of "structuring an area."

A more accurate strategy for comparing areas than visual estimation is superimposition. Children as young as three years have a rudimentary concept of area based on placing regions on top of one another, but it is not until five or six years that their strategy is accurate and efficient. As an illustration, asked to manipulate regions, preschoolers in one study used superimposition instead of the less precise strategies of laying objects side-by-side or comparing single sides, both of which use one dimension at best in estimating the area (Yuzawa, Bart, & Yuzawa, 2000). Again the facilitative effect of manipulation is shown. Children were given target squares or rectangles and asked to choose one which was equal to two standard rectangles in area. They performed better when they placed the standard figures on the targets than when they made perceptual judgments. They also performed better when one target could be overlapped completely with the standard figures (even in the perceptual condition, which suggests they performed a mental superposition).

Higher levels of thinking about area may have their roots in the internalization of such procedures as placing figures on one another, which may be aided by cultural tools (manipulatives) or scaffolding by adults (cf. Vygotsky, 1934/1986). For example, kindergartners who were given origami practice increased the spontaneous use of the procedure of placing one figure on another for comparing sizes (Yuzawa et al., 1999). Because origami practice includes the repeated procedure of folding one sheet into two halves, origami practice might facilitate the development of an area concept, which is related with the spontaneous use of the procedure.

EQUAL PARTITIONING

Partitioning is the mental act of "cutting" two-dimensional space into parts, with equal partitioning requiring parts of equal area (usually congruent). Teachers often assume that the product of two lengths structures a region into an area of two-dimensional units for students. However, the construction of a two-dimensional array from linear units is non-trivial. Young children often use counting as a basis for comparing (K. F. Miller, 1984) and do not partition two-dimensional surfaces into equal units of area.

UNITS AND UNIT ITERATION

Children often do not accurately tile the region with units and initially do not extend units over the boundaries when a subdivision of that unit is needed to fill the surface (Stephan et al., 2003). Even more limiting, children often choose units that physically resemble the region they are covering (Lehrer, 2003; Lehrer, Jenkins et al., 1998; Nunes et al., 1993). They sum the number of shapes used to cover, even if the covering shapes were of different sizes (84 percent of primary-grade children, Lehrer, Jenkins et al., 1998).

ACCUMULATION AND ADDITIVITY

Research suggests that primary-grade children may attempt to use mental superimposition to compare areas. However, even within a single session, about a fourth represented the area of two figures as a composition of shapes to compare areas, suggesting that such operations would be easily learned given appropriate experiences (Lehrer, Jenkins et al., 1998).

STRUCTURING SPACE

Spatial structuring is the mental operation of constructing an organization or form for an object or set of objects in space, a form of abstraction, the process of selecting, coordinating, unifying, and registering in memory a set of mental objects and actions. Based on Piaget and Inhelder's (1967) original formulation of coordinating dimensions, spatial structuring takes previously abstracted items as content and integrates them to form new structures. It creates stable patterns of mental actions that an individual uses to link sensory experiences, rather than the sensory input of the experiences themselves. Such spatial structuring precedes meaningful mathematical use of the structures, such as determining area or volume (Battista & Clements, 1996; Battista et al., 1998; Outhred & Mitchelmore, 1992).

The point is that working with lengths is often done too soon. In this study, eight- to nine-year-old students were more successful if they used tiles than if they used rulers (Nunes et al., 1993). With the latter, many students simply added the lengths. With tiles—especially in the condition in which students had tiles but not enough to cover the rectangles they were to measure—students were more likely to multiply with conceptual understanding. These constructions by the students were "isomorphism of measures" type of multiplicative concept, compared to the formula of multiplying length, which is the "product of measures" concept type (Vergnaud, 1983). That is, students' constructions were thinking about arrays of squares, not about multiplying one-dimensional measures to create a two-dimensional measure.

Spatial structuring involves the primitive notion that the region must be filled, with no gaps or overlaps; 73 percent of primary-grade students did not display this understanding, accepting circles placed within a square region as a viable way to measure area. They appear to use boundedness rather than space filling to judge adequacy of covering (Lehrer, Jenkins et al., 1998). Children develop through a series of levels in developing the difficult competence of learning to understand and spatially structure arrays of squares. These include the following (Battista et al., 1998; Mulligan, Prescott, Mitchelmore, & Outhred, 2005; Outhred & Mitchelmore, 2000; Outhred & Mitchelmore, 1992).

Area pre-recognizer Children at this level have not developed the ability to structure two-dimensional space. In a rectangular tiling task, they may not be able to tessellate the rectangle with squares, even with physical objects such as squares. In representational tasks, they may draw approximations of circles or other figures (Mulligan, Prescott et al., 2005).

Incomplete coverer Children understand that the goal is to cover the space. However, they have little or no ability to organize, coordinate, and structure two-dimensional space. They may be able to cover a rectangular space with physical tiles, because the tiles provide strong scaffolding for structuring the space and thus the task. However, they cannot represent that in a drawing. That is, these children cannot represent covering a rectangle with tiles without overlaps or gaps. This indicates that they are not interpreting arrays as composed of rows and columns, and they do not understand the need for units of equal size. Thus, their drawings capture a concatenation of approximately rectangular shapes, but their size (to be equal) and space-filling (to leave no gaps) are not constrained. Some fill the space only along the edges of the region, others attempt several rows of shapes, but leave gaps and do not align shapes between rows.

Primitive coverer Children can represent a complete covering of a region by drawing, without gaps or overlaps. Their alignment of shapes in one or two dimensions is intuitive, not constrained by a specific shape (square) or sizes or by an explicit concept of a row or column; therefore, rows and columns are not always accurately aligned. For similar reasons, children can not accurately count their shapes. For example, they lose track of which shapes were counted.

They may count around the border and then unsystematically count the internal shapes.

Primitive coverer and counter   Children can cover as in the previous level, but also count more accurately, but again with no row or column structuring. The local, incomplete use of rows or columns (e.g., counts some, but not all, rows as a unit) and the use of written labels provides structure that aids keeping track in counting.

Partial row structurer   Children make a significant advance when they structure the rectangle as a set of rows, understanding the collinearity of rows and the constraint that each row must have the same number of units. Some children revert to drawing individual squares (thus their drawing leaves gaps), others use repeated lines to demarcate rows. The entire array is not constructed (in geometric representation or in counting) as an iteration of rows; children are making progress with local structuring, but have not yet structured the array globally. They have begun the coordinating action of seeing a square as both a unit and a component of a unit of units (the row). Moreover, in tasks specific to measuring area that do not provide model units but provide a ruler, children may create rectangular shapes that are unrelated to the dimensions of the region (Outhred & Mitchelmore, 2000).

Row and column structurer   Children now have a mental construct of a row as consisting of a composite of aligned, congruent unit squares. They determine the number of squares by iterating those rows (e.g., counting each row of five, "five, 10, 15 . . ."). Within this level, they move from an intuitive iteration (based on the number of visual units in a column or an estimation) to iteration based on the number of squares in a column (e.g., skip counting by five or multiplying). At this level, they apply the concept of collinearity to both rows and columns and display the important advance of distributing the row over the elements of a column. They move from local to global structuring of the array, in which squares are seen as individual units, and as component of a unit of unit (e.g., a row; and also, eventually, they see it as a component of a column as well). To do so, they must coordinate the iteration of the unitized row (or column) with each unit element of an orthogonal column (or row). Alternatively, children may make a composite of two or more rows (e.g., combine two rows of five into a two-row unit of 10 and iterate that composite unit over each two-unit component of a column). In measurement contexts, they may measure one dimension to determine the size of the iterated squares and eventually both, to determine the number of rows needed, usually by marking off the units and drawing parallel lines using these marks. Thus, they apply the concept that the length of a line specifies the number of unit lengths that will fit along that line, but they still create a perceptual array to support their reasoning.

Array structurer   Children at this level understand that the rectangle's dimensions provide the number of squares in rows and columns and thus can meaningfully calculate the area from these dimensions without perceptual support. They have interiorized the spatial structuring, related the linear measures to their representation of each dimension, and thus can mentally decompose or recompose an array into rows, columns, or individual squares while retaining the array structure, even if provided only the linear measurements. Each square can thus be viewed as a unit, a component of at least two unit of units (a row and a column) and the unit of unit of units—the array. The distributive operation of iteration may be done on mental images that are spatial or symbolic in nature and eventually develops past iteration to a fully multiplicative concept. The area formula is understood and used as an abstraction of these operations.

Without this competence, students cannot use the area formula meaningfully. They are also more likely to confuse concepts such as perimeter and area; for example, believing that counting the units around a figure gives its area.

Students also must restructure the region to determine how to use known area measures to find the areas of non-rectangular areas. Only 20 percent of primary grade students in one study could do this (Lehrer, Jenkins et al., 1998).

CONSERVATION

Students have difficulty accepting that when they cut a given region and rearrange its parts to form another shape, the area remains the same (Lehrer, 2003). When shown two shapes, a square and a rhomboid, consisting of identical congruent right triangles, only 43 percent of children in grades 1–3 judged them as equal. One of the only cross-sectional developmental differences in area found was that children in grades 2–3 were more likely to conserve area mentally (Lehrer, Jenkins et al., 1998).

There are many other issues, including strategies for measuring irregular figures, subdividing the unit to fill a region, estimation, and so forth.

Experience and Education

As stated previously, the experiences of children in traditional U.S. instruction do not sufficiently build area concepts and skills. One group of children in typical instruction were followed for several years (Lehrer, Jenkins et al., 1998). They improved in space-filling and additive composition by grade 4, but not in other competencies, such as the confusion of area and length, using identical area-units, and finding measures of irregular shapes. In comparison, research-based activities taught second graders a wide range of area concepts and skills (Lehrer, Jacobson et al., 1998, see the companion book for details of the instructional activities).

Work with origami, because it involves folding and matching of multiple edges, may encourage children to use superimposition and see both dimensions in a figure (Yuzawa et al., 1999). In this study, the most effective use was folding to determine shape congruence. Girls were more interested and attentive than boys, and particularly increased their superimposition strategies; thus, origami may be an especially good geometric experience for girls.

The long developmental process usually only begins in the years before first grade. However, we should also appreciate the importance of these early conceptualizations. For example, three- and four-year-olds' use of a linear rating scale to judge area, (even if) using an additive rule, indicate an impressive level of quantitative ability, and, according to some, nascent mental structures for algebra at an early age (Cuneo, 1980).

Learning Trajectory for Area Measurement

Table 11.1 provides the developmental progression and the mental actions-on-objects for this learning trajectory.

Table 11.1 A Developmental Progression for Area Measurement

Age (years)	Developmental Progression	Actions on Objects
0–3	*Area/Spatial Structuring:* **Pre-Area Quantity Recognizer** Shows little specific concept of area. Uses side matching strategies in comparing areas (Silverman, York, & Zuidema, 1984). May draw approximation of circles or other figures in a rectangular tiling task. (Mulligan, Prescott, Mitchelmore, & Outhred, 2005) Draws mostly-closed shapes and lines with no indication of covering the specific region. 	Perceives space and objects within the space.
4	**Area Simple Comparer** May compare areas using only one side of figures, or estimating based on length plus (not times) width.	Using perceptual objects, internal bootstrap competencies compare extent.

Age (years)	Developmental Progression	Actions on Objects
	Asked which rectangular "candy" is the "same amount" as a bar 4 cm by 5 cm, one child chooses the 4 by 8 by matching the sides of the same length. Another child chooses the 2 by 7, intuitively summing the side lengths.	

Measures area with ruler, measuring a length, then moving the ruler and measuring that length again, apparently treating length as a 2-D space-filling attribute (Lehrer et al., 1998).

May compare areas if task suggests superposition or unit iteration.

Given square tiles and asked how many fit in a 4 by 5 area, child guesses 15.

A child places one sheet of paper over the other and says, "This one."

Area/Spatial Structuring: **Side-to-Side Area Measurer** Covers a rectangular space with physical tiles. However, can not organize, coordinate, and structure 2-D space without such perceptual support. In drawing (or imagining and pointing to count), can represent only certain aspects of that structure, such as approximately rectangular shapes next to one another.

With perceptual support, can visualize that regions can be covered by other regions. With strong guidance and perceptual support from pre-structured materials, can direct the covering of that space and recognize that covering as complete. Can represent approximate concatenations of rectangular shapes, aligning them (applied concept of collinearity), but often only intuitively and in one dimension.

Covers a region with physical tiles, and counts them by removing them one by one.

Draws within the region in an attempt to cover the region. May fill only next to existing guides (e.g., sides of region).

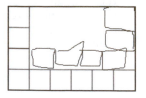

Continued Overleaf

Age (years)	Developmental Progression	Actions on Objects
	May attempt to fill region, but leave gaps and not align drawn shapes (or only align in one dimension). 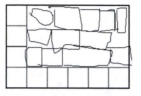	
5	*Area/Spatial Structuring:* **Primitive Coverer** Draws a complete covering, but with some errors of alignment. Counts around the border, then unsystematically in the interiors, counting some twice and skipping others. 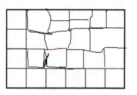	Applies explicit understanding that entire region must be covered with shapes. Implicit visual patterning of multiple concatenations of rectangles (and constraints of physical materials in physical tiling task) guides placement of squares in rows, approximately aligned with parallel rows.
	Area/Spatial Structuring: **Area Unit Relater and Repeater** Draws as above. Also, can tile area with manipulatives, and counts correctly aided by counting one row at a time and, often, by perceptual labeling.	Stronger constraints on object counting (counts all objects once and only once; see the Counting learning trajectory), and use of rows as an intuitive structure or explicit application of labeling as marker, allows child to keep track.
6	*Area/Spatial Structuring:* **Partial Row Structurer** Draws and counts some, but not all, rows as rows. May make several rows and then revert to making individual squares, but aligns them in columns. Does not coordinate the width and height. In measurement contexts, does not necessarily use the dimensions of the rectangle to constrain the unit size. 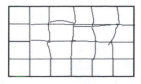	Builds, maintains, and manipulates *mental* images of composite shapes, structuring them as composites of individual shapes and as a single entity—a row (a unit of units). Applies this composite unit repeatedly, but not necessarily exhaustively, as its application remains guided by intuition.

Age (years)	Developmental Progression	Actions on Objects
7	*Area/Spatial Structuring:* **Row and Column Structurer**	Builds, maintains, and manipulates *mental* images of composite shapes, structuring them as composites of individual shapes and as a single entity—a row (a unit of units) of *congruent* squares. Applies this composite unit repeatedly *and exhaustively* to fill the array, possibly using mental imagery to "move" a row repeatedly over the rectangle to "fill" the array (or instantiating this operation symbolically)—coordinating this movement in 1-1 correspondence with the elements of the orthogonal column. If in a measurement context, applies the concept that the length of a line specifies the number of unit lengths that will fit along that line. May apply a skip counting scheme to determine the area.

Draws and counts rows as rows, drawing with parallel lines. Counts the number of squares by iterating the number in each row, either using physical objects or an estimate for the number of times to iterate. Those who count by ones usually do so with a systematic spatial strategy (e.g., by row).

If the task is to measure an unmarked rectangular region, measures one dimension to determine the size of the iterated squares and eventually measures both, to determine the number of rows needed in drawing. May not need to complete the drawing to determine the area by counting (most younger children) or computation (repeated addition or multiplication).

Area Conserver Conserves area and reasons about additive composition of areas (e.g., how regions that look different can have the same area measure) and recognize need for space-filling in most contexts (Lehrer et al., 1998).

(**NOTE:** Without high-quality instruction, this may not occur until nine years. E.g., there are serious deficiencies in many nine-year-olds' understanding of some of the most elementary concepts of area measurement. Students do not intuitively recognize the consequences of partitioning regions into units of measure. (Carpenter, Coburn, Reys, & Wilson, 1975).)

Continued Overleaf

Age (years)	Developmental Progression	Actions on Objects
8	*Area/Spatial Structuring:* **Array Structurer** With linear measures or other similar indications of the two dimensions, multiplicatively iterates squares in a row or column to determine the area. Drawings are not necessary. In multiple contexts, children can compute the area from the length and width of rectangles *and* explain how that multiplication creates a measure of area.	Builds, maintains, and manipulates composites (units of units of units) that operate in two dimensions. Mentally de/composes array into rows by columns or individual squares. The mental image may be of a spatial array or, at this level especially, a symbolic array. Applies repeated addition or multiplication to composites. Curtails these processes to apply multiplication and area formulas with understanding.

Volume

Volume not only introduces a third dimension and thus a significant challenge to students' spatial structuring, but also complexity in the nature of the materials measured. That is, solid units are "packed," such as cubes in a three-dimensional array, whereas a liquid "fills" three-dimensional space, taking the shape of the container. For the latter, the unit structure may be psychologically one-dimensional for some children (i.e., simple iterative counting that is not processed as geometrically three-dimensional), especially, for example, in filling a cylindrical jar in which the (linear) height corresponds with the volume (Curry & Outhred, 2005).

For children in grades 1–4, competence in "filling" volume (e.g., estimating and measuring the number of cups of rice that filled a container) was about equivalent with their competence in corresponding length tasks (Curry & Outhred, 2005). The relationship is consistent with the notion that the structure of the task is one-dimensional, exemplified by some students' treating the height of the rice in the container as if it were a unit length and iterating it, either mentally or using their fingers, up the side of the container. Some students performed better on length, others on filling volume, giving no evidence of a developmental relationship between the two. The task contained some extra demands, such as creating equal measurements; even many first graders made sure that the cup was not over- or under-filled for each iteration.

On the other hand, "packing" volume is more difficult than length and area (Curry & Outhred, 2005). Most students had little idea of how to estimate or measure on packing tasks. There were substantial increases from grades 2 to 4, but even the older students' scores were below the corresponding scores for the area task. Further there was a suggestion that understanding of area is a prerequisite to understanding packing volume.

This implies that a measure of packing volume requires that children build another layer onto their competence in spatial structuring, because the units must be defined, coordinated, and integrated in three dimensions. Work on spatial structuring described a variety of strategies students use to structure a three-dimensional array of cubes (Battista & Clements, 1998). Younger U.S. students often count only the faces of the cubes, often resulting in counting some cubes (e.g., those at the corners) multiple times and not counting cubes in the interior. The majority of fifth graders, but only 20 percent of third graders, structure the cubes constituting a rectangular prism as a series of layers, each of which is structured into rows and columns (similar to the two-dimensional structuring for area previously discussed). This spatial structuring strategy allows students to determine the number in one layer and then multiple or skip-count to obtain the total number of cubic units in the rectangular prism.

There is little research on volume that involves younger children. In one study, of all the measurable attributes tested (including number), one of the only relationships that was significant was surprising: number and volume. This may be because each task used a single basic strategy (different for number and volume), neither of which required units, for children from three years to nine years (K. F. Miller, 1984). That is, most children of all ages visually compared the levels of fluid. However, there are developmental differences. Younger children hold on to this strategy inappropriately, whereas older students will change to a more accurate strategy.

Another study indicated that three- and four-year-olds understand that object size affects the measurement of the volume of the object (Sophian, 2002). That is, they could tell that fewer larger than smaller objects would fit in a container. Children improved significantly from pre to posttest, with demonstrations in between, involving the experimenter saying "Let's see" and placing one object of each size in their respective containers, and saying, "This one (filled with large objects) is starting to get full, isn't it?" The degree of improvement was similar for three- vs. four-year olds and for Head Start children vs. children who attended private preschools. Head Start children, however, were less likely than peers attending private preschools to be able to articulate relevant quantitative features when asked to explain the outcomes that they observed during the training trials.

Experience and Education

As with length and volume, how students represent volume influences how they think of structuring volume. For example, compared to only a fifth of students without focused work on spatial structuring, *all* third graders with a wide range of experiences and representations of volume measure successfully structured space as a three-dimensional array (Lehrer, Strom, & Confrey,

2002). Most even developed the conception of area as the product of the area (i.e., length times width) and height. One third grader, for example, used squared grid paper to estimate the area of the base of a cylinder, then found the volume by multiplying this estimate by the height of the cylinder "to draw it [the area of the base] through how tall it is." This indicates that a developmental progression for spatial structuring, including packing volume, could reasonably be far more progressive than some cross-sectional studies of students in traditional instructional contexts would indicate.

Learning Trajectory for Volume Measurement

Table 11.2 A Developmental Progression for Volume Measurement

Age (years)	Developmental Progression	Actions on Objects
0–3	*Volume/Capacity:* **Volume Quantity Recognizer** Identifies capacity or volume as attribute. Says, "This box holds a lot of blocks!"	Perceives space and objects within the space.
4	**Capacity Direct Comparer** Can compare two containers. Pours one container into another to see which holds more.	Using perceptual objects, internal bootstrap competencies to compare linear extent (see the length trajectory for "Direct Comparer") or recognize "overflow" as indicating the container "poured from" contains more than that "poured into."
5	**Capacity Indirect Comparer** Can compare two containers using a third container and transitive reasoning. Pours one container into two others, concluding that one holds less because it overflows, and the other is not fully filled.	A mental image of a particular amount of material ("stuff") can be built, maintained, and manipulated. With the immediate perceptual support of the containers and material, such images can be compared. For some, explicit transitive reasoning may be applied to the images or their symbolic representations (i.e., object names).
6	*Volume/Spatial Structuring:* **Primitive 3-D Array Counter** Partial understanding of cubes as filling a space. Initially, may count the *faces* of a cube building, possibly double-counting cubes at the corners and usually not counting internal cubes. Eventually counts one cube at a time in carefully structured and guided contexts, such as packing a small box with cubes.	With perceptual support, can visualize that 3-D space can be filled with objects (e.g., cubes). With strong guidance and perceptual support from pre-structured materials, can direct the filling of that space and recognize that filling as complete, but often only intuitively. Implicit visual patterning and constraints of physical materials guides placement of cubes.

Age (years)	Developmental Progression	Actions on Objects
7	**Capacity Relater and Repeater** Uses simple units to fill containers, with accurate counting.	See the learning trajectory level, Length Unit Relater and Repeater.
	Fills a container by repeatedly filling a unit and counting how many.	
	With teaching, understands that fewer larger than smaller objects or units will be needed to fill a given container.	
7	*Volume/Spatial Structuring:* **Partial 3-D Structurer** Understands cubes as filling a space, but does not use layers or multiplicative thinking. Moves to more accurate counting strategies e.g.:	Builds, maintains, and manipulates *mental* images of composite shapes, structuring them as composites of individual shapes and as a single entity—a row (a unit of units), then a layer (a "column of rows" or unit of unit of units). Applies this composite unit repeatedly, but not necessarily exhaustively, as its application remains guided by intuition.
	Counts unsystematically, but attempts to account for internal cubes.	
	Counts systematically, trying to account for outside and inside cubes.	
	Counts the numbers of cubes in one row or column of a 3-D structure and using skip counting to get the total.	
8	*Area/Spatial Structuring:* **3-D Row and Column Structurer**	Builds, maintains, and manipulates *mental* images of composite shapes, structuring them as composites of individual shapes and as a single entity—a layer (a unit of units of units) of *congruent* cubes. Applies this composite unit repeatedly *and exhaustively* to fill the 3-D array— coordinating this movement in 1-1 correspondence with the elements of the orthogonal column. If in a measurement context, applies the concept that the length of a line specifies the number of unit lengths that will fit along that line. May applies a skip counting scheme to determine the volume.
	Counts or computes (row by column) the number of cubes in one row, and then uses addition or skip counting to determine the total.	
	Computes (row times column) the number of cubes in one row, and then multiplies by the number of layers to determine the total.	

Continued Overleaf

Age (years)	Developmental Progression	Actions on Objects
9	*Area/Spatial Structuring:* **3-D Array Structurer** With linear measures or other similar indications of the two dimensions, multiplicatively iterates squares in a row or column to determine the area.	Builds, maintains, and manipulates composites (a 3-D array—units of units of units of unit) that operate in two dimensions. Mentally de/composes 3-D array into layers, which themselves are de/composed into rows by columns. The mental image may be of a spatial array or, at this level especially, a symbolic array. Applies repeated addition or multiplication to composites. Curtails the process to use volume formulas with understanding.
	Constructions and drawings are not necessary. In multiple contexts, children can compute the volume of rectangular prisms from their dimensions *and* explain how that multiplication creates a measure of volume.	

Relationships Among Length, Area, and Volume

As the previous discussions show, length, area, and volume measurement have many similar cognitive features, such as general principles of measurement (unit iteration). They are also all *geometric* measurement, with the addition of similar features of conservation of units under spatial transformations, the inverse relation between unit size and the number of units, and spatial structuring. The measurement of area and volume leads to multiplicative relationships involving the lengths of the sides.

In a similar vein, developmental progressions for length, area, and volume measurement share features (Curry & Outhred, 2005). Early errors including difficulties with unit iteration, such as overlapping units, leaving gaps, using different size "units," and counting units twice or skipping units. Later, they have difficulty moving from physically filling space to using visualization and more abstract approaches (Battista & Clements, 1996, 1998; Bragg & Outhred, 2001; Curry & Outhred, 2005; Outhred & Mitchelmore, 2000).

Many curricula assume that children must learn length first, then area, then volume. However, research does not indicate there is a strict prerequisite relationship (K. Hart, 1984). The general developmental ordering has been found in other research (Curry & Outhred, 2005; Vasilyeva & Casey, 2007). Similarly, estimates of linear measurement are more accurate than for weight, liquid capacity, and volume, but poorer than for temperature. (Joram et al., 1998). However, there are several qualifications to this ordering. First, only "packing" volume is more difficult than length and area. Indeed, competence regarding "filling" volume seems to develop in parallel to competence regarding length (confirming that both involve one-dimensional thinking). Second, aspects of all three tasks are developing through the primary grades.

As another example, performing in the early levels of the developmental progressions in both length and area may be affected by how carefully children place iterated units and record the positions (Curry & Outhred, 2005), indicating the influence of a common feature of measurement for these domains. Therefore, it appears that it is the *spatial structuring* aspects of geometric measurement that could be effectively sequenced in learning length, then area, then volume. For example, most articles explicitly mention that a good foundation in *linear measurement* is a necessary condition for understanding area measurement. This seems clear in students' ability to understand the covering of one-dimensional space with units, as well as in *later* levels of understanding of area and volume, given that each, in their more sophisticated form, can be computed as the product of linear measurements. Similarly, a good understanding of two-dimension spatial structuring appears important to extend this competence to three dimensions (e.g., in stacking volume). But other aspects (e.g., using a filling unit to measure liquid volume) could develop in parallel (e.g., to measure length) and relatively independently. In summary, except for the development of spatial structuring in one, then two, and finally three dimensions, there seems to be no strict developmental sequence for length, area, and volume, but overlapping progress.

Angle and Turn Measure

As with length and area, children need to understand concepts such as equal partitioning and unit iteration to understand angle and turn measure. Whether defined more statically as the measure of the figure formed by the intersection of two rays or as turning, angle measure involves a relationship between components of shapes and therefore is a *property* as defined here. Given the complexity, it is unsurprising that students in the early and elementary grades often form separate concepts of angles as figures and turns (Lehrer, Jenkins et al., 1998), and may have separate notions for different turn contexts (e.g., unlimited rotation as a fan vs. a hinge) and for various "bends" (Mitchelmore, 1998; Mitchelmore & White, 1998).

Especially receiving only traditional instruction, students' misconceptions about angle and their measure abound. Children in grades 1, 2, and 3 believe that "straight" means no "bumps" or "bends" but many of those in grades 1 and 2 also believe that a line segment oriented 50° from the vertical is not straight (Lehrer, Jenkins et al., 1998). When discussing "bends," students are influenced by the lengths of the intersecting lines or their orientation, with the latter decreasing from grades 1 to 5, but the former a persistent error. That is, 67 percent of primary grade students claim that 30° and 60° angles are more similar to each other than to a 120° angle when the line segments of all three are equal in length, but when the length of the line segments of the 60° angle are decreased, only 43 percent judge the acute angles as most similar (see the illustration in the companion book). The influence of the irrelevant length of the line segments may be persistent (and orientation less so) because many students continue to believe that angles can be measured by the distance between the endpoints of two line segments that form angle. Even in contexts designed to evoke a dynamic image of turning, such as hinges or doors, most students used a static measure of the length between the endpoints.

A final rule-assessment task showed that most students in grades 1 and 2 (given traditional instruction) do not differentiate between angles based on their measure, although some do differentiate between small (e.g., 30° or 60°) and large (90° and 120°) angles. By grade 3, most children (69 percent) mentally decomposed figures to compare angles and could reliably compare all but the two most similar angles (30° and 60°). By grade 5, most could compare most angle pairs, but still only 9 percent even at this age could coordinate the relationships among all these angles.

Other research shows that students often hold other misconceptions, such as that a right angle is an angle that points to the right, or two right angles in different orientations are not equal in measure (Clements & Battista, 1992). They relate angle measure to not only the lengths of the line segments and distance between the endpoints, as already discussed, but also the slope or tilt of the top line segment, the area enclosed by the triangular region defined by draw sides, and the proximity of the sides (Clements & Battista, 1989). Some misconceptions decrease over the elementary years, such as orientation; but others, such as the effect of segment length, do not change, and some, such as the distance between end points, actually increase (Lehrer, Jenkins et al., 1998). By the third grade, most children can mentally decompose figures to allow identifying and distinguishing of one or more angles. Children's concept of images (Vinner & Hershkowitz, 1980) can be adversely affected by inappropriate instruction such as the limited illustrations they are shown.

Related topics include parallel and perpendicular lines. Both are difficult concepts for children in some applications. Children as young as three (Abravanel, 1977) and four years use parallelism in alignment tasks and six-year-olds can name parallel and non-parallel lines, although they have difficulty locating parallels in complex figures (Mitchelmore, 1992). Further, preschoolers use perpendicularity and parallelism in their informal play (H. P. Ginsburg et al., 1999). For example, they place blocks parallel and perpendicular to each other and even implicitly understand that the same length block will always bridge two long parallel blocks.

However, there appear to be initial foundations on which children can build. For example, children in pre-K use angles implicitly as in block building (H. P. Ginsburg et al., 1999). Children as young as five can use angles to represent locations of objects in a circle (i.e., an intuitive use of polar coordinates, Sandberg & Huttenlocher, 1996). In an early study, while five-year-olds showed no evidence of attention to angle in judging congruence, they could match angles in correspondence tasks (Beilin, 1984; Beilin et al., 1982). So, helping children mathematize their intuitive use of angle size, matching shapes by angles, and using angles to complete puzzles are all within the competence of most children from a very young age.

Thus, children do much more than recognize that geometric figures have corners. They can learn to reliably distinguish among angles of different measure, and can mentally decompose a figure into separate attributes of length and angle (Lehrer, Jenkins et al., 1998). Still, as noted previously, they often confound angle and length measures, so careful instructional attention must be given to angle and turn measure.

Experience and Education

This research might lead to the argument that angle and turn measure are both difficult and relatively esoteric mathematical concepts and therefore need not be introduced to young children. However, (a) children can and do compare angle and turn measures informally, (b) angle size is necessary to work with shapes, and (c) although only a small percentage of students learn angles well through elementary school in the U.S., young children *can* learn these concepts successfully (Lehrer, Jenkins et al., 1998).

Perhaps the most difficult step for students is to integrate turns, and, in general, a dynamic understanding of angle measure-as-rotation, into their understandings of angles. Computer manipulatives and tools can help children bring the concept of a turn to an explicit level of awareness (Sarama, Clements, & Vukelic, 1996).

Logo's turtle geometry involves specific angles measures. Logo use does not immediately develop strong angle concepts. Students' misconceptions about angle measure and difficulties coordinating the relationships between the turtle's rotation and the constructed angle have persisted for years, especially if not properly guided by their teachers (Hershkowitz et al., 1990; Hoyles & Sutherland, 1986; Kieran, 1986a; Kieran et al., 1986). In general, however, Logo experience appears to facilitate understanding of angle measure. Logo children's conceptualization of larger angles are more likely to reflect mathematically correct, coherent, and abstract ideas (Clements & Battista, 1989; Findlayson, 1984; Noss, 1987) and show a progression from van Hiele level 0 to level 2 in the span of the treatment (Clements & Battista, 1990). If Logo experiences emphasize the difference between the angle of rotation and the angle formed as the turtle traced a path, misconceptions regarding the measure of rotation and the measure of the angle may be avoided (Clements & Battista, 1989; Clements, Battista et al., 2001b; Lehrer et al., 1989).

Research indicates that the traditional Logo philosophy of body syntony, or connections with one's physical movements—is a critical instructional component. One study showed that children learned turn measure first through physical rotations, especially rotations of their own bodies (Clements, Battista et al., 1996). During the same time, they gained limited knowledge of assigning numbers to certain turns with turtle geometry, initially by establishing benchmarks. A synthesis of these two domains—turn-as-body-motion and turn-as-number—constituted a critical juncture in learning about turns for many primary-grade children. In a follow-up study, this developmental order was confirmed in students of above average ability and also extended it, revealing a process of psychological curtailment in which students gradually replace full rotations of their bodies with smaller rotations of an arm, hand, or finger (Clements & Burns, 2000). As they do this, they build mental images that can represent these physical movements. Eventually, these mental images become operational; that is, they can be created, maintained, and transformed internally. At this point, children have a "conceptual protractor" that they can mentally project onto objects and contexts to measure turns. Various factors (e.g., initial heading) affect students' strategy choice, with curtailment happening within each of several categories of problems.

These and other studies have used the Logo turtle to help children mathematize their physical experiences. In one study across grades K–6, the youngest children improved on certain turn and angle tasks the most relative to controls (Clements, Battista et al., 2001b). These tests involved difficult distracters, which demanded, for example, that children differentiate between greater angle measure and greater side length. Thus, thinking about angles and turns in turtle geometry helped children as young as kindergarten develop robust concepts of their measure. Again, the Logo activities were embedded in an instructional program designed to teach mathematics. In addition, Logo software specially designed to show the sweep of the ray as the turtle turns and provide other measurement tools has shown to be especially useful (Clements, Battista et al., 2001b; Clements & Sarama, 1995).

Learning Trajectory for Angle and Turn Measurement

To understand angles, children must understand the various aspects of the angle concept. They must overcome difficulties with orientation, discriminate angles as critical parts of geometric figures, and construct and represent the idea of turns, among others. Furthermore, they must construct a high level of *integration* among these aspects. A developmental progression, including the mental actions on objects, for angle and measurement is provided in Table 11.3.

Table 11.3 A Developmental Progression for Angle (and Turn) Measurement

Age (years)	Developmental Progression	Actions on Objects
2–3	**Intuitive Angle Builder** Intuitively uses some angle measure notions in everyday settings, such as building with blocks.	See the learning trajectory for motions and spatial sense.
	Places blocks parallel to one another and at right angles (with the perceptual support of the blocks themselves) to build a "road."	
4–5	**Implicit Angle User** Implicitly uses some angle notions, including parallelism and perpendicularity, in physical alignment tasks, construction with blocks, or other everyday contexts (Mitchelmore, 1989, 1992; Seo & Ginsburg, 2004). May identify corresponding angles of a pair of congruent triangles using physical models. Uses the word "angle" or other descriptive vocabulary to describe some of these situations.	See the learning trajectories for matching shapes and for motions and spatial sense. With immediate perceptual support of and feedback from action upon physical objects, places objects in approximate alignment (e.g., parallel). Such placement is influenced by an inborn sense of verticality and horizontality; for oblique placements, "not touching" is more heavily relied upon.
	Moves a long unit block to be parallel with another block after adjusting the distance between them so as to accurately place a perpendicular block across them, in anticipation of laying several other blocks perpendicularly across them.	
6	**Angle Matcher** Matches angles concretely. Explicitly recognizes parallels from non-parallels in specific contexts (Mitchelmore, 1992). Sorts angles into "smaller" or "larger" (but may be misled by irrelevant features, such as length of line segments).	With immediate perceptual support of and feedback from action upon physical objects, maintains an approximate visual image of a an angle, using this to choose another shape or angle that matches it. Similarly can create and maintain a visual trace of two separate lines, deciding that they are not parallel if the traces meet and that they are if the traces are approximately in the same direction according to an external framework.
	Given several noncongruent triangles, finds pairs that have one angle that is the same measure, by laying the angles on top of one another.	
7	**Angle Size Comparer** Differentiates angle and angle size from shapes and contexts and compares angle sizes. Recognizes right angles, and	Builds, maintains, and manipulates *mental* images of angles in which size is maintained even if those images undergo rigid motions.

Continued Overleaf

Age (years)	Developmental Progression	Actions on Objects
	then equal angles of other measures, in different orientations (Mitchelmore, 1989). Compares simple turns. (Note that without high-quality instruction, this and higher levels may not be achieved even by the end of the elementary grades.)	
	"I put all the shapes that have right angles here, and all the ones that have bigger or smaller angles over there."	
	Turns Logo turtle, using degree measurements.	
8+	**Angle Measurer** Understands angle and angle measure in both primary aspects and can represent multiple contexts in terms of the standard, generalizable concepts and procedures of angle and angle measure (e.g., two rays, the common endpoint, rotation of one ray to the other around that endpoint, and measure of that rotation).	Forms connections among, and eventually integrates, notions of angle (as intersection of two rays) and angle measure (as rotation between rays) across different contexts.

Final Words

Measurement is one of the principal real-world applications of mathematics. It bridges two critical realms of mathematics, geometry and real numbers. Number and operations are essential elements of measurement. The measurement process subdivides continuous quantities such as length to make them countable. Measurement provides a model and an application for both number and arithmetic operations. In this way, measurement helps connect the two realms of number and geometry, each providing conceptual support to the other.

Research on linear, area, volume, and angle and turn measurement indicates that measuring in general is more complex than learning the skills or procedures for determining a measure. The conceptual, mental activities of children as they engage in measuring contexts should be the focus of instruction. Learning specific measurement concepts and skills is intrinsically important, and it also helps children differentiate between two basic types of quantity, discrete and continuous, which are often confused by young children

(K. F. Miller, 1984; Piaget et al., 1960). That is, representing exact discrete quantities by counting, and more precise continuous quantities by measuring, may be instrumental in children's development of the distinction between and attributes of these two basic categories (Mix et al., 2002). This gradual integration and differentiation across domains supports the previously-described principle of *progressive hierarchization*, which appears consistently in studies of measurement. For example, recall that children who observed agreement between measurement and direct comparison were more likely to use measurement later than were children who observed both procedures but did not have the opportunity to compare them (P. E. Bryant, 1982). Children tend to learn about different aspects of measures of different attributes, and only with time do they form a set of related concepts. Only with high-quality instruction do they form generalizations about measurement across attributes. Such instruction integrates development of procedures and concepts. Finally, we repeat the caveat that although young children can develop early ideas in measurement of various attributes, such as area and angle, there is little research on how valuable it would be to invest instructional time in these areas rather than others. We believe that certain concepts, such as "right angle versus not right angle" are essential, but the age at which it is best to introduce more complex angle measurement concepts remains an open question.

This chapter concludes the main discussion of the three central content domains for early childhood mathematics: number, geometry, and geometric measurement. Part V contains two chapters that address (a) content domains not previously covered, and (b) processes.

Part V
Other Content Domains and Processes

Part V contains two chapters that address content domains and processes not previously covered. In both cases, the areas have already been discussed, sometimes extensively, in the context of the previous chapters. However, they are sufficiently important to require chapters focused exclusively on them. Chapter 12 describes two general areas, patterns—including repeating patterns, structure, and algebraic thinking—and data analysis. Chapter 13 focuses on the processes of reasoning, problem solving, classification, and seriation.

12
Other Content Domains

Patterns and Structure (Including Algebraic Thinking)

Previous chapters have discussed perceptual patterns, such as subitized patterns (Chapter 2); patterns in the number words of counting (Wu, 2007, see also Chapter 3); "one-more" pattern of counting (Chapter 3), which also connects counting with arithmetic, numerical patterns (see Chapters 2, 3, 5, and 6); arithmetic patterns (see Chapter 6, as well as other examples in Parker & Baldridge, 2004); and spatial patterns (Chapters 8 and 9), including array structures (Chapter 11). Noteworthy is that none of these are examples of the typical early childhood practice of patterning—repeated sequential patterns. However, they all reflect Lynne Steen's definition of mathematics as the "science of patterns"; that is, patterns in number and space (1988). The theory of mathematics, according to Steen, is built on relations among patterns and on applications derived from the fit between pattern and observations.

Because these chapters have dealt with these aspects of patterning extensively, we limit discussions of patterning in this chapter to sequential and other types of repeated patterns, and extend this focus only to include algebraic thinking, that content domain most clearly linked to early work with patterns. *Our own, however, is the broader view, that patterning is the search for mathematical regularities and structures, to bring order, cohesion, and predictability to seemingly unorganized situations and facilitate generalizations beyond the information directly available.* In this view, patterning is a domain of study, a process, and a habit of mind.

Pre-K children often engage in pattern-related activities and recognize patterns in their everyday environment. Recall that in the observational study of children at play, the category of mathematics, "pattern and shape" was the most frequently observed, 30 percent of the observed time (Ginsburg et al., 1999; Seo & Ginsburg, 2004). However, research also has revealed that an abstract understanding of patterns develops gradually during the early childhood years (B. A. Clarke et al., 2006; Klein & Starkey, 2004). Of children entering their first year of school in Australia, 76 percent could copy a repeating color pattern, but only 31 percent could extend or explain it (B. A. Clarke et al., 2006). Little else is known, except that patterns are one of many elements of teaching visual literacy with positive long-term impact in the Agam program (Razel & Eylon, 1990).

The recognition and analysis of patterns have been considered important components of the young child's intellectual development because they provide a foundation for the development of algebraic thinking. For example, early connections lie in the correspondences discussed in previous chapters—primitive versions of the basic algebraic notion of mapping (e.g., functions), at least developmentally. For example in counting (Chapter 3), people map each item of the "source" or "departure" set—the counting words—to items in the "arrival" set—the group of objects to be counted (Wagner & Walters, 1982).

Another key foundational ability for all topics in mathematics is the algebraic insight—the conscious understanding that one thing can represent another. Children develop this key idea at about three years of age in the simplest form; for example, as we have seen, understanding that a map or picture can represent another space. This ability develops considerably over the next several years, as children interact with symbols, and with other people using these symbols, in a variety of situations, from maps to spatial patterns to numerical patterns. (Early algebraic thinking is *not* early algebra.)

From this perspective, algebraic *thinking* can permeate much of the instruction of all the content domains, especially arithmetic (and the smaller amount of research done on such thinking should not determine its importance to the curriculum; more research is needed on that issue). That is, one common, albeit often underappreciated, route to algebra begins with a search for patterns. For example, the later months of kindergarten, it is possible that with guidance children can begin analyzing numerical patterns, just as primary grade students can do. These students learn to find and extend numerical patterns—extending their knowledge of patterns to thinking algebraically about arithmetic (Baroody, 1993). For example, even preschoolers and kindergartners can generalize that subtracting zero from any number gives that number, or that subtracting a number from itself gives zero (Baroody & Lai, 2007).

Moving into the primary grades, children can learn to find and extend numerical patterns—extending their knowledge of patterns to thinking algebraically about arithmetic (Baroody, 1993). Two central themes are making generalizations and using symbols to represent mathematical ideas and to represent and solve problems (Carpenter & Levi, 1999). For example, children might generalize that when you add zero to a number the sum is always that number or when you add three numbers it does not matter which two you add first (Carpenter & Levi, 1999). The ability of children to invent, learn, apply, justify, and otherwise reason about arithmetic problems, described extensively in Chapters 5 and 6, arguably demonstrates that algebraic thinking can be an implicit but significant component of early and primary children's learning of arithmetic. For example, children draw upon the fundamental properties of addition, subtraction, and multiplication, as well as the relations among the operations. They use the commutativity of addition to create counting-on-from-larger strategies. Similarly, associativity and the inverse relation between addition and subtraction are used extensively, if implicitly, in many of children's arithmetic strategies. The caveat of implicit use is important—children may not make these properties explicit, especially without guidance from the teacher. However, this, too, is possible (Carpenter & Levi, 1999).

Further, without teachers who understand young children's development of algebraic thinking, and are willing to promote it, children do not develop flexible, algebraic habits of thinking and, more unfortunately, develop limited and erroneous ideas. For example, they believe that the equal sign represents a one-way operation that produces an answer of the right side (and thus reject even simple number sentences such as $4 = 9 - 5$). One child said, "It's telling you, that, um, I think, the, um, the end is coming up ..." (Ginsburg, 1997, p. 24). Similarly, children often do not recognize the commutative and distributive properties in situations in which it is important to do so. Some researchers have explained such difficulties as cognitive developmental constraints. However, there are reasons to believe that a lack of experience, or mis-educative experiences (Dewey, 1938/1997), are the cause; that is, the source of this misconception is almost certainly that children never experience equal signs used in other ways than "give the answer." The first reason is that primary to intermediate grade children can and do recognize that equality is preserved if equivalent transformations are made on both "sides" of a situation, from balance scales to sets of objects, verbal problems, and written equations (Schliemann, Carraher, & Brizuela, 2007). High-SES children could give logical justifications for all contexts, but verbal contexts educed more logical and transformational justifications than the other contexts for all children, who tended to justify their responses based on calculations whenever possible. For example, if all numbers are known, children compute, whereas they would solve problems in which some quantities were unknown using other strategies, more likely to employ algebraic thinking.

A second reason to believe that cognitive developmental constraints are *not* a valid reason to postpone algebraic reasoning is that existence of successful educational interventions in which young children engage in algebraic thinking belie such an explanation (Schliemann et al., 2007). We discuss such interventions in the "Experience and Education" section of this chapter.

Consistent with such arguments, some mathematicians and researchers have claimed that an overemphasis on simple patterns can *impede* children's development (Blanton & Kaput, 2004). By emphasizing a single numeric progression, it may make it more difficult for children to learn the more mathematically important idea of co-variance between two variables. They describe functional thinking as representational thinking that relates two different quantities. For example, they asked children to suppose they were in a dog shelter and figure out, for a given number of dogs, how many eyes (or eyes and tails) they would see. Preschoolers (ages three to five) could use concrete representations to count, as the teacher wrote the numbers in a "t chart" such

Table 12.1 A T-Chart for Number of Dogs and Ears

Dogs	Eyes
1	2
2	4
3	6
4	8
. . .	

as in Table 12.1. Note how the two quantities relate. However, there was no sign they looked for patterns.

Kindergarteners used dots and numerals to represent this situation. The teacher again recorded the information in a t-chart and some students identified the pattern in the number of eyes as "counting by twos" or "every time we add one more dog, we get two eyes" (p. 137). In one class, children noticed that "We're skipping all the odd numbers" (p. 138). This is a further generalization and abstraction.

First graders also noticed counting by twos or threes (for eyes + tails) and skip-counted to find how many for seven dogs. Describing how quantities correspond is covariational thinking. Second graders provided multiplicative relationships using natural language: "You have to double the number of dogs to get the number of eyes" (p. 138). Third graders used letters as variables. Thus, even primary grade students could learn to use representations such as t-charts—fluently, by second or third grade—and show signs of functional thinking emerging in kindergarten. Note that first graders were often redirected to examine the pattern in just one column, perhaps because too much patterning work only deals with one quantity (Blanton & Kaput, 2004).

Note that the goal of this body of work is not to do algebra earlier but to develop toward algebraic thinking—the "ability to make effective and purposeful use of symbols in ways that are inherently sensible and meaningful. At times this means operating on symbols in ways that are purely syntactical. At times this means making meaningful use of the contexts and relations that gave rise to the symbols. The act of symbolizing itself may serve purposes of generalization, classification, or abstraction. Thinking algebraically means having access to various forms of representation, including symbolic representation; being able to move flexibly from one representation to another when one representation or another provides better affordances for the task at hand; being able to operate on the symbols meaningfully in context when called for, and according to the relevant syntactic rules when called for . . . algebraic thinking is a particular form of mathematical sense-making related to symbolization. It involves meaningful symbol use, whether the meaning is 'simply' guided by the syntactical rules of the symbol system being used or the meaning is related to the properties of a situation that have been represented by those symbols, or related to other representations of it" (Schoenfeld, 2008).

One final study in this section examined kindergartners' and first graders' knowledge of using symbols to represent number sentences (Mark-Zigdon & Tirosh, 2008). Kindergarteners could recognize legitimate number sentences, but had much difficulty producing them. First graders generally succeeded on both these tasks, although recognition was also easier for them than production. However, they found it difficult to recognize number sentences not written in the canonical form. Thus, there is a need for students to discuss the nature of addition and subtraction number sentences and the different symbols, the role they play, and their defining and nondefining properties.

In summary, students in the primary grades can learn to formulate, represent, and reason about generalizations and conjectures, although their justifications do not always adequately validate the conjectures they create (Davis, 1984; Kaput, Carraher, & Blanton, 2008; Schifter, 1999). This body of research on young children's understanding of patterns can be used to establish learning trajectories for pattern instruction in early mathematics education, more reliably for the simple case of sequential repeated patterns. Such a perspective on patterns and algebra as habits of mind or ways of thinking can form potentially useful connections between early and later school mathematics. That is, it creates a framework within which early work from correspondences, to analyzing relationships between quantities, noticing structure, studying change, generalizing, problem solving, modeling, justifying, proving, and predicting can be seen as building a bridge between these mathematical foundations and later formal algebraic work (see Kieran, 2006, for a detailed discussion). Again, the research is sparse regarding algebraic thinking and pre-algebra (arithmetic using letters to represent numbers, Parker & Baldridge, 2004). Some have argued that functional thinking within algebraic reasoning activities should be in the earliest of the elementary years (Blanton & Kaput, 2004). Although we believe this to be a fruitful perspective, we caution that little research is available that indicates whether this perspective—and the implied focus for curricula and teaching—is more efficacious and efficient than others. We need rigorous studies to test whether such an emphasis would be superior to other curricular approaches. The section on "Experience and Education" in this chapter describes some promising educational interventions based on this perspective.

Experience and Education

"When done properly (i.e., with understanding), engaging in mathematics is a coherent, sense-making activity. Actions are not arbitrary; one does what one does for good reason. If one understands those reasons, everything fits together.

Algebra represents one of humankind's great intellectual achievements—the use of symbols to capture abstractions and generalizations, and to provide analytic power over a wide range of situations, both pure and applied.

The fundamental purpose of early algebra should be to provide students with a set of experiences that enables them to see mathematics—sometimes called 'the science of patterns'—as something they can make sense of, and to provide them with the habits of mind that will support the use of the specific mathematical tools they will encounter when they study algebra. With the right kinds of experiences in early algebra, students will no longer find algebra to be a new and alien body of subject matter. Rather, they will find it to be the extension and codification of powerful modes of sense-making that they have already encountered in their study of mathematics."

(Schoenfeld, 2008, pp. 506–507)

The *Building Blocks* learning trajectories for this type of pattern is presented in Table 12.2. Such an approach could be successful, if teachers have the knowledge to build the mathematics learning from them, but several observational studies from Australia suggest caution. Teachers need to understand how to take advantage of the opportunities such vehicles present. Case studies of two teachers revealed that both thought patterning was important and that they knew enough about the patterning process. However, observations of their classrooms indicated that there were limited worthwhile patterning opportunities (Waters, 2004). For example, one teacher asked children to make clothing patterns; however, the examples of clothing she showed were colorful, but consisted of complex random designs that did not have any regularities. Other teachers ignored or did not elaborate on children's patterning (Fox, 2005, see specific examples in the companion volume).

Extending the conclusions of these research projects, we believe that teachers need to understand the learning trajectories of patterning in all its forms and the wider implications of patterning as a habit of mind. We agree that in patterning, as in all mathematical areas, there is a need to help teachers plan specific experiences and activities, capitalize on relevant child-initiated activities, and elicit and guide mathematically generative discussions in all settings (cf. Fox, 2005).

In reaction to these, innovative programs from Australia indicate that early patterning, algebraic thinking, and the learning of structure in mathematical thinking are important to young children's mathematical development and are best considered general cognitive characteristics (Mulligan, Mitchelmore, & Prescott, 2006; Mulligan, Prescott, Papic, & Mitchelmore, 2006). Descriptive studies have shown that the perception and representation of mathematical structure in children aged four to 6.7 years generalize across a range of mathematical domains, such as counting, partitioning, unitizing, patterning, measurement, space and graphing (Mulligan, Prescott, & Mitchelmore, 2004). The researchers also described four levels of development of patterning and structural thinking. At the first level, children might reproduce a clock as a picture with no math and a triangular arrangement of 6 chips as circles with no triangular shape, numerical pattern, or correct quantity of circles (levels of understanding of rulers are similar to those in Chapter 10 and levels of spatial structuring are similar to those in Chapter 11). The second level is emergent, with some elements of structure, such as a triangular form drawn as a "Christmas tree" without correct quantity or the correct number of dots but without the triangular shape. The third level shows partial structure, such as a clock face with numerals but not canonically arranged. The fourth level integrates mathematical and spatial structural features accurately. Between 80 percent and 95 percent of all responses could be unambiguously sorted into the four levels across all tasks—an impressive consistency of structural representations over quite different tasks. A longitudinal investigation supported these findings and showed that many low-structuring children continued to allow superficial features to "crowd" their images, so that some actually reverted to less sophisticated levels, as their higher-structuring peers moved up one or two levels. These studies imply that structuring is an important mathematical process that supports mathematics development across domains (Mulligan, Mitchelmore, & Prescott, 2005).

Preschoolers participating in the *Australian Pattern and Structure Mathematics Awareness Program* (*PASMAP*) show significant development of concepts and skills in mathematical structuring and patterning. The researchers are unsure whether children's awareness and use of pattern and structure is the cause or the effect of their learning of mathematical concepts and skill, but do claim that the more children have developed internal representations that are developed structurally, the more coherent, organized, and stable their external representations, and the more mathematically competent they are (Mulligan, Prescott et al., 2006). A quasi-experimental design showed that, on pretest, children in the comparison group were the more successful on all but one of the tasks, but after the *PASMAP*, the intervention group was more successful on all the tasks. This trend was maintained a year after the program ended (Papic & Mulligan, 2007). These were not randomized controlled trials designs, but strongly suggest that this approach contributed substantially to young children's mathematical development.

Generalizations about fundamental properties of number and arithmetic may arise spontaneously as students solve problems (Carpenter & Levi, 1999). However, this did not occur regularly in first and second grade classrooms, so the researchers used Bob Davis' activities from the Madison Project, in particular his activities involving true/false sentences (e.g., $22 - 12 = 10$, true or false?) and open number sentences ($x + y = 12$ or $x + x = 48$, see the companion book for elaborations). Results showed that such activities were successful. Students could make generalizations from the specific cases. Generalizations about zero were generated most easily. Some students made conjectures about arithmetic properties with "open sentences" such as a + b − b = a. Most of the students learned to deal with the equal sign as a relation, not just as indicating "here comes the answer"; however, they needed repeated experience with the number sentences with more than a single number after the equal sign. Further, many students had difficulty creating justifications that went beyond merely providing examples. With carefully guided conversations, however, second graders could make their implicit knowledge explicit in making and discussing conjectures (Carpenter, Franke, & Levi, 2003). The researchers believe that young children are capable of learning important, unifying ideas of mathematics that serve as the foundation for both arithmetic and algebra (Carpenter et al., 2003).

More recently, these researchers emphasize the importance of the content that is to be generalized and represented, including equality as a relation, relational thinking, articulating fundamental properties of number and operations, and justification (Franke, Carpenter, & Battey, 2008). We already discussed equality as a relation—understanding the equal sign not merely in a fixed, procedural (and often erroneous; e.g., for 7 + 3 = _ + 4 saying "14") manner, but as indicating a structural relationship. Relational thinking involves examining expressions and equations in their entirety rather than as just a step-by-step process. For example, solving 65 − 42 + 5 + 42 = _ relationally, students might understand that 42 − 42 = 0, so add the 65 and 5, rather than computing from left to right. Or, to solve 7 + 3 = _ + 4, students might not only answer correctly, but *reason* that given 4 is one more than 3, the answer should be one less than 7. This involves using the associative property of addition—implicitly. *Articulating* such fundamental properties of number and operations is the third content emphasis. Previously discussed true/false sentences can catalyze such dialog. The fourth emphasis, justification of conjectures, is the most difficult. At the lowest level, students appeal to authority, the teacher or textbook. More autonomous is the use of examples. Such use can be deceiving, but, appropriated pedagogically, it can help educe the highest level, the use of generalization. Naïve generalizations may appeal to ideas that appear self evident, such as n + 0 = n. Other arguments may use properties or generalizable models, such as a rotation of a rectangular array to show commutativity of multiplication. Such emphases are substantive extensions (from simple arithmetic) for teachers of the mathematical ideas and processes, and the pedagogical strategies that might be used.

These researchers have found that sequences of problems can be particularly important. For example, if a student correctly solves 43 + 28 = _ + 42, but using full computation, she might offer 14 + 15 − 14 + _, then 28 + 32 = 27 + _. Students soon realize how they can use relational thinking (Franke et al., 2008).

These and other studies (see the companion book) support the position that we stated previously, that one of the reasons to believe that cognitive developmental constraints are *not* a valid reason to postpone algebraic reasoning is that existence of successful educational interventions in which young children engage in algebraic thinking belie such an explanation (Schliemann et al., 2007). For example, children in grades 1 to 4 learned to use algebraic notation to solve verbal problems and performed better than the control children throughout their school years (Bodanskii, 1991). At the end of fourth grade, they showed better performance in algebra problem solving than sixth and seventh grades in traditional programs who were introduced to algebra only in sixth grade.

Similarly, although schools' introduction of algebra strongly affects the representations children use to solve algebraic problems, some primary-grade students also invented representational schemes (Brito-Lima & da Rocha Falcão, 1997). For example, one problem involved two groups of children, one of which built a number of kits in the morning and three times that number in the afternoon and the second built 24; knowing the two groups built the same number of kites, how many did the first group build in the morning (e.g., $x + ax = b$)? After a teacher wrote letters for morning, afternoon and the whole day, a second grader drew a kite to represent the number built in the morning, three identical kites for the afternoon, and correctly determined the number each kite represented. Another second grader drew one, then three more circles, and placed dots under each one until he reached 24; the number under the first, six, gave him the answer. Thus, although older children introduced to algebraic representations showed more sophistication and success, some students from all grades, first to sixth, developed written representations for algebraic problems, and, with guidance, solved linear equation problems using multiple solution strategies (Brito-Lima & da Rocha Falcão, 1997).

Third graders in the U.S. could use their understandings of equality to solve algebraic problems (Schliemann et al., 2007). For example, they were asked to solve problems such as Brito Lima's equations, $8 + x = 3x$ and $7 + y = 2 + y + x$. On one problem, two of 15 children solved it independently, but refused notation, using mental reasoning only, nine solved it with guidance from the adult, two tried to start a solution but could not complete it, and two said it could not be solved. Across all the problems, children showed two problems: a lack of familiarity with using notation to represent unknowns and a lack of experience approaching problems with unknown quantities. However, with guidance, many showed signs that they could develop trial-and-error strategies, and could remove an unknown from both sides of an equation, which may constitute initial steps toward algebraic procedures.

Instruction in algebra was provided to these children based on three ideas: arithmetic operations can be viewed as functions; generalizing lies at the heart of algebraic reasoning; and children can and should use letters to stand for unknown amounts and for variables. Pilot testing in the third grade classroom revealed that they could successfully solve "guess my rule" problems and understand notation such as $n \rightarrow n + 3$. They also learned to fill in tables representing relationships between unknown quantities using variables. Although they struggled, in their initial attempts, with the reference and meaning of the letter that represents those quantities, they came to understand it as representing "any number."

A particular difficulty of which educators should be aware is that of seeing numbers as the distance between ("space between") other numbers, that is, as *differences*. This has been reported in several projects (e.g., Wright, Stanger, Stafford, & Martland, 2006) and thus is probably a serious challenge to children, and to curriculum developers and teachers. In this study (Schliemann et al., 2007), for example, some children interpreted differences in heights as the absolute heights. Others learned to interpret as a difference in heights, but not initially as an interval along the dimension; instead, they had to reenact the act of comparing.

Representing quantities with letters was another challenge. After the class agreed to represent Tom's height as "T", some students resisted representing Mary's height as T + 4, instead representing it as "M." Two students solved the general case, but still said "T" stood for "Tall" or "10" (earlier, students' interpreted "n" as standing for "none," "nine," or "19").

Part of their difficulty was thinking of any letter as a *variable* amount, when the concrete situations used in the instruction implied that there was a *particular quantity*—unknown, perhaps, but not one that varies. That is, children could think of the value of a height, or the amount of money in a wallet as unknown, or a "surprise," but had difficulty thinking of it as a *range* of values. Thus, it should not be surprising to us to find that they benefitted from working with numerical relations *unassociated* with any physical context. A fecund activity was "guess my rule" games in which the focus was on number relationships. (A related suggestion was not to have input-output tables always in order, because children then used column-based strategies only; in "guess my rule" without ordered tables, they begin to formulate a general rule.) This is not to say that context does not help, but that pure number activities play a critical role, and that some contexts might be used as students are challenged to adapt their algebraic thinking to a variety of situations.

Finally, this was not an efficacy study, and there was no comparison group, much less random assignment. Nevertheless, it is interesting that scores on the state test showed these children performed better than students in other classrooms in the same school. Thus, the instruction appeared not only to improve students' algebraic thinking, but also and did no harm to their ability to solve more traditional mathematical problems and even enhanced the latter ability.

Another promising approach is to use measurement and "generalized diagrams" as a way to develop problem-solving ability and promote algebraic thinking (Dougherty & Slovin, 2004). Based on the work of Russian researchers, the notion is that children can think algebraically at a very young age, especially if they are given the opportunity to link concrete, pictorial (e.g., diagrams), and abstract (including symbolic) representations by having experiences that present all these simultaneously. The examples from Chapter 10 (pp. 287–288) illustrate this approach.

Other projects have reported similar results (with similar limitations; most all of these projects were, appropriately, exploratory only). An Australian project worked with children from second to sixth grade ("year," in Australia). The teaching included focus on algebra involving a variety of representation, such as natural language, figures/diagrams, symbols and, in later years, graphs, and to build students' abilities to switch between them. Children were to act out situations with physical materials and connect particular representations emerging from different perspectives, particularly an "arrow symbol system" for change with the equation system for relationships (T. J. Cooper & Warren, 2007). The first lessons taught the compensation principle for addition and subtraction. The addition compensation principle entails a notion of opposites, for example, if the first number is increased/decreased, then the second number is oppositely decreased/increased the same amount respectively to keep the sum of two numbers the same—algebraically $a + b = (a + n) + (b - n)$. The subtraction compensation principle is different; if the first number is increased/decreased, then the second number is increased/decreased the same amount to keep the difference between two numbers the same—algebraically, $a - b = (a + n) - (b + n)$. This was taught in five steps. Step one used the length model (lengths that were not measured or numbered). Two strips of paper were cut so that together they were the same length as the third. A piece was cut off one of them, and the students asked what had to happen to the third strip to keep it equal to the combined length of the other two. Step 2 used the set model (a numbered activity). Sets of five and four counters were compared with nine counters, a counter was removed from the set of four, and students were asked what had to happen to the five. In steps 3 and 4, the activity was repeated for equations, first with small and then larger numbers, asking the students what would have to happen if one of the numbers was increased and the sum remained the same. Step 5 repeated Steps 1 to 4 but here the quantities were increased rather than decreased.

Initial findings were that the unnumbered lengths model was the easiest for students to understand (yet another study supporting this Russian approach). Addition compensation was best illustrated by a relay race context, with students acting it out (if the first walker went farther, the second one walked a shorter distance). (See the research report for information about other grades and other representations, such as the balance beam with different colored small cans of food and cloth bags used to motivate study of equations.) In general, students could determine pattern rules for growing patterns from tables of numbers and visual structures of counters, with tables easier to teach. Development seemed to move from factual to contextual to algebraic. Analyzing pattern in terms of visuals resulted in better process generalization.

In summary, early algebra is not algebra done early; instead, it should be about teaching arithmetic and other mathematical topics more deeply, so that misconceptions and inflexible thinking are replaced with nascent algebraic thinking, developing from the earliest years. Typical, procedural-only instruction in arithmetic and procedural use of signs such as "=" does not provide a foundation for such generalization and symbolization, but appropriate instruction does (Kaput et al., 2008). Students in the primary grades can learn to formulate, represent, and reason about generalizations and conjectures, although their justifications do not always adequately validate the conjectures they create (Davis, 1984; Schifter, 1999). This body of research on young children's understanding of patterns can be used, in turn, to establish developmentally appropriate learning trajectories for pattern instruction in early mathematics education. We must also remember that patterning in mathematics goes beyond simple linear and arithmetic situations, to involve other knowledge and competencies we have discussed, such structuring of rectangular arrays (see pp. 296–299), and numerical and spatial structures in counting, partitioning, subitizing, grouping, and unitizing.

Learning Trajectory for Pattern and Structure

Table 12.2 provides the developmental progression and the mental actions-on-objects for this learning trajectory. As stated previously, this mostly concerns the simple, typical case of sequential repeated patterns, and the sequence here comes mainly from the few studies on patterning with young children, mostly our *Building Blocks* and TRIAD projects. Research is needed to extend this

Table 12.2 Developmental Progression for Patterns and Structure

Age (years)	Developmental Progression	Actions on Objects
2	**Pre-Explicit Patterner** Detects and uses patterning implicitly, but may not recognize sequential linear patterns explicitly or accurately.	Initial (bootstrap) sensitivity to regularity supports the implicit detection of patterns and expectations based on them.
	Names a striped shirt with no repeating unit a "pattern."	Connection is made between the term "pattern" and some visual, rhythmic, and other regularities.
3	**Pattern Recognizer** Recognizes a simple pattern.	The implicit cognitive capacity (and predisposition) to recognize patterns is representationally redescribed to allow explicit processes to operate on perceptual input and note regularities.
	"I'm wearing a pattern" about a shirt with black, white, black white stripes.	

Age (years)	Developmental Progression	Actions on Objects
4	**Pattern Fixer** Fills in missing element of pattern, first with ABAB patterns. Given objects in a row with one missing, ABAB_BAB, identifies and fills in the missing element.	The ability to name or describe the repeated items from perceptual input is used to continue the naming by continuing to produce the verbal sequence stored in the phonetic "buffer" (or, visually, through a visuospatial sketch pad).
	Pattern Duplicator AB Duplicates ABABAB pattern. May have to work close to the model pattern. Given objects in a row, ABABAB, makes their own ABABAB row in a different location.	The processes named above are sufficiently explicit to allow the reproduction of short pattern core units, as long as perceptual support is available for "checking" the duplication (although the core units themselves may not yet have been redescribed).
	Pattern Extender AB Extends AB repeating patterns. Given objects in a row, ABABAB, adds ABAB to the end of the row.	As above, but with less need for constant (duplicative) perceptual support.
	Pattern Duplicator Duplicates simple patterns (not just alongside the model pattern). Given objects in a row, ABBABBABB, makes their own ABBABBABB row in a different location.	As above, extended to longer and more complex core units.
5	**Pattern Extender** Extends simple repeating patterns. Given objects in a row, ABBABBABB, adds ABBABB to the end of the row.	As above, extended.
6	**Pattern Unit Recognizer** Identifies the smallest unit of a pattern. Can translate patterns into new media. Given objects in an ABBABBABB pattern, identifies the core unit of the pattern as ABB.	The pattern's core unit is representationally redescribed so that patterns are perceived not just as regularities and repetitions but explicitly conceived as repetitions of a core unit.
7	**Numeric Patterner** Describes a pattern numerically, can translate between geometric and numeric representation of a series. Given objects in a geometric pattern, describes the numeric progression.	A new executive process connects the processes of patterning and the patterning of number and arithmetic processes.

limited aspect of patterning to include other types of patterns (e.g., geometric patterns based on other symmetries, growing patterns) as well as *patterning* and algebraic thinking as habits of mind.

Data Analysis

There is a dearth of research on children's learning of data analysis in the early childhood years. From a small amount of research conducted with older students, we can describe in broad strokes the developmental continuum for data analysis. Importantly, the foundations for data analysis lie in other areas, such as counting and classification.

To understand data analysis per se, students must learn the dual concepts of expectation (averages and probabilities) and variation (uncertainty, "spread" of values; e.g., standard deviations). Data analysis has been called the search for signals (expectations) within the noise (variation) (Konold & Pollatsek, 2002). Children often initially see only the *individuals* in a data display. Children in the late primary or early intermediate grades can learn to view ranges in data or view the mode. Eventually, students can focus on features of the data set as a whole, including the relative frequencies, density, and location.

A large analysis of Australian students' understanding of both expectation and variation revealed that it was not until third grade that the majority of students even achieved level 3, called "inconsistent," in which they acknowledged both expectation and variation but had only initial notions of these concepts (J. M. Watson, Callingham, & Kelly, 2007). For example, they thought of expectation when asked to think about a container with 50 red, 20 yellow, and 30 green lollipops mixed up it in and how many would be red if you pulled out 10. They may have said "more red" but used inconsistent reasoning, with no explicit mention of proportion. Of variation, they might just say, "anything can happen" or they may use the same language of "more" to address this concept as well. In response to "Have you heard 'the winds are variable?" they might respond that this means they are "changing or something." There are few or no connections between the ideas of expectation and variation. Entering first graders are at the authors' level 1, a pre-recognition level in which neither concept is appreciated, or level 2, with only primitive or limited concepts of either. For example, children at level 1 might answer a problem because of the position that the red lollipops had in the container, or they might just say their age or favorite number. Regarding variation (what would happen if six children did this), the response might be, "5, because $5 + 5 = 10$." "Will it be the same every time?" "No. The red up the top will be gone. . . . You might get other colors." At level 2, termed "informal," students were just beginning to show thought about expectation and variation within the situations. Regarding expectation, they might say, after observing two different data sets, that one shows "more." They might make that decision based on visual comparison or summing up the values of two sets of equal size. They usually have little notion of variation and asked about repeated sampling of the lollipops, might draw pictures, single numbers, or draw a graph unrelated to the situation.

These authors present a complete developmental progression for these concepts (see J. M. Watson et al., 2007). Given the lack of evidence regarding the impact of complete learning trajectories (e.g., including instructional activities) for young children, and the low level of performance by young children on these and other measures, we decided not to present such a learning trajectory here. However, those wishing to investigate data analysis, statistics, and graphing should consult the work of Watson, Callingham, Kelly; Schwartz, and Cliff Konold.

Similarly, there is no consistent, complete body of research on young children's learning of probability concepts and processes and the usefulness of teaching such competencies to young children. There is intriguing data that probabilistic judgments, not unlike number and space, may be innate or early developing ("bootstrap") competencies, not based on sampling of past experiences (Téglás, Girotto, Gonzalez, & Bonatti, 2007). Also, some curriculum developers and teachers report success with beginning concepts such as classifying events into broad categories such as "must happen," "impossible—can't happen" and "might happen," or with activities such as use of spinners and dice. However, there is too little data to guide educational decisions in this area.

Experience and Education

The educational role of most of the processes has been described in previous chapters as it relates to specific topics (classifying and other processes are discussed in Chapter 13). The key issue is how much data representation in the canonical forms of graphs should be present in early childhood education. Research on data analysis in the classroom during the primary years, and especially *before* the primary years, is sparse. Most of what we have seen consists of anecdotal reports. They are promising, but limited. There is some evidence that preschoolers can understand discrete graphs as representations of numerosity based on one-to-one correspondence (Solomon, 2003). Similarly, although five- to six-year-olds were more accurate than four- to five-year-olds on most, but not all graphing tasks, all children could interpret the graphs and use them to solve mathematical problems (J. Cooper, Brenneman, & Gelman, 2005). Children performed better than in previous research, possibly because they were provided examples and given feedback, and that they were motivated by the task. Children performed better with discrete rather than continuous formats.

An exploratory study revealed a range of mathematical understandings and skills in over 1,000 inner-city four-year-olds (see Schwartz, 2004). The logical thinking skills and growing number sense evidenced in their work as they recorded data included: (a) coordinating one response to one data entry,

(b) sorting and grouping recorded information, (c) transforming information from verbal responses and concrete materials collections into graphs, (d) using a variety of ways to represent information, and (e) using numbers to summarize findings and interpret results. Children demonstrated varying levels of ability to interpret their recorded findings, identify missing information, and plan changes in their recording strategies. Many had the mathematical competencies to allow meaningful use of data and representations in graphs. (See the companion book for a description of the instruction, as well as a description of other projects.)

Final Words

As we saw, the "other topics" in mathematics discussed in this chapter are as much general habits of mind as they are about specific content. Teachers should appreciate that ideas such as *pattern as expectation* and *pattern as a predisposition to search for and use mathematical regularities and structures* needs to be considered beyond ideas of "more" or seasonal changes (J. M. Watson et al., 2007). Explicitly comparing and contrasting the use of pattern in pre-algebra and expectation in data settings may be useful. Similarly, the *processes* that are the focus of Chapter 13 are arguably best viewed as habits of mind that should pervade early childhood mathematics.

13

Mathematical Processes

"As important as mathematical content are general mathematical processes—problem solving, reasoning and proof, communication, connections, and representation; specific mathematical processes such as organizing information, patterning, and composing, and habits of mind such as curiosity, imagination, inventiveness, persistence, willingness to experiment, and sensitivity to patterns. All should be involved in a high-quality early childhood mathematics program."

(Clements, Sarama et al., 2004, p. 57)

Throughout this book, mathematical processes have been interwoven with content, as they should be. In this chapter, we focus on some of the core processes to synthesize those findings, describe research that addressed processes directly (with less attention to content), and to highlight the importance of these processes.

Reasoning and Problem Solving

"Reasoning is not a radically different sort of force operating against habit but the organization and cooperation of many habits, linking facts together. Reasoning is not the negation of ordinary bonds, but the action of many of them, especially of bonds with subtle elements of the situation. Almost everything in arithmetic should be taught as a habit that has connections with habits already acquired and will work in an organization with other habits to come. The use of this organized hierarchy of habits to solve novel problems is reasoning."

(Thorndike, 1922, pp.193–194)

Thorndike accurately reflects turn-of-the-century perspectives that learning mathematics was like mental exercising, building the mind like a muscle. This perspective was perhaps most problematic in generalizing that reasoning could be explained as stimulus-response bonds.

In contrast, others have thought that reasoning was merely logic, with uneducated people less knowledgeable of that domain. Descartes entitled his 1701 book on algebra, *Rules for the Operation of the Mind*. George Boole considered his research on pure mathematics and symbolic logic a central contribution to psychology as well, entitling his 1854 book, *An Investigation of the*

Laws of Thought. The Piagetians agreed. "In short, reasoning is nothing more than the propositional calculus itself" (Inhelder & Piaget, 1958, p. 305). Instead, as has already been illustrated in previous topically oriented sections, young children's reasoning is a complex cognitive process that depends on local and global knowledge and procedures. Space constraints prevent our doing more than the briefest of overviews of young children's mathematical processes in general, including reasoning, problem solving, and communication, with the goal of illustrating their complexity, impressive extent, and importance.

As some vignettes throughout this book have illustrated, even very young children can reason and solve problems if they have a sufficient knowledge base, if the task is understandable and motivating, and if the context is familiar (Alexander et al., 1997; DeLoache et al., 1998). Consistent with hierarchical interactionalism, there is no cogent evidence that these processes undergo substantive qualitative shifts. Instead, development occurs in interactive interplay among specific components of both general and specific knowledge and processes, together with an increasing effectiveness of these components.

Multiple types of reasoning processes can be identified in young children, although the various types overlap. Perceptual reasoning begins early, as similarity between objects is the initial relation from which children draw inferences, but it remains an important relation throughout development (see DeLoache et al., 1998, on which this summary is largely based). Once concepts are formed, children as young as toddlers build structural similarity relations, even between perceptually dissimilar objects, giving rise to analogies (Alexander et al., 1997). Analogies in turn increase knowledge acquisition, which increases information processing capacity through unitizing and symbolizing. Myriad represented relations give birth to reasoning with rules and symbolic relations, freeing reasoning from sensory-concrete experience and encouraging the appropriation of cultural tools, that vastly expand the possible realms of reasoning. Again, then, we see the mutual development of concepts and skills, with knowledge catalyzing new processes, which in turn facilitate knowledge growth.

A relatively sophisticated reasoning process is distinguishing between indeterminant and determinant evidence (i.e., situations in which evidence is sufficient for drawing conclusions). Children as young as four and five years perform surprisingly well except in one situation—an instance of positive evidence is presented simultaneously with an as-yet unexplored source of evidence (Klahr & Chen, 2003). For example, which of three closed boxes of same-colored beads was used to make a red necklace? When a box is opened with blue beads, most children know that one still can't tell which of the other two it could be. But when another box of red beads is opened, many mistakenly claim they know (not recognizing that the last closed box might also be red and this might actually be the one). Children (and in some situations, older students and adults) often mistakenly claim that the evidence is sufficient in this indeterminant situation. Giving a more meaningful context did not help children solve these types of problems correctly. However, repeated experience with feedback did, especially for five-year-olds, who also retained and trans-ferred their knowledge better than four-year-olds (many of whom also benefited, but not to the same degree). This reveals that educational experi-ences can help children learn reasoning skills that are significant throughout the lifespan, and suggests that children can learn from exposure to problems, figuring the solution out for themselves, and also from corrective feedback. Further, using multiple examples that vary in surface structure, but have the same underlying structure, may be an important path to developing reason abilities (in contrast to another popular approach of rich and varied content and structure).

In solving problems, children may often use most of these types of reason-ing, highlighting the overlap, and even lack of real distinction (except for adult purposes of classification or research) among them. One illustration researchers use is the task (described in the "Models and Maps" section of Chapter 7) in which children were shown a location of a toy on a scale model of a room and then asked to find the toy in the actual room (DeLoache, 1987). Perceptual similarity and concepts supported children's relating the model and room. Symbols were important—indeed, the picture was more useful to the youngest children because it served as a symbol. Children's inferring the toy's location was analogical, mapping a relationship in one space onto a similar relationship in the other.

Such strategies develop in generality and flexibility during the toddler and preschool years, enabling children to address problems of increasing complexity. For example, recall that kindergartners can solve a wide range of addition, subtraction, multiplication and division problems when they are encouraged to represent the objects, actions, and relationships in those situations (Carpenter et al., 1993). The researchers argue that modeling is a parsimonious and coherent way of thinking about children's mathematical problem solving that is accessible to teachers and children. An Australian study supported the notion that kindergartners could learn to solve a variety of quite difficult word problems (Outhred & Sardelich, 1998). Children used physical objects but were also required to draw and explain their representations, including the relationships among the elements. By the end of the year, they could pose and solve complex problems using a variety of strategies to repre-sent aspects of the problem, including showing combining and partitioning groups, and using letters and words to label elements of sets.

The ability to choose among alternative problem solving strategies also emerges early in life; for example, in early spatial planning (Wellman et al., 1985). At 18 months or earlier, for example, children can use multiple strategies to pull a toy into reach with a third object (DeLoache et al., 1998). As an example in a different domain, recall that young children from all income levels can make adaptive choices among arithmetic strategies, especially if the situations and strategies are meaningful for them (Siegler, 1993). In another study (Outhred & Sardelich, 1997), by the end of their kindergarten year, all children modeled arithmetic problems using sensory-concrete materials and accurately solved them. Their drawings showed a variety of strategies for representing the situations, including displaying properties (e.g., size), separating groups or crossing out items, partitioning sets, and drawing lines to indicate sharing relationships, drawing array structures to show equal groups, and using letters and words to label items in collections. They could write their own problems and represent problem situations symbolically (they only struggled to accurately represent multistep problems with symbols). All this was accomplished despite the small amount of time the teacher engaged the children in problem solving.

Classification and Seriation

The complex relationship between seriation and classification and the development of number concepts (Piaget & Szeminska, 1952) has already been discussed (see Chapters 2 and 3). Piagetian theory held that these operations also underlie logic and reasoning (Piaget, 1964). For example, the claim that the abilities to seriate, construct a correspondence between two series, and insert an element into a series developed synchronically was an argument for the Piagetian operational theory of intelligence. The research literature on these constructs is vast (Clements, 1984a); we will describe only some relevant findings.

Although research militates against any simple, direct causal relationship, there is also evidence that these processes do play important roles in the development of mathematical reasoning and learning (cf. Kamii, Rummelsburg, & Kari, 2005; Piaget, 1971/1974). For example, children who do not acquire basic competencies in classification (oddity—which one is not like the others), seriation, and conservation by kindergarten do not perform as well in mathematics in later schooling (Ciancio, Rojas, McMahon, & Pasnak, 2001; Lebron-Rodriguez & Pasnak, 1977; Pasnak et al., 1987). Similarly, assessments of Piagetian reasoning tasks in kindergarten were related to children's mathematics concepts years later (Silliphant, 1983).

Classification

At all ages, children classify informally as they intuitively recognize objects or situations as similar in some way (e.g., differentiating between objects they suck and those they do not at two weeks of age), and eventually label what adults conceive of as classes. Often, functional relationships (the cup goes with a saucer) are the bases for sorting (Piaget, 1964; Vygotsky, 1934/1986). In addition, even infants place objects that are different (six months), then alike (12 months), on some attribute together (Langer, Rivera et al., 2003). By 18 months, they form sets in which objects in each set are identical and objects in the other sets are different, and by two years, form sets with objects that are similar on some properties, but not necessarily identical. Some two-year-olds and all three-year-olds will substitute elements to reconstruct misclassified sets (Langer, Rivera et al., 2003). These are often partial arrangements with fluid criteria; nevertheless, they play an essential role in number, through the unitizing process.

Not until age three can most children follow verbal rules for sorting. For example, told two simple rules for sorting pictures, children aged 36 months could sort regardless of the type of category, but children even a few months younger could not (Zelazo & Reznick, 1991). Having relevant knowledge or having fewer memory demands were not significant in this case.

In the preschool ages, many children learn to sort objects according to a given attribute, forming categories, although they may switch attributes during the sorting (Kofsky, 1966; Vygotsky, 1934/1986). The end result may appear to reflect adult categorizations, but often has a different conceptual basis, such as general resemblance (Vygotsky, 1934/1986, calls these "pseudoconcepts"). Preschoolers appear to encode examples holistically, distributing their attention nonselectively across many stimulus features, and then generalize to new stimuli on the basis of their overall similarity to the stored examples (Krascum & Andrews, 1993). Even pre-K children can "hold fast" to a criterion for sorting and recognize that alternative bases for classification exist; however, they are not free from circumstantial constraints, nor predispositions to respond in certain ways (Clements, 1984a).

Not until age five or six years do children usually sort consistently by a single attribute and re-classify by different attributes. At this point they can sort consistently and exhaustively by an attribute, given or created, and use the terms "some" and "all" in that context (Kofsky, 1966). It is not until age nine that most master the hierarchical inclusion relationship (Inhelder & Piaget, 1958; Kofsky, 1966; Piaget & Szeminska, 1952). Children learn these skills in varying orders. School-age children may learn to simultaneously classify and count; for example, counting the number of colors in a group of objects. They may understand that the total number of objects in the subclasses is equal to the extension of the superordinate class. Further, they can learn to conscientiously sort according to multiple attributes, naming and relating the attributes, understanding that objects could belong to more than one group. This allows the completion of two-dimensional classification matrices or the formation of subgroups within groups.

Seriation

Young children also learn seriation from early in life. Preverbal infants are able to make perceptual size comparisons and from the age of 18 months or so, are able to respond to and use terms such as big, small, and more in ways that show they appreciate quantity differences (Resnick & Singer, 1993). By two or three years of age, children can compare numbers and number pairs on the basis of a common ordering relation (Bullock & Gelman, 1977). At three years, children can make paired comparisons, and four-year-olds can make small series, but may not seriate all objects (Clements, 1984a). Piaget & Inhelder reported that 55 percent make no attempt at seriation, and 47 percent build partial uncoordinated series (Inhelder & Piaget, 1958; 1967). At age five, 18 percent make no seriation, 61 percent build partial series, and 12 percent solve the problem, but only by trial and error. In a recent study, 43 percent of five-year-olds put six lengths in order by length (A. Klein et al., 1999, but note that Piaget's lengths were more difficult to distinguish perceptually). Most five-year-olds can insert elements into a series.

Children exhibit many strategies in seriation. Some choose the smallest (or largest) object to begin, then continue to select the next smallest (largest). Some place randomly selected objects in place. Others begin with the largest block, then select a proximate block, accepting it only if order is preserved, switching if it is not. Some analyses have claimed that those with less sophisticated, or even incorrect, strategies are not qualitatively different from seriators; they are just missing one or more rules (such as accepting any monotonic increase, rather than only unit differences).

There is also evidence that children can make transitive, deductive inferences, often considered to be the most difficult of the seriation tasks (if A is longer than B and B is longer than C, then A is longer than C). For example, four-year-olds do so if they are trained to code and retrieve the relevant information (Trabasso, 1975). The authors claim, as we claimed with reasoning and problem solving, that the cognitive processes of even young children are not that much different from those of the adults, at least in the nature of the strategies used. Surprisingly, kindergartners who conserved number did not perform better on a transitivity of order relations in number comparison tasks (D. T. Owens & Steffe, 1972). They did perform better on transitivity of the equivalence relation ("as many as"). Children performed better with "neutral" (objects arranged with no perceptual bias) than either screened or conflictive (items in columns in which the longer row contained fewer objects). Thus, conservation does not seem a prerequisite for developing some transitivity relations, and such reasoning does not develop at the same time, but appears to be acquired in one restricted situation at a time (D. T. Owens & Steffe, 1972), consistent with the hierarchic development tenet of hierarchic interactionalism.

As mentioned, Piaget claimed that seriation and serial correspondence (between two series) and reconstruction of ordinal correspondences (a similarity that has become numerical) are solved at approximately the same time (Piaget & Szeminska, 1952). Young children make global comparisons with seriation or correspondences. They then develop the ability to construct series and correspondences intuitively, but often fall back on perceptual correspondences. Only at the stage of concrete operations do they solve all the problems. They understand correspondences numerically, that is, the element n represents both the position n and the cardinal value n. Seriation and multiple seriation follow the development of classification and multiple classification, respectively. Generally, the developmental progressions within a domain (such as seriation) are supported, but few developmental concurrences across domains have been found (Clements, 1984a).

Studies involving both classification and seriation suggest that young children are more likely to abstract a property represented through literal comparisons. For example, both four- and six-year-olds can match three circles increasing in size with three squares that similarly increased in size, but only six-year-olds could match the circles to three circles that increased in color saturation, that is, match seriations across dimensions (Kotovsky & Gentner, 1996). If the four-year-olds are trained to mastery on the former, they can match across dimensions. Thus, as with counting and comparing number, we see a relational shift, in which children's early reliance on physical similarity develops into the ability to perceive purely relational commonalities, and the facilitative effects of both domain knowledge and language (Kotovsky & Gentner, 1996).

Experience and Education

"A curriculum focal point may draw on several connected mathematical content topics described in Principles and Standards for School Mathematics (NCTM 2000). It should be addressed by students in the context of the mathematical processes of problem solving, reasoning and proof, communication, connections, and representation. Without facility with these critical processes, a student's mathematical knowledge is likely to be fragile and limited in its usefulness."

(NCTM, 2006, p. 5)

Reasoning

Some have argued that developing reasoning and problem-solving abilities should be the main focus in any attempt to help babies and toddlers develop in mathematics (see, e.g., Kamii et al., 2004). Encouraging language can support the growth of reasoning abilities. For example, labeling situations ("big/little") led to a two-year-age gain in use of relational mapping in three-year-old children. The language invited children to form comparisons and provided a system of meanings and an index upon which to base these comparisons (Rattermann & Gentner, 1998). Presenting children with easy literal similarity matches also helps them solve more difficult analogical matches.

Similarly, helping preschoolers learn the properties and relationships in a mathematical situation allows them to solve analogies of various types, such as geometric analogy items (Alexander et al., 1997). The analogical processes themselves, encoding, inferring, mapping, and applying (Sternberg, 1985), may contribute to early mathematics reasoning and learning.

As other chapters have shown, having children explain and justify their solutions to mathematical problems is an effective way to develop mathematical (and general) reasoning.

Problem Solving[1]

Problem solving can also be facilitated. Even for the very young, there are substantial benefits of varied situations, encouragement of diverse strategies, discussions, simple justifications, and prompts and hints as needed (DeLoache et al., 1998). Children benefit from modeling a wide variety of situations and problem types with concrete objects, and also from drawing a representation to show their thinking, from explaining and discussing their solutions, and from connecting representations (Carpenter, Ansell, Franke, Fennema, & Weisbeck, 1993; Clements & Sarama, 2007, 2008; Dougherty & Slovin, 2004; Outhred & Sardelich, 1997; van Oers, 1994). Such direct modeling, along with reflection and discussion, probably elicits and develops schema for addition, subtraction, multiplication and division operations as well as developing positive beliefs about problem solving and mathematics in general. There is suggestive evidence that diagrams are especially useful in teaching children to link concrete and abstract representations and thus facilitate learning (e.g., Dougherty & Slovin, 2004).

Similar to this research, and to research from previous chapters, another study showed that young (five- to six-year-old) children successfully learned arithmetic problem solving when allowed to build on their invented strategies (Anghileri, 2001). Consistent with our theory of hierarchic interactionalism, they modified initially successful strategies to a more organized-oriented phase during which they exerted better control over the features of the addition tasks. Their procedures became more explicit, flexible, and organized when the children were given the opportunity to build on their own knowledge and inventions (Anghileri, 2001).

One study indicates that, besides the structure of the problem (e.g., see Chapter 5) the representation in which problems are given to children can affect their difficulty. Problems presented just with text, with decorative pictures, or with number lines, were of similar difficulty (Elia, Gagatsis, & Demetriou, 2007). Apparently, children ignored those two pictorial representations. This indicates that decorative pictures do *not* facilitate problem solving, as many critics of them assert. However, number lines do not help either—perhaps because children are confused by the dual representation of number as points and distances (or vectors). Solving problems presented with informational pictures was more difficult for these children. Therefore, presenting problems with written or oral text may be most effective and efficient, and specific instruction might be offered if the goal is to teach children to use number lines or to solve problems presented with informational pictures (Elia et al., 2007).

A final point is that concrete objects often make an important contribution, but are not guaranteed to help (Baroody, 1989b; Clements, 1999a). Children must see the structural similarities between any representation and the problem situation to use objects as tools. (These issues are discussed in Clements, 1999a, as well as Chapter 16 of the companion book.)

Classification and Seriation

Simple strategies for teaching classification and seriation can have a significant effect, especially for children with special needs. Pasnak and colleagues (Ciancio et al., 2001; Kidd & Pasnak, 2005; Lebron-Rodriguez & Pasnak, 1977) have used a simple learning set procedure, including demonstration, practice, and feedback with many varied concrete examples, to a variety of children, including blind and sighted, at-risk pre-K children and at-risk kindergarten children, and older blind children. All apparently enjoyed positive effects on instruments measuring intelligence quotient and mathematics achievement. (Other instructional approaches may also have these and other benefits as we shall see, Clements, 1984c; Kamii et al., 2005.)

A research review (DeLoache et al., 1998) stated that solving oddity problems requires making multiple comparisons, and, for children below the age of six, is difficult. Consistent with the learning set procedure, however, they also stated that telling the children the oddity rule quickly leads to success. Thus, children do not have difficulty following the rule, but inducing it. Game-like instruction may help children learn to induce simple rules. Again, evidence indicates that giving children clues concerning discussing a rule enables them to represent and follow it.

Beyond the youngest ages, many educational approaches have been tried, including direct verbal instruction, contingent feedback, and modeling by peers just one level above the target child's assessed level. Researchers disagreed as to the theoretical position their results supported, but all methods were found to be effective in at least some situations (Clements, 1984a). For example, between 28 percent and 66 percent of kindergarten children in a transitional level learned all classification including class inclusion following six training sessions on various classification competencies (P. Miller, 1967). The researcher claimed the training might have catalyzed cognitive reorganization. Approaches such as modeling, as well as verbal training (e.g., labeling, discussing attributes and classifying by more than one attribute) have been found to be effective for children from two to five years of age, but more consistently effective for the older children (Clements, 1984a).

Most of these approaches do not teach problem solving "in general" (Hofmeister, 1993). They embed problem solving in a specific domain of mathematics, and develop multiple components of knowledge of the content and processes simultaneously.

Children have to classify, at least implicitly, whenever they quantify a collection. We believe that counting proper subsets, such as all the blue marbles in a group of mixed colors, is valuable experience for young children. Research is lacking, unfortunately, on how competencies in quantification and classification co-develop (including number as a class, B. Russell, 1919) and if such educational experiences are particularly worthwhile. Research does suggest that teachers begin with literal representations, such as matching, classifying, and seriating in one dimension, and thereby help children build competencies before moving to two dimensions (Kotovsky & Gentner, 1996).

Several educational approaches have also been found effective in teaching seriation, which is often easier to teach than classification or number concepts such as conservation (Clements, 1984a). These approaches include televised modeling; developmentally sequenced lessons; use of Montessori materials; combinations of corrective feedback, attention to task stimuli, and cuing and cue fading; and discussion of children's own seriation strategies. Some studies report that only children in Piagetian transition stages make substantial gains.

A final issue is whether training in Piagetian foundational areas such as classification and seriation aids the development of number. Evidence is mixed. Several studies show positive effects. For example, teaching classification and seriation to kindergarten children improved their performance on tests of number concepts. (Lesh, 1972). Similarly, kindergarteners taught classification, seriation, and conservation with simple teaching procedures (Pasnak, 1987) made twice the gains of children receiving "traditional mathematics instruction" on measures of general learning and reasoning ability, and matched their gains on reading and mathematics achievement. These gains have held longitudinally (Pasnak et al., 1996). Other interventions had similar positive results (see Chapter 15 in the companion book for a discussion of the work of Adey, Robertson, & Venville, 2002).

Findings similar to those of Lesh and Pasnak et al. were reported for pre-K children. Four-year-old children were randomly assigned to one of three educational conditions for eight weeks: logical foundations (classification and seriation), number (counting), and control (Clements, 1984b). After engaging in activities teaching classification, multiple classification, and seriation operations, the logical foundations group significantly outperformed the control group both on measures of conservation and on number concepts and skills. However, inconsistent with Piagetian theory, the number group also performed significantly better than the control group on classification, multiple classification, and seriation tasks as well as on a wide variety of number tasks. Further, there was no significant difference between the experimental groups on the logical operations test and the number group significantly outperformed the logical foundations group on the number test. Thus, the transfer effect from number to classification and seriation was stronger than the reverse. The domains of classes, series, and number appear to be inter-dependent but experiences in number have priority (Clements, 1984b). Note that some number and logical foundation activities were structurally isomorphic, so children received implicit experience with classification and seriation in number activities. For example, in one activity, children counted the blue cars, the red cars, and all the cars. Thus, in meaningful counting situations, the child may have a familiar cognitive tool with which to construct the logical structures required.

Final Words

Research suggests that, especially for younger children, mathematical topics should not be treated as isolated topics; rather, they should be connected to each other, often in the context of solving a significant problem or engaging in an interesting project (Clements, 2001; Fuson, 2004). Thus, this book's main organization based on mathematical content should not be considered a de-emphasis on other aspects of mathematics.

This concludes the chapters on specific learning trajectories and those aligned with corresponding chapters in the companion volume. The last three chapters of the companion volume address issues essential to implementing the learning trajectories. The last chapter of this book, Chapter 14, addresses the critical issues of professional development: how teachers can be helped to learn and implement the learning trajectories.

14
Professional Development and Scaling Up

"Educational change depends on what teachers do and think—it's as simple and as complex as that."

(Fullan, 1982, p. 107).

Every chapter of this book has been concerned with professional development, directly or indirectly. Here we describe teachers' beliefs and opinions, as well as professional development strategies that have been verified by empirical research, especially those directly relevant to helping teachers use learning trajectories. We also provide references for those who perform professional development.

Teachers' Beliefs

Given the diversity of the teacher/caregiver population, professional development in early childhood mathematics is especially challenging. Teachers have quite different beliefs, and these beliefs affect their practice (Stipek & Byler, 1997), although not always in a straightforward manner (Sarama, Clements, Henry, & Swaminathan, 1996). For example, preschool and kindergarten teachers who had child-centered beliefs were less likely to engage in basic skills practice and more likely to have positive social climates than those who had a basic skills orientation (Stipek & Byler, 1997). They tended to polarize about those practices as well, compared to first grade teachers, who were less resistant to believing that both children-centered and basic skills were incompatible (Stipek & Byler, 1997). In another study, the overall quality of teachers' classrooms was lower for teachers with more adult-centered beliefs (Pianta et al., 2005). (Quality was also lower in classrooms with more than 60 percent of the children from homes below the poverty line, when teachers lacked formal training (or a degree) in early childhood education.)

A survey of early childhood care providers, including on issues concerning professional development provides some guidance (Sarama, 2002; Sarama & DiBiase, 2004). The providers included hundreds of teachers and caregivers from family and group day care, daycare centers, public and parochial schools, traditional nursery schools, and Head Start centers. The first question was:

"Are you at all interested in professional development in mathematics?" Ninety-four percent of the early childhood educators responded that they were. What is the best way to reach these busy professionals? Forty-three percent receive their information through mailings, and 31 percent from their workplace via supervisors, bulletin boards, and so forth. Of those who receive educational magazines or journals, 43 percent of respondents receive trade publications, such as *Mailbox*, and 22 percent receive the main journal published by the National Association for the Education of Young Children, *Young Children.*

Thirty-nine percent would prefer to meet every two weeks; an almost equal number (24 percent and 23 percent respectively) preferred to meet monthly or weekly. This was surprising, as expert advisors had suggested that monthly meetings might be "too much."

Although 60 percent of the participants preferred to meet in their workplace, 58 percent also chose a local college. Previous research has indicated that the collegiate atmosphere can be intimidating to providers (Copley & Padròn, 1999) Other popular choices included schools (44 percent) and teacher training centers (35 percent). Most respondents felt that attending inservice was not too difficult (63 percent), with fewer than 10 percent choosing either "very difficult" or "easy." Transportation did not seem to be an issue; only 14 percent stated that it would influence their decision on whether or not to attend a professional development opportunity. Ninety-two percent said that they would use their own car to attend.

Expert advisors have suggested that financial rewards and job advancement would be key motivators. Although 30 percent of the respondents did choose "increased pay" and 14 percent chose "job advancement," 66 percent chose "curriculum materials" and 43 percent chose "personal satisfaction." Forty-one percent of the respondents also chose a credential as a motivator and 31 percent chose college credit. (A caveat is that these are people who agree to respond.)

Another set of questions dealt with beliefs about mathematics education, answers to which could help inform any professional development effort. Asked at what age children should start large group mathematics instruction, the family and group care providers chose ages two or three most often, while the other group felt large group instruction should not start until age four. The survey asked whether teachers should have a "standard list of math topics that should be taught to preschoolers." Respondents agreed that it was important: 39 percent said "very important" and 47 percent said it was "important." Open-ended responses indicated a desire for general guidelines for the age-appropriateness of topics.

When asked about their main mathematics activities, 67 percent chose counting, 60 percent, sorting, 51 percent, numeral recognition, 46 percent, patterning, 34 percent, number concepts, 32 percent, spatial relations, 16 percent, making shapes, and 14 percent, measuring. Unfortunately, geometry and measurement concepts were the least popular.

Most teachers use manipulatives (95 percent), number songs (84 percent), basic counting (74 percent) and games (71 percent); few used software (33 percent) or workbooks (16 percent). They preferred children to "explore math activities" and engage in "open-ended free play" rather than participate in "large group lessons" or be "doing math worksheets." Other data for technology are promising in that 71 percent of the respondents have access to the Internet, 67 percent have a computer available for use by the children whom they teach, and 80 percent would be interested in some sort of distance learning.

Finally, respondents said they would be interested in attending professional development at a center specifically designed for mathematics and technology. Ninety-three percent were interested in visiting a model classroom. Having an outside agency keep track of professional development credits was more important to the respondents than was receiving credit for every course.

Another survey asked Head Start staff to identify practices that facilitate the transfer of their learning to their work with children (Wolfe, 1991). They recommended small group discussion and demonstration/modeling, followed by handouts, lecture, observing actual practice, games/simulations, role play, and video/movies. The least recommended instructional strategies were assignments and follow-up phone calls. Observing actual practice and follow-up assistance were ranked highest when participants were asked what strategies they felt would have the largest effect on their work with children. They ranked worksheets, follow-up letters, and panel discussions as the least likely to have an effect. These results confirm that what teachers desire and believe to be effective is not consistent with the current system of delivery (Cohen & Hill, 2000).

Another study interviewed prekindergarten teachers about their beliefs about early math education. All teachers shared the beliefs that there was pressure to teach children more number and arithmetic, that teaching and learning of it should be enjoyable and not pressured (e.g., involve interesting materials and be conducted in small groups with teachers sensitive to children's emotional well-being) (J. S. Lee & Ginsburg, 2007). Compared to those working with middle-SES children at private pre-kindergartens, those teaching low-SES children at publicly funded pre-kindergartens, believed that teachers needed a strong focus on specific goals so that children were prepared for kindergarten and primary school. Those teaching middle-SES children, in contrast, supported flexible mathematics education relying on a child-centered curriculum and child-initiated learning and opposed the instructional use of computers. They believed that even children behind in mathematics would be able to catch up later,

"My advice would be to not underestimate the importance of socializa-tion. . . . The math concepts, if we had to give up one thing, ultimately it would be those because the social piece is the piece that seems to be what we have with them at this age and what we can do. . . . If the children are not as interested, you let it go. Maybe they'll be interested in it in a month from now. Maybe they're not ready developmentally. . . . Maybe reintroduce it in another way, at another time, when they're more ready. . . . If I feel that the children aren't ready for something, I'll do it at another time, another day, or I'll put off for another month or two." (p. 13).

Given the differences between the typical low- and middle-SES child's prep-aration and backgrounds, Lee and Ginsburg (2007) claim that different emphases on academics vs. socialization reflect parental preferences and are reasonable.

However, much might stem from the lack of experience with mathematics and mathematics education. The authors state that "Some of the participating prekindergarten teachers commented on their somewhat careless attitude toward mathematics, especially when compared to literacy," quoting another teacher as saying: "Overall I'm feeling, I don't know much about teaching math. I know a little bit, you know, enough that, I know which materials to provide the children. But I really, you know, there are a lot of uh . . . This has made me think a lot about different aspects of teaching math that I haven't really thought of before in preschool." (p. 21).

The evidence suggests that teachers' preferences may hide (a) a dislike of mathematics, (b) a lack of reflection on its role, (c) a rationalization that it is already "covered" by providing materials and incidental exposure, and (d) a tendency to emphasize other domains. Consider this quote: "Well, math, it's hard. I don't think we actually do as much math as we should. You know, now that we're doing this [interview], I realize we don't . . . We do it. It's incorporated into everything that we do. But I don't think there's as much of a focus on it as there probably should be. There seems to be more reading, and writing, and knowing your letters, and colors" (p. 21).

Thus, professional development must illuminate children's interests and capabilities in mathematics. Teachers need to learn that appropriate mathe-matics for young children is wider and deeper than usually realized. Teachers of low-income children need help in how to achieve these goals (J. S. Lee & Ginsburg, 2007). They need to understand the learning trajectories of early mathematics, and how to move beyond superficial use of "themes" into which a random set of activities are often thrown. Teachers of middle-SES children need to understand that although their children tend to know more than low-SES children about mathematics, most children in the U.S. are not given the enriched opportunities offered to children in other countries (Starkey et al.,

1999). Further, limited beliefs in free play may limit their understanding and pedagogical use of the development of mathematical idea. Their rejection of computers shows a lack of knowledge of types of computer activities and the research on their effectiveness.

Research-Based Professional Development

> "Really to interpret the child's present crude impulses in counting, measuring, and arranging things in rhythmic series, involves mathematical scholarship— a knowledge of the mathematical formulae and relations which have, in the history of the race, grown out of such crude beginnings."
>
> (John Dewey 1902/1976, p. 282)

Teachers make a difference. Professional development—*high-quality* professional development—makes a difference for teachers. However, across the grades, what we know with certainty about professional development is slim. There are indications that certification alone is not a reliable predictor of high-quality teaching (Early et al., 2007; NMP, 2008), undoubtedly due to the wide variety of certification programs and the low quality of too many of them. For example, preservice education on math in early childhood/child development is often negligible or nonexistent. Most early childhood teacher training institutions require their teacher candidates to take only one course in mathematics, compared to several courses in language and literacy (Ginsburg et al., 2006). More *direct* measures of what the teachers know about mathematics and the learning and teaching of mathematics *do* predict the quality of their teaching (NMP, 2008). For example, first and third graders' math achievement gains were significantly related to their teachers' knowledge (Hill, Rowan, & Ball, 2005).

In a similar vein, a review of over 1,300 studies yielded only nine rigorous studies involving the effect of professional development on student achievement, and only four that had math outcomes (Yoon, Duncan, Lee, Scarloss, & Shapley, 2007). However, those yielded a significant effect size of .57. The average time given to professional development across the studies was 53 hours. This is important: Few teachers receive such intensive, sustained, and content-focused professional development in mathematics (Birman et al., 2007). The average most teachers received was 8.3 hours of professional development on how to teach mathematics and 5.2 hours on the "in-depth study" over a year. For early childhood teachers, the amount is even less, usually zero.

Thus, there is a critical need for professional development in early childhood mathematics education. Teachers and caregivers of young children have limited knowledge of mathematics and mathematics education and are not disposed to enjoy mathematical activity or learn more about it. Further, this is a serious equity concern, as teachers serving students who are lower SES, limited in English proficiency, or lower achieving de-emphasize mathematics in general and higher-level thinking in particular. Finally, most available programs do not focus on early childhood mathematics at all.

The good news is that we do have a growing research base regarding professional development. Research indicates that a focus on teachers' behaviors has less positive effect that a focus on teachers' knowledge of the subject, on the curriculum, or on how students learn the subject (Carpenter et al., 1988; Kennedy, 1998; Peterson et al., 1989). Successful professional development projects emphasize research on children's learning, made meaningful to teachers (Sarama, 2002). Most do this in the context of curriculum and reflection upon that curriculum. Most also involve collaborative efforts that involve extensive interactions among teachers and university professors, with some providing substantial modeling and mentoring in early childhood classrooms. Others balance summer programs with support provided during the school year. All integrate research and theory, connecting it closely to teachers' practice.

Prospective, or preservice, teachers appear to benefit from the same emphasis: How children learn mathematics (Philipp et al., 2007). In one study, the beliefs of college students who just observed classrooms changed less than those in a control group, but both of these groups changed their beliefs and knowledge less than a group who studied children's mathematical thinking, either through video or working with children on specific tasks, both designed to focus on what we call developmental progressions. Preservice teachers in Singapore had low mathematics pedagogical content knowledge at the beginning of their coursework, but improved substantially to desired levels, after the courses emphasizing inquiry, reflection, and constructive criticism (Kwong et al., 2007).

Research also supports an approach of encouraging sharing, risk taking, and learning from and with peers. This approach prepares participants to teach a specific curriculum and develops teachers' knowledge and beliefs that the curriculum is appropriate and its goals are valued and attainable. It situates work in the classroom, formatively evaluating teachers' fidelity of implementation and providing feedback and support from coaches in real time. (Bodilly, 1998; Borman, Hewes, Overman, & Brown, 2003; D. Clarke, 1994; Cohen, 1996; Elmore, 1996a; Garet, Porter, Desimone, Birman, & Yoon, 2001; Guskey, 2000; G. E. Hall & Hord, 2001; Kaser, Bourexis, Loucks-Horsley, & Raizen, 1999; Klingner, Ahwee, Pilonieta, & Menendez, 2003; Schoen, Cebulla, Finn, & Fi, 2003; Showers, Joyce, & Bennett, 1987.)

As we have said, success with *Building Blocks* is largely attributable to the focus on *learning trajectories* (Clements & Sarama, 2008). Several other projects also report success with variations of that approach (Bright, Bowman, & Vacc, 1997; Wright, 2000; Wright et al., 2002). All these projects were long term, with far more extensive and intensive professional development than the usual one-shot workshop, ranging from five to 14 full days (although one found diminishing returns, in that biweekly meetings were not enhanced by 30-minute meetings directly after lessons, McPhail, 2004).

Other successful projects also had similar characteristics (Bobis et al., 2005). First, they had research-based frameworks, including the use of developmental progressions of learning trajectories. Second, teachers learned about mathematics and the teaching and learning of early mathematics, in these cases, especially by conducting one-to-one interviews of children. Third, ongoing, reflective, professional development was conducted school wide (Bobis et al., 2005). Related research reports emphasized the combination of workshops, in-school support and modeling (G. Thomas & Tagg, 2004; Young-Loveridge, 2004).

Several reviews provide additional information (especially D. Clarke, 1994; Copley, 2004; Sarama & DiBiase, 2004, see also those cited previously and Seidel & Shavelson, 2007). They include, in addition to those already described, suggestions to emphasize cognitive models (Seidel & Shavelson, 2007), solicit teachers' commitment to participate actively, allow time for planning, reflection, and feedback, recognize that change is gradual, difficult, and often painful, and provide for support from peers and critical friends (D. Clarke, 1994). Across several studies, including the TRIAD/*Building Blocks* work, there is a sign that targeted coaching and mentoring is an essential piece (Certo, 2005; Clements & Sarama, 2008). Coaching reminds teachers that the project is a priority, that a commitment has been made to it, and that somebody cares about them (Hord, Rutherford, Huling-Austin, & Hall, 1987). Research indicates that when staff development includes ongoing coaching, classroom innovations continue at a 90 percent level after external funding ceases (Copley, 2004; Costa & Garmston, 1994; Nettles, 1993). A combination of use of theory, demonstrations, practice, and feedback, especially from coaches, may *quadruple* the positive effects of information-only training (Showers et al., 1987).

Survey research indicates that those in professional development have to branch out from the traditional publications, including not only trade publications but also such techniques as direct mailing. Although only a third of early childhood teachers used computers with their children, they had access to computers and the Internet, so professional development educators may be able to reach them through non-traditional means. Results strongly suggested that participants receive high-quality mathematics curriculum materials when attending professional development. Instructors should take care that participants receive enough experience with the materials to make sure they can be used effectively. Tying professional development to carefully documented credits that lead to a credential (early mathematics specialist) may also be a potent motivator. Finally, those who responded to the surveys had a limited view of appropriate and fun mathematics activities, which professional development educators might address.

In brief, we recommend those planning professional development in early childhood mathematics consider the following guidelines:

- Address both knowledge of, and beliefs about, mathematics and mathematics education.
- Develop knowledge and beliefs regarding specific subject-matter content, including deep conceptual knowledge of the mathematics teachers are to teach as well as the processes of mathematics.
- Respond to each individual's background, experiences, and current context or role.
- Be extensive, ongoing, reflective, and sustained.
- Actively involve teachers in observation, experimentation, and mentoring.
- Focus on common actions and problems of practice, and, as much as possible, be situated in the classroom.
- Focus on making small changes guided by a consistent, coherent, grand vision.
- Ground experiences in particular curriculum materials and allow teachers to learn and reflect on that curriculum, implement it, and discuss their implementation.
- Consider approaches such as research lessons and case-based teacher education.
- Focus on children's mathematical thinking and learning, including learning trajectories.
- Include strategies for developing higher-order thinking and for working with special populations.
- Address equity and diversity concerns.
- Involve interaction, networking and sharing with peers/colleagues.
- Include a variety of approaches.
- Use the early childhood professional career lattice as a means of encouraging professional development at all levels.
- Ensure the support of administration for professional development to promote sustained and wide-scale reform.
- Consider school-university partnerships, especially collaborative efforts involving extensive interactions among teachers and university professors.
- Sustain efforts to connect theory, research, and practice
- Investigate the use of non-traditional publications, including trade publications, direct mailing, and distance learning for communications.
- Provide participants with high-quality mathematics curriculum materials and ensure that participants receive adequate experience to use the materials effectively.
- Address economic, institutional, and regulatory barriers.

Professional development in early childhood mathematics is a national concern. Most professional development is not ongoing, continuous, reflective, and motivating. Research-based suggestions and models (such as the TRIAD model of professional development) hold the potential to make a significant difference in the learning of young children by catalyzing substantive change in the knowledge and beliefs of their teachers.

The TRIAD/*Building Blocks* Model

The TRIAD/*Building Blocks* projects are based on research from a variety of fields. The *Building Blocks* research model was presented above. However, although the successes of research-based, visionary educational practices such as *Building Blocks* have been documented, equally recognized is the "deep, systemic incapacity of U.S. schools, and the practitioners who work in them, to develop, incorporate, and extend new ideas about teaching and learning in anything but a small fraction of schools and classrooms" (see also Berends, Kirby, Naftel, & McKelvey, 2001; Cuban, 2001; Elmore, 1996a, p. 1; Tyack & Tobin, 1992). There may be no more challenging educational and theoretical issue than scaling up educational programs across a large number of diverse populations and contexts in the early childhood system in the U.S., avoiding the dilution and pollution that usually plagues such efforts to achieve broad success. That is the reason that we created the research-based TRIAD model (*T*echnology-enhanced, *R*esearchbased, *I*nstruction, *A*ssessment, and professional *D*evelopment) for successful scale up.

The goal of the TRIAD intervention is to increase math achievement in all young children, particularly those at risk, by means of a high-quality implementation of the *Building Blocks* math curriculum, with all aspects of the curriculum—teacher's guide, technology, and assessments—based on a common core of learning trajectories through which children develop mathematically. The TRIAD intervention provides (a) these curriculum materials *and* (b) ongoing professional development, including scalable distance education, an innovative *BBLT* site with extensive support for teaching based on learning trajectories, and classroom-based support by coaches during the school year; *and* (c) supportive roles and materials for parents and administrators. Building on this theoretical and empirical research base in the previous section, we summarize principles and guidelines that underlie the TRIAD model.

TRIAD Research-Based Guidelines for Scaling Up

The following are 10 research-based guidelines for successful scale up (Sarama, Clements, Starkey, Klein, & Wakeley, 2008):

- *Involve, and promote communication among, key groups around a shared vision of the innovation* (G. E. Hall & Hord, 2001). Emphasize connections between the project's goals, national and state standards, and greater societal need. Promote clarity of these goals and of all participants' responsibilities. School and project staff must share goals and a vision of the intervention (Cobb, McClain, de Silva, & Dean, 2003). This institutionalizes the intervention, for example the on-going socialization and training of new teachers (Elmore, 1996a; Fullan, 2000; Huberman, 1992; Kaser et al., 1999; Klingner et al., 2003; Sarama, Clements, & Henry, 1998).
- *Promote equity* through equitable recruitment and selection of participants, allocation of resources, and use of curriculum and instructional strategies that have demonstrated success with under-represented populations (Kaser et al., 1999).
- *Plan for the long term.* Recognizing that scale up is not just an increase in number, but also of complexity, provide continuous, adaptive support over an extended time. Use a dynamic, multilevel, feedback, and self-correction strategy (Coburn, 2003; Fullan, 1992; Guskey, 2000). Communicate clearly that change is not an event, but a process (G. E. Hall & Hord, 2001).
- *Focus on instructional change that promotes depth of children's thinking, placing learning trajectories at the core* of the teacher/child/curriculum triad to ensure that curriculum, materials, instructional strategies, and assessments are aligned with (a) national and state standards and a vision of high-quality math education, (b) each other, and (c) "best practice" as determined by research (Ball & Cohen, 1999; Bodilly, 1998; Clements, 2002; Fullan, 2000; Kaser et al., 1999).
- *Build expectations and camaraderie to support a consensus around adaptation.* Promote "buy-in" in multiple ways, such as dealing with all participants as equal partners and distributing resources to support the project. Establish and maintain cohort groups. Facilitate teachers visiting successful implementation sites. Build local leadership by involving principals and encouraging teachers to become teacher leaders (Berends et al., 2001; Borman et al., 2003; Elmore, 1996a; Fullan, 2000; G. E. Hall & Hord, 2001).
- *Provide professional development that is ongoing, intentional, reflective, focused on children's thinking, grounded in particular curriculum materials, and situated in the classroom.* Encourage sharing, risk taking, and learning from and with peers. Aim at preparing to teach a specific curriculum and develop teachers' knowledge and beliefs that the curriculum is appropriate and its goals are valued and attainable. Situate work in the classroom, formatively evaluating teachers' fidelity of implementation and providing feedback and support from coaches

in real time (Bodilly, 1998; Borman et al., 2003; Cohen, 1996; Elmore, 1996a; Garet et al., 2001; Guskey, 2000; G. E. Hall & Hord, 2001; Kaser et al., 1999; Klingner et al., 2003; Schoen et al., 2003; Showers et al., 1987).

- *Ensure school leaders are a central force supporting the innovation and provide teachers continuous feedback that children are learning what they are taught and that these learnings are valued.* Leaders must show that the innovation is a high priority, through statements, resources, and continued commitment to permanency of the effort. An *innovation champion* leads the effort within each organization (Bodilly, 1998; Elmore, 1996a; G. E. Hall & Hord, 2001; Rogers, 2003, p. 434; Sarama et al., 1998).
- *Give latitude for adaptation to teachers and schools, but maintain integrity.* Emphasize the similarities of the curriculum with sound early childhood practice and what teachers already are doing. Do not allow dilution due to uncoordinated innovations (i.e., productive adaptations, not lethal mutations, A. L. Brown & Campione, 1996; Fullan, 2000; Huberman, 1992; Sarama et al., 1998; Snipes, Doolittle, & Herlihy, 2002).
- *Provide incentives for all participants, including intrinsic and extrinsic motivators linked to project work,* such as external expectations—from standards to validation from administrators. Show how the innovation is advantageous to and compatible with teachers' experiences and needs (Berends et al., 2001; Borman et al., 2003; Cohen, 1996; Darling-Hammond, 1996; Elmore, 1996b; Mohrman & Lawler III, 1996; Rogers, 2003).
- *Maintain frequent, repeated communication, assessment ("checking up"), and follow-through efforts* emphasizing the purpose, expectations, and visions of the project, and involve key groups in continual improvement through cycles of data collection and problem solving (Fullan, 1992; G. E. Hall & Hord, 2001; Huberman, 1992; Kaser et al., 1999; Snipes et al., 2002).

TRIAD/Building Blocks *Professional Development*

The key guideline concerns professional development: *high-quality professional development is ongoing, intentional, reflective, focused on children's thinking, grounded in particular curriculum materials, and situated in the classroom.* That may sound promising, but what are the *details?* In TRIAD, teachers receive comprehensive, effective professional development, including training and coaching/mentoring. They participate in two full days of professional development during the summer, three days during the school day in the Fall and three days during the Spring for each of the first two years of the project. These sessions address learning trajectories for each math topic;

using learning trajectories for observation and other authentic formative assessment strategies; supporting mathematical development in the classroom; recognizing and supporting math throughout the day; setting up math learning centers; teaching with computers (including use of the management system and research-based teaching strategies); small-group activities; and supporting mathematical development in the home. The sessions include hands-on experience in rooms set up to mirror the structure of early childhood classrooms, with an emphasis on interactions with peers around common issues. The main technological tool is *Building Blocks Learning Trajectory (BBLT)* web application. *BBLT* provides scalable access to the learning trajectories via descriptions, videos, and commentaries. Each aspect of the learning trajectories—*developmental progressions* of children's thinking and connected *instruction*—are linked to the other. We describe this tool in a subsequent section.

Discussions of *BBLT's* best practice videos make explicit how such practice exemplifies research-based principles and will emphasize that even exemplary teachers continue to struggle—illustrating that high-quality teaching for understanding is both rewarding and challenging, and everyone can continue to improve and contribute to the profession (Heck et al., 2002; Weiss, 2002). Such virtual visits and discussion communicate the vision of the curriculum in action and make the ideas and processes accessible, memorable, engaging, and therefore usable.

COACHES AND MENTORS

Coaches and mentors work with teachers throughout the two-year period, visiting teachers in their classrooms no less than once per month. Coaching reminds teachers that the project is a priority, that a commitment has been made to it, and that somebody cares about them (Hord et al., 1987). The TRIAD coaching model is dynamic. Initial questionnaire data are helpful, but not sufficient, for knowing who will need additional assistance from coaches and mentors. For example, some teachers present themselves well and even misrepresent how much of the curriculum they are teaching; only coaching visits reveal and address such problems (with apologies to Leo Tolstoy, most happy classes resemble one another, but each unhappy class is unhappy in its own way, see Teddlie & Stringfield, 1993). Therefore we created a dynamic model in which additional attention by both mentors and coaches is given immediately until adequate fidelity of implementation is achieved. Several additional features also encourage sensitivity to individual needs of teachers, including (a) time to learn and work with cohort groups; (b) job-embeddedness—addressing concrete, immediate concern with practical problems of implementation; (c) opportunities for practice, receiving *individual*, non-threatening feedback from coaches; and (d) software and *BBLT* resources that facilitate individualization. Mentors will also coach teachers and will complete implementation fidelity evaluations and give immediate feedback to teachers on those evaluations.

BUILDING BLOCKS LEARNING TRAJECTORIES (BBLT) WEB APPLICATION

At the core of the TRIAD/*Building Blocks* model are the *learning trajectories* that have been the focus of this book (Clements & Sarama, 2008). The most important tool we have used to develop teachers' knowledge of the learning trajectories is the *Building Blocks Learning Trajectories* web application, BBLT (for a demonstration, see www.ubtriad.org). *BBLT* presents and connects all components of the innovation. Organized according to Learning Trajectories (LTs) (Clements & Sarama, 2004a), it encourages teachers to view the LTs through a curriculum or developmental (children's thinking) perspective. Each view is linked to the other. That is, teachers might choose the ╱ instruction ╲ view (below), then click an activity and not only see an explanation and video of the activity "in action," but also immediately see the level of thinking that activity is designed to develop, in the context of the entire LT. For example, below the user has selected Week 11. The activities are listed by type and a suggested weekly schedule is provided.

The user reads the description that appears on the right. If she chooses "More info" (╲ more info ☐☐▷ ╱) the screen "slides over" to reveal the expanded view shown below.

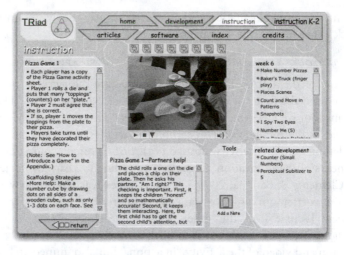

Here she can see multiple video examples, with commentary. Clicking on the related developmental level (child's level of thinking), ringed here, yields the view on the next page.

This developmental view likewise provides a description, video, and commentary on the developmental level—the video here is of a clinical interview task in which a child displays that *level of thinking*.

Alternatively, the user may have been studying developmental sequences themselves. After viewing the full list of the number topics on the left, she may have selected the same level of the Counting LT as above.

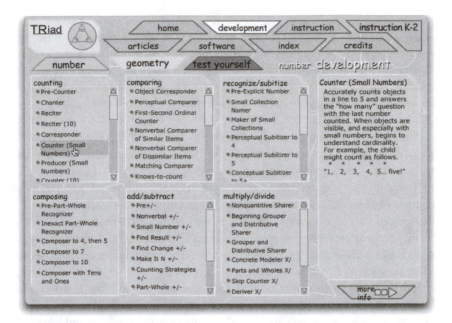

Pressing "More info" results in the same developmental view as above. The video commentary shown is just one of three commentaries, some by researchers, some by assessors, and still others by teachers. Further, the level is illustrated with assessment tasks *and* video of classroom activities in which children illustrate thinking at each level (the icons above the video allow the selection of alternative video), an approach that has received empirical support (Klingner et al., 2003).

Finally, this developmental level is connected to *all* correlated activities. Thus, a user in this view could jump to the "Make Buildings" activity *or* any of the activities whose goal is to develop that level of thinking.

Teachers also can test themselves over the developmental progressions component of the LTs by seeing videos and attempting to classify the level of thinking displayed; *assistive feedback* is offered on these attempts.

In this way, teachers may view a piece of video as an example of a curriculum activity and, later, when studying developmental sequences, see it again as an example of a particular child's level of thinking within. In each case, supporting text directs attention to each perspective and the connections between them. Such rich learning experiences promote flexible, integrated knowledge, as teachers learn to see and to integrate, the teaching and learning aspects of education. This results in multiple representations of, and perspectives on, complex phenomena that research shows is necessary for successfully applying concrete cases and the theories in which they are embedded in ill-structured domains (Feltovich, Spiro, & Coulson, 1997). The resulting cognitive flexibility positively impacts the variety of teaching strategies that people develop and ease with which they acquire new repertoires. (Showers et al., 1987).

BBLT provides professional development by bringing participating teachers into intimate contact with "best practice" classrooms, including instruction and assessment. On-line discussions (in a Blackboard-based course connected to *BBLT*) of the videos of best practice make explicit how such practice exemplifies research-based principles and emphasize that teachers considered exemplary continue to struggle—illustrating that high-quality teaching for understanding is both rewarding and challenging, and everyone can continue to improve and contribute to the profession (Heck et al., 2002; Weiss, 2002). Such "virtual visits" communicate the vision of our curriculum in action and make the ideas and processes accessible, memorable, engaging, and, therefore, usable. Results of project assessments are also interwoven.

BBLT is used in four related ways. The first two are main components supporting the course for teachers. First, it aids presentations of the trajectories and activities to teachers. Second, teachers observe, react to, test themselves on, and discuss (often online) specific trajectory levels, activities, or the relationship between the two. Third, coaches and mentors use the site in talking to teachers, often in their classrooms, about the trajectories, activities, or the relationship between the two. This is especially valuable in situations in which a teacher says, or demonstrates, that she or he did not fully understand a given activity's goals or structure. Fourth, teachers may voluntarily consult BBLT when they wish to refresh their memories on a particular activity they are to teach, or delve more deeply into understanding their children's thinking.

In summary, the TRIAD/*Building Blocks* professional development follows research-based guidelines and provides a combination of experiences. Multiple studies indicate it has had strong positive effects on both teachers and their children.

The first study was a "proof of concept" study in which we used a randomized field trial design to evaluate the first version of the TRIAD model. Children made substantially greater gains in mathematics achievement in the TRIAD, compared to the control, children, with an effect size of .62 (Sarama, Clements, Starkey, et al., 2008).

The second study was a randomized-trials design in which 36 preschool classrooms were assigned to experimental (TRIAD), comparison (a different preschool mathematics curriculum), or control conditions (Clements & Sarama, 2008). Only the TRIAD classroom had learning trajectories at the core of all components. Observational measures indicated that the curricula were implemented with fidelity, and the experimental condition had significant positive effects on classrooms' mathematics environment and teaching. The experimental group score increased significantly more than the comparison group score (effect size 0.47) and the control group score (effect size = 1.07).

Our present study is the largest evaluation of the TRIAD model. We are working with hundreds of teachers and more than 1000 children in three cities. The first year results are equally promising, with an effect size on children's mathematics achievement of .69. We are collecting longitudinal data at the time of this writing (see UBTRIAD.org for recent information).

Final Words

Research

Research in early mathematics has and continues to lead the way in investigating fundamental issues in epistemology, psychology, and education. Number and space are common topics of investigations by psychologists engaged in a debate among empiricist, nativist and interactionalist positions (Haith & Benson, 1998; Spelke, 2000). Further, researchers in mathematics education have emphasized the need to specify children's abilities to learn, and learn to learn, as well as the ecological influences on such learning, from sociocultural background to school learning experiences. There is as yet no consensus about exactly when knowledge begins, what it consists of, how it manifests itself, what causes it to emerge, or how it changes with growth and experience in the earliest years of life. Furthermore, reminiscent of introspective psychology of a century ago (Anderson, 2000), researchers' empirical evidence is consistent with their own theoretical orientation with uncomfortable frequency.[1] This is another reason why mathematics education research emphasizing curriculum research will be so valuable (Clements, 2007). Because it is result-centered, rather than theory-centered, curriculum research minimizes seductive theory-confirming strategies that tend to insidiously replace the intended theory-testing strategies, and maximizes strategies that attempt to produce specified patterns of data and thus mitigate confirmation bias, stimulating creative development of theory (Greenwald, Pratkanis, Leippe, & Baumgardner, 1986). Nevertheless, we already have a growing body of knowledge that is at the least suggestive about early competencies on which to build mathematics learning.

Through more than a century, research has moved from a cautious assessment of the number competencies of children entering school, to a Piagetian position that children were not capable of true numeric thinking, to the discovery of infant sensitivity to mathematical phenomena, to the present debate about the meaning of these contradictions and an attempt to synthesize ostensibly opposing positions. Frequent in the last two of these phases is the paradox of contradictions to Piagetian findings and confirmation of the basic constructivist Piagetian framework, the influence of which has been so fundamental that even substantive new theories were born in reaction to the monumental Piagetian corpus.

Often due to their reactions against certain Piagetian functions and the nature of their methods, researchers tended to create increasingly specialized and local theories. Recently, similarities among those theories have laid the groundwork for new hybrid theories that provide general frameworks, but are replete with local detail, including specific innate predispositions as well as competencies, conceptualizations, and strategies along developmental progressions. These progressions are at various levels of detail, both topical (e.g., "number" vs. "counting" vs. "specific counting competencies and errors at the *nth* level of development") and social-psychological (e.g., a broad level for goals, deeper for teachers, deeper for curriculum developers, deeper for researchers).

To develop such theories, we need to synthesize psychological and clinical approaches with others, such as those used in mathematics education research. The theoretical framework of *hierarchic interactionalism* that we proposed here is one such attempt. This framework connects *initial bootstraps* with a gradual development of conscious knowledge of systems of mathematical knowledge, depending on educational experiences. Thus, intellectual development results from an interplay between internal and external factors, including innate competencies and dispositions, maturation, experience with the physical environment, sociocultural experiences (as opposed to only "social transmission"), and self-regulatory processes (reflective abstraction). To be useful educationally, the roles and interactions of each of these factors must be described in detail within specific domains. The field of early mathematics is fortunate to include several research programs in which the development of such descriptions is underway. We need similar proposals and increased clinical, longitudinal, and educational studies of the usefulness of the theories. Studies and specific theories must avoid eclecticism (Newcombe & Huttenlocher, 2000), in which "everything matters," and garner empirical evidence that details development and the factors that influence it. Evaluating the theories' usefulness requires well-designed studies that connect specific pedagogical processes and contexts to outcomes to identify moderating and mediating variables and to compare the immediate and long-term outcomes of different approaches. Researchers should avoid the common mistake of limiting research to number and arithmetic so as to investigate young children's *mathematical* thinking.

Policy and Practice

There is much to gain, and little or nothing to lose, in engaging children from birth to elementary school, in foundational and mathematical experiences in number, space, geometry, measurement, and patterning, as well as the processes of mathematical thinking (Stewart et al., 1997). Piaget had reason to call the most important, most foundational type of knowledge "logico-mathematical knowledge" (Piaget, 1971/1974).

We need more and better early childhood programs (Barnett, 1995). We need relevant and rigorous professional development programs, both preservice and inservice. We need to use research-based curricula and develop better methods for evaluating all of these components.

Remember the girl in Chapter 1 who didn't know how old she was? After working in *Building Blocks* for a year, the research assistant who had talked to her at the beginning of the year asked her (purposively) about her age. She responded, "Oh, I'm four now. See [shows four fingers]. Next year I'll be five, then in, ummm, two years I'll be six. It's *just* counting."

Notes

Preface

1. Like most acronyms, TRIAD "almost" works; Julie Sarama always reminds people of the "silent p" from Professional Development.

Chapter 1

1. Terms for the preprimary years are not used consistently in the literature. We use "pre-K" for prekindergarten, the year before kindergarten entrance (in the U.S. pre-K children are usually four years of age); "pre-K children" and "preschoolers" are often used interchangeably, with plural phrases such as "the preschool years" explicitly meaning the pre-K year and the year before this year (three-year-olds); "toddlers" refers to one- to two-year-olds and "infants" to children below one year of age.

2. Such everyday foundational experiences form the intuitive, implicit conceptual foundation for later mathematics. Later, children represent and elaborate these ideas—creating models of an everyday activity with mathematical objects, such as numbers and shapes; mathematical actions, such as counting or transforming shapes; and their structural relations. We call this process "mathematization." A distinction between foundational and mathematized experiences is necessary to avoid confusion about the type of activity in which children are engaged (Kronholz, 2000).

3. *Building Blocks—Foundations for Mathematical Thinking, Pre-Kindergarten to Grade 2: Research-based Materials Development* was funded by NSF to create and evaluate mathematics curricula for young children based on a theoretically sound research and development framework. We describe the framework and research in detail in Chapter 15 of the companion book. (National Science Foundation Grant No. ESI-9730804 to D. H. Clements and J. Sarama "*Building Blocks—*Foundations for Mathematical Thinking, Pre-Kindergarten to Grade 2: Research-based Materials Development.") For the purposes of full disclosure, note that we have subsequently made this curriculum available through a publisher, and thus receive royalties. All research was conducted with independent assessors and evaluators.

4. This is the theory, of course. The developmental progressions described in this book range from those with considerable supportive evidence, to descriptions that are a "best professional judgment" of such a progression. Indeed, "progressions" may be determined by "natural ways of learning" more in some topics (e.g., number/counting) than others (geometric and spatial understandings). Further, even at best they are general descriptions and can be modified by cultural and individual differences. See the "frequently asked questions" section of the companion book for additional discussion and caveats.

5. Levels of thinking are theoretically nonrecurrent (Karmiloff-Smith, 1984); however, people not only can, but frequently do, "return" to earlier levels of geometric thinking in certain contexts. Therefore, we postulate the construct of *nongenetic*

levels (Clements et al., 2001). Nongenetic levels have two special characteristics. First, progress through nongenetic levels is determined more by social influences, and specifically instruction, than by age-linked development. (At this point, this only implies that progression does not occur by necessity with time, but demands, in addition, instructional intervention. Certain levels may develop under maturational constraints; further research is needed on this issue.) Second, although each higher nongenetic level builds on the knowledge that constitutes lower levels, its nongenetic nature does not preclude the instantiation and application of earlier levels in certain contexts (not necessarily limited to especially demanding or stressful contexts). For each level, there exists a probability of evoking each of numerous different sets of circumstances. However, this process is codetermined by conscious metacognitive control, and this control increases as one moves up through the levels. Therefore, people have increasing choice to override the default probabilities. The use of different levels is environmentally adaptive; thus, the adjective "higher" should be understood as a higher level of abstraction and generality, without the implication of either inherent superiority or the abandonment of lower levels as a consequence of the development of higher levels of thinking. Nevertheless, the levels would constitute veridical qualitative changes in behavior, especially in regard to the construction of mathematical schemes out of action.

Chapter 2

1. For a complementary review of historical changes in views of preschoolers' informal mathematics knowledge, see (Baroody et al., 2006).

Chapter 3

1. We also avoid the term "rational counting," as it was invented by Steffe to differentiate simple object counting from the ability to count on with understanding, but is now often used merely to mean "object counting" or "understanding object counting" (L. P. Steffe, personal communication, May 20, 2004).

Chapter 4

1. These were only computer activities, tested as the first working draft of possible *Building Blocks* activities. Given their limited impact, they were eliminated for future development or inclusion in the *Building Blocks* curriculum, illustrating the importance of following a model including substantive formative assessment (see Chapter 15 in the companion book).

Chapter 5

1. Several important and complex issues regarding manipulatives are discussed at length in Chapter 15 in the companion book.
2. Note that different cultures, such as Korean, Latino, and Mozambican have different methods for representing numbers with fingers (Draisma, 2000; Fuson, Perry, & Kwon, 1994).
3. Although simple counting practice transfers to addition and subtraction (Malofeeva, Day, Saco, Young, & Ciancio, 2004), counting skills should also include effortlessly (achieving automaticity on) counting forward and backward, counting in either direction starting with any number, naming the number before or after another number, counting-on-using-patterns, counting-on-keeping-track of the number of counts, and eventually embedded quantities within counting sequences.

Chapter 7

1. We use Wang and Spelke's (2002) term rather than Newcombe and Hutten-locher's (2000) term "dead reckoning" because the root of the latter is "deductive reasoning." With magnetic compasses, sailors could take compass bearings, or headings. Bearings on two landmarks were used to construct two intersecting lines, which determined a location. This starting point was then iteratively updated based on movement—direction and distance (speed times time). In both its implicit beginnings and navigational application, the difficulty is "drift"— small errors lead to increasingly inaccurate calculations. The common written abbreviation of deductive reckoning, "ded. reckoning," was misread by an early mariner and the name stuck as "dead reckoning." As a term, "path integration" has no implication of conscious deduction.

Chapter 8

1. We reserve the term "property" for those attributes that indicate a relationship between parts, or components, of shapes. Thus, parallel sides, or equal sides, are properties. We use "attributes" and features interchangeably to indicate any characteristic of a shape, including properties, other defining characteristics (e.g., straight sides) and nondefining characteristics (e.g., "right-side up").
2. We define "exemplars" as theoretically- and empirically-determined common forms of the class, and "variants" are other members of the class; "examples" are members of the class (and thus include exemplars and variants). We will call shapes that are not members of the class "distractors" ("palpable distractors" or "palpable nonexamples," are those without overall resemblance, such as ovals vs. triangles; "difficult distractors" are those that are highly visually similar to exemplars but lack at least one defining attribute); see the companion book for illustrations.
3. This sentence could be misconstrued to mean that students are controlled by the external environment. We assume students are always sense-making beings; however, during this phase in building a representation, they are actively making sense of their social and physical environments, rather than their representations, of which they are not yet conscious. This active sense-making is critical, in that it allows the students to differentiate between environments that do and do not assist goal attainment.
4. The first two steps, Information and Guided Orientation, of the van Hiele model's five-step instructional sequence would be, with some modification, consonant with the three phases of development described here. This topic is related to, but different from, the topics addressed here and will not be examined.
5. For more complete recent reviews, see (Clements, 1999b; Clements & Sarama, 1997b; McCoy, 1996).

Chapter 10

1. We focus on the geometric attributes here, but preschoolers can reason about other attributes in science, such as weight (see, e.g., Metz, 1993; Smith, Carey, & Wiser, 1985).

Chapter 13

1. Most of the information regarding teaching problem solving is integrated within the content chapters.

Chapter 14

1. A similar and contributing problem is the theoretical and empirical insularity of the various research communities. Research reviewed here indicates that mathematics education researchers are aware of some, but not all, of research from other fields, but those in various branches of psychology are not aware of relevant work in mathematics education research, even making discoveries or inventing "new" research methods that have a long history in mathematics education.

References

Abravanel, E. (1977). The figural simplicity of parallel lines. *Child Development, 48*, 708–710.

Acredolo, L. P. (1978). The development changes of spatial orientation in infancy. *Developmental Psychology, 14*, 224–234.

Acredolo, L. P., Adams, A., & Goodwyn, S. W. (1984). The role of self-produced movement and visual tracking in infant spatial orientation. *Journal of Experimental Child Psychology, 38*, 312–327.

Acredolo, L. P., & Evans, D. (1980). Developmental changes in the effects of landmarks on infant spatial behavior. *Developmental Psychology, 16*, 312–318.

Alexander, P. A., White, C. S., & Daugherty, M. (1997). Analogical reasoning and early mathematics learning. In L. D. English (Ed.), *Mathematical reasoning: Analogies, metaphors, and images* (pp. 117–147). Mahwah, NJ: Lawrence Erlbaum Associates.

Allen, G. L., & Ondracek, P. J. (1995). Age-sensitive cognitive abilities related to children's acquisition of spatial knowledge. *Developmental Psychology, 31*, 934–945.

Anderson, J. R. (1983). *The architecture of cognition.* Cambridge, MA: Harvard University Press.

Anderson, J. R. (2000). *Cognitive psychology and its implications* (5th ed.). New York: W. H. Freeman.

Anghileri, J. (2001). What are we trying to achieve in teaching standard calculating procedures? In M. v. d. Heuvel-Panhuizen (Ed.), *Proceedings of the 25th Conference of the International Group for the Psychology in Mathematics Education* (Vol. 2, pp. 41–48). Utrecht, The Netherlands: Freudenthal Institute.

Anooshian, L. J., Pascal, V. U., & McCreath, H. (1984). Problem mapping before problem solving: Young children's cognitive maps and search strategies in large-scale environments. *Child Development, 55*, 1820–1834.

Ansari, D., Donlan, C., Thomas, M. S. C., Ewing, S. A., Peen, T., & Karmiloff-Smith, A. (2003). What makes counting count? Verbal and visuo-spatial contributions to typical and atypical number development. *Journal of Experimental Child Psychology, 85*, 50–62.

Arcavi, A. (2003). The role of visual representations in the learning of mathematics. *Educational Studies in Mathematics, 52*, 215–241.

Arditi, A., Holtzman, J. D., & Kosslyn, S. M. (1988). Mental imagery and sensory experience in congenital blindness. *Neuropsychologia, 26*, 1–12.

Arnold, W. R., & Hale, R. (1971). An investigation of third-grade level pupil's ability in geometry. *Colorado Journal Of Educational Research, 10*(4), 2–7.

Aubrey, C. (1997). Children's early learning of number in school and out. In I. Thompson (Ed.), *Teaching and learning early number* (pp. 20–29). Philadelphia, PA: Open University Press.

Aunio, P., Ee, J., Lim, S. E. A., Hautamäki, J., & Van Luit, J. E. H. (2004). Young children's number sense in Finland, Hong Kong and Singapore. *International Journal of Early Years Education, 12*, 195–216.

Ball, D. L., & Cohen, D. K. (1999). *Instruction, capacity, and improvement.* Philadelphia, PA: Consortium for Policy Research in Education, University of Pennsylvania.

Barker, W. F., Merryman, J. D., & Bracken, J. (1988). Microcomputers, math CAI, Logo, and mathematics education in elementary school: A pilot study. New Orleans: American Educational Research Association.

Barnett, W. S. (1995). Long-term effects of early childhood programs on cognitive and school outcomes. *The Future of Children, 5*(3), 25–50.

Baroody, A. J. (1987). *Children's mathematical thinking.* New York: Teachers College.

Baroody, A. J. (1992). The development of preschoolers' counting skills and principles. In J. Bideaud, C. Meljac & J.-P. Fischer (Eds.), *Pathways to number: Developing numerical abilities* (pp. 99–126). Mahwah, NJ: Lawrence Erlbaum Associates.

Baroody, A. J. (1993). *Problem solving, reasoning, and communicating (K-8): Helping children think mathematically.* New York: Merrill/Macmillan.

Baroody, A. J. (2004). The developmental bases for early childhood number and operations standards. In D. H. Clements, J. Sarama & A.-M. DiBiase (Eds.), *Engaging young children in mathematics: Standards for early childhood mathematics education* (pp. 173–219). Mahwah, NJ: Lawrence Erlbaum Associates.

Baroody, A. J., & Lai, M.-l. (2007). Preschoolers' understanding of the addition-subtraction inverse principle: A Taiwanese sample. *Mathematical Thinking and Learning, 9*, 131–171.

Baroody, A. J., Lai, M.-L., & Mix, K. S. (2005, December). *Changing views of young children's numerical and arithmetic competencies.* Paper presented at the National Association for the Education of Young Children, Washington, DC.

Baroody, A. J., Lai, M.-l., & Mix, K. S. (2006). The development of young children's number and operation sense and its implications for early childhood education. In B. Spodek & O. N. Saracho (Eds.), *Handbook of research on the education of young children* (pp. 187–221). Mahwah, NJ: Lawrence Erlbaum Associates.

Battista, M. T. (1990). Spatial visualization and gender differences in high school geometry. *Journal for Research in Mathematics Education, 21*, 47–60.

Battista, M. T., & Clements, D. H. (1996). Students' understanding of three-dimensional rectangular arrays of cubes. *Journal for Research in Mathematics Education, 27*, 258–292.

Battista, M. T., Clements, D. H., Arnoff, J., Battista, K., & Borrow, C. V. A. (1998). Students' spatial structuring of 2D arrays of squares. *Journal for Research in Mathematics Education, 29*, 503–532.

Beaton, A. E., Mullis, I. V. S., Martin, M. O., Gonzalez, E. J., Kelly, D. L., & Smith, T. A. (1996, January 19, 1997). Mathematics achievement in the middle school years: IEA's third international mathematics and science study (TIMSS). from http://wwwcsteep.bc.edu/timss

Beilin, H. (1984). Cognitive theory and mathematical cognition: Geometry and space. In B. Gholson & T. L. Rosenthanl (Eds.), *Applications of cognitive-developmental theory* (pp. 49–93). New York: Academic Press.

Beilin, H., Klein, A., & Whitehurst, B. (1982). *Strategies and structures in understanding geometry.* New York: City University of New York.

Benson, K. A., & Bogartz, R. S. (1990). Coordination of perspective change in preschoolers. New Orleans, LA: Society for Research in Child Development.

Berends, M., Kirby, S. N., Naftel, S., & McKelvey, C. (2001). *Implementation and performance in New American Schools: Three years into scale-up.* Santa Monica, CA: Rand Education.

Bertenthal, B. I., Campos, J. J., & Kermoian, R. (1994). An epigenetic perspective on the development of self-produced locomotion and its consequences. *Current Directions in Psychological Sciences, 5*, 140–145.

Birman, B. F., LeFloch, K. C., Klekotka, A., Ludwig, M., Taylor, J., Walters, K., et al. (2007). *State and local implementation of the No Child Left Behind Act, volume II—Teacher quality under NCLB: Interim report.* Washington, D.C.: U.S. Department of Education, Office of Planning, Evaluation and Policy Development, Policy and Program Studies Service.

Bishop, A. J. (1980). Spatial abilities and mathematics achievement—A review. *Educational Studies in Mathematics, 11*, 257–269.

Bishop, A. J. (1983). Space and geometry. In R. A. Lesh & M. S. Landau (Eds.), *Acquisition of mathematics concepts and processes* (pp. 7–44). New York: Academic Press.

Bjonerud, C. (1960). Arithmetic concepts possessed by the preschool child. *The Arithmetic Teacher, 7*, 347–350.

Blades, M., & Spencer, C. (1989). Young children's ability to use coordinate references. *The Journal of Genetic Psychology, 150*, 5–18.

Blades, M., Spencer, C., Plester, B., & Desmond, K. (2004). Young children's recognition and representation of urban landscapes: From aerial photographs and in toy play. In G. L. Allen (Ed.), *Human spatial memory: Remembering where* (pp. 287–308). Mahwah, NJ: Lawrence Erlbaum Associates.

Blanton, M., & Kaput, J. J. (2004). Elementary students' capacity for foundational thinking. In M. J. Høines & A. B. Fuglestad (Eds.), *Proceedings of the 28th Conference of the International Group for the Psychology in Mathematics Education* (Vol. 2, pp. 135–142). Bergen, Norway: Bergen University College.

Blaut, J. M., & Stea, D. (1974). Mapping at the age of three. *Journal of Geography, 73*(7), 5–9.

Boardman, D. (1990). Graphicacy revisited: Mapping abilities and gender differences. *Educational Review, 42*, 57–64.

Bobis, J., Clarke, B. A., Clarke, D. M., Gill, T., Wright, R. J., Young-Loveridge, J. M., et al. (2005).

Supporting teachers in the development of young children's mathematical thinking: Three large scale cases. *Mathematics Education Research Journal, 16*(3), 27–57.

Bodanskii, F. (1991). The formation of an algebraic method of problem solving in primary school children. In V. V. Davydov (Ed.), *Soviet studies in mathematics education, Psychological abilities of primary school children in learning mathematics* (Vol. 6, pp. 275–338). Reston, VA: National Council of Teachers of Mathematics.

Bodilly, S. J. (1998). *Lessons from New American Schools' scale-up phase.* Santa Monica, CA: RAND Education.

Booth, D. (1984). Aspects of logic-mathematical intuition in the development of young children's spontaneous pattern painting. In B. Southwello, R. Eyland, M. Cooper, J. Conroy & K. Collis (Eds.), *Proceedings of the 8th Conference of the International Group for the Psychology in Mathematics Education* (pp. 225–237).

Borer, M. (1993). *Integrating mandated Logo computer instruction into the second grade curriculum.* Unpublished Practicum Report, Nova University, Fort Lauderdale, FL.

Borman, G. D., Hewes, G. M., Overman, L. T., & Brown, S. (2003). Comprehensive school reform and achievement: A meta-analysis. *Review of Educational Research, 73*, 125–230.

Bowerman, M. (1996). Learning how to structure space for language: A crosslinguistic perspective. In P. Bloom, M. A. Peterson, L. Nadel & M. F. Garrett (Eds.), *Language and space* (pp. 385–436). Cambridge, MA: MIT Press.

Bowman, B. T., Donovan, M. S., & Burns, M. S. (Eds.). (2001). *Eager to learn: Educating our preschoolers.* Washington, DC: National Academy Press.

Brade, G. (2003). *The effect of a computer activity on young children's development of numerosity estimation skills.* University at Buffalo, State University of New York.

Bredekamp, S. (2004). Standards for preschool and kindergarten mathematics education. In D. H. Clements, J. Sarama & A.-M. DiBiase (Eds.), *Engaging young children in mathematics: Standards for early childhood mathematics education* (pp. 77–82). Mahwah, NJ: Lawrence Erlbaum Associates.

Bremner, J. G., Andreasen, G., Kendall, G., & Adams, L. (1993). Conditions for successful performance by 4-year-olds in a dimensional coordination task. *Journal of Experimental Child Psychology, 56*(2), 149–172.

Bremner, J. G., Knowles, L., & Andreasen, G. (1994). Processes underlying young children's spatial orientation during movement. *Journal of Experimental Child Psychology, 57,* 355–376.

Bremner, J. G., & Taylor, A. J. (1982). Children's errors in copying angles: Perpendicular error or bisection error? *Perception, 11,* 163–171.

Bright, G. W., Bowman, A. H., & Vacc, N. N. (1997). Teachers' frameworks for understanding children's mathematical thinking. In E. Pehkonen (Ed.), *Proceedings of the 21st Conference of the International Group for the Psychology of Mathematics Education* (Vol. 2, pp. 105–112). Lahti, Finland: University of Helsinki.

Brito-Lima, A. P., & da Rocha Falcão, J. T. (1997). Early development of algebraic representation among 6–13 year-old children: The importance of didactic contract. In E. Pehkonen (Ed.), *Proceedings of the 21st Conference of the International Group for the Psychology of Mathematics Education* (Vol. 2, pp. 201–208). Lahti, Finland: University of Helsinki.

Brosnan, M. J. (1998). Spatial ability in children's play with Lego blocks. *Perceptual and Motor Skills, 87,* 19–28.

Brown, A. L., & Campione, J. C. (1996). Psychological theory and the design of innovative learning environments: On procedures, principles, and systems. In R. Glaser (Ed.), *Innovations in learning: New environments for education* (pp. 289–325). Mahwah, NJ: Lawrence Erlbaum Associates.

Brown, D. L., & Wheatley, G. H. (1989). Relationship between spatial knowledge and mathematics knowledge. In C. A. Maher, G. A. Goldin, & R. B. Davis (Eds.), *Proceedings of the eleventh annual meeting, North American Chapter of the International Group for the Psychology of Mathematics Education* (pp. 143–148). New Brunswick, NJ: Rutgers University.

Brown, M., Blondel, E., Simon, S., & Black, P. (1995). Progression in measuring. *Research Papers in Education, 10*(2), 143–170.

Brownell, W. A. (1941). *Arithmetic in grades I and II: A critical summary of new and previously reported research.* Durham, NC: Duke University Press.

Buckingham, B. R., & MacLatchy, J. (1930). The number abilities of children when they enter grade one. *Yearbook of the National Society for the Study of Education: Report of the Society's Committee on Arithmetic, 29,* 473–524.

Burger, W. F., & Shaughnessy, J. M. (1986). Characterizing the van Hiele levels of development in geometry. *Journal for Research in Mathematics Education, 17*, 31–48.

Bushnell, E. W., McKenzie, B. E., Lawrence, D. A., & Com, S. (1995). The spatial coding strategies of 1-year-old infants in a locomotor search task. *Child Development, 66*, 937–958.

Butler, D., & Close, S. (1989). Assessing the benefits of a Logo problem-solving course. *Irish Educational Studies, 8*, 168–190.

Butterworth, G. (1991). Evidence for the "geometric" comprehension of manual pointing. Seattle, WA: Society for Research in Child Development.

Callahan, L. G., & Clements, D. H. (1984). Sex differences in rote counting ability on entry to first grade: Some observations. *Journal for Research in Mathematics Education, 15*, 378–382.

Cannon, J., Levine, S. C., & Huttenlocher, J. (2007, March). *Sex differences in the relation between early puzzle play and mental transformation skill.* Paper presented at the Biennial Meeting of the Society of Research in Child Development, Boston, MA.

Carlson, G. R. (1976). Location of a point in Euclidian space by children in grades one through six. *Journal of Research in Science Teaching, 13*, 331–336.

Carlson, S. L., & White, S. H. (1998). The effectiveness of a computer program in helping kindergarten students learn the concepts of left and right. *Journal of Computing in Childhood Education, 9*(2), 133–147.

Carpenter, T. P., Ansell, E., Franke, M. L., Fennema, E. H., & Weisbeck, L. (1993). Models of problem solving: A study of kindergarten children's problem-solving processes. *Journal for Research in Mathematics Education, 24*, 428–441.

Carpenter, T. P., Coburn, T., Reys, R. E., & Wilson, J. (1975). Notes from National Assessment: Basic concepts of area and volume. *Arithmetic Teacher, 22*, 501–507.

Carpenter, T. P., Corbitt, M. K., Kepner, H. S., Lindquist, M. M., & Reys, R. E. (1980). National assessment. In E. Fennema (Ed.), *Mathematics education research: Implications for the 80s* (pp. 22–38). Alexandria, VA: Association for Supervision and Curriculum Development.

Carpenter, T. P., Fennema, E. H., Peterson, P. L., & Carey, D. A. (1988). Teacher's pedagogical content knowledge of students' problem solving in elementary arithmetic. *Journal for Research in Mathematics Education, 19*, 385–401.

Carpenter, T. P., Franke, M. L., Jacobs, V. R., Fennema, E. H., & Empson, S. B. (1998). A longitudinal study of invention and understanding in children's multidigit addition and subtraction. *Journal for Research in Mathematics Education, 29*, 3–20.

Carpenter, T. P., Franke, M. L., & Levi, L. (2003). *Thinking mathematically: Integrating arithmetic and algebra in elementary school.* Portsmouth, NH: Heinemann.

Carpenter, T. P., & Levi, L. (1999). Developing conceptions of algebraic reasoning in the primary grades. Montreal, Canada: American Educational Research Association.

Casey, M. B. (2005, April). *Evaluation of NSF-funded mathematics materials: use of storytelling contexts to improve kindergartners' geometry and block-building skills.* Paper presented at the National Council of Supervisors of Mathematics, Anaheim, CA.

Casey, M. B., & Erkut, S. (2005, April). *Early spatial interventions benefit girls and boys.* Paper presented at the Biennial Meeting of the Society for Research in Child Development, Atlanta, GA.

Casey, M. B., Nuttall, R. L., & Pezaris, E. (1997). Mediators of gender differences in mathematics college entrance test scores: A comparison of spatial skills with internalized beliefs and anxieties. *Developmental Psychology, 33*, 669–680.

Casey, M. B., Nuttall, R. L., & Pezaris, E. (2001). Spatial-mechanical reasoning skills versus mathematics self-confidence as mediators of gender differences on mathematics subtests using cross-national gender-based items. *Journal for Research in Mathematics Education, 32*, 28–57.

Certo, J. L. (2005). Support, challenge, and the two-way street: Perceptions of a beginning second-grade teacher and her quality mentor. *Journal of Early Childhood Teacher Education, 26*, 3–21.

Choi, S., & Bowerman, M. (1991). Learning to express motion events in English and Korean: The influence of language-specific lexication patterns. *Cognition, 41*, 83–121.

Choi, S., McDonough, L., Bowerman, M., & Mandler, J. (1999). Comprehension of spatial terms in English and Korean. *Cognitive Development, 14*, 241–268.

Ciancio, D. S., Rojas, A. C., McMahon, K., & Pasnak, R. (2001). Teaching oddity and insertion to Head Start children; an economical cognitive intervention. *Journal of Applied Developmental Psychology, 22*, 603 – 621.

Claessens, A., Duncan, G. J., & Engel, M. (2007). *Kindergarten skills and fifth grade achievement: Evidence from the ECLS-K.* Evanston, IL: Northwestern University.

Clarke, B. A. (2004). A shape is not defined by its shape: Developing young children's geometric understanding. *Journal of Australian Research in Early Childhood Education, 11*(2), 110–127.

Clarke, B. A., Clarke, D. M., & Cheeseman, J. (2006). The mathematical knowledge and under-standing young children bring to school. *Mathematics Education Research Journal, 18*(1), 81–107.

Clarke, D. (1994). Ten key principles from research for the professional development of mathe-matics teachers. In D. B. Aichele & A. F. Coxford (Eds.), *Professional development for teachers of mathematics* (pp. 37–48). Reston, VA: National Council of Teachers of Mathematics.

Clarke, D. M., Cheeseman, J., Clarke, B., Gervasoni, A., Gronn, D., Horne, M., et al. (2001). Under-standing, assessing and developing young children's mathematical thinking: Research as a powerful tool for professional growth. In J. Bobis, B. Perry & M. Mitchelmore (Eds.), *Numeracy and beyond (Proceedings of the 24th Annual Conference of the Mathematics Education Research Group of Australasia, Vol. 1)* (pp. 9–26). Reston, Australia: MERGA.

Clarke, D. M., Cheeseman, J., Gervasoni, A., Gronn, D., Horne, M., McDonough, A., et al. (2002). *Early Numeracy Research Project final report:* Department of Education, Employment and Training, the Catholic Education Office (Melbourne), and the Association of Independent Schools Victoria.

Clements, D. H. (1984a). Foundations of number and logic: Seriation, classification, and number conservation from a Piagetian perspective. *Psychological Documents (Ms. No. 2607), 14*(4).

Clements, D. H. (1984b). Training effects on the development and generalization of Piagetian logical operations and knowledge of number. *Journal of Educational Psychology, 76,* 766–776.

Clements, D. H. (1987). Longitudinal study of the effects of Logo programming on cognitive abilities and achievement. *Journal of Educational Computing Research, 3,* 73–94.

Clements, D. H. (1999a). "Concrete" manipulatives, concrete ideas. *Contemporary Issues in Early Childhood, 1*(1), 45–60.

Clements, D. H. (1999b). The future of educational computing research: The case of computer programming. *Information Technology in Childhood Education Annual, 1999,* 147–179.

Clements, D. H. (2001). Mathematics in the preschool. *Teaching Children Mathematics, 7,* 270–275.

Clements, D. H. (2002). Linking research and curriculum development. In L. D. English (Ed.), *Handbook of International Research in Mathematics Education* (pp. 599–636). Mahwah, NJ: Lawrence Erlbaum Associates.

Clements, D. H. (2004). Geometric and spatial thinking in early childhood education. In D. H. Clements, J. Sarama, & A.-M. DiBiase (Eds.), *Engaging young children in mathematics: Standards for early childhood mathematics education* (pp. 267–297). Mahwah, NJ: Lawrence Erlbaum Associates.

Clements, D. H. (2007). Curriculum research: Toward a framework for "research-based curricula". *Journal for Research in Mathematics Education, 38,* 35–70.

Clements, D. H., & Battista, M. T. (1989). Learning of geometric concepts in a Logo environment. *Journal for Research in Mathematics Education, 20,* 450–467.

Clements, D. H., & Battista, M. T. (1990). The effects of Logo on children's conceptualizations of angle and polygons. *Journal for Research in Mathematics Education, 21,* 356–371.

Clements, D. H., & Battista, M. T. (1991). *Logo geometry.* Morristown, NJ: Silver Burdett & Ginn.

Clements, D. H., & Battista, M. T. (1992). Geometry and spatial reasoning. In D. A. Grouws (Ed.), *Handbook of research on mathematics teaching and learning* (pp. 420–464). New York: Macmillan.

Clements, D. H., & Battista, M. T. (1994). Computer environments for learning geometry. *Journal of Educational Computing Research, 10*(2), 173–197.

Clements, D. H., Battista, M. T., & Sarama, J. (2001). Logo and geometry. *Journal for Research in Mathematics Education Monograph Series, 10.*

Clements, D. H., Battista, M. T., Sarama, J., & Swaminathan, S. (1996). Development of turn and turn measurement concepts in a computer-based instructional unit. *Educational Studies in Mathematics, 30,* 313–337.

Clements, D. H., Battista, M. T., Sarama, J., & Swaminathan, S. (1997). Development of students' spatial thinking in a unit on geometric motions and area. *The Elementary School Journal, 98,* 171–186.

Clements, D. H., Battista, M. T., Sarama, J., Swaminathan, S., & McMillen, S. (1997). Students' development of length measurement concepts in a Logo-based unit on geometric paths. *Journal for Research in Mathematics Education, 28*(1), 70–95.

Clements, D. H., & Burns, B. A. (2000). Students' development of strategies for turn and angle measure. *Educational Studies in Mathematics, 41*, 31–45.

Clements, D. H., & Conference Working Group. (2004). Part one: Major themes and recommendations. In D. H. Clements, J. Sarama & A.-M. DiBiase (Eds.), *Engaging young children in mathematics: Standards for early childhood mathematics education* (pp. 1–72). Mahwah, NJ: Lawrence Erlbaum Associates.

Clements, D. H., & McMillen, S. (1996). Rethinking "concrete" manipulatives. *Teaching Children Mathematics, 2*(5), 270–279.

Clements, D. H., & Meredith, J. S. (1993). Research on Logo: Effects and efficacy. *Journal of Computing in Childhood Education, 4*, 263–290.

Clements, D. H., & Meredith, J. S. (1994). Turtle math [Computer software]. Montreal, Quebec: Logo Computer Systems, Inc. (LCSI).

Clements, D. H., & Sarama, J. (1997a). Research on Logo: A decade of progress. In C. D. Maddux & D. L. Johnson (Eds.), *Logo: A retrospective* (pp. 9–46): Haworth Press.

Clements, D. H., & Sarama, J. (1997b). Research on Logo: A decade of progress. *Computers in the Schools, 14*(1–2), 9–46.

Clements, D. H., & Sarama, J. (2003a). *DLM Early Childhood Express Math Resource Guide.* Columbus, OH: SRA/McGraw-Hill.

Clements, D. H., & Sarama, J. (2003b). Young children and technology: What does the research say? *Young Children, 58*(6), 34–40.

Clements, D. H., & Sarama, J. (2004a). *Building Blocks* for early childhood mathematics. *Early Childhood Research Quarterly, 19*, 181–189.

Clements, D. H., & Sarama, J. (2004b). Hypothetical learning trajectories. *Mathematical Thinking and Learning, 6*(2).

Clements, D. H., & Sarama, J. (2004c). Learning trajectories in mathematics education. *Mathematical Thinking and Learning, 6*, 81–89.

Clements, D. H., & Sarama, J. (2007). Effects of a preschool mathematics curriculum: Summative research on the *Building Blocks* project. *Journal for Research in Mathematics Education, 38*, 136–163.

Clements, D. H., & Sarama, J. (2008). Experimental evaluation of the effects of a research-based preschool mathematics curriculum. *American Educational Research Journal, 45*, 443–494.

Clements, D. H., & Sarama, J. (2009). *Learning and teaching early math: The learning trajectories approach.* New York: Taylor & Francis.

Clements, D. H., Sarama, J., & DiBiase, A.-M. (2004). *Engaging young children in mathematics: Standards for early childhood mathematics education.* Mahwah, NJ: Lawrence Erlbaum Associates.

Clements, D. H., Swaminathan, S., Hannibal, M. A. Z., & Sarama, J. (1999). Young children's concepts of shape. *Journal for Research in Mathematics Education, 30*, 192–212.

Clements, D. H., Wilson, D. C., & Sarama, J. (2004). Young children's composition of geometric figures: A learning trajectory. *Mathematical Thinking and Learning, 6*, 163–184.

Cobb, P., McClain, K., de Silva, T., & Dean, C. (2003). Situating teachers' instructional practices in the institutional setting of the school and district. *Educational Researcher, 32*(6), 13–24.

Coburn, C. E. (2003). Rethinking scale: Moving beyond numbers to deep and lasting change. *Educational Researcher, 32*(6), 3–12.

Cohen, D. K. (1996). Rewarding teachers for student performance. In S. H. Fuhrman & J. A. O'Day (Eds.), *Rewards and reforms: Creating educational incentives that work* (pp. 61–112). San Francisco, CA: Jossey Bass.

Cohen, D. K., & Hill, H. C. (2000). Instructional policy and classroom performance: The mathematics reform in California. *Teachers College Record Volume, 102*, 294–343.

Confrey, J. (1996). The role of new technologies in designing mathematics education. In C. Fisher, D. C. Dwyer & K. Yocam (Eds.), *Education and technology, reflections on computing in the classroom* (pp. 129–149). San Francisco: Apple Press.

Confrey, J., & Kazak, S. (2006). A thirty-year reflection on constructivism in mathematics education in PME. In A. Gutiérrez & P. Boero (Eds.), *Handbook of research on the psychology of mathematics education: Past, present, and future* (pp. 305–345). Rotterdam, The Netherlands: Sense Publishers.

Cooper, J., Brenneman, K., & Gelman, R. (2005, April). *Young children's use of graphs for arithmetic.* Paper presented at the Biennial Meeting of the Society for Research in Child Development, Atlanta, GA.

Cooper, T. J., & Warren, E. (2007, April). *Developing equivalence of expressions in the early to middle elementary years.* Paper presented at the Research Presession of the 85th Annual Meeting of the National Council of Teachers of Mathematics, Atlanta, GA.

Cope, P., & Simmons, M. (1991). Children's exploration of rotation and angle in limited Logo microworlds. *Computers in Education, 16,* 133–141.

Copley, J. V. (2004). The early childhood collaborative: A professional development model to communicate and implement the standards. In D. H. Clements, J. Sarama & A.-M. DiBiase (Eds.), *Engaging young children in mathematics: Standards for early childhood mathematics education* (pp. 401–414). Mahwah, NJ: Lawrence Erlbaum Associates.

Copley, J. V., & Padròn, Y. (1999). Preparing teachers of young learners: Professional development of early childhood teachers in mathematics and science. In G. D. Nelson (Ed.), *Dialogue on early childhood science, mathematics, and technology education* (pp. 117–129). Washington, DC: American Association for the Advancement of Science.

Cornell, E. H., Heth, C. D., Broda, L. S., & Butterfield, V. (1987). Spatial matching in 1 1/2- to 4 1/2-year-old children. *Developmental Psychology, 23,* 499–508.

Costa, A., & Garmston, R. (1994). *The art of cognitive coaching: Supervision for intelligent teaching. Training syllabus.* Sacramento, CA: Institute for Intelligent Behavior.

Cronin, V. (1967). Mirror-image reversal discrimination in kindergarten and first grade children. *Journal of Experimental Child Psychology, 5,* 577–585.

Cuban, L. (2001). *Oversold and underused.* Cambridge, MA: Harvard University Press.

Dalke, D. E. (1998). Charting the development of representational skills: When do children know that maps can lead and mislead? *Cognitive Development, 70,* 53–72.

Darling-Hammond, L. (1996). Restructuring schools for high performance. In S. H. Fuhrman & J. A. O'Day (Eds.), *Rewards and reform: Creating educational incentives that work* (pp. 144–192). San Francisco: Jossey-Bass.

Davis, R. B. (1984). *Learning mathematics: The cognitive science approach to mathematics education.* Norwood, NJ: Ablex.

Dehaene, S., Izard, V., Pica, P., & Spelke, E. S. (2006). Core knowledge of geometry in an Amazonian indigene group. *Science, 311,* 381–384.

Dehaene, S., Spelke, E. S., Pinel, P., Stanescu, R., & Tsivkin, S. (1999). Sources of mathematic thinking: Behavioral and brain-imaging evidence. *Science, 284,* 970–974.

Del Grande, J. J. (1986). Can grade two children's spatial perception be improved by inserting a transformation geometry component into their mathematics program? *Dissertation Abstracts International, 47,* 3689A.

Delgado, A. R., & Prieto, G. (2004). Cognitive mediators and sex-related differences in mathematics. *Intelligence, 32,* 25–32.

DeLoache, J. S. (1987). Rapid change in the symbolic functioning of young children. *Science, 238,* 1556–1557.

DeLoache, J. S., & Burns, N. M. (1994). Early understanding of the representational function of pictures. *Cognition, 52,* 83–110.

DeLoache, J. S., Miller, K. F., & Pierroutsakos, S. L. (1998). Reasoning and problem solving. In D. Kuhn & R. S. Siegler (Eds.), *Handbook of Child Psychology (5th Ed.): Vol. 2. Cognition, Perception, & Language* (pp. 801–850). New York: Wiley.

DeLoache, J. S., Miller, K. F., Rosengren, K., & Bryant, N. (1997). The credible shrinking room: Very young children's performance with symbolic and nonsymbolic relations. *Psychological Science, 8,* 308–313.

Denis, L. P. (1987). Relationships between stage of cognitive development and van Hiele level of geometric thought among Puerto Rican adolescents. *Dissertation Abstracts International, 48,* 859A.

Denton, K., & West, J. (2002). Children's reading and mathematics achievement in kindergarten and first grade. 2002, from http://nces.ed.gov/pubsearch/pubsinfo.asp?pubid=2002125

Dewey, J. (1902/1976). The child and the curriculum. In J. A. Boydston (Ed.), *John Dewey: The middle works, 1899–1924. Volume 2: 1902–1903* (pp. 273–291). Carbondale, IL: Southern Illinois University Press.

Dewey, J. (1938/1997). *Experience and education.* New York: Simon & Schuster.

Doig, B., McCrae, B., & Rowe, K. (2003). *A good start to numeracy: Effective numeracy strategies from research and practice in early childhood.* Canberra ACT, Australia: Australian Council for Educational Research.

Dougherty, B. J., & Slovin, H. (2004). Generalized diagrams as a tool for young children's problem solving. In M. J. Høines & A. B. Fuglestad (Eds.), *Proceedings of the 28th Conference of* the *International Group for the Psychology in Mathematics Education* (Vol. 2, pp. 295–302). Bergen, Norway: Bergen University College.

Douglass, H. R. (1925). The development of number concept in children of preschool and kindergarten ages. *Journal of Experimental Psychology, 8*, 443–470.

Dowker, A. (2005). Early identification and intervention for students with mathematics difficulties. *Journal of Learning Disabilities, 38*, 324–332.

Draisma, J. (2000). Geture and oral computation as resources in the early learning of mathematics. In T. Nakahara & M. Koyama (Eds.), *Proceedings of the 24th Conference of the International Group for the Psychology in Mathematics Education* (Vol. 2, pp. 257–264).

du Boulay, B. (1986). Part II: Logo confessions. In R. Lawler, B. du Boulay, M. Hughes & H. Macleod (Eds.), *Cognition and computers: Studies in learning* (pp. 81–178). Chichester, England: Ellis Horwood Limited.

Duschl, R. A., Schweingruber, H. A., & Shouse, A. W. (Eds.). (2007). *Taking science to school: Learning and teaching sciences in grades K-8*. Washington, DC: National Academies Press.

Duval, R. (1999). Representation, vision and visualization: Cognitive functions in mathematical thinking. Basic issues for learning. In F. Hitt & M. Santos (Eds.), *Proceedings of the 21st annual meeting of the North American Chapter of the International Group for the Psychology of Mathematics Education* (pp. 3–26). Cuernavaca, Morelos, Mexico.

Early, D., Maxwell, K. L., Burchinal, M. R., Alva, S., Bender, R. H., Bryant, D., et al. (2007). Teachers' education, classroom quality, and young children's academic skills: Results from seven studies of preschool programs. *Child Development, 78*, 558–580.

Ebbeck. (1984). Equity for boys and girls: Some important issues. *Early Child Development and Care, 18*, 119–131.

Edwards, C., Gandini, L., & Forman, G. E. (1993). *The hundred languages of children: The Reggio Emilia approach to early childhood education*. Norwood, N.J.: Ablex Publishing Corp.

Edwards, L. D. (1991). Children's learning in a computer microworld for transformation geometry. *Journal for Research in Mathematics Education, 22*, 122–137.

Ehrlich, S. B., Levine, S. C., & Goldin-Meadow, S. (2005, April). *Early sex differences in spatial skill: The implications of spoken and gestured strategies*. Paper presented at the Biennial Meeting of the Society for Research in Child Development, Atlanta, GA.

Ehrlich, S. B., Levine, S. C., & Goldin-Meadow, S. (2006). The importance of gesture in children's spatial reasoning. *Developmental Psychology, 42*, 1259–1268.

Elia, I., Gagatsis, A., & Demetriou, A. (2007). The effects of different modes of representation on the solution of one-step additive problems. *Learning and Instruction, 17*, 658–672.

Eliot, J. (1987). *Models of psychological space*. New York: Springer-Verlag.

Elmore, R. F. (1996a). Getting to scale with good educational practices. *Harvard Educational Review, 66*, 1–25.

Elmore, R. F. (1996b). Getting to scale with good educational practices. In S. H. Fuhrman & J. A. O'Day (Eds.), *Rewards and reform: Creating educational incentives that work* (pp. 294–329). San Francisco: Jossey-Bass.

Fabricius, W. V., & Wellman, H. M. (1993). Two roads diverged: Young children's ability to judge distances. *Child Development, 64*, 399–414.

Feltovich, P. J., Spiro, R. J., & Coulson, R. L. (1997). Issues of expert flexibility in contexts characterized by complexity and change. In P. J. Feltovich, K. M. Ford & R. R. Hoffman (Eds.), *Expertise in context: Human and machine* (pp. xviii, 590 p.). Menlo Park, Calif.

Cambridge, Mass.: AAAI Press/The MIT Press.

Fennema, E. H., & Carpenter, T. P. (1981). Sex-related differences in mathematics: Results from National Assessment. *Mathematics Teacher, 74*, 554–559.

Fennema, E. H., Carpenter, T. P., Frank, M. L., Levi, L., Jacobs, V. R., & Empson, S. B. (1996). A longitudinal study of learning to use children's thinking in mathematics instruction. *Journal for Research in Mathematics Education, 27*, 403–434.

Fennema, E. H., & Sherman, J. (1977). Sex-related differences in mathematics achievement, spatial visualization and affective factors. *American Educational Research Journal, 14*, 51–71.

Fennema, E. H., & Sherman, J. A. (1978). Sex-related differences in mathematics achievement and related factors. *Journal for Research in Mathematics Education, 9*, 189–203.

Fey, J., Atchison, W. F., Good, R. A., Heid, M. K., Johnson, J., Kantowski, M. G., et al. (1984). *Computing and mathematics: The impact on secondary school curricula*. College Park, MD: The University of Maryland.

Filippaki, N., & Papamichael, Y. (1997). Tutoring conjunctions and construction of geometry concepts in the early childhood education: The case of the angle. *European Journal of Psychology of Education, 12*(3), 235–247.

Fischbein, E. (1987). *Intuition in science and mathematics.* Dordrecht, Holland: D. Reidel.

Fisher, N. D. (1978). Visual influences of figure orientation on concept formation in geometry. *Dissertation Abstracts International, 38,* 4639A.

Fodor, J. (1972). Some reflections on L. S. Vygotky's Thought and Language. *Cognition, 1,* 83–95.

Fox, J. (2005). Child-initiated mathematical patterning in the pre-compulsory years. In H. L. Chick & J. L. Vincent (Eds.), *Proceedings of the 29th Conference of the International Group for the Psychology in Mathematics Education* (Vol. 2, pp. 313–320). Melbourne, AU: PME.

Frank, R. E. (Cartographer). (1987). *The emergence of route map reading skills in young children*

Franke, M. L., Carpenter, T. P., & Battey, D. (2008). Content matters: Algebraic reasoning in teacher professional development. In J. J. Kaput, D. W. Carraher & M. L. Blanton (Eds.), *Algebra in the early grades* (pp. 333–359). Mahwah, NJ: Lawrence Erlbaum Associates.

Frazier, M. K. (1987). *The effects of Logo on angle estimation skills of 7th graders.* Unpublished master's thesis, Wichita State University.

Friedman, L. (1995). The space factor in mathematics: Gender differences. *Review of Educational Research, 65*(1), 22–50.

Fullan, M. G. (1982). *The meaning of educational change.* New York: Teachers College Press.

Fullan, M. G. (1992). *Successful school improvement.* Philadelphia, PA: Open University Press.

Fullan, M. G. (2000). The return of large-scale reform. *Journal of Educational Change, 1,* 5–28.

Fuson, K. C. (1988). *Children's counting and concepts of number.* New York: Springer-Verlag.

Fuson, K. C. (1992). Research on whole number addition and subtraction. In D. A. Grouws (Ed.), *Handbook of research on mathematics teaching and learning* (pp. 243–275). New York: Macmillan.

Fuson, K. C. (2004). Pre-K to grade 2 goals and standards: Achieving 21st century mastery for all. In D. H. Clements, J. Sarama & A.-M. DiBiase (Eds.), *Engaging young children in mathematics: Standards for early childhood mathematics education* (pp. 105–148). Mahwah, NJ: Lawrence Erlbaum Associates.

Fuson, K. C., Carroll, W. M., & Drueck, J. V. (2000). Achievement results for second and third graders using the *Standards*-based curriculum *Everyday Mathematics. Journal for Research in Mathematics Education, 31,* 277–295.

Fuson, K. C., & Hall, J. W. (1982). The acquisition of early number word meanings: A conceptual analysis and review. In H. P. Ginsburg (Ed.), *Children's mathematical thinking* (pp. 49–107). New York: Academic Press.

Fuson, K. C., & Murray, C. (1978). The haptic-visual perception, construction, and drawing of geometric shapes by children aged two to five: A Piagetian extension. In R. Lesh & D. Mierkiewicz (Eds.), *Concerning the development of spatial and geometric concepts* (pp. 49–83). Columbus, OH: ERIC Clearinghouse for Science, Mathematics, and Environmental Education.

Fuson, K. C., Perry, T., & Kwon, Y. (1994). Latino, Anglo, and Korean children's finger addition methods. In J. E. H. Van Luit (Ed.), *Research on learning and instruction of mathematics in kindergarten and primary school* (pp. 220–228). Doetinchem, Netherlands: Graviant.

Fuson, K. C., Wearne, D., Hiebert, J. C., Murray, H. G., Human, P. G., Olivier, A. I., et al. (1997). Children's conceptual structures for multidigit numbers and methods of multidigit addition and subtraction. *Journal for Research in Mathematics Education, 28,* 130–162.

Fuys, D., Geddes, D., & Tischler, R. (1988). The van Hiele model of thinking in geometry among adolescents. National Council of Teachers of Mathematics.

Gagatsis, A. (2003). Young children's understanding of geometric shapes: The role of geometric models. *European Early Childhood Education Research Journal, 11,* 43–62.

Gagatsis, A., & Patronis, T. (1990). Using geometrical models in a process of reflective thinking in learning and teaching mathematics. *Educational Studies in Mathematics, 21,* 29–54.

Gagatsis, A., Sriraman, B., Elia, I., & Modestou, M. (2006). Exploring young children's geometrical strategies. *Nordic Studies in Mathematics Education, 11*(2), 23–50.

Gallou-Dumiel, E. (1989). Reflections, point symmetry and Logo. In C. A. Maher, G. A. Goldin & R. B. Davis (Eds.), Proceedings of the eleventh annual meeting, North American Chapter of the International Group for the Psychology of Mathematics Education (pp. 149–157). New Brunswick, NJ: Rutgers University.

Garet, M. S., Porter, A. C., Desimone, L., Birman, B. F., & Yoon, K. S. (2001). What makes professional development effective? Results from a national sample of teachers. *American Educational Research Journal, 38*, 915–945.

Gauvain, M. (1991). The development of spatial thinking in everyday activity. Seattle, WA: Society for Research in Child Development.

Gay, P. (1989). Tactile turtle: Explorations in space with visually impaired children and a floor turtle. *British Journal of Visual Impairment, 7*(1), 23–25.

Geary, D. C. (1994). *Children's mathematical development: Research and practical applications.* Washington, DC: American Psychological Association.

Geary, D. C. (2006). Development of mathematical understanding. In D. Kuhn, R. S. Siegler, W. Damon & R. M. Lerner (Eds.), *Handbook of child psychology: Volume 2: Cognition, perception, and language (6th ed.)* (pp. 777–810). Hoboken, NJ: Wiley.

Geary, D. C. (2007). An evolutionary perspective on learning disability in mathematics *Developmental Neuropsychology, 32*, 471–519.

Geary, D. C., Bow-Thomas, C. C., Fan, L., & Siegler, R. S. (1993). Even before formal instruction, Chinese children outperform American children in mental addition. *Cognitive Development, 8*, 517–529.

Gelman, R. (1990a). First principles organize attention to and learning about relevant data: Number and animate-inanimate distinction as examples. *Cognitive Science, 14*, 79–106.

Gelman, R. (1990b). Structural constraints on cognitive development. *Cognitive Science, 14*, 39.

Gelman, R., & Gallistel, C. R. (1978). *The child's understanding of number.* Cambridge, MA: Harvard University Press.

Gelman, R., & Williams, E. M. (1997). Enabling constraints for cognitive development and learning: Domain specificity and epigenesis. In D. Kuhn & R. Siegler (Eds.), *Cognition, perception, and language. Volume 2: Handbook of Child Psychology* (5th ed., pp. 575–630). New York: John Wiley & Sons.

Gerhardt, L. A. (1973). *Moving and knowing: The young child orients himself in space.* Englewood Cliffs, NJ: Prentice-Hall.

Ginsburg, H. P. (1977). *Children's arithmetic.* Austin, TX: Pro-ed.

Ginsburg, H. P. (1997). Mathematics learning disabilities: A view from developmental psychology. *Journal of Learning Disabilities, 30*, 20–33.

Ginsburg, H. P., Choi, Y. E., Lopez, L. S., Netley, R., & Chi, C.-Y. (1997). Happy birthday to you: The early mathematical thinking of Asian, South American, and U.S. children. In T. Nunes & P. Bryant (Eds.), *Learning and teaching mathematics: An international perspective* (pp. 163–207). East Sussex, England: Psychology Press.

Ginsburg, H. P., Inoue, N., & Seo, K.-H. (1999). Young children doing mathematics: Observations of everyday activities. In J. V. Copley (Ed.), *Mathematics in the early years* (pp. 88–99). Reston, VA: National Council of Teachers of Mathematics.

Ginsburg, H. P., Kaplan, R. G., Cannon, J., Cordero, M. I., Eisenband, J. G., & Galanter, M. (2006). Helping early childhood educators to teach mathematics. In M. Zaslow & I. Martinez-Beck (Eds.), *Critical issues in early childhood professional development* (pp. 171–202). Baltimore, MD: Paul H. Brookes.

Ginsburg, H. P., & Russell, R. L. (1981). Social class and racial influences on early mathematical thinking. *Monographs of the Society for Research in Child Development, 46*(6, Serial No. 193).

Glasersfeld, E. v. (1995). Sensory experience, abstraction, and teaching. In L. P. Steffe & J. Gale (Eds.), *Constructivism in education* (pp. 369–383). Mahwah, NJ: Lawrence Erlbaum Associates.

Golbeck, S. L., Rand, M., & Soundy, C. (1986). Constructing a model of a large scale space with the space in view: Effects of guidance and cognitive restructuring. *Merrill-Palmer Quarterly, 32*, 187–203.

Goodrow, A., Clements, D. H., Battista, M. T., Sarama, J., & Akers, J. (1997). *How long? How far? Measurement.* Palo Alto, CA: Dale Seymour Publications.

Goodson, B. D. (1982). The development of hierarchic organization: The reproduction, planning, and perception of multiarch block structures. In G. E. Forman (Ed.), *Action and thought* (pp. 165–201). New York: Academic Press.

Gopnik, A., & Meltzoff, A. N. (1986). Words, plans, things, and locations: Interactions between semantic and cognitive development in the one-word stage. In S. A. Kuczaj II & M. D. Barrett (Eds.), *The development of word meaning: Progress in cognitive development research* (pp. 199–223). New York: Springer-Verlag.

Gordon, P. (2004). Numerical cognition without words: Evidence from Amazonia. *Science, 306,* 496–499.

Gouteux, S., & Spelke, E. S. (2001). Children's use of geometry and landmarks to reorient in an open space. *Cognition, 81,* 119–148.

Gray, E. M., & Pitta, D. (1999). Images and their frames of reference: A perspective on cognitive development in elementary arithmetic. In O. Zaslavsky (Ed.), *Proceedings of the 23rd Conference of the International Group for the Psychology of Mathematics Education* (Vol. 3, pp. 49–56). Haifa, Isreal: Technion.

Greabell, L. C. (1978). The effect of stimuli input on the acquisition of introductory geometric concepts by elementary school children. *School Science and Mathematics, 78*(4), 320–326.

Greeno, J. G., Riley, M. S., & Gelman, R. (1984). Conceptual competence and children's counting. *Cognitive Psychology, 16,* 94–143.

Greenough, W. T., Black, J. E., & Wallace, C. S. (1987). Experience and brain development. *Child Development, 58,* 539–559.

Greenwald, A. G., Pratkanis, A. R., Leippe, M. R., & Baumgardner, M. H. (1986). Under what conditions does theory obstruct research progress? *Psychological Review, 93,* 216–229.

Griffin, S., & Case, R. (1997). Re-thinking the primary school math curriculum: An approach based on cognitive science. *Issues in Education, 3*(1), 1–49.

Griffin, S., Case, R., & Capodilupo, A. (1995). Teaching for understanding: The importance of the Central Conceptual Structures in the elementary mathematics curriculum. In A. McKeough, J. Lupart & A. Marini (Eds.), *Teaching for transfer: Fostering generalization in learning* (pp. 121–151). Mahwah, NJ: Lawrence Erlbaum Associates.

Griffin, S., Case, R., & Siegler, R. S. (1994). Rightstart: Providing the central conceptual pre-requisites for first formal learning of arithmetic to students at risk for school failure. In K. McGilly (Ed.), *Classroom lessons: Integrating cognitive theory and classroom practice* (pp. 25–49). Cambridge, MA: MIT Press.

Guay, R. B., & McDaniel, E. (1977). The relationship between mathematics achievement and spatial abilities among elementary school children. *Journal for Research in Mathematics Education, 8,* 211–215.

Guskey, T. R. (Ed.). (2000). *Evaluating professional development.* Thousand Oaks, CA: Corwin Press.

Gutiérrez, A., & Jaime, A. (1988). *Globality versus locality of the van Hiele levels of geometric reasoning.* Unpublished manuscript, Universidad De València, Valencia, Spain.

Haith, M. M., & Benson, J. B. (1998). Infant cognition. In W. Damon, D. Kuhn & R. S. Siegler (Eds.), *Handbook of child psychology (5th edition), Cognition, perception, and language* (Vol. 2, pp. 199–254). New York: Wiley.

Hall, G. E., & Hord, S. M. (2001). *Implementing change: Patterns, principles, and potholes.* Boston, MA: Allyn and Bacon.

Hall, G. S. (1891). The content of children's minds on entering school. *Pedagogical Seminary, 1,* 139–173.

Han, Y., & Ginsburg, H. P. (2001). Chinese and English mathematics language: The relation between linguistic clarity and mathematics performance. *Mathematical Thinking and Learning, 3,* 201–220.

Hannibal, M. A. Z., & Clements, D. H. (2008). Young children's understanding of basic geometric shapes. *Manuscript submitted for publication.*

Harris, L. J. (1981). Sex-related variations in spatial skill. In L. S. Liben, A. H. Patterson & N. Newcombe (Eds.), *Spatial representation and behavior across the life span* (pp. 83–125). New York: Academic Press.

Hart, B., & Risley, T. R. (1995). *Meaningful differences in the everyday experience of young American children.* Baltimore, MD: Paul H. Brookes.

Heck, D. J., Weiss, I. R., Boyd, S., & Howard, M. (2002). Lessons learned about planning and implementing statewide systemic initiatives in mathematics and science education. New Orleans, LA: American Educational Research Association.

Hegarty, M., & Kozhevnikov, M. (1999). Types of visual-spatial representations and mathematical problems-solving. *Journal of Educational Psychology, 91,* 684–689.

Hermer, L., & Spelke, E. (1996). Modularity and development: The case of spatial reorientation. *Cognition, 61,* 195–232.

Hershkowitz, R., Ben-Chaim, D., Hoyles, C., Lappan, G., Mitchelmore, M. C., & Vinner, S. (1990). Psychological aspects of learning geometry. In P. Nesher & J. Kilpatrick (Eds.), *Mathematics and cognition: A research synthesis by the International Group for the Psychology of Mathematics Education* (pp. 70–95). Cambridge, U.K.: Cambridge University Press.

Hershkowitz, R., & Dreyfus, T. (1991). Loci and visual thinking. In F. Furinghetti (Ed.), *Proceedings of the fifteenth annual meeting International Group for the Psychology of Mathematics Education* (Vol. II, pp. 181–188). Genova, Italy: Program Committee.

Heuvel-Panhuizen, M. v. d. (1996). *Assessment and realistic mathematics education.* Utrecht, The Netherlands: Freudenthal Institute, Utrecht University.

Hiebert, J. C. (1986). *Conceptual and procedural knowledge: The case of mathematics.* Hillsdale, NJ: Lawrence Erlbaum.

Hiebert, J. C. (1999). Relationships between research and the NCTM Standards. *Journal for Research in Mathematics Education, 30,* 3–19.

Hill, H. C., Rowan, B., & Ball, D. L. (2005). Effects of teachers' mathematical knowledge for teaching on student achievement. *American Educational Research Journal, 42,* 371–406.

Hillel, J., & Kieran, C. (1988). Schemas used by 12-year-olds in solving selected turtle geometry tasks. *Recherches en Didactique des Mathématiques, 8/1.2,* 61–103.

Hinkle, D. (2000). *School involvement in early childhood.* Washington, DC: National Institute on Early Childhood Development and Education, U.S. Department of Education Office of Educational Research and Improvement.

Hofmeister, A. M. (1993). Elitism and reform in school mathematics. *Remedial and Special Education, 14*(6), 8–13.

Hord, S., Rutherford, W., Huling-Austin, L., & Hall, G. (1987). *Taking charge of change.* Alexandria, VA: Association for Supervision and Curriculum Development.

Horne, M. (2005). The effects of number knowledge at school entry on subsequent number development: A five year longitudinal study. In P. Clarkson, A. Downtown, D. Gronn, M. Horne, A. McDonough, R. Pierce & A. Roche (Eds.), *Building connections: Research, theory and practice (Proceedings of the 28th annual conference of the Mathematics Education Research Group of Australasia)* (pp. 443–450). Melbourne, Australia: MERGA.

Howell, R. D., Scott, P. B., & Diamond, J. (1987). The effects of "instant" Logo computing language on the cognitive development of very young children. *Journal of Educational Computing Research, 3*(2), 249–260.

Hoyles, C., & Healy, L. (1997). Unfolding meanings for reflective symmetry. *International Journal of Computers for Mathematical Learning, 2,* 27–59.

Hoyles, C., & Noss, R. (1987). Synthesizing mathematical conceptions and their formalization through the construction of a Logo-based school mathematics curriculum. *International Journal of Mathematics Education, Science, and Technology, 18,* 581–595.

Hoyles, C., & Noss, R. (1992). A pedagogy for mathematical microworlds. *Educational Studies in Mathematics, 23,* 31–57.

Hoyles, C., & Sutherland, R. (1986). *When 45 equals 60.* London, England, University of London Institute of Education, Microworlds Project.

Huberman, M. (1992). Critical introduction. In M. G. Fullan (Ed.), *Successful school improvement* (pp. 1–20). Philadelphia, PA: Open University Press.

Huttenlocher, J., & Newcombe, N. (1984). The child's representation of information about location. In C. Sophian (Ed.), *The origin of cognitive skills* (pp. 81–111). Hillsdale, NJ: Lawrence Erlbaum Associates.

Huttenlocher, J., Newcombe, N., & Sandberg, E. H. (1994). The coding of spatial location in young children. *Cognitive Psychology, 27*(2), 115–147.

Huttenlocher, J., Newcombe, N. S., & Vasilyeva, M. (1999). Spatial scaling in young children. *Psychological Science, 10,* 393–398.

Ibbotson, A., & Bryant, P. E. (1976). The perpendicular error and the vertical effect in children's drawing. *Perception, 5,* 319–326.

Iverson, J. M., & Goldin-Meadow, S. (1997). What's communication got to do with it? Gesture in children blind from birth. *Developmental Psychology, 33,* 453–567.

Johnson, M. (1987). *The body in the mind.* Chicago: The University of Chicago Press.

Johnson, P. A. (1986). *Effects of computer-assisted instruction compared to teacher-directed instruction on comprehension of abstract concepts by the deaf.* Unpublished doctoral dissertation, Northern Illinois University.

Johnson-Gentile, K., Clements, D. H., & Battista, M. T. (1994). The effects of computer and non-computer environments on students' conceptualizations of geometric motions. *Journal of Educational Computing Research, 11*(2), 121–140.

Joram, E., Subrahmanyam, K., & Gelman, R. (1998). Measurement estimation: Learning to map the route from number to quantity and back. *Review of Educational Research, 68,* 413–449.

Jordan, N. C., Huttenlocher, J., & Levine, S. C. (1992). Differential calculation abilities in young children from middle- and low-income families. *Developmental Psychology, 28,* 644–653.

Jordan, N. C., Kaplan, D., Oláh, L. N., & Locuniak, M. N. (2006). Number sense growth in kindergarten: A longitudinal investigation of children at risk for mathematics difficulties. *Child Development, 77,* 153–175.

Jovignot, F. (1995). Can 5–6 year old children orientate themselves in a cave? *Scientific Journal of Orienteering, 11*(2), 64–75.

Kabanova-Meller, E. N. (1970). The role of the diagram in the application of geometric theorems. In J. Kilpatrick & I. Wirszup (Eds.), *Soviet studies in the psychology of learning and teaching mathematics (Vols. 4)* (pp. 7–49m). Chicago: University of Chicago Press.

Kamii, C., & Housman, L. B. (1999). *Young children reinvent arithmetic: Implications of Piaget's theory* (2nd ed.). New York: Teachers College Press.

Kamii, C., Miyakawa, Y., & Kato, Y. (2004). The development of logico-mathematical knowledge in a block-building activity at ages 1–4. *Journal of Research in Childhood Education, 19,* 13–26.

Kamii, C., Rummelsburg, J., & Kari, A. R. (2005). Teaching arithmetic to low-performing, low-SES first graders. *Journal of Mathematical Behavior, 24,* 39–50.

Kaput, J. J., Carraher, D. W., & Blanton, M. L. (Eds.). (2008). *Algebra in the early grades.* Mahwah, NJ: Lawrence Erlbaum Associates.

Karmiloff-Smith, A. (1984). Children's problem solving. In M. E. Lamb, A. L. Brown & B. Rogoff (Eds.), *Advances in developmental psychology (Vol. 3)* (pp. 39–90). Mahwah, NJ: Lawrence Erlbaum Associates.

Karmiloff-Smith, A. (1986). From meta-processes to conscious access: Evidence from children's metalinguistic and repair data. *Cognition, 23,* 95–147.

Karmiloff-Smith, A. (1990). Constraints on representational change: Evidence from children's drawing. *Cognition, 34,* 57–83.

Karmiloff-Smith, A. (1992). *Beyond modularity: A developmental perspective on cognitive science.* Cambridge, MA: MIT Press.

Kaser, J. S., Bourexis, P. S., Loucks-Horsley, S., & Raizen, S. A. (1999). *Enhancing program quality in science and mathematics.* Thousand Oaks, CA: Corwin Press.

Kay, C. S. (1987). *Is a square a rectangle? The development of first-grade students' understanding of quadrilaterals with implications for the van Hiele theory of the development of geometric thought.*

Kellman, P. J., & Banks, M. S. (1998). Infant visual perception. In W. Damon, D. Kuhn & R. S. Siegler (Eds.), *Handbook of child psychology (5th ed.), Cognition, perception, and language* (Vol. 2, pp. 103–146). New York: Wiley.

Kelly, G. N., Kelly, J. T., & Miller, R. B. (1986–87). Working with Logo: Do 5th and 6th graders develop a basic understanding of angles and distances? *Journal of Computers in Mathematics and Science Teaching, 6,* 23–27.

Kennedy, M. (1998). *Form and substance of inservice teacher education (Research Monograph No. 13).* Madison, WI: National Institute for Science Education, University of Wisconsin—Madison.

Kersh, J., Casey, B., & Young, J. M. (in press). Research on spatial skills and block building in girls and boys: The relationship to later mathematics learning. In B. Spodek & O. N. Saracho (Eds.), *Mathematics, science, and technology in early childhood education.*

Kieran, C. (1986a). Logo and the notion of angle among fourth and sixth grade children. In C. Hoyles & L. Burton (Eds.), *Proceedings of the tenth annual meeting of the International Group for the Psychology in Mathematics Education* (pp. 99–104). London: City University.

Kieran, C. (1986b). Turns and angles: What develops in Logo? In G. Lappan & R. Even (Eds.), *Proceedings of the eighth annual meeting of the North American Chapter of the International Group for the Psychology of Mathematics Education* (pp. 169–177). East Lansing, MI: Michigan State University.

Kieran, C. (2006). Research on the learning and teaching of algebra. In A. Gutiérrez & P. Boero (Eds.), *Handbook of research on the psychology of mathematics education: Past, present, and future* (pp. 11–49). Rotterdam, The Netherlands: Sense Publishers.

Kieran, C., & Hillel, J. (1990). "It's tough when you have to make the triangles angles": Insights from a computer-based geometry environment. *Journal of Mathematical Behavior, 9*, 99–127.

Kieran, C., Hillel, J., & Erlwanger, S. (1986). Perceptual and analytical schemas in solving structured turtle–geometry tasks. In C. Hoyles, R. Noss & R. Sutherland (Eds.), *Proceedings of the Second Logo and Mathematics Educators Conference* (pp. 154–161). London: University of London.

Kilpatrick, J., Swafford, J., & Findell, B. (2001). *Adding it up: Helping children learn mathematics.* Washington, DC: National Academy Press.

Klahr, D., & Chen, Z. (2003). Overcoming the positive-capture strategy in young children: Learning about indeterminacy. *Child Development, 74*, 1275–1296.

Klein, A., & Starkey, P. (2004). Fostering preschool children's mathematical development: Findings from the Berkeley Math Readiness Project. In D. H. Clements, J. Sarama & A.-M. DiBiase (Eds.), *Engaging young children in mathematics: Standards for early childhood mathematics education* (pp. 343–360). Mahwah, NJ: Lawrence Erlbaum Associates.

Klein, A., Starkey, P., & Ramirez, A. B. (2002). *Pre-K mathematics curriculum.* Glenview, IL: Scott Foresman.

Klingner, J. K., Ahwee, S., Pilonieta, P., & Menendez, R. (2003). Barriers and facilitators in scaling up research-based practices. *Exceptional Children, 69*, 411–429.

Konold, C., & Pollatsek, A. (2002). Data analysis as the search for signals in noisy processes. *Journal for Research in Mathematics Education, 33*, 259–289.

Kosslyn, S. M. (1983). *Ghosts in the mind's machine.* New York: W. W. Norton.

Kosslyn, S. M., Reiser, B. J., & Ball, T. M. (1978). Visual images preserve metric spatial information: Evidence from studies of image scanning. *Journal of Experimental Psychology: Human Perception and Performance, 4*(1), 47–60.

Kotovsky, L., & Gentner, D. (1996). Comparison and categorization in the development of relational similarity. *Child Development, 67*, 2797–2822.

Kouba, V. L., Brown, C. A., Carpenter, T. P., Lindquist, M. M., Silver, E. A., & Swafford, J. O. (1988). Results of the fourth NAEP assessment of mathematics: Measurement, geometry, data interpretation, attitudes, and other topics. *Arithmetic Teacher, 35*(9), 10–16.

Krajewski, K. (2005, April). *Prediction of mathematical (dis-)abilities in primary school: A 4-year German longitudinal study from Kindergarten to grade 4* Paper presented at the Biennial Meeting of the Society for Research in Child Development, Atlanta, GA.

Kraner, R. E. (1977). The acquisition age of quantitative concepts of children from three to six years old. *Journal of Experimental Education, 46*(2), 52–59.

Kronholz, J. (2000, May 16). See Johnny jump! Hey, isn't it math he's really doing? *The Wall Street Journal*, p. A1; A12.

Krutetskii, V. A. (1976). *The psychology of mathematical abilities in schoolchildren.* Chicago: University of Chicago Press.

Kühne, C., van den Heuvel-Panhulzen, M., & Ensor, P. (2005). From the Lotto game to subtracting two-digit numbers in first-graders. In H. L. Chick & J. L. Vincent (Eds.), *Proceedings of the 29th Conference of the International Group for the Psychology in Mathematics Education* (Vol. 3, pp. 249–256). Melbourne, AU: PME.

Kull, J. A. (1986). Learning and Logo. In P. F. Campbell & G. G. Fein (Eds.), *Young children and microcomputers* (pp. 103–130). Englewood Cliffs, NJ: Prentice-Hall.

Kwong, C. W., Joseph, Y. K. K., Eric, C. C. M., Khoh, L.-T. S., Gek, C. K., & Eng, N. L. (2007). Development of mathematics pedagogical content knowledge in student teachers. *The Mathematics Educator, 10*(2), 27–54.

Kynigos, C. (1991). Can children use the turtle metaphor to extend their learning to include non-intrinsic geometry? In F. Furinghetti (Ed.), *Proceedings of the 15th annual meeting of the International Group for the Psychology of Mathematics Education* (Vol. II, pp. 269–276). Genova, Italy: Program Committee, 15th PME Conference.

Landau, B. (1988). The construction and use of spatial knowledge in blind and sighted children. In J. Stiles-Davis, M. Kritchevsky & U. Bellugi (Eds.), *Spatial cognition: Brain bases and development* (pp. 343–371). Mahwah, NJ: Lawrence Erlbaum Associates.

Landau, B. (1996). Multiple geometric representations of objects in languages and language learners. In P. Bloom, M. A. Peterson, L. Nadel & M. F. Garrett (Eds.), *Language and space* (pp. 317–363). Cambridge, MA: MIT Press.

Landau, B., Gleitman, H., & Spelke, E. (1981). Spatial knowledge and geometric representation in a child blind from birth. *Science, 213*, 1275–1277.

Lappan, G. (1999). Geometry: The forgotten strand. *NCTM News Bulletin, 36*(5), 3.

Lawler, R. (1985). *Computer experience and cognitive development: Children's learning in a computer culture.* New York: John Wiley & Sons.

Lean, G., & Clements, M. A. (1981). Spatial ability, visual imagery, and mathematical performance. *Educational Studies in Mathematics, 12*, 267–299.

Learmonth, A. E., Newcombe, N. S., & Huttenlocher, J. (2001). Toddlers' use of metric informaiton and landmarks to reorient. *Journal of Experimental Child Psychology, 80*, 225–244.

Lebron-Rodriguez, D. E., & Pasnak, R. (1977). Induction of intellectual gains in blind children. *Journal of Experimental Child Psychology, 24*, 505–515.

Lee, J. S., & Ginsburg, H. P. (2007). What is appropriate mathematics education for four-year-olds? *Journal of Early Childhood Research, 5*(1), 2–31.

Lee, V. E., & Burkam, D. T. (2002). *Inequality at the starting gate.* Washington, DC: Economic Policy Institute.

Leeb-Lundberg, K. (1996). The block builder mathematician. In E. S. Hirsh (Ed.), *The block book* (3rd ed., pp. 35–60). Washington, DC: National Association for the Education of Young Children.

Lehrer, R., Jenkins, M., & Osana, H. (1998). Longitudinal study of children's reasoning about space and geometry. In R. Lehrer & D. Chazan (Eds.), *Designing learning environments for developing understanding of geometry and space* (pp. 137–167). Mahwah, NJ: Lawrence Erlbaum Associates.

Lehrer, R., Randle, L., & Sancilio, L. (1989). Learning pre-proof geometry with Logo. *Cognition and Instruction, 6*, 159–184.

Lehrer, R., & Smith, P. C. (1986). Logo learning: Are two heads better than one? San Francisco, CA: American Educational Research Association.

Lester, F. K., Jr., & Wiliam, D. (2002). On the purpose of mathematics education research: Making productive contributions to policy and practice. In L. D. English (Ed.), *Handbook of International Research in Mathematics Education* (pp. 489–506). Mahwah, NJ: Lawrence Erlbaum Associates.

Leushina, A. M. (1974/1991). *The development of elementary mathematical concepts in preschool children* (Vol. 4). Reston, VA: National Council of Teachers of Mathematics.

Levine, S. C., Huttenlocher, J., Taylor, A., & Langrock, A. (1999). Early sex differences in spatial skill. *Developmental Psychology, 35*(4), 940–949.

Liben, L. S. (1978). Performance on Piagetian spatial tasks as a function of sex, field dependence, and training. *Merrill-Palmer Quarterly, 24*, 97–110.

Liben, L. S. (1988). Conceptual issues in the development of spatial cognition. In J. Stiles-Davis, M. Kritchevsky & U. Bellugi (Eds.), *Spatial cognition: Brain bases and development* (pp. 145–201). Mahwah, NJ: Lawrence Erlbaum Associates.

Liben, L. S., & Downs, R. M. (1989). Understanding maps as symbols: The development of map concepts in children. In H. W. Reese (Ed.), *Advances in child development and behavior: Vol. 22* (pp. 145–201). San Diego: Academic Press.

Liben, L. S., Moore, M. L., & Golbeck, S. L. (1982). Preschoolers' knowledge of their classroom environment. Evidence from small-scale and life-size spatial tasks. *Child Development, 53*, 1275–1284.

Liben, L. S., & Myers, L. J. (2007). Developmental changes in children's understanding of maps: What, when, and how? In J. M. Plumert, & J. P. Spencer (Eds.), *The emerging spatial mind* (pp. 193–218). Oxford, UK: Oxford University Press.

Liben, L. S., & Yekel, C. A. (1996). Preschoolers' understanding of plan and oblique maps: The role of geometric and representational correspondence. *Child Development, 67*(6), 2780–2796.

Lockman, J. J., & Pick, H. L., Jr. (1984). Problems of scale in spatial development. In C. Sophian (Ed.), *Origins of cognitive skills* (pp. 3–26). Mahwah, NJ: Lawrence Erlbaum Associates.

Loeb, S., Bridges, M., Bassok, D., Fuller, B., & Rumberger, R. (in press). How much is too much? The influence of preschool centers on children's development nationwide. *Economics of Education Review.*

Loewenstein, J., & Gentner, D. (2001). Spatial mapping in preschoolers: Close comparisons facilitate far mappings. *Journal of Cognition and Development, 2*, 189–219.

Logan, G. (1994). Spatial attenion and the apprehension of spatial relations. *Journal of Experimental Psychology: Human Perception and Performance, 20,* 1015–1036.

Lourenco, S. F., Huttenlocher, J., & Vasilyeva, M. (2005). Toddlers' representations of space. *Psychological Science, 16,* 255.

Mackay, C. K., Brazendale, A. H., & Wilson, L. F. (1972). Concepts of horizontal and vertical: A methodological note. *Developmental Psychology, 7,* 232–237.

Magnuson, K. A., Meyers, M. K., Rathbun, A., & West, J. (2004). Inequality in preschool education and school readiness. *American Educational Research Journal, 41,* 115–157.

Malofeeva, E., Day, J., Saco, X., Young, L., & Ciancio, D. (2004). Construction and evaluation of a number sense test with Head Start children. *Journal of Education Psychology, 96,* 648–659.

Mark-Zigdon, N., & Tirosh, D. (2008). What is a legitimate arithmetic number sentence? The case of kindergarten and first-grade children. In J. J. Kaput, D. W. Carraher & M. L. Blanton (Eds.), *Algebra in the early grades* (pp. 201–210). Mahwah, NJ: Lawrence Erlbaum Associates.

Mayberry, J. (1983). The van Hiele levels of geometric thought in undergraduate preservice teaching. *Journal for Research in Mathematics Education, 14,* 58–69.

McClelland, J. L., Rumelhart, D. E., & the PDP Research Group. (1986). *Parallel distributed processing: Explorations in the microstructure of cognition. Volume 2: Psychological and biological models.* Cambridge, MA: MIT Press.

McCoy, L. P. (1996). Computer-based mathematics learning. *Journal of Research on Computing in Education, 28,* 438–460.

McDonough, L. (1999). Early declarative memory for location. *British Journal of Developmental Psychology, 17,* 381–402.

McGee, M. G. (1979). Human spatial abilities: Psychometric studies and environmental, genetic, hormonal, and neurological influences. *Psychological Bulletin, 86,* 889–918.

McLaughlin, K. L. (1935). Number ability of preschool children. *Childhood Education, 11,* 348–353.

McPhail, D. (2004). Professional learning in the teaching of area. In I. J. Putt, R. Faragher & M. McLean (Eds.), *Mathematics education for the third millennium: Towards 2010 (Proceedings of the 27th annual conference of the Mathematics Education Research Group of Australasia)* (pp. 359–366). Townsville, Australia: MERGA.

Metz, K. E. (1993). Preschoolers' developing knowledge of the pan balance: From new representation to transformed problem solving. *Cognition and Instruction, 11,* 31–93.

Millar, S., & Ittyerah, M. (1992). Movement imagery in young and congenitally blind children: Mental practice without visuo-spatial information. *International Journal of Behavioral Development, 15,* 125–146.

Miller, K. F., Smith, C. M., Zhu, J., & Zhang, H. (1995). Preschool origins of cross-national differences in mathematical competence: The role of number-naming systems. *Psychological Science, 6,* 56–60.

Miller, P. (1967). The effects of age and training on children's ability to understand certain basic concepts. *Dissertation Abstracts International, 28,* 2161B–2162B.

Miller, R. B., Kelly, G. N., & Kelly, J. T. (1988). Effects of Logo computer programming experience on problem solving and spatial relations ability. *Contemporary Educational Psychology, 13,* 348–357.

Minsky, M. (1986). *The society of mind.* New York: Simon and Schuster.

Mitchelmore, M. C. (1989). The development of children's concepts of angle. In G. Vergnaud, J. Rogalski, & M. Artique (Eds.), *Proceedings of the 13th Conference of the International Group for the Psychology of Mathematics Education* (pp. 304–311). Paris: City University.

Mitchelmore, M. C. (1992). Children's concepts of perpendiculars. In W. Geeslin & K. Graham (Eds.), *Proceedings of the 16th Conference of the International Group for the Psychology in Mathematics Education* (Vol. 2, pp. 120–127). Durham, NH: Program Committee of the 16th PME Conference.

Mitchelmore, M. C. (1993). The development of pre-angle concepts. In A. R. Baturo & L. J. Harris (Eds.), *New directions in research on geometry* (pp. 87–93). Brisbane, Australia: Centre for Mathematics and Science Education, Queensland University of Technology.

Mitchelmore, M. C. (1998). Young students' concepts of turning and angle. *Cognition and Instruction, 16,* 265–284.

Mix, K. S. Huttenlocher, J., & Levine, S. C. (1996). Do preschool children recognize auditory-visual numerical correspondences? *Child Development, 67,* 1592–1608.

Mix, K. S. Huttenlocher, J., & Levine, S. C. (2002). *Quantitative development in infancy and early childood*. New York: Oxford University Press.

Mix, K. S. Levine, S. C. & Huttenlocher, J. (1997). Numerical abstraction in infants: Another look. *Developmental Psychology, 33*, 423–428.

Mix, K. S., Sandhofer, C. M., & Baroody, A. J. (2005). Number words and number concepts: The interplay of verbal and nonverbal processes in early quantitative development. In R. Kail (Ed.), *Advances in Child Development and Behavior* (Vol. 33, pp. 305–345). New York: Academic Press.

Mohrman, S. A., & Lawler III, E. E. (1996). Motivation for school reform. In S. H. Fuhrman & J. A. O'Day (Eds.), *Rewards and reform: Creating educational incentives that work* (pp. 115–143). San Francisco: Jossey-Bass.

Morrongiello, B. A., Timney, B., Humphrey, G. K., Anderson, S., & Skory, C. (1995). Spatial knowledge in blind and sighted children. *Journal of Experimental Child Psychology, 59*, 211–233.

Moyer, J. C. (1978). The relationship between the mathematical structure of Euclidean transformations and the spontaneously developed cognitive structures of young children. *Journal for Research in Mathematics Education, 9*, 83–92.

Moyer, P. S., Niezgoda, D., & Stanley, J. (2005). Young children's use of virtual manipulatives and other forms of mathematical representations. In W. Masalski & P. C. Elliott (Eds.), *Technology-supported mathematics learning environments: 67th Yearbook* (pp. 17–34). Reston, VA: National Council of Teachers of Mathematics.

Muir, S. P., & Cheek, H. N. (1986). Mathematics and the map skill curriculum. *School Science and Mathematics, 86*, 284–291.

Mulligan, J., Mitchelmore, M. C., & Prescott, A. (2005). Case studies of children's development of structure in early mathematics: A two-year longitudinal study. In H. L. Chick & J. L. Vincent (Eds.), *Proceedings of the 29th Conference of the International Group for the Psychology of Mathematics Education* (Vol. 4, pp. 1–8). Melbourne, AU: PME.

Mulligan, J., Mitchelmore, M. C., & Prescott, A. (2006). Integrating concepts and processes in early mathematics: The Australian Pattern and Structure Awareness Project (PASMAP). In J. Novotná, H. Moraová, M. Krátká & N. a. Stehlíková (Eds.), *Proceedings of the 30th Conference of the International Group for the Psychology in Mathematics Education* (Vol. 4, pp. 209–216). Prague, Czecho: Charles University.

Mulligan, J., Prescott, A., & Mitchelmore, M. C. (2004). Children's development of structure in early mathematics. In M. J. Høines & A. B. Fuglestad (Eds.), *Proceedings of the 28th Conference of the International Group for the Psychology in Mathematics Education* (Vol. 3, pp. 393–401). Bergen, Norway: Bergen University College.

Mulligan, J., Prescott, A., Mitchelmore, M. C., & Outhred, L. (2005). Taking a closer look at young students' images of area measurement. *Australian Primary Mathematics Classroom, 10*(2), 4–8.

Mulligan, J., Prescott, A., Papic, M., & Mitchelmore, M. C. (2006). Improving early numeracy through a Pattern and Structure Mathematics Awareness Program (PASMAP). In P. Clarkson, A. Downtown, D. Gronn, M. Horne, A. McDonough, R. Pierce & A. Roche (Eds.), *Building connections: Theory, research and practice (Proceedings of the 28th annual conference of the Mathematics Education Research Group of Australia)* (pp. 376–383). Melbourne, Australia: MERGA.

Mullis, I. V. S., Martin, M. O., Beaton, A. E., Gonzalez, E. J., Kelly, D. L., & Smith, T. A. (1997). *Mathematics achievement in the primary school years: IEA's third international mathematics and science study (TIMSS)*. Chestnut Hill, MA: Center for the Study of Testing, Evaluation, and Educational Policy, Boston College.

Munakata, Y. (1998). Infant perseveration and implications for object permanence theories: A PDP model of the AB task. *Developmental Science, 1*(2), 161–211.

Murata, A., & Fuson, K. C. (2006). Teaching as assisting individual constructive paths within an interdependent class learning zone: Japanese first graders learning to add using 10. *Journal for Research in Mathematics Education, 37*, 421–456.

Murphy, C. M., & Wood, D. J. (1981). Learning from pictures: The use of pictorial information by young children. *Journal of Experimental Child Psychology, 32*, 279–297.

Myers, L. J., & Liben, L. S. (2008). The role of intentionality and iconicity in children's developing comprehension and production of cartographic symbols. *Child Development.*

Nadel, L., & Moscovitch, M. (1998). Hippocampal contributions to cortical plasticity. *Neuropharmacology, 37*, 431–439.

Natriello, G., McDill, E. L., & Pallas, A. M. (1990). *Schooling disadvantaged children: Racing against catastrophe*. New York: Teachers College Press.

NCES. (2000). *America's kindergartners (NCES 2000070)*. Washington, DC: National Center for Education Statistics, U.S. Government Printing Office.

NCTM. (1989). *Curriculum and evaluation standards for school mathematics*. Reston, VA: National Council of Teachers of Mathematics.

NCTM. (2000). *Principles and standards for school mathematics*. Reston, VA: National Council of Teachers of Mathematics.

NCTM. (2006). *Curriculum focal points for prekindergarten through grade 8 mathematics: A quest for coherence*. Reston, VA: National Council of Teachers of Mathematics.

Nettles, S. M. (1993). Coaching in community settings. *Equity and Choice, 9*(2), 35–37.

Newcombe, N. S. (1989). The development of spatial perspective taking. In H. W. Reese (Ed.), *Advances in Child Development and Behavior* (Vol. 22, pp. 203–247). New York: Academic Press.

Newcombe, N. S., & Sanderson, H. L. (1993). *The relation between preschoolers' everyday activities and spatial ability*. New Orleans, LA: Society for Research in Child Development.

Newcombe, N. S. (2002). The nativist-empiricist controversy in the context of recent research on spatial and quantitative development. *Psychological Science, 13*(5), 395–401.

Newcombe, N. S., & Huttenlocher, J. (2000). *Making space: The development of spatial representation and reasoning*. Cambridge, MA: MIT Press.

Newcombe, N. S., Huttenlocher, J., Drummey, A. B., & Wiley, J. G. (1998). The development of spatial location coding: Place learning and dead reckoning in the second and third years. *Cognitive Development, 13*, 185–200.

Newcombe, N. S., & Sluzenski, J. (2004). Starting points and change in early spatial development. In G. L. Allen (Ed.), *Human spatial memory: Remembering where* (pp. 25–40). Mahwah, NJ: Lawrence Erlbaum Associates.

Nieuwoudt, H. D., & van Niekerk, R. (1997). The spatial competence of young children through the development of solids. Chicago: American Educational Research Association.

NMP. (2008). *Foundations for Success: The Final Report of the National Mathematics Advisory Panel*. Washington D.C.: U.S. Department of Education, Office of Planning, Evaluation and Policy Development.

Noss, R. (1987). Children's learning of geometrical concepts through Logo. *Journal for Research in Mathematics Education, 18*, 343–362.

Noss, R., & Hoyles, C. (1992). Afterword: Looking back and looking forward. In C. Hoyles & R. Noss (Eds.), *Learning mathematics and Logo* (pp. 427–468). Cambridge, MA: MIT Press.

NRC. (2006). *Learning to think spatially*. Washington, DC: National Research Council, National Academy Press.

O'Keefe, J., & Nadel, L. (1978). *The hippocampus as a cognitive map*. Oxford, U.K.: Oxford University Press.

Olive, J. (1991). Logo programming and geometric understanding: An in-depth study. *Journal for Research in Mathematics Education, 22*, 90–111.

Olive, J., Lankenau, C. A., & Scally, S. P. (1986). *Teaching and understanding geometric relationships through Logo: Phase II. Interim Report: The Atlanta–Emory Logo Project*. Altanta, GA: Emory University.

Olson, A. T., Kieren, T. E., & Ludwig, S. (1987). Linking Logo, levels, and language in mathematics. *Educational Studies in Mathematics, 18*, 359–370.

Olson, J. K. (1985). Using Logo to supplement the teaching of geometric concepts in the elementary school classroom. *Dissertation Abstracts International, 47*, 819A.

Osborne, R. T., & Lindsey, J. M. (1967). A longtitudinal investigation of change in the factorial composition of intelligence with age in young children. *Journal of Genetic Psychology, 110*, 49–58.

Outhred, L. N., & Sardelich, S. (1997). Problem solving in kindergarten: The development of representations. In F. Biddulph & K. Carr (Eds.), *People in Mathematics Education. Proceedings of the 20th Annual Conference of the Mathematics Education Research Group of Australasia* (Vol. 2, pp. 376–383). Rotorua, New Zealand: Mathematics Education Research Group of Australasia.

Owens, K. (1992). Spatial thinking takes shape through primary-school experiences. In W. Geeslin

& K. Graham (Eds.), *Proceedings of the 16th Conference of the International Group for the Psychology in Mathematics Education* (Vol. 2, pp. 202–209). Durham, NH: Program Committee of the 16th PME Conference.

Owens, K. (1999). The role of visualization in young students' learning. In O. Zaslavsky (Ed.), *Proceedings of the 23rd Conference of the International Group for the Psychology of Mathematics Education* (Vol. 1, pp. 220–234). Haifa, Isreal: Technion.

Papic, M., & Mulligan, J. (2007). The growth of early mathematical patterning: An intervention study. In J. Watson & K. Beswick (Eds.), *Mathematics: Essential research, essential practice (Proceedings of the 30th annual conference of the Mathematics Education Research Group of Australasia, Hobart)* (pp. 591–600). Adelaide, Australia: MERGA.

Parker, T. H., & Baldridge, S. J. (2004). *Elementary mathematics for teachers.* Quebecor World, MI: Sefton-Ash Publishing.

Pasnak, R., Brown, K., Kurkjian, M., Mattran, K., Triana, E., & Yamamoto, N. (1987). Cognitive gains through training on classification, seriation, conservation. *Genetic, Social, and General Psychology Monographs, 113,* 295–321.

Peisner-Feinberg, E. S., Burchinal, M. R., Clifford, R. M., Culkins, M. L., Howes, C., Kagan, S. L., et al. (2001). The relation of preschool child-care quality to children's cognitive and social developmental trajectories through second grade. *Child Development, 72,* 1534–1553.

Perham, F. (1978). An investigation into the effect of instruction on the acquisition of transformation geometry concepts in first grade children and subsequent transfer to general spatial ability. In R. Lesh & D. Mierkiewicz (Eds.), *Concerning the development of spatial and geometric concepts* (pp. 229–241). Columbus, OH: ERIC Clearinghouse for Science, Mathematics, and Environmental Education.

Perry, B., & Dockett, S. (2002). Young children's access to powerful mathematical ideas. In L. D. English (Ed.), *Handbook of International Research in Mathematics Education* (pp. 81–111). Mahwah, NJ: Lawrence Erlbaum Associates.

Peterson, P. L., Carpenter, T. P., & Fennema, E. H. (1989). Teachers' knowledge of students' knowledge in mathematics problem solving: Correlational and case analyses. *Journal of Educational Psychology, 81,* 558–569.

Philipp, R. A., Ambrose, R., Lamb, L. L. C., Sowder, J. T., Schappelle, B. P., Sowder, L., et al. (2007). Effects of early field experiences on the mathematical content knowledge and beliefs of prospective elementary school teachers: An experimental study. *Journal for Research in Mathematics Education, 38,* 438–476.

Piaget, J. (1971/1974). *Understanding causality.* New York: Norton.

Piaget, J., & Inhelder, B. (1967). *The child's conception of space* (F. J. Langdon & J. L. Lunzer, Trans.). New York: W. W. Norton.

Piaget, J., & Inhelder, B. (1971). *Mental imagery in the child.* London, U.K.: Routledge and Kegan Paul.

Piaget, J., Inhelder, B., & Szeminska, A. (1960). *The child's conception of geometry.* London: Routledge and Kegan Paul.

Piaget, J., & Szeminska, A. (1952). *The child's conception of number.* London: Routledge and Kegan Paul.

Pianta, R. C., Howes, C., Burchinal, M. R., Bryant, D., Clifford, R., Early, D., et al. (2005). Features of pre-kindergarten programs, classrooms, and teachers: Do they predict observed classroom quality and child–teacher interactions? *Applied Developmental Science, 9,* 144–159.

Pillow, B. H., & Flavell, J. H. (1986). Young children's knowledge about visual perception: Projective size and shape. *Child Development, 57,* 125–135.

Pinel, P., Piazza, D., Le Bihan, D., & Dehaene, S. (2004). Distributed and overlapping cerebral representations of number, size, and luminance during comparative judgments. *Neuron, 41,* 983–993.

Plumert, J. M., & Nichols-Whitehead, P. (1996). Parental scaffolding of young children's spatial communication. *Developmental Psychology, 32*(3), 523–532.

Poag, C. K., Cohen, R., & Weatherford, D. L. (1983). Spatial representations of young children: The role of self- versus adult-directed movement and viewing. *Journal of Experimental Child Psychology, 35,* 172–179.

Porter, A. C. (1989). A curriculum out of balance: The case of elementary school mathematics. *Educational Researcher, 18,* 9–15.

Presmeg, N. C. (1997). Generalization using imagery in mathematics. In L. D. English (Ed.),

Mathematical reasoning: Analogies, metaphors, and images (pp. 299–312). Mahwah, NJ: Lawrence Erlbaum Associates.

Presson, C. C. (1982). Using matter as a spatial landmark: Evidence against egocentric coding in infancy. *Developmental Psychology, 18*, 699–703.

Presson, C. C. (1987). The development of spatial cognition: Secondary uses of spatial information. In N. Eisenberg (Ed.), *Contemporary topics in developmental psychology* (pp. 77–112). New York: John Wiley & Sons.

Presson, C. C., & Somerville, S. C. (1985). Beyond egocentrism: A new look at the beginnings of spatial representation. In H. M. Wellman (Ed.), *Children's searching: The development of search skill and spatial representation* (pp. 1–26). Mahwah, NJ: Lawrence Erlbaum Associates.

Prigge, G. R. (1978). The differential effects of the use of manipulative aids on the learning of geometric concepts by elementary school children. *Journal for Research in Mathematics Education, 9*, 361–367.

Pylyshyn, Z. W. (1973). What the mind's eye tells the mind's brain: A critique of mental imagery. *Psychological Bulletin, 80*, 1–24.

Pylyshyn, Z. W. (1981). The imagery debate: Analogue media versus tacit knowledge. *Psychological Review, 88*, 16–45.

Pylyshyn, Z. W. (2003). *Seeing and visualizing: It's not what you think.* Cambridge, MA: MIT Press/Bradford Books.

Razel, M., & Eylon, B.-S. (1986). Developing visual language skills: The Agam Program. *Journal of Visual Verbal Languaging, 6*(1), 49–54.

Razel, M., & Eylon, B.-S. (1990). Development of visual cognition: Transfer effects of the Agam program. *Journal of Applied Developmental Psychology, 11*, 459–485.

Rea, R. E., & Reys, R. E. (1971). Competencies of entering kindergarteners in geometry, number, money, and measurement. *School Science and Mathematics, 71*, 389–402.

Regier, T., & Carlson, L. (2002). Spatial language: Perceptual constraints and linguistic variation. In N. L. Stein, P. J. Bauer & M. Rabinowitz (Eds.), *Representation, memory, and development. Essays in honor of Jean Mandler* (pp. 199–221). Mahwah, NJ: Lawrence Erlbaum Associates.

Resnick, L. B. (1994). Situated rationalism: Biological and social preparation for learning. In H. L. A. & S. A. Gelman (Eds.), *Mapping the mind. Domain-specificity in cognition and culture* (pp. 474–493). Cambridge, MA: Cambridge University Press.

Reys, R. E., & Rea, R. E. (1970). The comprehensive mathematics inventory: An experimental instrument for assessing the mathematical competencies of children entering school. *Journal for Research in Mathematics Education, 1*, 180–186.

Rieser, J. J. (1979). Spatial orientation of six-month-old infants. *Child Development, 50*, 1078–1087.

Rieser, J. J., Doxsey, P. A., McCarrell, N. S., & Brooks, P. H. (1982). Wayfinding and toddlers' use of information from an aerial view. *Developmental Psychology, 18*, 714–720.

Rieser, J. J., Garing, A. E., & Young, M. F. (1994). Imagery, action, and young children's spatial orientation: It's not being there that counts, it's what one has in mind. *Child Development, 65*, 1262–1278.

Rittle-Johnson, B., & Siegler, R. S. (1998). The relation between conceptual and procedural knowledge in learning mathematics: A review. In C. Donlan (Ed.), *The development of mathematical skills* (pp. 75–110). East Sussex, UK: Psychology Press.

Roberts, R. J., Jr., & Aman, C. J. (1993). Developmental differences in giving directions: Spatial frames of reference and mental rotation. *Child Development, 64*, 1258–1270.

Robinson, N. M., Abbot, R. D., Berninger, V. W., & Busse, J. (1996). The structure of abilities in math-precocious young children: Gender similarities and differences. *Journal of Educational Psychology, 88*(2), 341–352.

Rogers, E. M. (2003). *Diffusion of innovations* (Fourth ed.). New York: The Free Press.

Rosser, R. A. (1994). The developmental course of spatial cognition: Evidence for domain multidimensionality. *Child Study Journal, 24*, 255–280. .

Rosser, R. A., Ensing, S. S., Glider, P. J., & Lane, S. (1984). An information-processing analysis of children's accuracy in predicting the appearance of rotated stimuli. *Child Development, 55*, 2204–2211.

Rosser, R. A., Horan, P. F., Mattson, S. L., & Mazzeo, J. (1984). Comprehension of Euclidean space in young children: The early emergence of understanding and its limits. *Genetic Psychology Monographs, 110*, 21–41.

Rosser, R. A., Lane, S., & Mazzeo, J. (1988). Order of acquisition of related geometric competencies in young children. *Child Study Journal, 18,* 75–90.

Salem, J. R. (1989). Using Logo and BASIC to teach mathematics to fifth and sixth graders. *Dissertation Abstracts International, 50,* 1608A.

Sandberg, E. H., & Huttenlocher, J. (1996). The development of hierarchical representation of two-dimensional space. *Child Development, 67*(3), 721–739.

Sandhofer, C. M., & Smith, L. B. (1999). Learning color words involves learning a system of mappings. *Developmental Psychology, 35,* 668–679.

Sarama, J. (2002). Listening to teachers: Planning for professional development. *Teaching Children Mathematics, 9,* 36–39.

Sarama, J., & Clements, D. H. (2005, April). *Mathematics knowledge of low-income entering pre-schoolers.* Paper presented at the American Educational Research Association, Montreal, Canada.

Sarama, J., & Clements, D. H. (2008). Mathematics knowledge of low-income entering pre-schoolers. *Manuscript submitted for publication.*

Sarama, J., Clements, D. H., & Henry, J. J. (1998). Network of influences in an implementation of a mathematics curriculum innovation. *International Journal of Computers for Mathematical Learning, 3,* 113–148.

Sarama, J., Clements, D. H., Henry, J. J., & Swaminathan, S. (1996). Multidisciplinary research perspectives on an implementation of a computer-based mathematics innovation. In E. Jakubowski, D. Watkins & H. Biske (Eds.), *Proceedings of the 18th annual meeting of the North America Chapter of the International Group for the Psychology of Mathematics Education* (Vol. 2, pp. 560–565). Columbus, OH: ERIC Clearinghouse for Science, Mathematics, and Environmental Education.

Sarama, J., Clements, D. H., Starkey, P., Klein, A., & Wakeley, A. (2008). Scaling up the imple-mentation of a pre-kindergarten mathematics curriculum: Teaching for understanding with trajectories and technologies. *Journal of Research on Educational Effectiveness, 1,* 89–119.

Sarama, J., Clements, D. H., Swaminathan, S., McMillen, S., & González Gómez, R. M. (2003). Development of mathematical concepts of two-dimensional space in grid environments: An exploratory study. *Cognition and Instruction, 21,* 285–324.

Sarama, J., Clements, D. H., & Vukelic, E. B. (1996). The role of a computer manipulative in foster-ing specific psychological/mathematical processes. In E. Jakubowski, D. Watkins & H. Biske (Eds.), *Proceedings of the 18th annual meeting of the North America Chapter of the Inter-national Group for the Psychology of Mathematics Education* (Vol. 2, pp. 567–572). Columbus, OH: ERIC Clearinghouse for Science, Mathematics, and Environmental Education.

Sarama, J., & DiBiase, A.-M. (2004). The professional development challenge in preschool mathematics. In D. H. Clements, J. Sarama & A.-M. DiBiase (Eds.), *Engaging young children in mathematics: Standards for early childhood mathematics education* (pp. 415–446). Mahwah, NJ: Lawrence Erlbaum Associates.

Saxe, G. B., Guberman, S. R., & Gearhart, M. (1987). Social processes in early number development. *Monographs of the Society for Research in Child Development, 52*(2, Serial #216).

Schifter, D. (1999). Reasoning about operation: Early algebraic thinking in grades K-6. In L. V. Stiff (Ed.), *Developing mathematics reasoning in grades K-12, 1999 Yearbook of the National Council of Teachers of Mathematics* (pp. 62–81). Reston, VA: National Council of Teachers of Mathematics.

Schliemann, A. C. D., Carraher, D. W., & Brizuela, B. M. (2007). *Bringing out the algebraic character of arithmetic.* Mahway, NJ: Lawrence Erlbaum Associates.

Schoen, H. L., Cebulla, K. J., Finn, K. F., & Fi, C. (2003). Teacher variables that relate to student achievement when using a standards-based curriculum. *Journal for Research in Mathematics Education, 34*(3), 228–259.

Schoenfeld, A. H. (2008). Algebra in the early grades. In J. J. Kaput, D. W. Carraher & M. L. Blanton (Eds.), (pp. 479–510). Mahwah, NJ: Lawrence Erlbaum Associates.

Scholnick, E. K., Fein, G. G., & Campbell, P. F. (1990). Changing predictors of map use in way-finding. *Developmental Psychology, 26,* 188–193.

Schultz, K. A., & Austin, J. D. (1983). Directional effects in transformational tasks. *Journal for Research in Mathematics Education, 14,* 95–101.

Schwartz, S. (2004) "Explorations in Graphing with Prekindergarten Children", in *International Perspectives on Learning and Teaching Mathematics.* National Center for Mathematics, Goteborg University, Box 160, SE-405 30 Goteborg, Sweden. p. 83–96.

Seidel, T., & Shavelson, R. J. (2007). Teaching effectiveness research in the past decade: The role of theory and research design in disentangling meta-analysis results. *Review of Educational Research, 77*(4), 454–499.

Senk, S. L. (1989). Van Hiele levels and achievement in writing geometry proofs. *Journal for Research in Mathematics Education, 20*, 309–321.

Seo, K.-H., & Ginsburg, H. P. (2004). What is developmentally appropriate in early childhood mathematics education? In D. H. Clements, J. Sarama & A.-M. DiBiase (Eds.), *Engaging young children in mathematics: Standards for early childhood mathematics education* (pp. 91–104). Mahwah, NJ: Lawrence Erlbaum Associates.

Serbin, L. A., & Connor, J. M. (1979). Sex-typing of children's play preferences and patterns of cognitive performance. *The Journal of Genetic Psychology, 134*, 315–316.

Shavelson, R. J., & Towne, L. (Eds.). (2002). *Scientific research in education.* Washington, DC: National Research Council, National Academy Press.

Shepard, R. N. (1978). The mental image. *American Psychologist, 33*, 125–137.

Shepard, R. N., & Cooper, L. A. (1982). *Mental images and their transformations.* Cambridge, MA: The MIT Press.

Showers, B., Joyce, B., & Bennett, B. (1987). Synthesis of research on staff development: A framework for future study and a state-of-the-art analysis. *Educational Leadership, 45*(3), 77–87.

Shusterman, A., & Spelke, E. (2004). Investigations in the development of spatial reasoning: Core knowledge and adult competence.

Siegel, A. W., & Schadler, M. (1977). The development of young children's spatial representations of their classrooms. *Child Development, 48*, 388–394.

Siegel, A. W., & White, S. H. (1975). The development of spatial representations of large-scale environments. In H. W. Resse (Ed.), *Advances in Child Development and Behavior* (Vol. 10, pp. 9–55). New York: Academic Press.

Siegler, R. S. (1993). Adaptive and non-adaptive characteristics of low income children's strategy use. In L. A. Penner, G. M. Batsche, H. M. Knoff & D. L. Nelson (Eds.), *Contributions of psychology to science and mathematics education* (pp. 341–366). Washington, DC: American Psychological Association.

Siegler, R. S. (1996). *Emerging minds: The process of change in children's thinking.* New York: Oxford University Press.

Siegler, R. S., & Alibali, M. W. (2005). *Children's thinking.* Englewood Cliffs, NJ: Prentice-Hall.

Siegler, R. S., & Booth, J. L. (2004). Development of numerical estimation in young children. *Child Development, 75*, 428–444.

Silliphant, V. (1983). Kindergarten reasoning and achievement in grades K-3. *Psychology in the Schools, 20*, 289–294.

Silverman, I. W., York, K., & Zuidema, N. (1984). Area-matching strategies used by young children. *Journal of Experimental Child Psychology, 38*, 464–474.

Simon, M. A. (1995). Reconstructing mathematics pedagogy from a constructivist perspective. *Journal for Research in Mathematics Education, 26*(2), 114–145.

Skemp, R. (1976, December). Relational understanding and instrumental understanding. *Mathematics Teaching, 77*, 20–26.

Smith, C. L., Carey, S., & Wiser, M. (1985). On differentiation: A case study of the development of the concepts of size, weight, and density. *Cognition, 21*, 177–237.

Smith, C. L., Wiser, M., Anderson, C. W., & Krajcik, J. S. (2006). Implications of research on children's learning for standards and assessment: A proposed learning progression for matter and the atomic-molecular theory. *Measurement, 14*(1&2), 1–98.

Snipes, J., Doolittle, F., & Herlihy, C. (2002). *Foundations for success: Case studies of how urban school systems improve student achievement.* Washington, DC: Council of the Great City Schools.

Solomon, T. (2003, April). *Early development of the ability to interpret graphs.* Paper presented at the Biennial Meeting of the Society for Research in Child Development, Tampa, FL.

Somerville, S. C., & Bryant, P. E. (1985). Young children's use of spatial coordinates. *Child Development, 56*, 604–613.

Somerville, S. C., Bryant, P. E., Mazzocco, M. M. M., & Johnson, S. P. (1987). *The early development of children's use of spatial coordinates.* Baltimore, MD: Society for Research in Child Development.

Sophian, C., & Crosby, M. E. (1998). *Ratios that even young children understand: The case of spatial proportions.* Ireland: Cognitive Science Society of Ireland.

Sowell, E. J. (1989). Effects of manipulative materials in mathematics instruction. *Journal for Research in Mathematics Education, 20*, 498–505.

Spelke, E. S. (2000). Nativism, empiricism, and the origns of knowledge. In D. Muir & A. Slater (Eds.), *Infant development: The essential readings* (pp. 36–51). Malden, MA: Blackwell Publishers.

Spelke, E. S. (2002). Conceptual development in infancy: The case of containment. In N. L. Stein, P. J. Bauer & M. Rabinowitz (Eds.), *Representation, memory, and development. Essays in honor of Jean Mandler* (pp. 223–246). Mahwah, NJ: Lawrence Erlbaum Associates.

Spencer, J. P., Smith, L. B., & Thelen, E. (2001). Dynamic systems account of the A-not-B error: The influence of prior experience on the spatial memory abilities of two-year-olds. *Child Development, 72*, 1327–1346.

Starkey, P., & Klein, A. (1992). Economic and cultural influence on early mathematical development. In F. L. Parker, R. Robinson, S. Sombrano, C. Piotrowski, J. Hagen, S. Randoph & A. Baker (Eds.), *New directions in child and family research: Shaping Head Start in the 90s* (pp. 440). New York: National Council of Jewish Women.

Starkey, P., Klein, A., Chang, I., Qi, D., Lijuan, P., & Yang, Z. (1999, April). *Environmental supports for young children's mathematical development in China and the United States.* Paper presented at the Society for Research in Child Development, Albuquerque, NM.

Steen, L. A. (1988). The science of patterns. *Science, 240*, 611–616.

Steffe, L. P. (1991). Operations that generate quantity. *Learning and Individual Differences, 3*, 61–82.

Steffe, L. P. (2004). PSSM From a constructivist perspective. In D. H. Clements, J. Sarama & A.-M. DiBiase (Eds.), *Engaging young children in mathematics: Standards for early childhood mathematics education* (pp. 221–251). Mahwah, NJ: Lawrence Erlbaum Associates.

Steffe, L. P., & Cobb, P. (1988). *Construction of arithmetical meanings and strategies.* New York: Springer-Verlag.

Sternberg, R. (1985). *Beyond IQ.* Cambridge, MA: Cambridge University Press.

Stevenson, H. W., Lee, S.-Y., & Stigler, J. W. (1986). Mathematics achievement of Chinese, Japanese, and American children. *Science, 231*, 693–699.

Stevenson, H. W., & McBee, G. (1958). The learning of object and pattern discrimination by children. *Journal of Comparative and Psychological Psychology, 51*, 752–754.

Stewart, R., Leeson, N., & Wright, R. J. (1997). Links between early arithmetical knowledge and early space and measurement knowledge: An exploratory study. In F. Biddulph & K. Carr (Eds.), *Proceedings of the Twentieth Annual Conference of the Mathematics Education Research Group of Australasia* (Vol. 2, pp. 477–484). Hamilton, New Zealand: MERGA.

Stigler, J. W., Lee, S.-Y., & Stevenson, H. W. (1990). *Mathematical knowledge of Japanese, Chinese, and American elementary school children.* Reston, VA: National Council of Teaching of Mathematics.

Stiles, J. (2001). Spatial cognitive development. In C. A. Nelson & M. Luciana (Eds.), *Handbook of developmental cognitive neuroscience* (pp. 399–414). Cambridge, MA: Bradford.

Stipek, D. J., & Byler, P. (1997). Early childhood teachers: Do they practice what they preach? *Early Childhood Research Quarterly, 12*, 305–325.

Teddlie, C., & Stringfield, S. (1993). *Schools make a difference: Lessons learned from a 10-year study of school effects.* New York: Teachers College Press.

Téglás, E., Girotto, V., Gonzalez, M., & Bonatti, L. L. (2007, April). *Intuitions of probabilities shape expectations about the future at 12 months and beyond.* Paper presented at the Society for Research in Child Development, Boston, MA.

Thelen, E., & Smith, L. B. (1994). *A dynamic systems approach to the development of cognition and action.* Cambridge, MA: MIT Press.

Thirumurthy, V. (2003). *Children's cognition of geometry and spatial thinking—A cultural process.* Unpublished doctoral dissertation, University of Buffalo, State University of New York.

Thomas, B. (1982). *An abstract of kindergarten teachers' elicitation and utilization of children's prior knowledge in the teaching of shape concepts:* Unpublished manuscript, School of Education, Health, Nursing, and Arts Professions, New York University.

Thomas, G., & Tagg, A. (2004). *An evaluation of the Early Numeracy Project 2003.* Wellington, Australia: Ministry of Education.

Thomas, G., & Ward, J. (2001). *An evaluation of the Count Me In Too pilot project.* Wellington, New Zealand: Ministry of Education.

Thomas, H., & Jamison, W. (1975). On the acquisition of understanding that still water is horizontal. *Merrill-Palmer Quarterly, 21*, 31–44.

Thomson, S., Rowe, K., Underwood, C., & Peck, R. (2005). *Numeracy in the early years: Project Good Start.* Camberwell, Victoria, Australia: Australian Council for Educational Research.

Thorndike, E. L. (1922). *The psychology of arithmetic.* New York: Macmillan.

Tibbals, C. (2000). Standards for Preschool and Kindergarten Mathematics Education. Arlington, VA: Conference on Standards for Preschool and Kindergarten Mathematics Education.

Try, K. M. (1989). *Cognitive and social change in young children during Logo activities: A study of individual differences.* Unpublished Doctoral dissertation, The University of New England, Armidale, New South Wales, Australia.

Tyack, D., & Tobin, W. (1992). The "grammar" of schooling: Why has it been so hard to change? *American Educational Research Journal, 31,* 453–479.

Tyler, D., & McKenzie, B. E. (1990). Spatial updating and training effects in the first year of human infancy. *Journal of Experimental Child Psychology, 50,* 445–461.

Tyler, R. W. (1949). *Basic principles of curriculum and instruction.* Chicago: University of Chicago Press.

U.S. Department of Education, N. C. E. S. (2000). *The condition of education 2000.* Washington, DC: U.S. Government Printing Office.

Ungerleider, L. G., & Mishkin, M. (1982). Two cortical visual systems. In D. J. Ingle, M. A. Goodale & R. J. W. Mansfield (Eds.), *Analysis of visual behavior* (pp. 549–586). Cambridge, MA: MIT Press.

Uttal, D. H. (1996). Angles and distances: Children's and adults' reconstruction and scaling of spatial configurations. *Child Development, 67*(6), 2763–2779.

Uttal, D. H. (2000). Seeing the big picture: Map use and the development of spatial cognition. *Developmental Science, 3*(3), 247–286.

Uttal, D. H., Gregg, V. H., Tan, L. S., & Sines, A. (2001). Connecting the dots: Children's use of a systematic figure to facilitate mapping and search. *Developmental Psychology*(37), 338–350.

Uttal, D. H., & Wellman, H. M. (1989). Young children's representation of spatial information acquired from maps. *Developmental Psychology, 25,* 128–138.

Van de Rijt, B. A. M., & Van Luit, J. E. H. (1999). Milestones in the development of infant numeracy. *Scandinavian Journal of Psychology, 40,* 65–71.

Van de Walle, G. A., Carey, S., & Prevor, M. (2000). Bases for object individuation in infancy: Evidence from manual search. *Journal of Cognition and Development, 1,* 249–280.

Van Horn, M. L., Karlin, E. O., Ramey, S. L., Aldridge, J., & Snyder, S. W. (2005). Effects of developmentally appropriate practices on children's development: A review of research and discussion of methodological and analytic issues. *Elementary School Journal, 105,* 325–351.

van Oers, B. (1994). Semiotic activity of young children in play: The construction and use of schematic representations. *European Early Childhood Education Research Journal, 2,* 19–33.

Vergnaud, G. (1982). A classification of cognitive tasks and operations of thought involved in addition and subtraction problems. In T. P. Carpenter & J. M. Moser (Eds.), *Addition and subtraction: A cognitive perspective* (pp. 39–59). Hillsdale, NJ: Lawrence Erlbaum Associates.

Vinner, S., & Hershkowitz, R. (1980). Concept images and common cognitive paths in the development of some simple geometrical concepts. In R. Karplus (Ed.), *Proceedings of the Fourth International Conference for the Psychology of Mathematics Education* (pp. 177–184). Berkeley, CA: Lawrence Hall of Science, University of California.

Vurpillot, E. (1976). *The visual world of the child.* New York: International Universities Press.

Vygotsky, L. S. (1934/1986). *Thought and language.* Cambridge, MA: MIT Press.

Vygotsky, L. S. (1935/1978). *Mind in society: The development of higher psychological processes.* Cambridge, MA: Harvard University Press.

Wagner, S. W., & Walters, J. (1982). A longitudinal analysis of early number concepts: From numbers to number. In G. E. Forman (Ed.), *Action and Thought* (pp. 137–161). New York: Academic Press.

Wang, R. F., & Spelke, E. S. (2002). Human spatial representation: Insights from animals. *Trends in Cognitive Sciences, 6,* 376–382.

Waters, J. (2004). Mathematical patterning in early childhood settings. In I. J. Putt, R. Faragher & M. McLean (Eds.), *Mathematics education for the third millennium: Towards 2010 (Proceedings of the 27th annual conference of the Mathematics Education Research Group of Australasia)* (pp. 565–572). Townsville, Australia: MERGA.

Watson, J. A., & Brinkley, V. M. (1990/91). Space and premathematic strategies young children adopt in initial Logo problem solving. *Journal of Computing in Childhood Education, 2,* 17–29.

Watson, J. A., Lange, G., & Brinkley, V. M. (1992). Logo mastery and spatial problem-solving by young children: Effects of Logo language training, route-strategy training, and learning styles on immediate learning and transfer. *Journal of Educational Computing Research, 8,* 521–540.

Watson, J. M., Callingham, R. A., & Kelly, B. A. (2007). Students' appreciation of expectation and variation as a foundation for statistical understanding. *Mathematical Thinking and Learning, 9,* 83–130.

Weaver, C. L. (1991). *Young children learn geometric and spatial concepts using Logo with a screen turtle and a floor turtle.* Unpublished doctoral dissertation, State University of New York at Buffalo.

Weiss, I. R. (2002). Systemic reform in mathematics education: What have we learned? Research presession of the 80th annual meeting of the National Council of Teachers of Mathematics.

Wellman, H. M., Fabricius, W. V., & Sophian, C. (1985). The early development of planning. In H. M. Wellman (Ed.), *Children's searching: The development of search skill and spatial representation* (pp. 123–149). Hillsdale, NJ: Lawrence Erlbaum Associates.

West, J., Denton, K., & Reaney, L. (2001). The kindergarten year: Findings from the Early Childhood Longitudinal Study, kindergarten class of 1998–1999. 2004, from http://nces.ed.gov/pubsearch/pubsinfo.asp?pubid=2002125

Wheatley, G. (1996). *Quick draw: Developing spatial sense in mathematics.* Tallahassee, FL: Mathematics Learning.

Wheatley, G. H. (1990). Spatial sense and mathematics learning. *Arithmetic Teacher, 37*(6), 10–11.

Wheatley, G. H., Brown, D. L., & Solano, A. (1994). Long term relationship between spatial ability and mathematical knowledge. In D. Kirshner (Ed.), *Proceedings of the sixteenth annual meeting North American Chapter of the International Group for the Psychology of Mathematics Education* (Vol. 1, pp. 225–231). Baton Rouge, LA: Louisiana State University.

Williford, H. J. (1972). A study of transformational geometry instruction in the primary grades. *Journal for Research in Mathematics Education, 3,* 260–271.

Wolfe, B. (1991). *Effective practices in inservice education: An exploratory study of the perceptions of head start participants.* Unpublished Dissertation, University of Wisconsin-Madison, Wisconsin.

Wright, B. (1991). What number knowledge is possessed by children beginning the kindergarten year of school? *Mathematics Education Research Journal, 3*(1), 1–16.

Wright, R. J. (2000). Professional development in recovery education. In L. P. Steffe & P. W. Thompson (Eds.), *Radical constructivism in action: Building on the pioneering work of Ernst von Glasersfeld* (pp. 134–151). London: RoutledgeFalmer.

Wright, R. J., Martland, J., Stafford, A. K., & Stanger, G. (2002). *Teaching number: Advancing children's skills and strategies.* London: Paul Chapman Publications/Sage.

Wright, R. J., Stanger, G., Stafford, A. K., & Martland, J. (2006). *Teaching number in the classroom with 4–8 year olds.* London: Paul Chapman Publications/Sage.

Wu, H. (2007). *Whole numbers, fractions, and rational numbers.* Berkeley, CA: University of California.

Yackel, E., & Wheatley, G. H. (1990). Promoting visual imagery in young pupils. *Arithmetic Teacher, 37*(6), 52–58.

Yoon, K. S., Duncan, T., Lee, S. W.-Y., Scarloss, B., & Shapley, K. L. (2007). *Reviewing the evidence on how teacher professional development affects student achievement (Issues & Answers Report, REL 2007–No. 033).* Washington, DC: U.S. Department of Education, Institute of Education Sciences, National Center for Education Evaluation and Regional Assistance, Regional Educational Laboratory Southwest.

Young-Loveridge, J. M. (2004). *Patterns of performance and progress on the Numeracy Projects 2001–2003: Further analysis of the Numeracy Project data.* Wellington, Australia: Ministry of Education.

Yuzawa, M., Bart, W. M., Kinne, L. J., Sukemune, S., & Kataoka, M. (1999). The effects of "origami" practice on size comparison strategy among young Japanese and American children. *Journal of Research in Childhood Education, 13*(2), 133–143.

Zorzi, M., Priftis, K., & Umiltà, C. (2002). Neglect disrupts the mental number line. *Nature, 417,* 138.

Zykova, V. I. (1969). Operating with concepts when solving geometry problems. In J. Kilpatrick & I. Wirszup (Eds.), *Soviet studies in the psychology of learning and teaching mathematics (Vols. 1)* (pp. 93–148). Chicago: University of Chicago.

Index